D0754293

CLASSICS OF BUDDHISM AND ZEN

The Collected Translations of
Thomas Cleary

CLASSICS OF BUDDHISM AND ZEN

CLASSICS OF BUDDHISM AND ZEN

SHAMBHALA
Boston & London
2005

SHAMBHALA PUBLICATIONS, INC.
Horticultural Hall
300 Massachusetts Avenue
Boston, Massachusetts 02115
www.shambhala.com

© 1986, 1994, 1998, 1999 by Thomas Cleary

Shōbōgenzō: Zen Essays by Dōgen is reprinted by special arrangement with
University of Hawai'i Press.
The Ecstasy of Enlightenment is reprinted by special arrangement with
Samuel Weiser, Inc.

All rights reserved. No part of this book may be
reproduced in any form or by any means, electronic or
mechanical, including photocopying, recording, or by any
information storage and retrieval system, without permission
in writing from the publisher.

9 8 7 6 5 4 3 2 1

FIRST PAPERBACK EDITION
Printed in the United States of America

⊚ This edition is printed on acid-free paper that meets the American National
Standards Institute z39.48 Standard.

Distributed in the United States by Random House, Inc., and in Canada by
Random House of Canada Ltd

LIBRARY OF CONGRESS CATALOGING-IN-PUBLICATION DATA
Cleary, Thomas.
Classics of Buddhism and Zen: the collected translations of Thomas Cleary /
Thomas Cleary.—1st ed.
p. cm.
ISBN 1-57062-831-9 (v. 1).—ISBN 1-57062-832-7 (v. 2).—ISBN 1-57062-833-5
(v. 3).—ISBN 1-57062-834-3 (v. 4).—ISBN 1-57062-838-6 (v. 5).—ISBN 1-59030-218-4
(v. 1 paperback).—ISBN 1-59030-219-2 (v. 2 paperback).—ISBN 1-59030-220-6 (v. 3
paperback).—ISBN 1-59030-221-4 (v. 4 paperback).—ISBN 1-59030-222-2 (v. 5
paperback).
1. Zen Buddhism. 2. Buddhism. I. Title.
BQ9258 .C54 2001
294.3'927—dc21
2001034385

CONTENTS

CONCORDIA UNIVERSITY LIBRARY
PORTLAND. OR 97211

PUBLISHER'S NOTE

The works contained in The Collected Translations of Thomas Cleary were published over a period of more than twenty years and originated from several publishing houses. As a result, the capitalization and romanization of Chinese words vary occasionally from one text to another within the volumes, due to changes in stylistic preferences from year to year and from house to house. In all cases, terms are rendered consistently within each text.

TEACHINGS OF ZEN

INTRODUCTION

Zen Buddhism emerged in China some fifteen centuries ago, to become one of the most dynamic spiritual movements of Asia for more than a thousand years.

After generations of experimentation with Buddhism, Zen masters found that enlightenment cannot be attained simply by literal adherence to dogma, or by mechanical performances of fixed systems of practices.

Returning to the source of Buddhism in personal experience of enlightenment, Zen teaching emphasized the liberation of subtle mental capacities from bondage to conditioned thinking habits and crude psychological propensities.

Conventional religious formats had externalized Buddhist teachings in the forms of myth, doctrine, and ritual. Zen masters internalized Buddhist teachings as allegories for perceptions, practices, and experiences of metaphysical principles, mental postures, psychological processes, psychic states, and spiritual capacities.

In projecting such interpretations of Buddhism, Zen teachers were not really innovating but concentrating on certain core teachings of the Buddhist scriptures. Even the hallmark Zen teaching that "mind is Buddha" is not a Zen invention, but is found in scriptural sources.

Although they have been called iconoclastic, Zen masters did not oppose the practice of conventional religion, except where obsession with formalities of dogma and ritual inhibited spiritual experience of formless truth.

On a deeper level, Zen masters sought to restore and express the living meaning of religion and philosophy; the Zen teaching was to "study the living word, not the dead word." Not only did Zen reawaken Buddhism in this way, but it also revitalized Taoism, Confucianism, Shintoism, and shamanism, bringing out their higher spiritual dimensions.

The essentialist approach to Zen in practical presentation of the classical allegories and principles of Buddhism is illustrated with unparalleled clarity and simplicity by the great master Bankei (1622–1693), who had both Chinese and Japanese teachers but claimed to have rediscovered the spiritual reality of Zen through his own experience:

> When we look back on this life, we see that when people are born, no one has thoughts of joy, sadness, hatred, or bitterness. Are we not in the state of the buddha mind bequeathed by our parents? It is after birth that intelligence develops, and people learn bad habits from others in the course of seeing and hearing them. As they grow up, their personal mental habits emerge, and they turn the buddha mind into a monster because of biased self-importance.
>
> People are born with nothing but the unconceived buddha mind, but because of self-importance they want to get their own way, arguing and losing their temper yet claiming it is the stubbornness of others that makes them mad. Getting fixated on what others say, they turn the all-important unique buddha mind into a monster, mulling over useless things, repeating the same thoughts over and over again. They are so foolish they will not give up on things even if getting their own way would in any case prove to be futile. Folly is the cause of animality, so they are inwardly changing the all-important unique buddha mind into a paragon of animality.
>
> Everyone is intelligent, but through lack of understanding they turn the buddha mind into all sorts of things—hungry ghost, monster, animal. Once you've become an animal, even if you hear truth you don't listen, or even if you do listen, being animal-like, you can't retain what you've heard.
>
> Going from one hellish state to another, from one animalistic state to another, from one ghostly state to another, from darkness to darkness in an endless vicious cycle, you go on experiencing infinite misery for the bad things you have done, with never a break.
>
> This can happen to anyone, once you've gone astray. Just understand the point of not turning the buddha mind into something else.

As soon as a single thought gets fixated on something, you become ordinary mortals. All delusion is like this. You pick up on something confronting you, turn the buddha mind into a monster because of your own self-importance, and go astray on account of your own ego.

Whatever it is confronting you, let it be. As long as you do not pick up on it and react with bias, just remaining in the buddha mind and not transforming it into something else, then delusion cannot occur. This is constant abiding in the unconceived buddha mind.

Everyone makes the mistake of supposing that acquired delusions produced by selfish desire and mental habits are inborn, and so they are unable to avoid confusion. . . .

As I listen to the people who come to me, all of them make the mistake of turning the buddha mind into thoughts, unable to stop, piling thoughts upon thoughts, resulting in the development of ingrained mental habits, which they then believe are inborn and unalterable.

Please understand; this is very important. Once you have unconsciously drifted into delusion, if your state of mind degenerates and you flow downward like a valley stream in a waterfall, there is no way back after you have fallen into vicious cycles.

Again, suppose that you have developed mental habits based on selfish desires. When people criticize things that suit your selfish mentality, you become angry and defensive—since they are, after all, bad things—and you rationalize them as good. When people praise things that do not suit your selfish mentality, you reject them—being, of course, good things—and you retort that they are bad.

Everything is like this. Delusion can make a defect seem like a virtue. Having fallen into ignorance, you go through all sorts of changes, degenerating further and further until you fall into hell, with precious little chance of regaining your humanity.

The most important thing is not to be self-centered; then you cannot fail to remain in the buddha mind spontaneously.

To want to be at least as good as others in everything is the worst thing there is. Wanting to be at least as good as others is called egotistic pride. As long as you don't wish to be superior to others, then you won't be inferior either.

Also, when people mistreat us, it is because we have pride. When we consider mistreatment from others to be due to our own defects and so we examine ourselves, then no one in the world is bad.

When angry thoughts arise, they turn the buddha mind into a monster. But anger and delight both, being self-centered, obscure and confuse the luminous buddha mind, so that it goes around in vicious circles. Without subjective bias the buddha mind remains unconceived, so it does not revolve in circles. Let everyone understand this.

The following pages contain essential Zen teachings on realizing this original buddha mind in all of us. These teachings have been selected from the voluminous Zen canon for their accessibility, their clarity, and above all their practical effectiveness in fostering Zen concentrations and insights. This is Zen guidance presented by the masters for over a thousand years.

Teachings of Zen

THE MIND MONARCH

Observe the empty monarch of mind; mysterious, subtle, unfathomable, it has no shape or form, yet it has great spiritual power, able to extinguish a thousand troubles and perfect ten thousand virtues. Although its essence is empty, it can provide guidance. When you look at it, it has no form; call it, and it has a voice. It acts as a great spiritual leader; mental discipline transmits scripture.

Like salt in water, like adhesive in coloring, it is certainly there, but you don't see its form; so is the monarch of mind—dwelling inside the body, going in and out the senses, it responds freely to beings according to conditions, without hindrance, succeeding at all it does.

When you realize the fundamental, you perceive the mind; when you perceive the mind, you see Buddha. This mind is Buddha; the Buddha is mind. Keeping mindful of the buddha mind, the buddha mind is mindful of Buddha. If you want to realize early attainment, discipline your mind, regulate yourself. When you purify your habits and purify your mind, the mind itself is Buddha; there is no Buddha other than this mind monarch.

If you want to attain buddhahood, don't be stained by anything. Though the essence of mind is empty, the substance of greed and anger is solid. To enter this door to the source, sit straight and be Buddha. Once you've arrived at the other shore, you will attain the perfections.

People who seek the way, observe your own mind yourself. When you know the Buddha is within, and do not seek outside, then mind itself is Buddha, and Buddha is the mind. When the mind is clear, you perceive Buddha and understand the perceiving mind. Apart from mind is not Buddha; apart from Buddha is not mind. If not for Buddha, nothing is fathomed; there is no competence at all.

If you cling to emptiness and linger in quiescence, you will bob and sink herein: the buddhas and bodhisattvas do not rest their minds this way. Great people who clarify the mind understand this mystic message; body and mind naturally sublimated, their action is unchanging. Therefore the wise release the mind to be independent and free.

Do not say the mind monarch is empty in having no essential nature; it can cause the physical body to do wrong or do right. Neither being nor nonbeing, it is concealed and revealed without fixation. Although the essence of mind is empty, it can be ordinary and can be saintly: therefore I urge you to guard it yourself carefully—a moment of contrivance, and you go back to bobbing and sinking.

The knowledge of the pure clean mind is as yellow gold to the world; the spiritual treasury of wisdom is all in the body and mind. The uncreated spiritual treasure is neither shallow nor deep. The buddhas and bodhisattvas understand this basic mind; for those who have the chance to encounter it, it is not past, future, or present.

FU SHAN-HUI (487–569)

FIVE TYPES OF MEDITATION METHOD

Know the essence of mind. Its intrinsic essence is pure clarity. It is essentially the same as a buddha.

Know the functions of the mind. Its functions produce the treasury of teachings. When its activity is always silent, myriad illusions become suchness.

Constantly be aware, without stopping. When the aware mind is present, it senses the formlessness of things.

Constantly see your body as empty and quiet, inside and outside communing in sameness. Plunge the body into the realm of reality, where there has never been any obstruction.

Keep to unity without shifting. With constant presence, whether active or still, the student can see the buddha nature clearly.

TAO-HSIN (580–651)

LET YOUR MIND BE FREE

It has been asked, "How should those who enter the path apply their minds?"

All things are originally uncreated and presently undying. Just let your mind be free; you don't have to restrain it.

See directly and hear directly; come directly and go directly. When you must go, then go; when you must stay, then stay.

This is the true path. A scripture says, "Conditional existence is the site of enlightenment, insofar as you know it as it really is."

NIU-T'OU HUI-CHUNG (683–769)

NO PERFORMANCE

It has been asked, "If one wants to practice the path now, what technique should one perform to attain liberation?"

People who see buddhahood immediately realize the mind source without performing techniques. When you clearly see buddha nature, this very mind is Buddha, because it is neither illusory nor real. A scripture says, "Directly abandoning expedients, just expound the unsurpassed way."

HUI-CHUNG

THE NORMAL MIND IS THE WAY

The way does not require cultivation; just don't defile it. What is defilement? As long as you have a fluctuating mind, artificiality, or compulsive tendencies, all of this is defilement.

If you want to understand the way directly, the normal mind is the way. What I call the normal mind is free from artificiality: in it there is no right or wrong, no grasping or rejection, no extinction or permanence, no banality or sanctity. A scripture says, "Neither the conduct of ordinary people nor the conduct of saints, it is the conduct of enlightening beings."

Right now, as you walk, stand, sit, and recline, responding to situations and dealing with people, all is the way. The way is the realm of reality. No matter how many the countless inconceivable functions, they are not beyond the realm of reality. If it were not so, how could we speak of the teaching of the ground of mind, how could we speak of the inexhaustible lamp?

All phenomena are mental phenomena; all names are named by mind. All phenomena arise from mind; mind is the root of all phenomena. A scripture says, "When you know the mind and arrive at the root source, in that sense you may be said to be a devotee."

The equivalency of terms, the equivalency of meanings, and the equivalency of all truths are wholly one, without adulteration. If you can attain situational free mastery of the teachings, when you define the realm of reality, all is the realm of reality; when you define true suchness, all is true suchness. If you speak in terms of abstract designs, all realities are abstract designs; if you speak in terms of concrete facts, all realities are concrete facts. Bring up one, and a thousand follow; abstract principle and concrete fact are no different. All are inconceivable functions; there is no other principle. All derive from the operation of mind.

Metaphorically, it is like the fact that there is a plurality of reflections of the moon but no plurality in the real moon. There is a plurality of water sources but not a plurality in the essence of water. There is plurality in myriad forms, but there is no plurality in space. There is plurality in principles expounded but no plurality in uninhibited intelligence.

All kinds of establishments derive from one mind: you may set them up, and you may dismantle them; both are inconceivable functions, and inconceivable functions are all your own. If there is no place to stand apart from reality, then where you stand is real; all is the structure of your own house. If anyone is otherwise, then who is it?

All things are Buddhist teachings; all things are liberating. Liberation is true suchness, and nothing is apart from true suchness. Walking, standing, sitting, and reclining are all inconceivable acts.

This does not depend on the time: scripture says, "Everywhere, everyplace, is Buddha considered to be." A buddha is one who is capable of humanity, who has knowledge and wisdom, who accurately perceives potentials and states of mind and can cut through the web of doubts of all living beings, getting out of entanglements such as being and nonbeing, so that both profane and sacred feelings end, and personality and phenomena are both empty: then a buddha turns the incomparable wheel of teaching that transcends calculation and measurement, unobstructed in action, communicating both concrete facts and abstract principles.

It is like clouds rising in the sky: suddenly there, then gone without a trace. And it is like drawing a pattern on water: it neither is born nor passes away. This is cosmic peace and eternal rest. When it is enclosed, it is called the matrix of the realization of suchness; when it emerges from enclosure, it is called the cosmic body of reality.

The body of reality is infinite; its substance neither increases nor decreases. It can be great or small, square or round; it manifests visible forms in accordance with things and beings, like the moon reflected in water. Its effusive function does not plant roots: it does not exhaust deliberate action and does not dwell in non-doing. Deliberate action is a function of nonartificiality; nonartificiality is the basis of deliberate action. Because of not being fixated on the basis, one is said to be independent, like space.

As for the meanings of birth and death of mind and true suchness of mind, the true suchness of mind is like a clear mirror reflecting images: the mind is like the mirror, the images are like phenomena. If the mind grasps phenomena, then it gets involved in external causes and conditions; this is the meaning of the birth and death of mind. If it does not grasp phenomena, this is the meaning of true suchness of mind.

Followers hear about seeing buddha nature; enlightening beings see buddha nature with their eyes. When you realize nonduality, terms are equivalent, having no difference in essence but not being the same in usage. What is called consciousness in a state of delusion is called knowledge in the enlightened state; following principle is called enlightenment, following things is called delusion.

When you are deluded, that means you have lost sight of your own original mind. When you are enlightened, that means you have realized your own original mind. Once enlightened you are forever enlightened and do not become deluded anymore. It is like when the sunlight comes out, it does not combine with darkness; when the sunlight of knowledge and wisdom emerge, they are not together with the darkness of afflictions.

When you understand mind and objects, then idle imaginings do not arise. When idle imaginings do not arise, this is acceptance of the uncreated. What is fundamentally there is there now; you don't need to cultivate the path and sit meditating. Not cultivating and not sitting is the pure meditation of those who realize suchness.

Now, if you see this principle truly and accurately and do not fabricate any actions but pass your life according to your lot, fulfilling your minimal needs wherever you are, disciplined conduct increasingly taking effect, accumulating pure actions—as long as you can be like this, why worry about not attaining mastery?

MA-TSU (709–788)

THE BODY OF REALITY

The essence of mind is formless; this itself is the subtle body of reality. The essenceof mind is inherently empty; this itself is the infinite body of space. Demonstrating arrays of practices is the body of reality of virtues. The body of reality is the root of myriad emanations, which are named according to the situation. Its knowledge and function are endless; this is the inexhaustible treasury.

TA-CHU (EIGHTH CENTURY)

GET THE ROOT

You should each individually clarify your own mind, getting to the root without pursuing the branches. Just get the root, and the branches come of themselves. If you want to get the root, just get to know your mind. This mind is basically the root of all mundane and supramundane phenomena. As long as the mind does not become obsessed with all good and bad, you will realize that all things are basically just so.

TA-MEI (CA. 805)

VERBAL TEACHINGS

All verbal teachings are just to cure diseases. Because diseases are not the same, the remedies are also different. That is why it is sometimes said that there is Buddha, and sometimes it is said that there is no Buddha.

True words are those that actually cure sickness; if the cure manages to heal, then all are true words. If they can't effectively cure sickness, all are false words.

True words are false words when they give rise to views. False words are true words when they cut off the delusions of sentient beings. Because disease is unreal, there is only unreal medicine to cure it.

PAI-CHANG (720–814)

INWARD AND OUTWARD VIEWS

To cling to oneself as Buddha, oneself as Zen or the way, making that
an understanding, is called clinging to the inward view. Attainment
by causes and conditions, practice and realization, is called the outward view. Master Pao-chih said, "The inward view and the outward
view are both mistaken."

PAI-CHANG

SEEKING

A buddha is one who does not seek. In seeking this, you turn away
from it. The principle is the principle of nonseeking; when you seek
it, you lose it.

If you cling to nonseeking, this is the same as seeking. If you cling
to nonstriving, this is the same as striving.

Thus the *Diamond Cutter Scripture* says, "Do not grasp truth, do
not grasp untruth, and do not grasp that which is not untrue."

It also says, "The truth that the buddhas find has no reality or unreality."

PAI-CHANG

LIBERATION IN ALL PLACES

Don't seek a buddha, don't seek a teaching, don't seek a community.
Don't seek virtue, knowledge, intellectual understanding, and so on.
When feelings of defilement and purity are ended, still don't hold to
this nonseeking and consider it right. Don't dwell at the point of ending, and don't long for heavens or fear hells. When you are unhindered
by bondage or freedom, then this is called liberation of mind and body
in all places.

PAI-CHANG

A METHOD OF AWAKENING

First set aside all involvements and concerns; do not remember or
recollect anything at all, whether good or bad, mundane or transcen-

dental. Do not engage in thoughts. Let go of body and mind, setting them free.

When the mind is like wood or stone, you do not explain anything, and the mind does not go anywhere, then the mind ground becomes like space, wherein the sun of wisdom naturally appears. It is as though the clouds had opened and the sun emerged.

Just put an end to all fettering connections, and feelings of greed, hatred, craving, defilement and purity, all come to an end. Unmoved in the face of inner desires and external influences, not choked up by perception and cognition, not confused by anything, naturally endowed with all virtues and the inconceivable use of spiritual capacities, this is someone who is free.

Having a mind neither stilled nor disturbed in the presence of all things in the environment, neither concentrated nor distracted, passing through all sound and form without lingering or obstruction, is called being a wayfarer.

Not setting in motion good or evil, right or wrong, not clinging to a single thing, not rejecting a single thing, is called being a member of the great caravan.

Not being bound by any good or evil, emptiness or existence, defilement or purity, striving or nonstriving, mundanity or transcendence, virtue or knowledge, is called enlightened wisdom.

Once affirmation and negation, like and dislike, approval and disapproval, and all various opinions and feelings come to an end and cannot bind you, then you are free wherever you may be. This is what is called a bodhisattva at the moment of inspiration immediately ascending to the stage of buddhahood.

PAI-CHANG

THIS ABUNDANT LIGHT

You guard a spiritual thing: it isn't something you could make, and it isn't something you can describe. In this ground of ours, there is no Buddha, no nirvana, and no path to practice, no doctrine to actualize. The way is not within existence or nonexistence—what method would one then practice? This abundant light, wherever you are, in every situation, is itself the great way.

TAN-HSIA (739-824)

MYSTIC UNDERSTANDING

Mystic understanding of truth is not perception or cognition. That is why it is said that you arrive at the original source by stopping the mind, so it is called the enlightened state of being as is, the ultimately independent free individual.

NAN-CH'UAN (748–834)

ABSOLUTE TRUTH

The body of truth is not constructed; it does not fall into any category. Truth is unshakable; it does not depend on the objects of the six senses. Therefore scripture says buddha nature is constant, while mind is inconstant. That is the sense in which knowledge is not the way and mind is not Buddha.

For now, do not say mind is Buddha; do not understand in terms of perception and cognition. This thing originally does not have all those names.

NAN-CH'UAN

PRACTICE

Someone asked Nan-ch'uan, "How does one cultivate practice?"

Nan-ch'uan replied, "It cannot be thought up. To tell people to cultivate in such and such a way, or to practice in such and such a way, is very difficult."

The questioner now asked, "Then will you let students cultivate practice at all?"

Nan-ch'uan answered, "I cannot stop you."

"How should I practice?"

Nan-ch'uan said, "Do what you have to do; don't just follow behind others."

FORMLESS MIND

The formless mind can operate brilliance, responding to sound, responding to form, illuminating wherever it is directed. Even though it may be localized, it is not local; while going along with the flow high and low, it is altogether inconceivable. If you look for it, it has no head; and it has no tail: where do its surges of radiant light come from? Just this right now is all mental: the mind is used to clarify mind, and mind reverts to spontaneity. Since it does not abide anywhere, where can you look for it? Its operation has no tracks and no traces. Get to know the person who is clearly seeking right now—don't disregard this and seek another aim.

KAO-CH'ENG (N.D.)

SPIRITUALITY

If there were any object, any doctrine, that could be given to you to hold on to or understand, it would reduce you to bewilderment and externalism. It's just a spiritual openness, with nothing that can be grasped; it is pure everywhere, its light clearly penetrating, outwardly and inwardly luminous through and through.

TE-SHAN (D. 867)

LIBERATION

Don't love sagehood; sagehood is an empty name. There is no special truth but this radiant spiritual openness, unobstructed and free. It is not attained by adornment and cultivated realization. From the buddhas to the Zen masters, all have transmitted this teaching, by which they attained liberation.

TE-SHAN

THE BUSINESS OF ZEN

One day the governor of the province asked Mu-chou (780–877), "What is the business of Zen?"

Mu-chou said, "Come here, come here."

The governor approached; Mu-chou said, "You sure can talk nonsense!"

The governor was speechless. Finally Mu-chou asked, "Whom have you seen?"

The governor said that he had seen such-and-such an old adept. Mu-chou asked, "What else?" The governor replied that he had read scriptures. Mu-chou suddenly hit his chair and said, "In the teachings, what is this called?"

The governor said, "It is not spoken of in the teachings."

Mu-chou said, "In the teachings it says, 'Productive labor as a means of livelihood is not contrary to the truth.' What about that?"

The governor had no reply.

EVALUATING TEACHERS

When I was journeying, I didn't choose communities on the basis of whether or not they had material provisions; I was only concerned with seeing whether their perception indicated some capacity. If so, then I might stay for a summer or a winter; but if they were low-minded, I'd leave in two or three days. Although I called on more than sixty prominent teachers, barely one or two had great perception. The rest hardly had real true knowledge—they just want your donations.

TA-SUI (834–919)

THE ESSENTIAL NATURE

The essential nature is originally pure and endowed with myriad virtues, but there come to be differentiations because of following conditions that are tainted or pure. Therefore sages realize this and only use it in pure ways, thus attaining enlightenment, while ordinary people miss it and only use it in tainted ways, sinking into moribund routines. Their essence is not two; that is why the scriptures on transcendent wisdom say that "there is no duality, no division, because there is no disjunction, no separateness."

TA-SUI

A PRICELESS JEWEL

Each of you has a priceless jewel in your own body. It radiates light through your eyes, shining through the mountains, rivers, and earth. It radiates light through your ears, taking in all sounds, good and bad. It radiates light through your six senses day and night. This is also called absorption in light. You yourself do not recognize it, but it is in your physical body, supporting it inside and out, not letting it tip over. Even if you are carrying a double load of rocks over a single-log bridge, it still doesn't let you fall over. What is this? If you seek in the slightest, then it cannot be seen.

TA-AN (D. 883)

FREE-FLOWING

All things are free-flowing, untrammeled—what bondage is there, what entanglement? You create your own difficulty and ease therein. The mind source pervades the ten directions with one continuity; those of the most excellent faculties understand naturally.

TZU-HU (800–880)

INDEPENDENCE

There is no other task but to know your own original face. This is called independence; the spirit is clear and free. If you say there is some particular doctrine or patriarchy, you'll be totally cheated. Just look into your heart; there is a transcendental clarity. Just have no greed and no dependency and you will immediately attain certainty.

YEN-T'OU (828–887)

DEGENERATION OF ZEN

Ninety years ago, I saw more than eighty teachers from the school of the great master Ma-tsu. Each of them was an adept, unlike the teachers today who produce branches and tendrils upon branches and tendrils. The generality of them are far from sagehood, and each generation is worse than the last.

How about Nan-ch'uan's usual saying that we should act in the midst of different kinds? How do you understand this? Nowadays yellow-mouthed punks give complicated talks at crossroads in exchange for food to eat, seeking obeisance, gathering crowds of three to five hundred, saying, "I am the teacher, you are the students."

CHAO-CHOU (778–897)

The Normal Mind

Chao-chou was asked, "Is a person with a normal mind still to be taught?"

Chao-chou said, "I don't go through such a person's door."

The questioner asked, "Then wouldn't it be someone sunk into the beyond?"

Chao-chou retorted, "A fine 'normal mind'!"

No Fooling

You come here looking for sayings and talks, novel expressions and elegant lines, uselessly taking to verbalization. I am old and my energy is not up to par; I'm a dull speaker and have no idle talk for you. If you ask me questions, I answer in accord with your questions, but I have no mysterious marvel that can be conveyed to you, and I won't have you get fixated.

I never assert the existence of Buddha and Dharma, of ordinary person and sage, either in the beyond or the here and now; and I have no intention of sitting here tying you people down. You go through a thousand changes, but all of it is you people conceiving interpretations, carrying them with you, experiencing the results of your own doings. I have nothing here for you, and nothing exoteric or esoteric to explain to you, no appearance or intention to represent to you.

T'OU-TZU (819–914)

Natural

To speak of practicing the path is an expression of encouragement, a term of inducement; there has never been any doctrine to give people, just transmission of various expedient techniques. These are for expressing the essential idea, to get people to know their own minds. Ultimately there is no doctrine to get, no path to practice. Therefore it is said, "The path of enlightenment is natural."

LUNG-YA (834–920)

THE OCEAN OF KNOWLEDGE

Have you gotten familiar with the ocean of intuitive knowledge of the essence and forms of pure original suchness? If you have not gotten familiar with it, how about the green mountains here before your eyes—do you see them?

If you say you see them, how do you see? If you say you don't see, how can the green mountains be called invisible?

Do you understand? It is simply that your ocean of intuitive knowledge of the essence and forms of pure original suchness is equipped with seeing and hearing.

If you understand, it is simply as such; if you don't understand, it is still simply as such.

HSUAN-SHA (NINTH TO TENTH CENTURY)

YOUR OWN EXPERIENCE

Every reality is eternal, every essence is as is: just don't seek outwardly. If you have a great root of faith, the buddhas are just states of your own experience; whether you are walking, standing, sitting, or lying down, never is it not this.

My speaking directly to you now is already pressing the free into servitude. Would you agree to speak thus? And how do you understand agreeing or not agreeing?

HSUAN-SHA

NO THING

There is no thing to Buddhism—it can enliven people, and it can kill people too. Seeing essential nature and becoming enlightened penetrates all time.

HSUAN-SHA

THE REALITY OF MIND

The earth and the sky are entirely composed of mind, but how do you explain the principle of being composed of mind? And how do you explain the reality of mind without form pervading the ten direc-

tions? There is no part that does not come from compassion producing knowledge, there is no part that does not come from knowledge
activating compassion, and there is no part that does not come from
compassion and knowledge equally illumining the ocean of essential
nature, pervading the universe, completely fluid and free.

Knowing the light and the dark, matter and emptiness, compassion
and knowledge equally wind up at the door of concentration of kindness, with reward, response, and reality, independent and free, widely
benefiting the world. The whole earth and open space are both manifestations of the door of concentration of kindness. That is why it is
said that the reality of mind without form pervades the ten directions.

HSUAN-SHA

WIDE OPEN

The way of buddhas is wide open, without any stages. The door of
nothing is the door to liberation; having no intention is the will to
help others. It is not within past, present, and future, so it cannot rise
and sink; setups are counter to reality, because it is not in the realm
of the created.

Move, and you produce the root of birth and death; be still, and
you get drunk in the village of oblivion. If movement and stillness
are both erased, you fall into empty annihilation; if movement and
stillness are both withdrawn, you presume upon buddha nature.

You must be like a dead tree or cold ashes in the face of objects and
situations while acting responsively according to the time, without
losing proper balance. A mirror reflects a multitude of images without their confusing its brilliance; birds fly through the sky without
mixing up the color of the sky.

HSUAN-SHA

THE GREAT TASK

As long as you have not accomplished the great task and are not in
communion with the bloodline of the source, you must avoid memorizing sayings and living inside conceptual consciousness. Has it not
been said, "Concepts act as robbers, consciousness becomes waves"?

Everyone has been swept away and drowned. There is no freedom in that.

If you have not mastered the great task, nothing compares to stopping, in the sense of quiet cessation, the purifying and quieting of the body and mind. At all times avoid dwelling obsessively on things, and it will be easy to unveil *this*.

KU-SHAN (D. CA. 940)

THE OBJECT OF INVESTIGATION

Ku-shan was asked, "What is the basic object of investigation?"
He replied, "How one has gotten to such a state."

NAMES AND ACTUALITIES

An ancient said, " 'Buddha' and 'Dharma' are constructed teaching methods; the terms *Zen* and *Tao* are talk for pacifying children." The names have no relation to actualities, actualities have no relation to names; if you cling to names, you will be blocked from the mystery.

That is why I have told you that sayings do not correspond to potential, words do not set forth actualities. Those who accept words perish; those who linger over sayings get lost. When you have caught the fish, you forget the trap; when you have gotten the meaning, you forget the words. We use a net to catch fish; the fish are not the net.

KU-SHAN

WHAT IS DISTURBING YOU

What is disturbing you and making you uneasy is that there are things outside and mind inside. Therefore even when the ordinary and the holy are one reality, there still remains a barrier of view. So it is said that as long as views remain you are ordinary; when feelings are forgotten you're a buddha. I advise you, don't seek reality, just stop views.

FA-YEN (885-958)

THE EYE OF THE HEART

To expound the vehicle to the source and bring out the great teaching, it is necessary to attain thorough clarity of the objective eye; only then can you perceive the distinction between the initiate and the naive. Because reality and falsehood have the same source, it's hard to tell them apart, like water and milk in the same vessel. I always use the eye in my heart to observe external appearances. I keep observing until I discern the true from the false. How could anyone who doesn't do this be called a teacher?

TUNG-SHAN SHOU-CH'U (CA. 910/15–990/95)

THE NORMAL MIND

Tung-shan was asked, "The normal mind is the way; what is the normal mind?"

He replied, "Not picking things up along the road."

EXCESS

If you want to seek too much, it may hinder the way. For your part, can you say your work is done? If not, then a thousand kinds of clever talk do not enhance your mind; what is the reason for ten thousand kinds of thought?

CHIH-MEN (FL. CA. 1000–1020)

THE PIVOTAL POINT

"When you try to set your mind on it, you miss it; when you stir your thoughts, you turn away from it. If you do not try and do not stir, you are making your living in stagnant water. What is the pivotal point for a Zennist?" Is there any benefit in this ancient saying? If you say there is benefit, it binds you fatally with words. If you say there is no benefit, what is the intention?

This is why it is said, "The heart of nirvana is easy to realize; knowledge of differentiation is hard to clarify."

CHIH-MEN

WHAT THING

What thing is not attained when painstakingly sought?
  What thing comes of itself without being sought?
  What thing does not break under the blow of an iron hammer?
  What thing closes by night and opens by day?

CHIH-MEN

TRUTH AND WORDS

There is originally no word for truth, but the way to it is revealed by words. The way originally has no explanation, but reality is made clear by explanation. That is why the buddhas appeared in the world with many expedient methods; the whole canon dispenses medicines according to diseases.

SHIH-SHUANG (986–1039)

THE CAUSE OF MISERY

Greed is the basic cause of misery; if you extinguish greed, then it has no basis. If you have no greed, you are clean and free wherever you are; the mountains, rivers, and earth do not block the light of your eyes.

SHE-HSIEN (TENTH TO ELEVENTH CENTURY)

EYES FOR STUDY

Zen study can only be done with the eyes for Zen study; if you are simply attracted to others' sayings and memorize them, you will not be able to cut through yourself.

SHEN-TING (TENTH TO ELEVENTH CENTURY)

NO SECTARIAN STYLE

I have no sayings or statements to have you understand, and no sayings or statements to have you study. And I have no sectarian style to have you set up. I just distinguish right and wrong for you, so that you will not jump to conclusions and think you have attained when you have not.

CH'ENG-KU (FL. CA. 1037)

LOOK INTO YOURSELF

Space has no inside or outside; the same is so of the reality of mind. If you comprehend space, this is arriving at the principle of reality as such.

This was the way of the ancient masters, but later descendants couldn't continue it. That is because it is easy to understand but hard to see.

To understand as soon as it's brought up is called conceiving interpretation according to words; it's also called dependent penetration. It is also called parrot understanding. It is not personal realization and personal awakening. Therefore feelings of doubt do not stop.

Because they have no basis to rely on, and their habit-ridden consciousness is manic, people produce idiosyncratic views. They say, "I won't enter this deep pit of liberation," and "What end is there to running around in this spiritual realm? Why not seek a way out?" Or they say, "I have something transcendental within me," or "I have the road to penetrating liberation within me." When asked what the road to penetrating liberation is, some say, "Donkeys pick wet spots to piss," or "In spring the grass is deep green." Taking up the way of the ancient masters, instead they uphold verbal teachings as the ultimate model.

This is called slighting mind and esteeming doctrine, abandoning the root and pursuing the branches, like a dog chasing a clod. For a hundred and ten years now, everyone's been like this. Master Hsueh-feng said, "The grand masters have passed away, buried in the weeds by you people today."

If you manage to enter in by the way of the ancient masters, that will be like a hundred thousand suns and moons, liberating all sentient beings in the universe. If you enter into verbal teachings, that will be like the light of a firefly, and you won't even be able to save yourself. Why? Because it is still sterile wisdom. Detach from literal knowledge and look into yourself.

CH'ENG-KU

Whoring for Appearances

If you don't know there is an original self, and do not know there is such a thing as the road beyond, and instead learn to question and answer based on writings and words, what relevance is there? With three or five notebooks of extracts and notes, wherever you go to spend the summer or winter in the congregation of a master, you ask for more instruction on every item, right from the start, and talk about ascent and descent, perception and function, vertical and horizontal, becoming a clear Zennist, not relying on a single thing. You say the issue of your own self is clear, and keep it in your chest as the ultimate rule. Eventually you want to be called a Zen master and to open eyes for later people. How much you bury away the ancient masters and misguide later people! If you try to counter birth and death with things like this, will it work? Even if you immediately have a great insight and a great awakening, and can talk like clouds and rain, all you have gained is a slippery tongue—you are further and further from the way. That's what is called being a whore for appearances.

CH'ENG-KU

Cease and Desist

It is essential for you to cease and desist from your previously held knowledge, opinions, interpretations, and understandings. It is not accomplished by stopping the mind; temporary relinquishment is not the way—it fools you into wasting body and mind, without accomplishing anything at all in the end.

I suggest to you that nothing compares to ceasing and desisting. There is nowhere for you to apply your mind. Just be like an imbecile twenty-four hours a day. You have to be spontaneous and buoyant, your mind like space, yet without any measurement of space. You have to be beyond light and dark, no Buddhism, body, or mind, year in and year out. If anything is not forgotten, you've spent your life in vain. That is why it is said, "Even if you learn things pertaining to buddhahood, that too is misuse of mind. You have to be free of preoccupations; you have to be normal."

Nevertheless, even so, it is undeniably hard to find people. Not just now—it has always been hard to find people. It was hard even in ancient times; how much the more so nowadays when people who study things are all drawn into weeds by ignorant old baldies! That is why it is said, "Our eyes were originally right, but went wrong because of teachers."

CH'ENG-KU

FACING SUCHNESS

Fog lacks the endless sky, wind rises over the vast plains; all plants and trees roar the great lion's roar, expounding universal wisdom; the buddhas of past, present, and future are at your feet, turning the wheel of the great teaching.

If you can understand, you will not expend effort at random. If you do not understand, don't say this mountain is steep—the highest peak is still ahead.

YANG-CH'I (992–1049)

THE PRIMORDIAL

"There is something before heaven and earth, formless and basically silent; the master of all forms, it does not fade along with the seasons." Tell me, what is this? Do you know? If you know, the whole universe and everything in it is luminously clear. If you don't know, when confronted by things you cannot turn around.

TAO-WU WU-CHEN (FL. CA. 1025–1060)

WHERE WILL YOU SEEK?

What is there to Buddhism? Old masters have said, "There is no matter, so be unconcerned," and "The body of truth is uncreated and is not subsumed by any categories." An ancient worthy said, "When you don't believe in Buddha or bodhi, understanding of emptiness is foremost." That is why it is said, "Speaking of buddhas and Zen masters, talking about mysteries and marvels, is all saying too much or too little."

This being so, then where will you seek? You must have the eye to journey before you can.

FA-HUA (FL. CA 1000-1056)

STRAIGHT AND TRUE

Sit straight, and before you buy shoes measure your feet. Looking around this way and that isn't worth a cent.

TA-YÜ SHOU-CHIH (D. CA. 1060)

WAKING UP

When you know illusion, you become unattached, without exercising any technique. When you detach from illusion, you wake up, without going through any process. Shakyamuni Buddha opened up a thousand gates and ten thousand doors all at once; someone who is spiritually sharp will immediately act on that. As for those who shilly-shally, you and I are going in different directions.

TSU-HSIN (ELEVENTH CENTURY)

HEART OF HEARTS

This very mind, heart of hearts, is Buddha, the most spiritual being in the universe. Wondrous functions free in all ways may be charming, but the whole lot of it is not as good as authentic truth of mind.

Do not have the arrogance to pretend you are seeking enlightenment; enlightenment cannot be seen. Do not have the arrogance to pretend you are getting rid of afflictions; afflictions have no front or back. Before the appearance of signs, there is fundamentally no change. If you speak of understanding or nonunderstanding, it is all three necks and two heads. If you go on asking "How?" and "Huh?"— what a pain, this Buddha!

TSU-HSIN

EYES AND FEET

If you only understand your self and not the environment, you have eyes but no feet. If you understand the environment but not your self, you have feet but no eyes. In either case there is something on your chest all the time. Since there is something on your chest, uneasiness is always present, and you get stuck along the way. How can you attain peace? A spiritual ancestor said, "If you cling to it, you lose measure and inevitably fall into a false path. Let it go and be natural; essence neither goes nor stays."

TSU-HSIN

TESTING SEEKERS

I have tested all the Zen seekers in the world with four pivotal sayings:
"There is life within death."
"There is death within life."
"There is permanent death in death."
"There is permanent life in life."
Now tell me, what do all the Zen seekers in the world use to test me?

SSU-HSIN (ELEVENTH CENTURY)

HUMAN SENTIMENT

Buddhism does not obey human sentiments. The elders everywhere all open their mouths wide, saying "I understand Zen, I understand Tao!" But tell me, do they understand or not?

As for those who sit in cesspits for no reason, deceiving spirits and fooling ghosts, even if you killed a thousand or ten thousand of them and fed them to the dogs, what would be wrong with that?

There's also a type of Zen followers who get bewitched by those foxes with their eyes wide open, quite unaware of it themselves. Plunging into pouring piss, they don't even feel disgusted.

Hey! You are all adults! How can you accept this? What should you do yourself?

CHEN-CHING (EXILED 1080)

INDIVIDUAL REALIZATION

This thing cannot be learned, cannot be taught, cannot be transmitted; it can only be attained by individual realization. Once you've attained realization, you are content, unpreoccupied, thoroughly lucid, clear and at ease. All spiritual capacities and miracle working are inherent endowments and need not be sought elsewhere.

CHEN-CHING

PREPAREDNESS

It's hard to find people ready for Buddhism. Some do not believe in the fact of the Buddha within themselves, only relying on a little bit of the influence of the ancients, on imitation wisdom. The domain of their knowledge is doctrines on characteristics of meditation; in action, they turn away from enlightenment and get mixed up in the dust, stuck and unable to get free. If students come to them, it is like an imprint stamping clay; they successively hand on the imprint, not only fooling themselves but also fooling others.

I have no Buddhism to give anyone. I just have a sword—whoever comes, I cut down, so their lives cannot go on and their seeing and hearing disappear: then I meet them before their parents gave birth to them. If I see them go forward, I cut them off.

However, though the sword is sharp, it does not cut the innocent. Is there anyone who is innocent?

CHEN-CHING

THE PURE LUMINOUS BODY

Shakyamuni Buddha said that the continuing birth and death of all beings is because they don't know the pure luminous body of the eternal true essence of mind, and employ all sorts of false thoughts; because these thoughts are not real, there is habitual repetition.

Do you want birth and death not to continue, the falsely thinking mind to die out? Just directly get to know the pure luminous body of the eternal true essence of mind in yourself. Then birth and death naturally will not continue, and everyone will rejoice together. This is what is called attainment once and for all time.

If you cannot believe in it and won't listen, then you remain sunk in habit-ridden consciousness, an ocean of ignorance.

CHEN-CHING

REMOVING BONDS

I do not understand Zen, I do not understand Tao: I only know how to dissolve glue and remove bonds, to give medicines according to ailments.

There is no Zen to study, no Tao to learn. Abandoning the fundamental to pursue trivia, busily working on externals, is not as good as coming back to get to know your own citadel.

In the citadel is your own spiritual monarch to honor, who answers a hundredfold when called once, who wants all people to wake up themselves.

Come, come! What you must do is put down your previous knowledge and views of Buddhism all at once; then the mental stamp of your own cosmic Buddha will be clear through and through.

CHEN-CHING

ONLY MIND

Before you have realized objects are only mind, you produce all sorts of discriminations; after you have realized objects are only mind, discrimination does not arise. When you know all things are only mind, then you let go of the forms of external objects. But what about the earth, the mountains and rivers, light and dark, matter and space: with all things right before you, what principle of letting go can you speak of?

Even if you understand this, you are still just halfway. You must realize there is yet another opening going beyond.

YUN-FENG WEN-YUEH (D. CA. 1060)

TRUTH AND THE WAY

The way is the perennial Way, the truth is the perennial Truth; don't misapply body and mind chasing after sayings. This is why it is said that "even the slightest object is dust; as soon as you arouse intent, you're confused by hallucination."

YUN-FENG

STOP

If you can stop right now, then stop; if you seek a time of completion, there is no time of completion. If you make up intellectual understanding of this matter based on words, or try to figure it out conceptually, you are as far from it as the sky is from earth.

For people of great power, cutting in two with one slash is not yet attainment; how much less is being called away by someone else to give muddled explanations in an abbot's room, citing scripture and treatise, bringing up senses and objects, material phenomena, transcendence and immanence, being and nonbeing, gain and loss! Some day you will die without having found your place.

YUN-FENG

WARPED UNDERSTANDING

In recent times there is another kind of Zen master who enjoys fame for twenty or thirty years just telling people not to pay attention to the sayings of others, calling this "passing through sound and form." When they are asked about the east, they answer about the west, considering that "expression beyond convention." Passing on this warped understanding, they have thus confused and damaged Zen teaching, fooling and deluding younger generations.

YUN-FENG

ABSOLUTE AND RELATIVE

When the absolute is absolute, it is incomplete; within completeness there is also the relative. When the relative is relative, it is not material; even within matter, completeness remains. Deep in the night, there's the energy that brings on dawn; when the sun is at its peak, it lights up the skies.

I-CH'ING (1032–1083)

CONCEPTS AND EMOTIONS

Zen is not in conceptual understanding; how can the way be sought by emotions?

I-CH'ING

ORIGINAL ZEN

In the original Zen school, an authentic meeting was not a matter of climbing up into a high pulpit and setting out verbal points. Why? This is why it is said that if verbal points miss, home's ten thousand miles away.

You simply have to let go over a cliff, willingly accept the experience, and revive after annihilation. It will be impossible to deceive you.

This is why past sages skillfully employed expedient techniques, eventually setting out many methods, setting them up on a nonabiding basis. Since the basis is nonabiding, it can respond to a multitude of conditions, just like an enormous bell sounding when struck, like the moonlight reflecting in a thousand rivers. This is unconditional compassion responding sensitively according to potential, a nondual message divided according to faculties and natures. Although the teachings take many tracks, the ideal goal is one.

HUI-LIN (1020–1099)

THE PATH

Truth has no this or that, the path has no ordinary or holy: throughout the ages it has been smooth, beyond all cultivation and realization. Those who get it produce lotuses in scarlet flames, those who lose it grasp at reflections in aquamarine pools.

The reason you have not attained it yet is generally because of the present time. I will sweep away thoughts of both good and bad all at once for you, and even get you not to make extinction your home, not to make emptiness your seat, and not to make myriad practices your clothing, so in action you are like the flight of a bird, and in stillness you are like open space.

FU-JUNG (1042–1118)

A SHORTCUT

A shortcut into the path is to be inwardly empty and outwardly quiet, like water that is clear and still, myriad images reflecting in it, neither sinking nor floating, all things spontaneously so.

FU-JUNG

AVOIDING RESIDUAL TROUBLE

"All realities are uncreated, all realities are imperishable"—if you can understand thus, the buddhas are always present. You should take the mind that frantically seeks every day and use it to investigate this matter. After a long, long time it will naturally become clear. If you do not do this, you are living and dying in vain. An ancient said, "Make an effort; you must understand in this life. Don't subject yourself to residual trouble over the ages."

HUAI-SHAN (FL. CA. 1115)

SIX ROADS

There are six roads before you: one is suitable for travel, five are not.

First, don't rub your eyes and create optical illusions on the subtle ground of the sages.

Second, don't take servant for master on the ground of ordinary reality.

Third, don't play with physical energy in a state of light.

Fourth, don't be an escapist in the room of nothing.

Fifth, don't talk of yellow and red in a nest of complications.

The sixth road is the only one I'd let you go on. But tell me, how do you travel this road?

Understand?

If not for your footgear's wearing out, how do you notice the forked road is long?

HUAI-SHAN

SELF-DEFEAT

The ultimate way is without difficulty; those who seek it make their own hardship. The true mind is originally pure; those who exercise it make their own defilement.

HUI-K'UNG (1096–1158)

THE LIVING EYE

The living eye of Zen sees clearly through the heavens: the livelihood of the six senses takes place everywhere, without borrowing the form or appearance of another.

TZU-TE (1090–1159)

LOOKING FOR AND LOOKING AT

I have something here: when you look at it, it's there, but when you look for it, it's not. What is it?

TZU-TE

THE BLACK PEARL

When you are completely clear, there is no subjective distortion; when you are completely pure, there is true perception. But even if you are thus through and through, this is still not the transcendental key. When the wind and waves have died out, the ocean of mind is as is; when you get to the bottom of the ocean of mind, for the first time you see the black pearl.

TZU-TE

FABRICATIONS

As I see people pursuing the path today, none of them seem to be in accord with it. Why is this so? Some of them control their minds to make them settled within, others gather in their thoughts to induce stabilization. All of them are fabrications. In reality, this is not inner mastery at all.

If they are able to want to see, these people have to turn around this mindless state; would they have no understanding? This is why scripture says, "Bodhisattvas entering concentration are not yet free of the phenomenon of this concentration."

Scripture also says, "Having realized the purity of the realm of reality by permanent detachment through laborious meditation, that understanding of purity then becomes self-obstruction. You should know there is an even deeper mind."

TZU-TE

THE BLIND LEADING THE BLIND

There are some white-robed lay devotees who keep up the discipline of not eating after noon as if they were saints, yet are completely wrapped up in profiteering, ruining commoners and kinfolk. When they die, every one of them will be like turtles with their shells stripped off alive, winding up like foxes and badgers skinned alive, going right to uninterrupted hell, to be sunk forever without a break. An ancient said, "When one who is blind leads many who are blind, they lead each other into a pit of fire." The *Scripture of Complete Enlightenment* says, "It is not people's fault, but the error of false teachers."

P'U-AN (D. 1169)

THIS MIND

Bodhidharma came from the West and just pointed to the human mind, to show its nature and enlighten it. That was undeniably direct and economical, but when seen with the absolute eye, it is already all mixed up. There is no choice for now but to make some medicine for a dead horse.

This mind that is simply pointed to is precisely what the Buddha could not express in forty-nine years of lectures and talks. It is extremely rarefied, extremely subtle; few are able to find the true pulse.

This mind cannot be transmitted but can only be experienced in oneself and understood in oneself. When you get to the point where there is neither delusion nor enlightenment, you simply dress and eat as normal, without a bunch of arcane interpretations and lines of doctrine jamming your chest, so you're clear and uncluttered.

YING-AN (D. 1163)

AN INEXHAUSTIBLE TREASURY

Correctness in self-management is in the self; the most important step of a thousand-mile journey is the first one. If you manage both of these well, then you have graduated the infinite subtle doctrines of the hundred thousand doors of the teaching. Therefore this is called concentration of an inexhaustible treasury.

YING-AN

The Experience of the True Human Being

The founding teacher came from the West and pointed directly at the human mind to show its nature and foster enlightenment, but in Zen this is like digging a hole in the ground and burying people alive. It was out of temporal necessity that medicine for a dead horse was made, with talk about Buddha, Zen masters, mind, and nature, like switching sweet fruit for bitter gourd.

As for powerful people, they cut in two with one blow of the sword, stepping back into themselves, seeing through to the original face before a single thought is conceived, illuminating the universe, penetrating everywhere. Then they are no different from Shakyamuni Buddha. This is called the crowning royal concentration, it is called the bonfire, it is called the diamond sword, it is called the crouching lion, it is called the poison drum; it is referred to by various names.

At this time, who makes birth and death? Who makes coming and going? Who makes good and bad? Who makes opposition and harmony? Who makes right and wrong? Who makes heaven and hell? Who makes the various states of being? The whole world is a door of liberation; the whole thing is the experience of the true human being with no position.

YING-AN

Moon and Clouds

Comprehending illusion from within enlightenment is like the moon stamping a thousand peaks; wishing for enlightenment from within illusion is like clouds dotting the endless sky.

P'U-AN

One True Source

People who have yet to understand use mind to seek mind and make Buddha seek Buddha. They have no prospect of attainment. What they don't realize is that all conscious beings are of the same one true source.

P'U-AN

DIRECT EXPERIENCE

You must detach from forms and labels before you can learn the way. When your learning reaches the effortless knowledge that is not learned, the path is not a fixed path—the mind itself is the buddha-mind. Maximum capacity becomes accessible; not from formal externals, but experienced directly.

P'U-AN

ADEPTS AND SHOW-OFFS

Venerable adepts since ancient times worked on this thing until they had passed through to where there is no trouble at all; only then did they dare to take up positions as guides for others. How could they be compared with those today who show off for fame and profit, blinding people with confusion?

YING-AN

NONCOMPETITIVENESS

The way the old adepts of ancient times asked about the path was not competitive or contentious; they would inquire of anyone with some strength, even a child. Only thus may people be called students of the way.

Followers of Zen in recent times may say they are going traveling solely to investigate the great concerns of life and death, but though they may imitate the appearances of the ancients, they remain very competitive and contentious. Once you have this problem, the source of direct pointing cannot be understood.

It is like the case of archers: if they start out competing, they'll never achieve good marksmanship. It is after long practice without thought of winning or losing that they can hit the target. So it is with study of the path: if even a single thought of winning and losing abides in the heart, you will be chained by winning and losing.

YING-AN

UNDERSTANDING

First of all, do not predefine understanding, and do not make a principle of nonunderstanding.

YING-AN

GOING BEYOND

When you get to the point where even a thousand people, even ten thousand people, cannot trap you or cage you, that is still not expertise. You must go on to the beyond and activate the transcendental key, never injuring your hand against the sharp edge, bringing everyone in the world to life.

YING-AN

ZEN AND GENDER

The Transcendental path is not masculine or feminine.

YING-AN

CHARLATANS

Pay close attention. An ancient worthy said, "A swift hound does not bare its teeth, but hardly do you make a move before it's on you right away!" Students in recent times insist on preaching Zen as religion before they have understood their own selves. They are all charlatans.

HUAI-T'ANG (TWELFTH CENTURY)

DETERIORATION

If pilgrims have no spiritual bones, their eyes do not know people, and they do not meet a real true Zen master to open their minds, they plunge into a bag of curios: gathering in groups of two or three hundred, they make wild cries and talk wild talk, discoursing on mind and nature, lecturing on Zen and the way, criticizing and extolling ancients and moderns. They call this Buddhism and consider it the essence of the teaching, but this is actually slandering the universal vehicle, creating seeds of hell.

Such people are very numerous; they are to be pitied. Our path has deteriorated!

HUAI-T'ANG

THE IMPASSABLE BARRIER

Even if you attain realization of the emptiness of persons and things, this does not measure up to the way of Zen. Even if you embody complete function and complete perception, this is still not the essential wonder of Zen. You must break through the impassable barrier and get to know the opening beyond.

FO-HSING T'AI (TWELFTH CENTURY)

NO ACTUAL DOCTRINE

If we are to discuss this matter, the simple fact is that there is nothing whatsoever to point out to people. If there were anything at all to indicate to people, Buddhism would not have reached the present day. For this reason the successions of buddhas extending a hand and the successions of Zen masters passing on transmission have done so for lack of practical choice; there has never been an actual doctrine.

FU-AN (TWELFTH CENTURY)

TRUE SPEECH

The sun may cool off and the moon may heat up, but all the bedevilments there are cannot destroy true speech.

What is true speech? Ninety percent accuracy is not as good as silence.

YUEH-LIN (THIRTEENTH CENTURY)

PAY ATTENTION

It is presented right to your face, wholeheartedly imparted: if you have keen faculties and higher wisdom, you will carry it with your whole body, with unavoidable strictness. As soon as you get involved in thought, formalizing it in writing and verbal conventions, you have lost contact. Therefore it is said, "The way is nearby, yet you seek it afar."

Just manage to pay attention twenty-four hours a day, whatever you may be doing, stepping back into yourself and silently bringing up over and over again the contemplation "What is this?" Keep contemplating throughout your comings and goings, contemplating until you reach the point where there is no flavor, and no place to get a grip or a foothold, and your body and mind are like space, yet do not seem like space. Suddenly you lose your footing and stomp over the scenery of the original ground, breaking out in a sweat. This makes your life joyful!

Then you can respond to people according to potential, picking up what comes to hand, saying what comes to mind, putting to use what is right there, having a way out in every expression. Buddhism and things of the world become one. Then you go to another genuine teacher to make sure of the profound depths; it is like going into the oceans: the further you go, the deeper it is. The moment there is any clinging, any conceit or dependence on others, you are the same as an outsider. The reason those who study the path in the present time are not as advanced as earlier ones is often because they gain a little and consider it enough.

SUNG-YUAN (1139–1209)

QUINTESSENTIAL ZEN

Since time immemorial, when buddhas or Zen masters have dealt with sharp and clear people with the keen faculties appropriate to the higher vehicle, they have simply required transcendence of feelings, detachment from views, and liveliness of functions, knowing something before it's brought up, understanding something before it's said, cutting through appearances, never pursuing thought in the conceptual faculty, making body and mind empty, immaterially spiritual, serenely sublimated, inwardly clarifying independent individual perception, outwardly unattached to anything at all. When inside and outside are clear, there is only one true reality: not being companion to myriad things, not congregating with the thousand sages, you are independently liberated, transcendent, independent, and free.

SUNG-YUAN

SELF-OBSTRUCTION

The essence of the message that is specially transmitted outside of doctrine is present in all states, and the true mind is in all consciousness; the radiant light of its powers, freedoms, and total functioning shines brilliantly day and night without interruption. Yet people do not consciously know it; they make their own obstructions, blowing it off to the back of their brains. Then they go elsewhere to ask about Buddha, to ask about mastery, to seek Zen, to seek the path. For this reason they are called pitiful.

P'O-AN (1136–1211)

STAND ON YOUR OWN

Zennists are spontaneously able to roar the lion's roar while still in their mothers' wombs. Only when you are like this can you uphold this school. As for those who are conceited yet rely on others, depending on instructions from another, memorizing the sayings of others as if this were the way to the source, all of them are destroyers of Buddhism.

The fact that this path has not been flourishing in recent times is because teachers and disciples give each other approval and recognition, ignoring cause and effect and duping the people, claiming themselves able to uphold this school. It is like sculpting a "sandalwood" icon out of dung—no matter how long a time passes, it simply stinks.

You should get away from such people as soon as possible. Apply your own concentrated attention, apply your own eyes and brains; develop yourself, stand on your own. One day your own eyes will clear and will radiate light shining through the whole world. Only then will you live up to the aim of your journey.

When a master craftsman instructs people, he can give them compass and ruler but cannot give them skill. The function of Zen teachers is otherwise: first they take away your compass and ruler, then wait until you can cut squares and circles freehand, spontaneously conforming to compass and ruler; thus the skill is therein.

Even so, this too is a temporary byroad, a little resting place. Going through the gate of Zen, you still have to study for thirty years.

CH'IH-CHUEH (FL. CA. 1208–1225)

THE REALM OF BUDDHAHOOD

An ancient said, "If people want to know the realm of buddhahood, they should make their minds clear as open space, detaching from all false thoughts and all grasping, making their minds unobstructed wherever they turn." What is the realm of buddhahood? Basically it is the normal course of one's own mind in everyday life; it's just that one daily buries one's head in things and events and is swept along under the influence of objects.

If you want to harmonize with the realm of buddhahood, if you can just keep mindful twenty-four hours a day, not giving up through every state of mind, one day it will be like meeting an old friend in a busy city: "Oh! So here you are!"

When you get to this state, errant thoughts and all grasping melt right away, and everything becomes your own subtle function.

CH'IH-CHUEH

THE FAILURE OF ZEN

The failure of the Zen path comes from teachers without deep attainment just setting forth sayings and showing off knowledge as a tool to capture students, and from students with no great aspiration just following popular fads and current customs, content to sink themselves in the domain of intellectual knowledge and verbiage, not knowing how to return. The "teachers" and "students" bewitch each other.

CH'IH-CHUEH

The Normal Course

The normal course of everyday life is not in events and things; the source not transmitted by a thousand sages is not confined to the realm of mystic wonder. If you don't have your feet on the real ground, with the wonder in the turning point, how are you worth talking to about this?

If in the midst of events and things you see all the way through, then the source not transmitted by a thousand sages appears every moment; if you can shed the realm of mystic wonder, then the normal course of everyday life will fit into the groove.

Ch'ih-chueh

The Mind

How great the mind is! It is so vast it is all-encompassing, so fine it is all-pervading. Enhancement doesn't make excess; minimization doesn't make lack. Silently it operates spontaneously; serenely it responds skillfully. It is swift without speeding; it arrives without going. Location and mass cannot contain it; measurements and numbers cannot plumb it.

It is clearly there in the midst of everyday activities, but students cannot avail themselves of it because emotional thoughts stultify them and desire for gain dulls them. In subtle ways, they are compelled by creation, subsistence, change, and extinction; in crude ways, they are compelled by earth, water, fire, and air. Forgetting themselves, they pursue things; abandoning the real, they pursue the artificial. Ultimately swept away irrevocably, everyone in the world is like this.

If you can get rid of the veils over the mind, restore the root of nature, and clearly see the mind in the midst of everyday life, then emotions, thoughts, and desires; creation, subsistence, change, and extinction; earth, water, fire, and air, are all your own subtle functions.

Ch'ih-chueh

INSIDE AND OUTSIDE

"There is no thing before the eyes"—a long sword against the sky. "The idea is before the eyes"—a thousand peals of thunder roar. Whether you get it or not, you still do not escape losing your life.

This matter is so vast it contains the universe, so fine it penetrates atomic particles. It is not comprehended by perception and cognition, not understood by worldly knowledge and intellectual brilliance. Yuan-wu said, "It should not be that it exists when you speak of it but not when you don't." Miao-hsi said, "It cannot be that it is there when you're sitting on a cushion and not there when you get off the meditation seat."

Here, turn over the tongues of these two elders, and then you will know there is a living road right in front of you. Twenty-four hours a day, throughout all of your activities, you "enter the forest without disturbing the grasses, go into the water without stirring up waves." Even in an urban environment, you are not caged or bridled by sound and form; even if prosperous and well positioned, you are not moved or changed by the glory of success. Thus it is said, "Break out from inside, and your power is strong; break in from outside, and your power is weak."

FO-CHIH (FL. CA. 1228)

ACTION AND STILLNESS

Let your actions be like clouds going by; the clouds going by are mindless. Let your stillness be as the valley spirit; the valley spirit is undying. When action accompanies stillness and stillness combines with action, then the duality of action and stillness no longer arises.

PEI-CHIEN (1185–1246)

DISCOVERY OF MIND

Teachers have appeared in the world to uphold this thing, spreading a net to bring in those of the very highest capacity. When you find out their essential subtlety, it is not beyond the discovery of each individual's own mind.

Once the mind is clear, this very word *clarity* doesn't stick anywhere anymore; it is like a snowflake on a red-hot fireplace.

When you get to such a state, you still need long-term refinement and polishing to reach complete maturity.

Once the roots are firm, there is no need to worry that the branches might not flourish. Only then can you deal with important matters and take on great responsibilities. Life and death, calamity and fortune, cannot move you at all; whether you are in adversity or prosperity, withdrawn or expansive, in activity or in quietude, you hit the target in every case.

In action, you adapt to changes with intuitive penetration and complete fluidity without bound. In stillness, you are open and clear, independently illumined, not imprisoned by special wondrous states. This is what is meant by the saying "All times and all places are my livelihood."

WU-CHUN (D. 1249)

DAILY ACTIVITIES

The path is in daily activities, but if you linger in daily activities, then you are taking a thief for your son. If you seek some special life outside of daily activities, that is like brushing aside waves to look for water.

WU-CHUN

THE PATH AND THE END

The path cannot be sought—the important thing is just to stop the mind. However, this stopping is not to be forced. You need to search morning and night until you reach the point where the road of conception comes to an end, whereupon you'll suddenly spontaneously stop. After this stopping, the racing and seeking mind stops.

It is like a traveler stopping at an inn. In his desire to get where he's going, he puts his effort into traveling, for if he doesn't travel he won't get there. Once he's arrived, all the toils and pains of the road come to an end and he goes running off no more.

WU-CHUN

THE PIVOT OF THE ZEN GATE

The pivot of the Zen gate is not a matter of going from group to group; how does the guiding principle of Zen seekers need taking on one teacher after another?

If you see horns on the other side of a fence, clearly there's an inference to be made. If you still want to depict it in words, that's like the case of a master painter making a lifelike portrait of an ox—after all it's not a live ox.

I have heard that the verbal teachings of the Zen masters are for orienting the efforts of people of the time: if their efforts are not disoriented, don't bother to orient them. The verbal teachings of Zen masters and buddhas are prescriptions for curing the insane; if the mind and spirit are not deranged, don't bother to cure them.

The only words to be said to those who know are *urgency* and *intentness*. If you don't clearly understand your own self, you have no way to fend off birth and death; if you do not understand the surroundings, how can you tell right from wrong?

CHUEH-AN (1250s)

WORLDLY AFFAIRS

Men of affairs who are in positions of wealth and rank yet are not trapped by wealth and rank, and are also able to break through the iron face of the mortal being and focus their minds on this path, must already have the seed of wisdom; otherwise, how could they reach this?

The trouble is not being able to do real true work in deadly earnest. We see many who think and compare, consciously anticipating enlightenment, trying deliberately to achieve cessation, rejoicing when others privately acknowledge them, wanting people to praise them. As soon as you give rise to these thoughts, this is the root of birth and death.

HSI-SOU (FL. CA. 1249)

AWAKEN ON YOUR OWN

Learning the path of Zen study has no special mysterious gateway or essential road: it requires individuals to awaken on their own. If you have awakened correctly once, you see mountains are not mountains and rivers are not rivers; then after that you see mountains are mountains and rivers are rivers. If you are not awakened, when you see things you are obstructed by seeing, influenced by things, confused by objects. This is what is called restlessness of habit-ridden consciousness, in which there is no reliable basis.

YUN-KU (FL. CA. 1256)

THE GREAT WAY

The great way is right before our eyes, but it is still hard to see what is right before our eyes. If you want to know the true substance of the great way, it is not apart from sound and form, words and speech.

WU-MEN (1183–1260)

BUDDHISM AND HUMAN SENTIMENT

Even if one's body is wrapped in hot iron, and molten copper is poured down one's throat, one should never equate Buddhism with human sentiment.

When human sentiments are thick, the sense of truth is slight. What does the world know of true capacities and human sentiments? Where there are only vain human sentiments, there is no real capacity; how long can human sentiments last?

WU-MEN

THOROUGH COOKING

Once three scholars on the way to the civil service examination stopped to buy refreshments from a woman who sold pastries by the wayside. One man was calm and quiet, while the other two argued over literature. The woman asked where they were going. The latter two told her they were going to take the civil service examination. She said, "You two scholars won't pass the exam; that other man will." The two men swore at her and left.

When the results of the examination turned out as the woman had predicted, the two scholars who had failed went back to find out how she had known they would not pass, while the third man would.

They asked her if she knew physiognomy. "No," she said, "all I know is that when a pastry is thoroughly cooked, it sits there quietly, but before it's finished it keeps on making noise."

WU-MEN

NOMINAL ZEN STUDY

Master Shih-t'ou said, "A thousand kinds of sayings and ten thousand sorts of explanations are just intended to teach you to always be unconfused." What is popular in groups nowadays is just nominal Zen study; to try to find even one person who is always unconfused is like trying to pick the moon from the sky.

TUAN-CH'IAO (CA. 1241)

LIFE AND DEATH

The matter of life and death is important; impermanence is swift. Aspirants of Zen all understand the path, but when you ask them why we live and why we die, ten out of ten are dumbstruck. If you go on this way, even if you journey throughout the whole world, what will it accomplish?

TUAN-CH'IAO

DAILY ACTIVITIES

The way is in daily activities; it is used every day, unknowingly. That is why it is said, "Knowing is false consciousness, not knowing is indifference." At this point, tell me, is knowing right or is not knowing right?

The elders since time immemorial and the pilgrims all over the world have all scraped through the bottoms of their rice bags and worn out their footgear, but I have never seen anyone who could get through this double barrier.

If you can't get through, it's better to just walk when walking, just sit when sitting.

HSUEH-YEN (FL. CA. 1253)

CLARIFYING MIND

What is most essential to Buddhism is based on clarifying the mind. If you want your mind to be clear, it is important to put opinions to rest. If opinions are not stopped, then wrong and right are confused; if the mind is not clear, reality and illusion are mixed up. If you stop opinions and clear the mind, then reality and illusion are both empty, wrong and right do not stand.

HSUEH-YEN

THREE TYPES OF LEARNING

The Buddhist path has its source in the three types of learning—discipline, concentration, and insight. Discipline holds the mind with regulations, concentration illumines the mind with stillness, insight clarifies the mind with wisdom.

If one has insight without concentration or discipline, then one remains unrestrained, uselessly engaging in verbalization without being able to stop repetitive routines and shed birth and death.

If one has concentration without discipline or insight, then one remains in empty stillness and uselessly lingers in blank emptiness and cannot elucidate the great teaching to guide people.

If one has discipline but no concentration or wisdom, then one continues clinging, uselessly getting mired in rules, unable to unify right and wrong and equalize others and self.

Nevertheless, insight is concentration, and concentration is discipline: discipline can produce concentration, concentration can produce insight.

Insight, concentration, and discipline originate in one mind. If the mind fundamentally does not exist, where do discipline, concentration, and insight come from?

So it exists without existing, vast as cosmic space: all worlds of the whole universe, all the plants, trees, and forests, the birds, beasts, and people, as well as the eighty-four thousand troubles of the world, are all none other than this mind.

When the mind is not aroused, this is discipline; when the mind is unmoved, this is concentration; when the mind is not obscured, this is insight.

HSUEH-YEN

THE EYES FOR THE JOURNEY

To journey, you must have eyes for the journey; if you don't have eyes, the old baldies sitting in carved wood chairs everywhere will set out used furniture from the past before you, putting big prices on them, boasting in a hundred ways that they are rare and marvelous treasures. You may lose your eyes and brains all at once; unable to get anywhere, you may not avoid being confused by them and getting into a bunch of antique curios, never to emerge.

HSI-YEN (1198–1262)

WHERE IS THE PROBLEM?

When people spend ten or twenty years, or even a whole lifetime, just clarifying this matter, detached from the world and forgetful of objects, and yet they do not penetrate through to freedom, where is the problem? Genuine seekers should try to bring it out.

Is it lack of spiritual potential? Is it not having met an enlightened teacher? Is it inconsistency? Is it inferiority of faculties and weakness of will? Is it floating and sinking in mundane toils? Is it settling in emptiness and stagnating in stillness? Is it that miscellaneous poisons have gotten into the mind? Is it that the time has not yet arrived? Is it failure to wonder about sayings? Is it that they think they have attained what they have not, or think they have realized what they have not?

KAO-FENG (1260s)

THE FIRE OF ZEN

This thing is like an enormous fire, fierce flames pervading the sky, with never the slightest interruption. Everything in the world is thrown into it, immediately evaporating away like a fleck of snow.

KAO-FENG

TURNING DOCTRINE INTO SICKNESS

Those who have spent ten or twenty years brushing aside the weeds looking for the way and yet have not seen the buddha nature often say they are trapped by oblivion and excitement. What they don't realize is that the substance of this very oblivion and excitement is itself buddha nature.

It is a pity that deluded people do not understand; they arbitrarly cling to doctrines and turn them into sicknesses, using sickness to attack sickness. They make it so they get further estranged from buddha nature the more they seek it. The more they hurry, the more they're delayed.

Even if one or two turn their attention around, look back into themselves and realize their error, empty out and forget both medicine and disease so that their eyes emerge and they clearly understand the simple message of Zen, seeing into their original buddha nature, in my estimation this is still something on the shore of birth and death. If you would talk about the road of transcendence, you should know it is even beyond the green mountains.

KAO-FENG

DON'T CLING TO THE CUSHION

It is essential in Zen study that you do not cling to a sitting cushion for practice. If you sink into oblivion or distraction, or plunge into ease and tranquillity, totally unawares, not only will you waste time, you will not be able to digest the offerings of donors. When the light of your eyes falls to the ground one day, in the end what will you rely on?

KAO-FENG

THE INEXHAUSTIBLE TREASURY

This matter is like a pile of trash under the eaves of someone's house; from morning to night rain beats on it, wind blows on it, but nobody pays attention to it. They do not realize there is an inexhaustible treasure trove within it; if they could avail themselves of it, they could take from it and put it to use for a hundred aeons and a thousand lifetimes without exhausting it.

You should know that this treasury doesn't come from outside; it all emerges from your faith. If you can have complete faith in it, you certainly won't be cheated. If you do not have complete faith, you will never realize it even in countless aeons. So I ask you to have faith in this way, so you can avoid being destitute beggars.

But tell me, where is this treasury right now?

If you don't go into the tiger's den, how can you catch a tiger cub?

KAO-FENG

THE LIMIT OF EFFORT

When you investigate this matter, the extreme limit of effort is like planting flowers in the sky or fishing for the moon in the water: there is simply no place for you to set about it, no place to apply your mind. Time and again people beat the drum of retreat as soon as they run into this state; they don't realize that this is actually news of getting home.

If they are bold, people face the state where there's no place to set to work, when the mind cannot be applied, like great generals in the midst of huge armies, directly capturing their adversaries, mindless of gain or loss. If you truly have such a grasp of the essential, and such keenness, you can achieve success in a fingersnap, attaining sagehood instantly.

KAO-FENG

THREE BARRIERS

The bright sun is in the sky, shining on everything; why is it blocked by a cloud?

Everyone has a shadow, which never leaves; why can't you step on it?

The whole world is a fire pit; attaining what state of mind can you avoid being burned?

KAO-FENG

STUDY THE LIVING WORD

If you want to reach this state, you should immediately get rid of your previous learned understanding, both that which is clear and that which is obscure, gradually making your whole body like a hot iron ball, next door to death: take up a saying of an ancient and toss it in front of you, looking at it like a born enemy. Day and night be as if you were sitting in thorns, and someday you will naturally have a breakthrough.

Do not under any circumstances stick to the form of sitting. When you do sit, you must employ expedient means; if you do it without inner mastery, you belabor your spirit in vain. An ancient said, "When the mind is vacant and the surroundings are still, it is just because of stagnation. When you study Zen, you should study the living word, not the dead word. If you understand through the dead word, you cannot even save yourself."

HSU-T'ANG (1185–1269)

THE SCENERY OF THE ORIGINAL GROUND

The scenery of the original ground is completely fluid and without bounds before mortals and buddhas are there; suddenly it is obscured by false perceptions, whereupon we stagnate and sink into mundane toils, grasping all objects, until we are infected by psychological afflictions. If you are unable to turn attention around to illumine the self right away, how can you pass through so many myriad entanglements?

Whether in adverse or favorable situations, neither grasp nor cling; cut right through speech and silence, being and nothingness, action and stillness. When dealing with things, responding to potentials, like a flying sword discus, like a blazing fire, you leave no shadow or trace at all. Thus you are empty and spiritual, tranquil and sublime; with one perception you illumine myriad distinctions, a thousand differentiations. Arriving directly at a state of great peace, you find there is no stagnation at all.

HAI-YIN (CA. 1282)

FULFILLMENT

Virtue has no fixed teacher—focus on goodness is the teacher. If teachers are effective, then you know they are to be regarded as teachers.

You find out the truth and fulfill your nature to arrive at your destiny; to transcend at once, without going through a process, you need to find out the ultimate.

A monk asked Chao-chou, "Does a dog have buddha nature or not?" Chao-chou said, "No." This is not "no" meaning nonexistence of an existence, nor is it "no" meaning pure nonexistence. It is a non-rational mystic razor, a sublime method of transforming life's fortunes.

Go right ahead and bring it up; right away you'll empty out. Like a silver mountain, an iron wall, you'll be impervious to gain and loss, praise and blame; neither honor nor censure, neither pain nor pleasure, can trap you.

You do not plunge into the sentiments of the ordinary, nor do you fall into the understanding of the sage. Empty and spiritual, serene and sublime, you do not tarry anywhere but attain fulfillment everywhere.

At this time, you should know there is a final statement; only then are you a mature person. Completing the task of the mature person is called transcending the world in the midst of the world, highest of all.

HAI-YIN

DELUSION AND ENLIGHTENMENT

When deluded, you are deluded about the contents of enlightenment; when enlightened, you are enlightened about the contents of delusion. When delusion and enlightenment are both forgotten, it is like a man cutting off his own head: if his head is cut off, there's no one to do the cutting.

If you see this clearly, right away you'll have no second thought. An ancient said, "Clearly, clearly there is no enlightenment; if there is any dogma, it is delusion." When you get here, you can't take a stand and you can't stay: if you take a stand you will be in peril; if you stay, you will be blind.

Just do not react automatically to the outside world, and do not take refuge in voidness within. Do not pursue trivialities outside, and do not stay in trance inside.

It is imperative that ideas do not inhibit mystery, expressions do not inhibit ideas, and functions do not inhibit potentials. Once these three things are clear, they naturally appear everywhere without need for concentration, naturally clear everywhere without need for special attention.

In this state, frequently meeting is not intimacy, transcendent aloofness is not estrangement. When dealing with them accordingly, one is not obstructed by events; when sitting quietly, one is not lost in the noumenon. Being the master wherever one may be, one finds the source in everything, appearing and disappearing, now reserved, now expansive, having attained great freedom.

And yet one must also know there is an opening beyond.

HAI-YIN

EXPEDIENTS

"Faith is the basis of the path, the mother of virtue; it nourishes all roots of goodness."

Every word uttered by sages of yore as expedient methods were medicines given in accordance with particular ailments—when was there ever any actual dogma to bind people?

If you are confused, there are a thousand differentiations, ten thousand distinctions. If you are enlightened, everything is the same one family.

WU-CHIEN (FL. CA. 1265–1300)

DIRECTED EFFORT

Unexcelled sublime enlightenment is originally in-herent in everyone, but because of accumulated ages of arbitrary ideas and clinging attachments, people cannot clarify the scenery of the original state all at once. People of great strength should employ real true directed effort, bringing up an ancient saying in all situations, secretly evoking it without interruption through successive states of mind. When you suddenly break through the feeling of doubt, for the first time you will have some freedom.

WU-CHIEN

LIBERATION AND BLOCKAGE

The ancients circulate verbal teachings of buddhas and Zen masters for the edification of later learners, with the subtlety to pull out nails, remove stakes, dissolve stickiness, and remove bonds. When it came to taking care of details over and over, making unconventional changes for effectiveness, they were like rolling round boulders down mountains ten miles high. Perpetuating such examples among those of later ages was for no other reason than to remove mental clinging, contentiousness, intellectual opinion, and theoretical understanding, to place people in the empty and clear, clean and naked, bare and untrammeled state of great liberation.

Now it is otherwise. There tend to be those who are blocked by worldly knowledge and intellectual sharpness, divided into those who argue forcefully and those who overcome themselves; and there are ascetics who fall into quietism or ambitious activism. When you observe their behavior, they all claim to have the claws and fangs of time immemorial, but when it comes to situational adaptation in contact with conditions at large, they are invariably living in ghost caves in mountains of darkness.

This matter is certainly not to be rushed. It is essential that the individual be clear and precise in getting the gist, and after that not leak at all twenty-four hours a day. Only then is it appropriate to go to another for certain discernment, lest one still be blown by the wind of intellectual understanding. If one is unwilling to give up what one has treasured, it will become a serious problem in the future.

Even more problematic is when one wants to clarify this matter without a genuine basis and without the necessary attainments. How is that different from worms dancing in hopes of soaring into the misty clouds and undergoing a miraculous transformation? Can they do it?

KU-LIN (FL. CA. 1297–1308)

NAMELESS AND TRACELESS

When mind does not stick to things and consciousness does not dwell in mystery, great knowledge is nameless, true emptiness is traceless. So where do you place your feet twenty-four hours a day? If you are immediately unconcerned, you fall into perception and cognition; yet as soon as you get into deliberate arrangement, you do not escape dependence and attachment.

KU-LIN

COLLECTING CONVERSATION PIECES

Fen-yang called on more than seventy teachers: only one or two had insight and vision; the rest were nothing to talk about. Recently there are some people whose knowledge is not clear and who have not learned their own fundamental task; unable to make an existential investigation, instead they work from books, trying to get a supply of things to talk about. They are mistaken—they have thrown away real gold to go after rubble.

KU-LIN

TOTAL ZEN

Zen is your original face; there is no special Zen to study other than this. And there is nothing to see or hear either—the totality of this seeing and hearing is Zen; outside of Zen, no other seeing or hearing can be found.

MING-PEN (1263–1323)

A METHOD OF STOPPING

Zen is the teaching of the true ground of mind. If you are sure you want to comprehend the great matter of life and death, you should know that with a single thought of doubt or confusion you fall into the realm of demons.

When you are concentrating, if your thoughts are mixed up, and random ideas are in a jumble, don't mind them at all, regardless of whether they're good or bad, true or false. Just turn to a saying, until you reach the point where as soon as you resort to the saying it stops torpor, distraction, and miscellaneous thoughts flying in confusion. After a long time of this, they will spontaneously stop.

Even if they don't stop, you still don't need to forcibly suppress them; just keep concentrated right mindfulness continuous, and that's all. If concentrated right mindfulness is stable and continuous, thoughts will naturally dissolve. When thoughts dissolve, then there is hope of transcendent realization of sudden enlightenment.

Once you have attained enlightenment, you will naturally have insight: it can be said that in your own mind you will naturally comprehend the near future, the distant future, what is false and what is not false, and whether there are so many great and small awakenings. You won't need to ask anyone else.

If you haven't awakened yet, for now do not idly ponder this trivia—it will only increase your torpor and distraction.

MING-PEN

TURNING ATTENTION AROUND TO LOOK WITHIN

Turning the attention around to look within is the domain of independent liberation from ordinary sentiments and transcendent access to the realm of great enlightenment. If your work has not yet reached this state, how is attention turned around? How does one look within?

If you have not yet arrived at the stage of true enlightenment, if there is any theory of turning around or introspection, it is all self-deception. When you are thoroughly enlightened, the light of mind turns around without depending on being turned around, awareness introspects without depending on being introverted.

Because there is no dependence, there is no light to turn around and no looking to direct within. This is called absorption in one practice. The buddhas and Zen masters have all dug in their heels here—it is quite unattainable by conceptual consciousness and emotional illusion.

Nowadays some ignoramuses go to quiet, isolated places and gather in their looking and listening, cutting off seeing and hearing, so that they are like wood or stone, and they call that turning the attention around and looking within. They can go on "looking" this way for thirty years, wishing every moment to shed birth and death, but they will not succeed.

MING-PEN

LOOKING INTO A SAYING

Just believe in yourself, and bring up the saying you are looking into. Keep on looking into it no matter how long it takes, and you will naturally penetrate someday. While you are looking into it, don't give rise to any doubtful thinking, and don't give rise to any hurry for enlightenment.

When you are doing the work looking into a saying, whatever extraordinary marvels or effects you may perceive or experience, these are all bedeviling entanglements; as long as you do not let your mind pursue them, they will eventually dissolve of themselves. If you suddenly conceive a momentary feeling of enjoyment or attachment, from this you will fall into the realm of bedevilment. You may think you've awakened, but actually you're deranged.

Enlightenment is like someone returning home: everything is familiar, so one is naturally comfortable and clear about everything, without any further thoughts of doubt or confusion at all. If there is still half a speck of doubt or confusion, it certainly isn't your home. Then you must toss it away and seek elsewhere; otherwise you'll get conceited and develop idiosyncratic views.

MING-PEN

NO ARRANGEMENT

Mind is originally clear and calm, fundamentally free from pollution; and there is no difference between doing and not doing concentration. In all activities it is only essential to understand one's own mind clearly.

This mind does not come under any arrangement at all; it must be experienced by realization. If it is not realized by way of authentic enlightenment, whatever the myriad mystical understandings or thousand kinds of thoughts you may have, you are "like someone trying to rub space with your hands." How can you apprehend the body of space for you to rub?

MING-PEN

REALITY AND IMITATIONS

It is imperative to speak according to reality and act according to reality; only that constitutes harmonization.

We regularly see Zen teachers of recent times teaching people to bring up a saying: "Myriad things return to one; where does one return?" They also teach people to contemplate this story: A monk asked Chao-chou, "Does a dog have buddha nature or not?" Chao-chou said, "No." They make them come for interrogation morning and evening, and keep them wondering, calling this great doubt, necessitating great enlightenment. Although this is a clever expedient for a period of time, nevertheless it has added increased obstruction.

On this acount, complete ignoramuses have disguised themselves as Zen monks: they don't know the scriptural teachings, don't keep the precepts, and are utterly at a loss when questoned; they just say they have asked for instruction from a teacher. Bringing up a saying, they recite it and think about it, like a village school teaching children to repeat after an adult. While they're awake they remember, then when they fall asleep they forget. Some concentrate too hard, and become more confused the more they doubt, eventually reaching the point where they lose their minds and go crazy.

Some fabricate prognostications, saying strange things to deceive and threaten the ignorant. Some spend their whole lives in unknowing quietism in a ghost cave in a mountain of blackness, never attaining the slightest empowerment. They still don't realize that it's like an ox drawing a cart; if the cart isn't moving, do you hit the cart or the ox?

Also, Buddha said that if you cling to anything, this is called conceptual attachment, whereby you fall into the notion of permanence; but if you are totally mindless, that is called naturalism, fallen into a nihilistic view.

HSIAO-YIN (FL. CA. 1330)

SHARP BUT INCONSPICUOUS

To learn this path it is important to be sharp yet inconspicuous. When you are sharp, you are not confused by people; when you are inconspicuous, you don't contend with people. Not being confused by people, you are empty and spiritual; not contending with people, you are serene and subtle.

LIAO-AN (FL. CA. 1330)

FUNCTIONS OF ZEN

Zen is a razor to cut off birth and death; Zen is a bodkin to undo knots; Zen is a mirror to distinguish the beautiful and the ugly; Zen is a sword to cut off error and delusion; Zen is an axe to cut down a forest of brambles; Zen is a strategy for defeating enemies; Zen is a basis for attaining enlightenment and exercising mastery.

LIAO-AN

NO DOGMA

When the ancients uttered a word or half a phrase, it was to resolve sticking points, untie bonds, pull out nails, and remove stakes; how could they have had any dogma to bind people? We see many students who cling to the pointing finger, taking it for the moon; they seek mastery and marvel, they seek intellectual understanding, instead of a way to the source. They are to be deeply pitied.

So for people of superior faculties and keen insight, this matter is not hard to see. As for those of lesser potential and capacity who are also lazy and pursue trivia in neglect of the fundamental, they have no hope of attainment. In reality, they exclude themselves.

LIAO-AN

BEYOND MEASURE

The essence of mind is unpolluted, basically complete in itself. Just detach from false mental objects and there is the Buddha of being as is.

When deluded, you deviate from the real and pursue the false; when enlightened, you abandon the false and return to the real.

After you have reached the point where reality and falsehood both melt and delusion and enlightenment lodge nowhere, then you use up your old karma according to conditions, trusting essence and enjoying natural reality, exercising kindness and compassion, helping out the orphaned and the unsheltered, forgetting subject and object, annihilating shadow and form, becoming a person beyond measure, living in a realm of experience beyond measure, and doing a task beyond measure.

LIAO-AN

CURING MADNESS

The teachings of the whole vast canon are all prescriptions for curing the mad. If you see through the origin, the mad mind abruptly stops, and you may spontaneously burst out in a laugh.

LIAO-AN

THE FUNDAMENTAL

Just get the fundamental, don't worry about the outgrowths. What is the root, what are the outgrowths? Knowing the mind and seeing its essence is the root; explaining Zen and expounding the path are outgrowths. If you know the mind and see its essence, you may speak at will and go where your feet take you—nothing is not the path.

LIAO-AN

MISTAKING A THIEF FOR YOUR SON

"People studying the way do not know the real simply because they have been acknowledging the conscious mind. The root of infinite aeons of birth and death, ignorant people call it the original human being." If learners do not distinguish skillfully, and mistake the conscious mind for the self, this is what is referred to in the teachings as taking a thief for one's son—the family fortune will never be established.

LIAO-AN

A PLACE TO START

If beginners studying Zen fear they have as yet no place to start and no direction, even so, there's nothing else to say but that you each have an original face, which you have never recognized. This original face is one with all buddhas: twenty-four hours a day, as you are speaking, silent, active, quiet, walking, standing, sitting, and lying down, all of this is due to its empowerment. Just recognize this inwardly, and there you have a place to start; there you have direction.

WEI-TSE (D. 1348)

THE SUBTLE PATH

The subtle path of buddhas and Zen masters is not an irrational creation of knotty problems, nor is it eccentricity or weirdery. And it is not something that is very lofty and hard to practice: it is just what you presently use all the time in your everyday activities. If we have to give it a name, we might call it the natural real Buddha in your own nature, or the master within your own self.

In everyday terms, at all times and in all places, you see and hear with Shakyamuni Buddha's eyes and ears, you speak and breathe with Zen founder Bodhidharma's tongue and nose. In ultimate terms, the individual lives of all the buddhas and Zen masters of the ten directions are all in your grip—whether to gather them together or let them disperse is all up to you.

WEI-TSE

AWARENESS ITSELF

The subtle, perfect essence of awareness is basically spontaneously open and calm, equanimous and pure, vast as space. It cannot be pointed out in terms of any concrete form, it cannot be approached in terms of location. It cannot be entered into by any door or road, it cannot be depicted or copied by the colors of the spectrum.

WEI-TSE

STOPPING AND SEEING

"Calmness and insight develop through stilling thoughts: the mind of the buddhas manifests therein." This saying seems to refer to cessation and observation, or stopping and seeing.

The ocean of nature to which all things alike return is essentially united, quiet, always clear and calm. When it is stirred by the influences of conditions, then billows of consciousness and waves of emotion well up in ten thousand ways. If not for stopping, there is no way to clarify its clarity and calm its calmness.

The cosmos of reality completely manifesting unity is always evident and always clear when views are gone and things disappear: as soon as it is obscured by the dust of behavioral and intellectual obstructions, then the fog of confusion and clouds of delusion coalesce into myriad forms. If not for seeing, there is no way to bring to light its evident clarity.

When all agitations have ceased and not a single wave arises, myriad phenomena are clear, without confusion, without obstruction. Thus seeing is not separate from stopping. Once the layers of obscurity have been cleared and no clouding occurs, the ten directions are empty, without stirring, without agitation. Thus stopping is not outside of seeing.

Stopping is like concentration, seeing is like insight. Insofar as we see by stopping, concentration is the catalyst of insight; insofar as we stop by seeing, insight is the basis of concentration. When the catalyst of insight does not run dry, stopping is sufficient to assist the function of seeing; when the basis of concentration is not lacking, seeing is adequate to fulfill the achievement of stopping.

Stopping without seeing may deteriorate into stagnation; seeing without stopping may degenerate into inquisitiveness. Stopping is of course stopping motion, but it is also the root of motion: so when stopping without seeing, one either falls into empty quiescence, or distraction arises. Seeing is of course illumining the obscure, but it is also the root of obscurity: so when seeing without stopping, either one drifts into thought and reflection, or immersion in illusion occurs. Therefore stopping and seeing need each other; neither one can be neglected.

So this stopping is not intrinsic stopping: it depends on motion and stillness to manifest its achievement. And this seeing is not independent seeing: it depends on obscurity and clarity to reveal its function. Since they are not beyond achievement and function, how can they be called true stopping and true seeing?

If stopping and achievement are not set up, and seeing and function are both forgotten, after that both motion and stillness are stopping with true seeing, and both darkness and light are seeing with true stopping.

When stopping with true seeing merges motion and stillness, then the hundreds of thousands of buddhas enter into right concentration in the midst of billows of feeling and waves of consciousness, which do not harm that which is essentially unified and silent. When seeing with true stopping merges darkness and light, then the eighty thousand methods of practice illumine right knowledge in the midst of the fog of confusion and clouds of illusion, which do not inhibit that which causes views to vanish and things to disappear.

When you get to this, then thoughts become still without being stilled, calmness and insight arise without being produced, the mind of the buddhas appears without being revealed. To try to liken it to the body of cosmic space or the light of a thousand suns would be to be further away than the sky is from the earth.

WEI-TSE

THE GREAT WAY

People who study the path today do not understand the great way—they only strive to fulfill greed and ambition. At the very outset of their inspiration to study the way, their initial understanding is already mistaken.

The way is the path of fundamental purity: for immense aeons, and even up to the present day, it has no gain or loss, no new or old, no light or dark, no form or name. It is not more in the buddhas and not less in ordinary people. To insist on calling it the way is already defiling; to say something is accomplished by methods of learning the way is what I have called mistaken. It was for lack of choice that the ancients referred to people heading for transcendence as students of the way. The study is that there is nothing to study; the way is that there is nothing to be a way. Since there is nothing to study, there is no clinging; since there is nothing to be a way, there is no following. If one idly slips and says the word *Buddha*, one must simply wash out one's mouth for three years—only thus can one be called a real student of the way.

Nan-ch'uan said, "The way is not in the province of knowing, nor in the province of unknowing. Knowing is false consciousness, unknowing is indifference. If you truly arrive at the way without doubt, it is like cosmic space—how can you insist on affirmation and denial?"

SHU-CHUNG (D. 1386)

THE ORIGINAL FACE

What was my original face before my parents gave birth to me? This *kung-an* is a sharp sword for cutting through the net of birth and death, a giant axe for felling the tree of afflictions. Just look into it closely at all times, whatever you are doing, never forgetting it for a moment. After a long time at this, it will naturally become unmixed, coming up spontaneously without being brought up, coming to mind spontaneously without being brought to mind: from head to heels, the whole body is just this one saying.

When you get to this point, you cannot even find any arising of previous mundane toils and false ideas. Suddenly the bottom falls out of the bucket of lacquer, before and after are cut off; then you will attain realization.

Even so, there is still a final revelation.

NAN-SHIH (FL. CA. 1368–1425)

REAL TRUTH

Generally speaking, on this path it is important to work on real truth. When real truth stamps the mind, the path becomes self-evident. If the mind is not true, then even if you attend lectures every day and discuss the path constantly, this just provides topics of conversation and is ultimately of no benefit on the path.

So what is real truth? It is just a matter of looking back into the purity of your own mind in the course of daily activities, not being influenced by anything wrong. That is because mind is like a monkey, consciousness like a horse: without the chain and bridle of great awareness watching them, it will be truly hard to control them no matter how clever your devices.

But when you have whipped and thrashed them into submission, so they merge back into oneness, and all traces of birth and extinction disappear, then you naturally realize basic subtle illumination, thoroughly empty yet uncannily penetrating and effective.

Actuality itself is mind—there is nothing extra. Speech and action both accord with perfect objectivity. Only then can it be said that you are not deceiving your mind.

When you reach the point of not deceiving your mind, then all things, whether mundane or transcendental, are Buddha teachings; whether it is aroused or unaroused, your mind is the buddha mind.

HUI-CHING (1528–1598)

GENUINE SEEKERS

Genuine seekers of true enlightenment should first question themselves and discover their inherent spiritual light. Then they must meet others to find out the handle of going beyond. As they penetrate the subtle crux of being and nonbeing, grasping and rejection are both empty; as they pass through the dark machinations of gain and loss, they devote no energy to matters of glory and disgrace.

HUI-CHING

CLARITY AND CALMNESS

When stopping and seeing have no entryways, then oblivion and distraction are used for doors. When oblivion and distraction have no ground, clarity and calmness are the sources. Thus those who travel the way unfailingly make skillful use of the fire of stopping and seeing to burn off the dross of oblivion and distraction. Once the refinement is complete, the essence of stopping and seeing becomes concentration and insight.

Thus sages may overturn heaven and earth without being disturbed; this is the power of concentration. They make penetrating investigation into all things without getting confused; this is the efficacy of insight.

If this is so, then in ordinary people clarity and calm are oblivion and distraction, while in sages oblivion and distraction are concentration and insight.

TZU-PO (1543–1604)

DISCOVERING THE LIGHT OF MIND

Beginners learning the way should make their will firm and strong: twenty-four hours a day, wield the sword of positive energy to over-come demons and curses, cutting off psychological afflictions. When you look into a saying continuously, you spontaneously discover the light of mind, containing heaven and earth, every land completely revealed.

CHIEN-JU (1549–1619)

TWO TESTS

I have tested people by means of two things, and have never yet seen anyone pass through. What are these two things? One is testing them by writings. These writings are the body of teachings consisting of the sayings of the buddhas. If you say you have experienced realiza-tion, this must be realization of your own mind. One's own mind is itself the buddha mind; if you have realized the buddha mind, you should understand the words of buddhas. If you understand the words of buddhas, then you must be able to immediately understand the teachings of the scriptures expounded by the buddhas, as well as the diverse stories of the Zen masters, without doubt or confusion. If any have doubts, then their claims of realization are not necessarily so.

The second thing is testing the mind in the course of daily activi-ties and interactions. There seem to be some who act as masters to some extent, to whom people resort, but they are not really enlight-ened. But leaving them aside, what about when in tranquil quietude detached from things, or while sitting in meditation; there seems to be something there, going up and down—that is, right and wrong, gain and loss, doubt and confusion, grasping and rejecting. Can you be at peace? If you are at peace, then even if every plant and tree in the world turned into a human being, each with infinite tongues, with countless challenging questions of infinite complexity on every tongue, all posed simultaneously, it would only require a fingersnap to answer them all. That would be considered attainment of great confidence and freedom.

If you are as yet unable to be at peace, not only are you unable to interact with keen liveliness—even when you are at rest with nothing to do you are already mixed up. Therefore it is said, "For others to approve me is easy; for me to approve myself is hard."

YUAN-CHENG (CA. 1570S–1620S)

PURE EYES

Learners use the teachings of the canon to open their own pure eyes; if one's own eyes are fundamentally pure, what is the need to open them any further? The teachings are expounded for those who have not understood. The *Scripture of Complete Enlightenment* says, "Buddhahood is only attained after permanent cessation of ignorance by means of purity of panoramic awareness." If you know that ignorance is originally nonexistent and the nature of consciousness is unreal, then mountains and rivers do not block the light of your eyes—how can senses and objects damage the body of awareness? Seeing through countless worlds does not seem hard.

YUAN-LAI (1575–1630)

NATURAL REAL BUDDHA NATURE

The natural real buddha nature is always inherently complete and luminous; it was thus before our parents gave birth to us, it is thus right now, and it will always be thus forever.

Originally there is not a single thing. Since there's not a single thing, what is to be called original? If you can see into this, you will save the most mental energy.

When divergent thoughts arise, adamantly cut them off yourself. This is expediently called concentration and insight, but it is not a reality; this mind itself is inherently concentrated and inherently insightful.

Huang-po said, "This mind is always intrinsically round and bright, illuminating everywhere. People of the world don't know it, and just recognize perception and cognition as mind. Empty perception and cognition, and the road of mind comes to an end." He also said, "If you want to know the mind, it is not apart from perception and cognition; and yet the original mind does not belong to perception and cognition either."

When you come to this, it is really essential for you to look into yourself; it is not a matter of verbal explanation. The more the talk, the further removed from the way. Those who are successful at introspection know for themselves when the time comes and do not need to ask anyone—all false imaginations and emotional thoughts naturally disappear. This is the effect of learning the way.

A thousand falsehoods do not compare to a single truth. If you are not thus, even if you consciously apply your mind, seeking effectiveness daily, it is all in the realm of impermanence, becoming and passing away. A master teacher said, "If you want to cultivate practice and seek to become a buddha, I don't know where you will try to seek the real." If you can see reality within the mind spontaneously, having reality is the basis of attaining buddhahood. If you seek Buddha externally without seeing your own essential nature, you are an utter ignoramus.

TA-TU (SEVENTEENTH CENTURY)

THE SPIRITUAL LIGHT

"The spiritual light shines independently, transcendentally liberated from organs and objects of sense." This statement has said it all. If you can understand this, how could I presume to talk a lot? If you can't, then I'll go on and make some complications for now.

The spiritual light of living beings originally has no obstruction, yet deluded feelings arise in confusion. From this there are six sense organs within and objects of the six senses outside: with the opposition of organs and objects, false consciousness arises uncontrolled, producing good and bad, initiating virtuous and evil actions. Because of these actions, living beings revolve in a variety of mundane states, like a pulley wheel, wave after wave, age after age, emerging and sinking, with no end to it. The buddhas took pity on them and expounded the great teaching to them, all just to clarify this independent shining of spiritual light.

If the spiritual light is not obscured, organs and objects suddenly disappear, mind is forgotten, and the world is silent: panoramic awareness all-embracing, the substance of awakening is being as is.

If the light is not revealed, you need a method. The method is not asking someone to explain, it is not studying scriptures, it is not doing a lot of charitable acts, it is not closing the eyes and sitting as if dead. Just look intently into the question of what your original face is in the course of daily life. Don't think about whether it is hard or easy, or remote or near; and don't worry that your own faculties and potential are slow and dull, or that you are too heavily obstructed by past habits. Just go right ahead and do it; after a long time, eventually you will bump into it all of a sudden.

YUAN-HSIEN (1618–1697)

EFFORT IN STUDY

Everyone has a torch giving off great light: originally it spontaneously illumines heaven and earth; there is no distance to which it does not reach. It is no different from the buddhas and Zen masters, but when it gets covered by false ideas and material toils, so that it cannot come out, it is therefore necessary to use effort in study to polish it.

What is effort in study? It means placing your everyday mental and physical energies on one saying, without allowing any deviation. After a long time, not only will your mental and physical energies congeal into one mass; the whole earth, mountains and rivers, and the space of the ten directions will also congeal into a single mass, like an iron pill.

One day, through some chance event, the iron pill will explode, producing the eyes of Zen; then the mountains, rivers, and whole earth are all one vast treasury of light.

YUAN-HSIEN

PARTICIPATION

The path of Zen values participation. What participation means is that it cannot be ordered by teachers and elders, it cannot be done for you by colleagues, it cannot be adulterated by external energies, it cannot be confined by outward form; it is only in the power of your own mind.

Go right ahead boldly and fiercely like a great warrior with a single sword mounted on a lone horse, plunging into a million-man army to kill the commander. That would be outstanding, would it not?

But if you think about whether it will be hard or easy, and worry about whether it is far or near, anxious about whether you will suc-

ceed or fail, then you cannot even stand on our own, let alone partici-
pate in Zen.

YUAN-HSIEN

TRUE MIND

There are not many arts to Zen study: it just requires knowing your
own true mind. Now observe that within this body the physical elements combine temporarily, daily heading for extinction: where is
the true mind?

The flurry of ideas and thoughts arising and passing away without
constancy is not the true mind.

That which shifts and changes unstably, sometimes good, sometimes bad, is not the true mind.

That which wholly depends on external things to manifest, and is
not apparent when nothing is there, is not the true mind.

The heart inside the body cannot see itself, blind to the internal; it
is not the true mind.

What is unaffected by feelings outside the body, cut off from the
external, is not the true mind.

Suppose you turn the light of awareness around to look within,
and sense a recondite tranquillity and calm oneness; do you consider
this the true mind? You still do not realize that this recondite tranquillity and calm oneness are due to the perception of the false mind:
there is the subjective mind perceiving and the object perceived—so
this recondite tranquillity and calm oneness totally belong to the
realm of inner states. This is what is meant by the *Heroic Progress
Scripture* when it says, "Inwardly keeping to recondite tranquility is
still a reflection of discrimination of objects." How could it be the
true mind?

So if these are not the true mind, what is the true mind? Try to see
what your true mind is, twenty-four hours a day. Don't try to figure
it out, don't try to interpret it intellectually, don't try to get someone
to explain it to you, don't seek some other technique, don't calculate
how long it may take, don't calculate the degree of your own
strength—just silently pursue this inner investigation on your own:
"Ultimately what is my own true mind?"

YUAN-HSIEN

EMPTY AND QUIET

People learning the way should first empty and quiet their minds. This is because the mind must be empty and quiet before it can mystically understand the subtle principle. If the mind is not emptied, it is like a pitcher full of donkey milk—how can you also fill it with lion milk? If the mind is not quiet, it is like a lamp in the wind, or like turbulent water—how can it reflect myriad forms?

Therefore learners should first stop cogitation and minimize objects of attention, making the mind empty and quiet. After that you have a basis for attaining the way. As Te-shan said, "Just have no mind on things and no things in your mind, and you will naturally be empty and spiritual, tranquil and sublime."

Nevertheless, you should not settle in empty quietude, sitting relaxed and untrammeled in nothingness. You must be truly attentive, investigating diligently, before you can break through the barrier of illusion and accomplish the great task. People's forces of habit, accumulated since beginningless time, are deep-seated; if you want to uproot them today, it will not be easy. You need to have a firm will constantly spurring you on. Strive to make progress in the work, without thinking about how much time it may take. When you have practiced for a long time, you will naturally become peaceful and whole. Why seek any other particular method?

YUAN-HSIEN

AVOIDING FOXES AND DOGS

The basic essential nature inherent in all people is clearly evident when you constantly perceive it within yourself; if you pursue external objects, then it becomes obscured; you get confused and are not awake.

That is why people of old would look into a saying—immediately attention is gathered on one point, and you are not drawn by the external world. Eventually the world is forgotten and objects disappear; then the original inherent light naturally comes through revealed.

If you arbitrarily start trying to figure the saying out, you immediately enter a mistaken path. If you want to ask other people, that too increases your confusion and distress. Therefore the method of looking into a saying is just to keep your mind on it, with a feeling of doubt that does not dissipate. Great doubt results in great enlightenment, small doubt results in small enlightenment, no doubt results in no enlightenment. This is an established fact.

People nowadays are unwilling to look into sayings: they just get together in groups to discuss this and that saying as being thus and so, calling it great enlightenment when they've managed to explain them clearly. Since the teachers have no true insight, when they see a resemblance in the words of others, they give them useless stamps of approval, saying they are people of attainment. The teachers and their followers are engaging in a mutual deception, defrauding each other.

That is why the way of Zen today has deteriorated and died out, while gangs of foxes and packs of dogs claim honor everywhere, fooling the whole world. They will go to hell like an arrow shot. If you want to study Zen, be sure not to fall into the company of those gangs of devils.

YUAN-HSIEN

List of Zen Masters

Fu Shan-hui (487–569)
Tao-hsin (580–651)
Niu-t'ou Hui-chung (683–769)
Ma-tsu (709–788)
Ta-chu (eighth century)
Ta-mei (ca. 805)
Pai-chang (720–814)
Tan-hsia (738–824)
Nan-ch'uan (747–834)
Kao-ch'eng (n.d.)
Te-shan (d. 867)
Ta-sui (800–880)
Ta-an (d. 883)
Tzu-hu (ninth century)
Yen-t'ou (827–887)
Chao-chou (778–897)
T'ou-tzu (845–914)
Lung-ya (834–920)
Hsuan-sha (ninth to tenth century)
Ku-shan (d. ca. 940)
Fa-yen (885–958)
Tung-shan Shou-ch'u (910/15–990/95)
Chih-men (fl. ca. 1000–1020)
Shih-shuang (986–1039)
She-hsien (tenth to eleventh century)
Sheng-ting (tenth to eleventh century)
Chieng-ku (fl. ca. 1037)
Yang-ch'i (992–1049)
Tao-wu Wu-chen (fl. ca. 1025–1060)
Fa-hua (fl. ca. 1000–1056)

Ta-yü Shou-chih (d. ca. 1060)
Tsu-hsin (eleventh century)
Ssu-hsin (eleventh century)
Chen-ching (exiled 1080)
Yun-feng Wen-yueh (d. ca. 1060)
I-ch'ing (1032–1083)
Hui-lin (1020–1099)
Fu-jung (1042–1118)
Huai-shan (fl. ca. 1115)
Hui-k'ung (1096–1158)
Tzu-te (1090–1159)
P'u-an (d. 1169)
Ying-an (d. 1163)
Huai-t'ang (twelfth century)
Fo-hsing T'ai (twelfth century)
Fu-an (twelfth century)
Yueh-lin (thirteenth century)
Sung-yuan (1140–1209)
P'o-an (1136–1211)
Ch'ih-chueh (fl. ca. 1208–1225)
Fo-chih (fl. ca. 1228)
Pei-chien (1185–1246)
Wu-chun (d. 1249)
Chueh-an (1250s)
Hsi-sou (fl. ca. 1249)
Yun-ku (fl. ca. 1256)
Wu-men (1183–1260)
Tuan-ch'iao (ca. 1241)
Hsueh-yen (fl. ca. 1253)
Hsi-yen (1198–1262)
Kao-feng (1260s)
Hsu-t'ang (1185–1269)
Hai-yin (ca. 1282)
Wu-chien (fl. ca. 1265–1300)
Ku-lin (fl. ca. 1297–1308)
Ming-pen (1263–1323)
Hsiao-yin (fl. ca. 1330)
Liao-an (fl. ca. 1330)
Wei-tse (d. 1348)

Shu-chung (d. 1386)
Nan-shih (fl. ca. 1368–1425)
Hui-ching (1528–1598)
Tzu-po (1543–1604)
Chien-ju (1549–1619)
Yuan-cheng (ca. 1570s–1620s)
Yuan-lai (1575–1630)
Ta-tu (seventeenth century)
Yuan-hsien (1618–1697)

Further Reading

Zen Essence: The Science of Freedom. Translated and edited by Thomas Cleary. In *Classics of Buddhism and Zen*, vol. 1. Boston: Shambhala Publications, 2001.

Zen Lessons: The Art of Leadership. Translated by Thomas Cleary. In *Classics of Buddhism and Zen*, vol. 1. Boston: Shambhala Publications, 2001.

Minding Mind: A Course in Basic Meditation. Translated by Thomas Cleary. In *Classics of Buddhism and Zen*, vol. 1. Boston: Shambhala Publications, 2001.

Instant Zen: Waking Up in the Present. Translated by Thomas Cleary. In *Classics of Buddhism and Zen*, vol. 1. Boston: Shambhala Publications, 2001.

Zen Letters: Teachings of Yuanwu. Translated by J.C. Cleary and Thomas Cleary. In *Classics of Buddhism and Zen*, vol. 2. Boston: Shambhala Publications, 2001.

Buddhist Yoga: A Comprehensive Course. Translated by Thomas Cleary. Boston: Shambhala Publications, 1995.

The Observing Self: Mysticism and Psychotherapy. By Arthur J. Deikman, M.D. Boston: Beacon Press, 1982.

ZEN READER

INTRODUCTION

Zen is traditionally called the School of the Awakened Mind, or the Gate to the Source. The premise of Zen is that our personality, culture, and beliefs are not inherent parts of our souls, but "guests" of a recondite "host," the Buddha-nature or real self hidden within us. We are not limited, in our essence or mode of being, to what we happen to believe we are, or what we happen to believe the world is, based on the accidental conditions of our birth and upbringing.

This realization may not seem to have positive significance at first, until it is remembered how much anger, antagonism, and grief arises from the ideas of "them" and "us" based on historically conditioned factors like culture, customs, and habits of thought. Any reasonable person knows these things are not absolute, and yet the force of conditioning creates seemingly insurmountable barriers of communication.

By actively awakening a level of consciousness deeper than those occupied by conditioned habits of perception, the realization of Zen removes the strictures of absolutism and intolerance from the thinking and feeling of the individual. In doing so, Zen realization also opens the door to impartial compassion and social conscience, not in response to political opportunity, but as a spontaneous expression of intuitive and empathic capacities.

This book is a collection of quotations from the great Eastern masters of Zen. It has no beginning, middle, or end. The masters talk about the practicalities of Zen realization in many different ways, speaking as they did to different audiences in different times, but all of them are talking about waking up, seeing for yourself, and standing on your own two feet. Start anywhere; eventually you'll come full circle.

Zen Reader

Entry into the Way, by the Founder of Zen

There are many avenues of entry into the way, but they are essentially of just two types, referred to as principle and conduct.

Entry by principle is when you realize the source by way of the teachings and deeply believe that all living beings have the same real essential nature, but it is veiled by outside elements and false ideas and cannot manifest completely. If you abandon falsehood and return to reality, abiding stably in impassive observation, with no self and no other, regarding ordinary and holy as equal, persisting firmly, immovable, not following other persuasions, then you deeply harmonize with the principle. Having no false notions, being serene and not striving, is called entry by way of principle.

Entry by conduct refers to four practices in which all other practices are included. What are the four? First is compensation for opposition. Second is adapting to conditions. Third is not seeking anything. Fourth is acting in accord with truth.

The practice of compensation for opposition means that when people cultivating the way are beset by suffering, they should think how in past times they themselves neglected the fundamental and pursued the trivial over countless ages, flowing in waves of existences, arousing much enmity and hatred, with no end of offense and injury. Although they may be innocent right now, they think of their suffering as the results of their own past evil deeds, not something inflicted upon them by gods or humans. Thus they accept contentedly, without enmity or complaint. Scripture says, "There is no anxiety when experiencing suffering, because of perfect knowledge." When this attitude is developed, you are in harmony with the way. Because we make progress on the way by comprehending opposition, this is called the practice of compensating for opposition.

Second is the practice of adapting to conditions. Living beings have no absolute self; they are all influenced by conditions and actions. Their experiences of pain and pleasure both come from conditions. Even if they attain excellent rewards, things like prosperity and fame, these are effects of past causes only now being realized. When the conditions wear out, they return to nothing, so what is there to rejoice about? Gain and loss come from conditions; there is no increase or decrease in the mind. When the influence of joy does not stir you, there is profound harmony with the way; therefore, this is called the practice of adapting to conditions.

Third is the practice of not seeking anything. Worldly people wander forever, becoming attached by greed here and there. This is called seeking. The wise realize that the principle of absolute truth is contrary to the mundane. Mentally at ease in nonstriving, physically they adapt to the turns of fate.

All existents are empty; there is nothing to hope for. Blessings and curses always follow each other. Living in the world is like a house on fire, all corporeal existence involves pain—who can be at peace? Because of understanding this point, we let go of all existences, stop thinking, and seek nothing. Scripture says, "Seeking is all painful; not seeking anything is bliss." Not seeking anything is clearly the conduct of the way, so it is called the practice of not seeking anything.

Fourth is the practice of acting in accord with truth. The principle of purity of essential nature is called truth. In terms of this principle, all appearances are empty; so there is no infection, no attachment, no this, no that. Scripture says, "In truth there are no beings, because it is free from the defilement of beings. In truth there is no self, because it is free from the defilement of self."

Therefore, if the wise can believe in this principle, they should act in accord with truth. The substance of truth has no stinginess: practicing charity with one's person, life, and goods, the mind has no regret. Liberated from empty personality and things, independent and unattached, with the sole purpose of getting rid of defilement, edifying people informally, this constitutes your own practice, and can also help others. It can also adorn the path of enlightenment.

As this is true of charity, it is also thus with the other five perfections, or ways of transcendence. Practicing the six ways of transcendence in order to get rid of false ideas, without objectivizing practices, is called practice in accord with truth.

BODHIDHARMA

FORM AND SHADOW

Shadows arise from forms, echoes come from sounds. If we fiddle with shadows and ignore the forms, we do not recognize that the forms are the roots of the shadows. If we raise our voices to stop echoes, we are not cognizant of the fact that sounds are the roots of the echoes. To try to head for nirvana by getting rid of afflictions is like removing forms to look for shadows. To seek Buddhahood apart from living beings is like seeking echoes by silencing sounds.

So we know that illusion and enlightenment are one road. Ignorance and knowledge are not separate. We make names for what has no name. Because we go by the names, judgments of right and wrong arise. We make rationalizations for what has no reason. Because we rely on the rationalizations, argument and discussion arise. Illusion is not real: who is right, who is wrong? The unreal is not actual: what is empty, what exists? Thus I realize that attainment gains nothing, and loss loses nothing.

LAYMAN HSIANG

NONDUALITY

When the illusory body faces a mirror and its form is reflected, the reflected form is not different from the illusory body. If you only want to get rid of the reflection but leave the body, you do not realize the body is fundamentally the same as space.

The body is basically not different from the reflection. You cannot have one without the other: If you try to keep one and get rid of the other, you'll be forever estranged from the truth. Even more, if you love the holy and hate the ordinary, you'll bob in the ocean of birth and death.

Afflictions have reasons based on mind; when mindless, where can afflictions abide? If you do not bother to discriminate and grasp appearances, you will attain the way naturally in an instant. While dreaming, you act in dreams; when you awaken, dreamland doesn't exist. If you think back to waking and dreaming, they are not different from deluded dualism.

If you seek to gain by reforming illusion and grasping awakening, how is that different from involvement in commerce? When movement and stillness are both forgotten, and you are ever serene, then you spontaneously merge with reality as it is.

If you say that sentient beings are different from Buddha, then you are forever alienated from Buddha. Buddha and sentient beings are not two; this naturally comprehends all.

PAO-CHIH

THE NONDUALITY OF GOOD AND EVIL

My own mind and body are blissful and happy, calm and serene, without good or evil. The body of reality is independent, without location; whatever strikes the eye is none other than true awakening.

The objects of sense are originally empty and null; ordinary people arbitrarily create attachments and fixations. Nirvana and samsara are equal; who in the world gets differential treatment? The uncontrived Great Way is natural and spontaneous; you don't need to use your mind to figure it out.

Enlightening beings are untrammeled, spiritually effective. Whatever they do is always imbued with sublime awareness. Seekers clinging to method sitting in meditation are like silkworms spitting out thread binding themselves. The essence of reality is originally completely clear; when the sickness is healed, what is the need to cling to the medicine? When you know all things are equal, you are serenely clear and open, blissfully happy.

PAO-CHIH

THE NONDUALITY OF QUIETUDE AND DISTURBANCE

Seekers who disdain clamor to seek quietude are as it were throwing away flour but seeking cake. Cake is originally flour, which changes according to use.

Afflictions are not other than enlightenment. When there is no minding, there are no objects. Samsara is not different from nirvana. Craving and anger are like flames, like shadows.

The wise have no mind to seek Buddha. The ignorant cling to wrong and right. Passing all their lives in wasted toil, they do not see the sublime peak of realization of being as is. If you realize the essence of lust is empty, then even hellfire is cool.

PAO-CHIH

THE NONDUALITY OF PHENOMENA AND NOUMENON

The mind-monarch is independent and serene; the real nature is originally unbound. Everything without exception is Buddha-work; why should you concentrate thought in sitting meditation? Errant imaginations are originally empty and null; one need not cut off attention to objects.

The wise have no mind to be grasped; they are naturally noncontentious and peaceful. If you do not know the Great Way of noncontrivance, when can you realize the hidden mystery?

Buddhahood and ordinary life are of one kind; ordinary beings are themselves Buddhas. The common man creates arbitrary distinctions, clinging to the existence of what has none, rushing in confusion. When you realize desire and wrath are void, what place is not a door to reality?

PAO-CHIH

THE NONDUALITY OF BUDDHAHOOD AND ORDINARY LIFE

Ordinary life and Buddhahood have no distinction. Great knowledge is not different from ignorance. Why should one seek outwardly for a treasure, when the field of the body has its own bright jewel?

The right way and wrong ways are not two. When perfectly known, ordinary and sage are on the same road. Illusion and enlightenment originally have no distinction; nirvana and samsara are one suchness.

In the final analysis, clinging to objects is empty and null; only seek clear spaciousness of mind and thought. There is not a single thing that can be attained; serenely, spontaneously, you enter the ultimate.

PAO-CHIH

THE NONDUALITY OF DISCIPLINE AND LICENSE

The actions of great people are uninhibited, not controlled by precepts and regulations. Discipline and license basically have no origin of their own, yet ignorant people are bound by them. The doings of those who know are all empty; followers get stuck on the road.

The physical eyes of enlightening beings are completely perceptive; the celestial eyes of individual illuminates have cataracts. If you arbitrarily cling to being and nonbeing in emptiness, you will not arrive at the noninterference of matter and mind.

Enlightening beings live with ordinary people; their purity is never stained by the world. Ignoramuses are greedy for nirvana; for the knowers, life and death are ultimate reality.

The nature of things is empty and has no verbal explanation; there is nothing at all in interdependent occurrence. The hundred-year-old without knowledge is a child; the child with knowledge is a hundred years old.

PAO-CHIH

THE NONDUALITY OF ENLIGHTENMENT AND AFFLICTION

People who do not know how to practice the way therefore want to get rid of afflictions. Afflictions are originally void and null; you are trying to use the way to seek the way beyond.

The instantaneous mind is it. What is the need to seek somewhere else? The Great Way is right before the eyes; the ignorant who are deluded do not comprehend.

Buddha-nature is natural and spontaneous; it is not caused, conditioned, or fabricated. If you do not know the three poisons are unreal, you grasp at random and flounder in life, growing old. Before, when you were deluded, it wasn't too late; now you finally realize it isn't too early.

PAO-CHIH

WASTE OF EFFORT

Seekers cut off contusion in every state of mind, but the mind that does the cutting off is a thief. When one thief sends off another, when will you ever realize the basis of speech and silence? You may recite a thousand scrolls of scripture without understanding how the scripture applies to yourself; if you do not understand the comprehensive completeness of what the Buddha taught, you are just wasting effort following lines and counting ink marks.

Ascetic exercises and austere practices may be done seeking meritorious qualities in later life, but seeking is itself a barrier to wisdom; how could the Great Way be attained thereby? It is like crossing a river in a dream: the boatman, having crossed over the river, suddenly awakens to find he's been sleeping in bed, and has lost the way to ferry the boat. The boatman and the people he ferries over never know each other.

Sentient beings, confused and bound up, come and go in the realms of desire, form, and abstraction, to the extremes of exhaustion. When they realize that life and death are like dreams, all their sense of seeking will spontaneously stop.

PAO-CHIH

VANITY

How many ignorant people in the world try to seek the Way by means of the Way! Searching widely amongst a profusion of doctrines, they cannot even save themselves. Only pursuing the confused explanations of others' writings, they claim to have arrived at the subtlety of noumenon.

Wasting a life in idle labors, they sink forever in birth and death. When polluted attachment binds the mind unrelentingly, the mind of pure knowledge afflicts itself; the forest of the cosmos of realities turns into a wasteland of brambles.

As long as you cling to yellow leaves as gold, you won't know to give up the gold for jewels. The reason you lose your mind and run around crazily is that you forcibly try to keep up appearances; you may be reciting scriptures and treatises in your mouth, but in your heart you're always lifeless.

If you realize the original mind is empty some day, the fullness of reality as is will not leave you lacking.

PAO-CHIH

SEEK NOTHING

The inner view and the outer view are both wrong; the way of Buddhas and the way of demons are both mistaken. If you are subject to these two evils, then you will reject suffering and seek pleasure. When you awaken to the root, birth and death are essentially empty; where can Buddhas or demons stay?

It is just because of the discriminations of arbitrary feelings that successive lives are isolated and alienated. The repetitious routines of mundane ways go on unceasing; if you form compulsive habits, you cannot get rid of them. The reasons for flowing in the waves of birth and death all come from arbitrary production of schemes for control.

The body is fundamentally empty and unreal; when you go back to the basis, who is calculating? Being and nonbeing can be done on your own; don't bother figuring with a confused mind. The body of sentient beings is the same as cosmic space; where can afflictions stay? Just seek nothing at all, and afflictions will naturally fall away.

PAO-CHIH

PRINCIPLE AND PRACTICE

The Great Way is not attained by practice; talk of practice is for the ordinary and the ignorant. When you have found the principle and look back on practice, for the first time you will realize you have misused time and effort.

As long as you have not realized the great principle that permeates all, it is essential that speech and action should support each other. Do not hold to the intellectual understanding of others; turn the light of awareness back to the root, and it is not there at all.

Who understands this talk? I'll have you turn to yourself to seek. After having seen past faults and gotten rid of the sores of sensual desires, liberated, roaming free and independent, wherever I may be I sell refinement on the cheap; whoever is inspired to buy will get to be carefree just like me.

PAO-CHIH

THE NATURE OF THINGS

The nature of things is fundamental perpetual silence, open and clear, without limits or boundaries. If you place your mind in the midst of grasping and rejecting, you will be under the influence of those two states.

If you concentrate, enter trance, and sit in meditation, focusing on an objective, setting your mind on awareness and contemplation, practicing the way like a mechanical mannequin, when will you ever arrive at the goal?

All things are fundamentally empty; there is nothing to stick to. Objects are like floating clouds, certain to disperse. When you realize the basic emptiness of fundamental essence, that will be like a fever's breaking. Don't speak of it to the ignorant, or they'll beat your body to pieces.

PAO-CHIH

FALSE BUDDHAS

A gold Buddha can't get through a furnace, a wood Buddha can't get through a fire, and a clay Buddha can't get through water. The real Buddha sits within: enlightenment, nirvana, suchness, and Buddha-nature are all clothes sticking to the body. They are also called afflictions; don't ask and there is no vexation.

In the noumenal ground of reality, where is there to grasp? When the individual mind is not aroused, myriad things have no fault. Just sit investigating the truth for twenty or thirty years; if you don't understand, then cut off my head.

It is useless to bother to try to grasp dreams, illusions, and false appearances. If the mind does not differ, myriad things are also thus. Since it is not gotten from outside, what is there to get wrapped up in or hung up on any more? Why go on being like goats, picking up things at random and putting them in your mouth?

CHAO-CHOU

TRANSCENDING DUALISM

If you want to avoid experiencing reversal, just cut off dualism; then measurements cannot govern you. You are neither Buddha nor sentient being; you are not near or far, not high or low, not equal or even, not going or coming. Just do not cling to written letters that obstruct

It, and neither side can hold you. You will escape both pain and pleasure, and escape the opposition of light and dark.

The true principle is that even reality is not really real, and even falsehood is not unreal. It is not something calculable. Like space, it cannot be cultivated. If any intellectual fabrication occurs in the mind, then it is governed by measurements. This is like divination signs—they are governed by metal, wood, water, fire, and earth. It is also like sticky glue; the king demon can grab you, stuck in five places, and go home freely.

PAI-CHANG

PROVISIONAL TEACHINGS

If a Buddha would not speak, then people would have no hope of liberation; but if a Buddha speaks, then people pursue the words and create interpretations, so there would be little advantage and much disadvantage. That is why the Buddha said, "I would rather not explain the truth, but enter into extinction right away."

But then afterwards he thought back on all the Buddhas of the past, who had all taught the doctrines of three vehicles. After that he made temporary use of verses to explain, and provisionally established names and terms.

Originally it is not Buddha, but he told people, "This is Buddha." Originally it is not enlightenment, but he told people, "This is enlightenment peace, liberation," and so on. He knew people couldn't bear a burden of ten thousand pounds, so for the time being he taught them the incomplete teaching. And he realized the spread of good ways, which was still better than evil ways.

But when the limits of good results are fulfilled, then bad consequences ensue. Once you have "Buddha," then there are "sentient beings." Once you have "nirvana," then there is "birth and death." Once you have light, then there is darkness. As long as cause and effect with attachment continue to operate, there is nothing that does not have consequences.

PAI-CHANG

THREE STEPS

The words of the teachings all have three successive steps: the elementary, the intermediate, and the final good.

At first, it is just necessary to teach people to develop a good mind. In the intermediate stage, they break through the good mind. The last stage is finally called really good.

This is what is meant by the sayings, "An enlightening being is not an enlightening being, but is called an enlightening being; the truth is not truth, yet is not other than truth." Everything is like this.

If, however, you teach only one stage, you will cause people to go to hell. If all three stages are taught at once, they'll go to hell on their own. This is not the work of a real teacher.

PAI-CHANG

ELEMENTARY, INTERMEDIATE, AND FINAL GOOD

Realizing that the present mirroring awareness is your own Buddha is the elementary good. Not to keep dwelling in the immediate mirroring awareness is the intermediate good. Not to make an understanding of nondwelling either is the final good.

Such a person is one of the Buddhas, neither an ordinary person nor a sage. Yet do not mistakenly state that a Buddha is neither an ordinary person nor a sage. The founder of Zen said, "With no ability and no sagacity, this is enlightened sagehood." Yet if you say a Buddha is a sage, that is also wrong.

PAI-CHANG

DIFFERENCES IN MEANING

The gradations of the language of the teachings—haughty, relaxed, rising, descending—are not the same. What are called desire and aversion when one is not yet enlightened or liberated are called enlightened wisdom after enlightenment. That is why it is said, "One is not different from who one used to be; only one's course of action is different from before."

PAI-CHANG

CLEANING THE MIND

Zen study is like washing a dirty garment. The garment is originally there; the dirt comes from outside.

Having heard it said that all sound and form, existent or not, are such filth, do not set your mind on any of it at all.

The thirty-two marks of greatness and eighty refinements of the idealized Buddha under the tree of enlightenment are all in the province of form; the twelve sections of doctrines of the canon are all in the province of sound. Right now cut off the flow of sound and form, existent or not, and your mind will be like space.

You should study in this way as attentively as you would save your head from burning. Only then will you be capable of finding a road already pre-prepared to go upon when you come to the end of your life.

If you have not accomplished that yet, if you try to compose yourself to start learning this when you get to the moment of death, you will have no hope of success.

PAI-CHANG

FACING THE END

When facing the end, generally beautiful scenes appear. According to your mental inclinations, the most impressive are experienced first. If you do not do bad things right now, then there will be no unpleasant scenes when you face death. Even if there are some unpleasant scenes, they too will change into pleasant scenes.

If you fear that you will go mad with terror at the moment of death and will fail to attain freedom, then you should first be free right now. Then you'll be all right. Right now, in respect to each and every thing, don't have any obsession at all, and do not remain fixated on intellectual interpretation. Then you will be free.

PAI-CHANG

Now and Forever

The cause is right now; the result is at the moment of death. When the resultant action is already manifest, how can you fear? Fear is over the past and present; since the past had a present, the present must have a past. Since there has been enlightenment in the past, there must also be enlightenment in the present. If you can attain now and forever the single moment of present awareness, and this one moment of awareness is not governed by anything at all, whether existent or nonexistent, then from the past and the present the Buddha is just human, and humans are just Buddhas.

This is, furthermore, meditation concentration. Don't use concentration to enter concentration, don't use meditation to think of meditation, don't use Buddha to search for Buddhahood. As it is said, "Reality does not seek reality, reality does not obtain reality, reality does not practice reality, reality does not see reality; it finds its way naturally." It is not attained by attainment.

That is why awakening people should thus be properly mindful, subsisting alone in the midst of things, composed, yet without knowledge of the fact of subsisting alone.

The nature of wisdom is such as it is of itself; it is not disposed by causes. It is also called the knot of essence, or the cluster of essence. It is not known by knowledge, not discerned by consciousness. It is entirely beyond mental calculation. Still and silent, essence totally realized, thought and judgment are forever ended. Just as if the flow of the ocean had stopped, waves do not rise again.

PAI-CHANG

The Sphere of the Enlightened

It is like the water of the ocean: even without wind there are waves everywhere. Suddenly knowing of the waves all around is the gross within the subtle; letting go of knowledge in the midst of knowing is like the subtle within the subtle. This is the sphere of the enlightened.

From this point on you really know. This is called the pinnacle of Zen, the sovereignty of Zen. It is also called knowledge of what is knowable; it produces all the various states of meditation, and anoints the heads of all spiritual princes. In all fields of form, sound, fragrance, flavor, feeling, and phenomena, you realize complete perfect enlightenment. Inside and outside are in complete communion, without any obstruction at all.

PAI-CHANG

STOPPING AND SEEING

Before the cosmic net is spread, how can its thousands of pearls be seen? When it is suddenly raised by its universal rope, the myriad eyes spontaneously open. When mind and Buddha are both observed, that is seeing; when mind and Buddha are both forgotten, that is stopping. Once concentration and insight are balanced, what mind is not Buddha, what Buddha not mind? Mind and Buddha being thus, then myriad situations, myriad conditions, are all meditation.

TS'AO-T'ANG

TACIT ACCORD

Nan-ch'uan was asked, "If the Great Way is not in the realm of perception or cognition, how is it realized?"

Nan-ch'uan said, "It is necessary to realize how to reach it spontaneously by tacit accord with it."

He continued, "The basis of realization does not come from perception or cognition. Perception and cognition involve objects, and only exist in relation to things. The spiritual subtlety is inconceivable; it is not relative. That is why it is said that the subtle function is mastered spontaneously, not depending on something else.

"So it is said that this is not a matter of light or dark, and is apart from being and nonbeing. It is penetrated mystically by plunging into the noumenon, unbeknownst to anyone."

THE SUBSTANCE OF MIND

The substance of your mind is apart from annihilation and apart from eternity; its essence is neither polluted nor pure. Calm and complete, it is equal in ordinary people and sages, functioning responsively without convention. All realms of experience and all states of being are only manifestations of your own mind—do the moon reflected in water or images in a mirror have origination and extinction?

If you actually know this, you are fully equipped. The reason that the sages have manifested a spiritual presence to provide exemplars, and have set forth a wide variety of puzzling sayings, is simply to illustrate the fundamental peace of the body of reality, bringing about a return to the root.

SHIH-T'OU

BEYOND MINDLESSNESS

Don't say mindlessness is itself Zen; there is an even more recondite road herein. After you have overturned the donkey-tethering stake, as you hit the south you move the north.

HUAI-SHAN

UNDERSTANDING

Questions are endless, and answers are inexhaustible: if it's a matter of curing illness, it doesn't take a donkey load of medicine.

What does that mean? When sages of yore passed on a word or half a phrase, it was something they did only because they had no other choice. If you talk a lot about different points of view, that is contrary to the essence of the way.

Indeed, the subtlety is beyond all images; the principle unifies all methods. Even while presenting many approaches, the light is hidden in the absolute.

So it seems that the way depends on the mind's awakening; it is not in words. Continuously evident, it has never been cut off. Not belaboring the mind, turn your own light around for a while. Daily activities are completely included—how can opposition stand?

Therefore it is said that the whole universe is just an illusion, unless you immediately realize the vehicle of truth and attain the mystic path all at once, forgetting all about subject and object, arriving at basic unminding, seeing through worldly troubles, understanding gangs of devils. If you effectively understand thus, it will make you

happy for life. If you still don't understand, it's just because you yourselves are avoiding it.

HUI-LIN

APPLICATION

Ch'eng-t'ien was asked, "How should I apply my mind twenty-four
hours a day?"

He replied, "When chickens are cold, they roost in trees; when
ducks are cold, they plunge into water."

The questioner said, "Then I don't need cultivated realization, and
won't pursue Buddhahood or Zen mastery."

Ch'eng-t'ien responded, "You've saved half my effort."

AWAKENING

Once you realize universal emptiness, all objects are spontaneously
penetrated: integrating the world and beyond, it contains all states of
being within. If you lose the essence, there is nothing after all; if you
attain the function, there is spiritual effect. The genuine path of unminding is not a religion for the immature.

FEN-YANG

BODY AND MIND

Do you want to know what my body is? My body is the same as the
whole earth.

Do you want to know what my mind is? My mind is the same as
space itself.

Do you want to know what my vision is? I see there is nothing to
see.

Do you want to know what I hear? I hear the unheard.

Since I have been seeing and hearing, why then do I speak of the
unheard? "If you listen with your ears, after all you cannot understand; when you hear through your eyes, only then will you know."

SSU-HSIN

THE PRIMORDIAL BUDDHA

The sun rises in the east, the moon sets in the west. When one rises, one sets. From ancient times until now, people like you all know this and see this. The primordial cosmic Buddha is infinitely boundless, independent in all circumstances, in a thousand different daily affairs—why do you not see it?

It is because you still have calculation in your mind and your views are limited to effect and cause: you are not yet able to transcend religious sentiments and get beyond the shadows and traces. If you instantly understand that conditional occurrence is uncreated, you will shine with illumination like the sun and moon, envelop and support like the sky and earth.

HUANG-LUNG HUI-NAN

SUBJECTIVE FEELINGS

When subjective feelings arrange your effort, and activity is obsessed with objects, the matter of your self is neglected; not believing in true universal knowledge in oneself, you'll never attain true awakening.

CHEN-CHING

MATTER AND EMPTINESS

Seeing matter itself as emptiness produces great wisdom so one does not dwell in birth and death; seeing emptiness as equivalent to matter produces great compassion so one does not dwell in nirvana.

YUN-FENG

EXPEDIENTS AND REALITY

Stop, stop! Once the Great Form had disappeared and the Pure Sound had died out, the door of expedients was opened to convey the influence of truth indirectly. With this the Three Baskets and Five Vehicles set up teachings in response to potentials. Like a nation's military forces, they were only used when unavoidable.

After that, Bodhidharma came from the West solely transmitting the mind seal. One flower blossomed in five petals, and Zen spread all over China. It was much like those born deaf becoming dumb. Why? Because you each have something that shines through all time, open as space, clear as a bright mirror: It can be experienced now, and there is certainly no possibility of it deceiving people's eyes.

But what are your eyes? Can you experience it? If you can experience it, then countless Buddhas, the Three Vehicles, the Twelve Parts of the Teachings, the six generations of Grand Masters, and the teachers everywhere all shatter to smithereens in your eyes.

If you cannot experience it, ahead is Mt. An, behind is Mt. Chu.

YUN-FENG

ABSOLUTE AND RELATIVE

When the absolute is absolute, it is incomplete; within completeness there is also the relative. When the relative is relative, it is not material; even within matter, completeness remains. Deep in the night, there's the energy that brings on dawn; when the sun is at its peak, it lights up the skies.

I-CH'ING

WHO'S GOT THE PEARL?

Remain silent, and you sink into a realm of shadows; speak, and you fall into a deep pit.

Try, and you're as far away as sky from earth; give up, and you'll never attain.

Enormous waves go on and on, foaming breakers flood the skies: who's got the bright pearl that calms the oceans?

I-CH'ING

MEANINGLESS TALK

Bottomless in depth, boundlessly vast, foaming waves flood the sky; how can you determine the current of the water? If you can discern the current of the water then you will know the source. If you don't yet know the source, for now I am speaking meaningless talk to you.

But how do you understand this "meaningless talk?" Is it that I tend to criticize people? Is this meaningless talk? Is it that speaking about worldly judgments and comparisons is meaningless talk? This is not the point.

As I see you, you are a sorry bunch. You leap up idly, and nine times out of ten crudely, merely having remembered a useless saying or an outworn speech. When you are confronted with a challenge, though, you cannot clear it up.

Nowadays there's a kind of elder who likes to instruct people by means of sayings, like giving out verbal orders in a small village. That is called slandering universal insight. It is truly hard to repent. Why don't you search your own guts? When you are lying sick and helpless on your death bed, none of the sayings you learned all your life will be of any use at all.

SSU-HSIN

ZEN AND THE TEACHINGS

Dharma Master Chao said, "Wisdom has the perception to find out the recondite, without any knowledge; spirit has the function of responsive understanding, without any rumination."

Even in speaking thus, the ancient certainly expended a lot of effort! How can that compare to sitting near the fireplace when it's cold, and sitting by bamboo groves and valley streams when it's hot?

Even so, I ask you, what about the ultimate matter?

YUN-FENG

EYE AND CATARACT

Do you want to understand? The whole world is one of your eyes, the body produced by your parents is a cataract. All ordinary people ignore the indestructible, marvelously clear, unfailingly mirroring eye, and cling fast to the dust cataract produced by the relationship of their father and mother. Therefore they take illusions for realities, and grasp at reflections as the physical forms themselves.

P'U-AN

GREAT WISDOM

Those of superior faculties and great wisdom get the point right off the bat—guidance doesn't mean gumbeating and lip-flapping. Truly awakened people with clear eyes would just laugh.

The great masters of India and China only met mind to mind—from the first there was never any "mind" to attain. But if you make a rationale of mindlessness, that is the same as having a certain mentality.

YING-AN

SPIRITUAL KNOWLEDGE

The great enlightenment that broke down the ultimate particle manifested both substance and functions completely, expounding 5,048 scrolls of teachings, each word embodying truth, pointing out 84,000 subtle ways to truth, all ending up in the ocean of essential nature. Its application is not in vain. Fact and principle are universally included, freely concentrating and expanding.

Primordially there is just a single energy, temporally expressed by means of provisional terms. It contains all things, and pervades all times. Beyond all natures and characterizations, It is a solitary light, the source of completeness, spiritual knowledge. From the eon of the void right up to now it has never perished and never been born, never increased and never decreased.

Originally there are no four kinds of birth and six courses of being; all of them arise from false ideas. Ancient sages, out of compassion and mercy, bequeathed scriptures and established classics, wanting to get people to return to themselves. Provisionally designating the names Confucianism, Buddhism, and Taoism, they set up images to represent the heart, employed words to lead to the essential.

Thus the Confucians take Confucius and Mencius as models, Taoists study Lao-tzu and Chuang-tzu, and Buddhists search out true emptiness. The three are basically one body: that body is neither void nor material, neither existent nor nonexistent. It contains heaven and earth, including everything. It benefits sentient beings, its constant radiance shining independently.

This subtle basis is rarely expounded. The sages are long gone, and falsehood is deep; bedevilment is strong, while true teaching is weak. After Bodhidharma came from the West, not insisting on writings but just pointing to the human mind for perception of its nature and attainment of enlightenment, fortunately we had one flower blossom in five petals. When the fruit had formed, the sixth grand master disseminated it throughout the land. The mutual objective recognition of minds was called transmission of the lamp. Perfectly clear spiritual knowledge taught in accord with potentials.

There were some, however, who sunk into voidness and lingered in stillness. There were some who went frantically seeking, clinging to forms; they took up walking sticks and traveled over a thousand mountains and ten thousand rivers, not knowing for themselves that the body is the site of enlightenment. Their every thought was on objects, turning away from awakening. Retreating and forgetting halfway along the path, they sank forever into the realm of devils.

P'U-AN

Transmission of Zen

Have you not read how Bodhidharma faced a wall for nine years when he first went to Shao-lin, absolutely inscrutable?

The future second grand master stood in the snow and cut off his arm, yet Bodhidharma still would not trust him.

The second grand master said, "Please pacify my mind."

Bodhidharma said, "Bring me your mind and I will pacify it for you."

The second grand master said, "Having looked for my mind, I cannot find it."

Bodhidharma said, "I have pacified your mind for you."

The mind of the second grand master opened up, and he attained great enlightenment.

When your original mind is all-pervasive, only then will you understand the meaning of Bodhidharma's coming from the West. It was transmitted successively, reaching the sixth grand master.

Teaching nowadays can hardly be compared with the wise ones of old; there is the name without the reality. Who among latter-day students knows they are turning away from awakening and getting mixed up in objects?

P'U-AN

ZEN SEEKING

A grand master said, "With uniform equanimity, everything disappears of itself." Only then do you attain great effectiveness. When you come to the boundary of life and death, you calmly become absolutely still, without any further effort whatsoever. Just being so, like a polar mountain—does that not hit the mark?

Zen students in recent times may call themselves seekers, but wherever they take up residence they just keep false ideas in their minds, making contentious disputation a way of life. They are really pitiful.

Genuine seekers are not like this. Observe how the ancient sages since time immemorial went from community to company, got to know genuine spiritual friends, and spent ten or twenty years retreating into themselves, like dead ashes and withered trees, carefully finding out what's at the root and the stem. They had to find reality before they could adapt to conditions while remaining natural and spontaneous, worthy of the name of a Zen student or high-minded pilgrim.

If your state of mind is not clear, how can you stop arousing your mind and stirring thoughts twenty-four hours a day, like countless waves lapping all around? How can you dissolve them away?

At this point, if you have no penetrating liberation, you are just an ignorant thief stealing the community's food. When your time is up, all the mechanical knowledge and intellectualism you have acquired in your life will be of no use at all in facing death.

Even if you do countless good works all your life, you will have less and less hope of transcending birth and death. You will only get human or heavenly blessings and rewards; when the rewards are finished, as before you have no way out.

YING-AN

LIONS AND GEESE

In olden times, Ta-sui called on over seventy teachers. Those who had great vision were only one or two; the rest had accurate knowledge and perception.

Hsiang-lin associated with Yun-men for eighteen years, working as an attendant; every word, even half a phrase, he would record on his paper robe.

By these two extremes we can see how sincere the ancients were about truth. When they reached penetration, they were empowered, transcending beyond all traps, devices, strategies, and emotional and intellectual interpretation. This is what is meant by the saying that the lion king does not roar at random.

In recent times, the Zen schools are weak and dilute. What is their problem? The problem lies in individual lack of self-trust. And where does this problem come from?

It generally comes from the basis not being correct. As long as the basis is not correct, even if you put yourself in a Zen community, you will see the Zen community as an inn; even if you talk about studying Zen and learning Zen, you will be like geese hearing thunder.

From these two extremes we can also see the difference between people of the present and people of olden times.

YING-AN

BAD FRIENDS

Recently a kind of devil has emerged, referred to in the teachings as bad friends. They each expound different interpretations, claiming to help people.

Some teach people to stop their minds and not think at all, cutting off any stirring thought the moment it arises.

Some teach people to do nothing at all, not even burn any incense or perform any prostrations.

Some only teach people to rationally understand past and present, just like bumbling professors.

Some refer to what the ancient adepts held forth with naked hearts, and claim they were setting up schools.

Some see a student come and utter a saying that seems right, then half a day later pose a question with another saying; the student presents another saying, and if it fits they say this one has penetration.

Now tell me—do these ways of "helping people" actually live up to direct pointing to mind? Clearly there is no connection at all.

YING-AN

Dreaming and Waking

Delusion is dreaming; enlightenment is awakening. When you're deluded, you don't know it's a dream; when you wake up from the dream, then you realize it was a dream.

An ancient worthy said, "When you're in a dream, how can you know the dream is unreal? When you wake up, then you become conscious that what was in the dream doesn't exist. When you're deluded, it's like something in a dream; when you're enlightened, it's the same as waking up."

Delusion and enlightenment are originally nonexistent; it's just that the Buddhas spoke of them for remedial purposes after they had realized enlightenment.

That is why there are sayings and writings, expedient means for helping people, explaining delusion from the point of view of enlightenment, in accord with the mutual quelling of medicine and disease.

Once people are enlightened, there is fundamentally no delusion; what is the use of talking about medicine?

P'U-AN

Solitary Shining

If people who study the path are intending to concentrate on Zen, they should only concentrate on the Zen of the "solitary shining of a lone lamp in the hall of nirvana." Do not set up specific periods, hoping to awaken to the path within a certain time. That is laughable.

This Zen has no trouble and no pain: the only important thing is to step back and trust completely; hang your pack high and break your staff. Stiffen your spine, and be like wood or stone inside, and like open space outside.

Suddenly the tub of lacquer comes apart, and the five clusters and eighteen elements are washed clear and clean; all beings are suddenly liberated.

Once you have seen this highway, it is not the place to stop: when you arrive at clear understanding of universal truth, only then will you find true and false, right and wrong, clearly distinguished in every case. This is called insuperably great independent spiritual mastery.

YING-AN

STEPS ON THE WAY

Those who would learn Buddhahood should just break through the seeds of karma by means of the power of great devotion, then recognize cause and effect and be wary of sin and virtue.

Detach from all mental objects, stop all thoughts: do not let either good thoughts or bad thoughts enter your thinking, do not keep either Buddhist teachings or worldly phenomena in mind.

Let go of body and mind, until you reach a state of great rest, like letting go over a cliff ten miles high, being like open space. And don't produce representations of discriminations of random thoughts arising and passing away; the moment a view sticks in your mind, use the sword of wisdom to cut it right off, not letting it continue.

HUAI-T'ANG

COVER THE UNIVERSE

Zen is not thought, the path has no achievement; yet if not thought it is not Zen, and without achievement it is not the path.

At this point, where do you arrive?

When you have cut through your conceptual faculty, how do you discriminate?

When you do not fall into consciousness, how do you approach?

As soon as you get into the clusters and elements, you're already a lifetime away.

What you must do is cover the whole universe, with no opinion about Buddha or doctrine, bringing it up in the midst of sharp edges, putting it to use in heated situations.

Just trust in it thus, and naturally every step will tread on the real ground; you can hold still and be the master, go along with things or spurn things, setting out and setting aside according to the time.

When you turn upward, Buddhas and devils disappear without a trace; mountains and seas vanish.

When you turn downward, clerics are clerics, lay folk are lay folk.

You transcend seeing and hearing, get rid of all dependence, and ride at leisure on top of sound and form, mastering that which startles the crowd.

HUAI-T'ANG

INWARD AND OUTWARD VIEWS

To cling to oneself as Buddha, oneself as Zen or the way, making that an understanding, is called clinging to the inward view.

Attainment by causes and conditions, practice and realization, is called the outward view.

Master Pao-chih said, "The inward view and the outward view are both mistaken."

PAI-CHANG

OBJECTIVITY AND SUBJECTIVITY

Things have never declared themselves empty, nor do they declare themselves form; and they do not declare themselves right, wrong, defiled, or pure. Nor is there a mind that binds and fetters people.

It is just because people themselves give rise to vain and arbitrary attachments that they create so many kinds of understanding, produce so many kinds of opinion, and give rise to many various likes and fears.

Just understand that things do not originate of themselves. All of them come into existence from your own single mental impulse of imagination mistakenly clinging to appearances.

If you know that mind and objects fundamentally do not contact each other, you will be set free on the spot. Everything is in a state of quiescence right where it is; this very place is the site of enlightenment.

PAI-CHANG

INHERENT NATURE

Inherent nature cannot be named. Originally it is not mundane, nor is it holy; it is neither defiled nor pure. It is not empty or existent either, and it is not good or bad.

When it is involved with impure things, it is called the two vehicles of divinity and humanity.

When mental involvement in purity and impurity is ended, the mind does not dwell in bondage or liberation; it has no mindfulness of striving or nonstriving, or of bondage or liberation.

Then, even though it is within birth and death, the mind is free; ultimately it does not commingle with all the vanities, the empty illusions, material passions, life and death, or media of sense.

Transcendent, without abode, it is not constrained by anything at all; it comes and goes through birth and death as through an open door.

PAI-CHANG

REALIZATION

The basic attainment is not produced by production. Manjushri said, "It is only realized by realization, not produced by production." The immemorial tradition has been only to teach people to understand the way, and not seek anything else. If you think about it and rationalize, that all belongs to statement and doctrine.

All the principles of the three vehicles and five natures I call points of practice: if you can apply them sufficiently wherever you are, that will do. If you discourse on the way, that is not it; if you get obsessed, you will be imprisoned by that knowledge. That is also to be called worldly knowledge. The teaching says that those who are obsessed with canonical studies are hunters and fishers, who kill universal Buddhism for profit.

NAN-CH'UAN

THE EYE OF THE LIVING

Someone asked T'ou-tzu, "What is the eye of the living?"
T'ou-tzu said, "No warmth."

SUPERFICIAL IMITATION

A student asked T'ou-tzu, "What is avoiding superficial imitation?"
T'ou-tzu said, "I'm not fooling you."
The student asked, "What do you mean?"
T'ou-tzu said, "It won't do to teach you superficial imitation."

Subject and Object

Someone asked T'ou-tzu, "How is it when subject and object are both forgotten?"

T'ou-tzu said, "No such thing. Don't entertain such an understanding."

Bedevilment

What is bedevilment? Bedevilment means error. If you conceive intent to grasp the external, this is error. If you conceive intent to grasp the internal, this is error. If the mind is not aroused, then it is not agitated; if the mind is not agitated, this is correct.

Fu Shanhui

The Burden of Nothing

A student asked T'ou-tzu, "How about when I don't bring a single thing?"

T'ou-tzu said, "Where did you get this?"

Transformation

A single pill of alchemical elixir transmutes iron into gold; a single word of ultimate truth transforms an ordinary person into a sage. This being true even of worldly phenomena, I ask you, what is the principle behind transforming ordinary people into sages? Try to express it to everyone.

Even if you are not forthcoming, you have already said it in your gut. What is the principle behind transformation of ordinary people into sages? For now, tell me what is transformed! Don't sleep! What is it?

Is it a shout or a caning? Views like this are tantamount to the view of those who beat iron gongs on the street, telling beads and chanting.

For your part, what should you do? You must have eyes before you can discern right from wrong. Don't just go on as you are. Time does not wait for anyone. You should make earnest effort. When you wake up after sleeping, try to see—what principle is this?

TUNG-SHAN

THE WHOLE EXPERIENCE

High-minded mystics and pilgrims should have the eyes of Zen. When they open their mouths, they exhaust the senses of a thousand sages, make a thousand mental objects unbinding; father and mother both die, guest and host do not stand.

If you understand in this way, it is still just a little bit of Zen perceptive understanding, not the whole experience of Zen.

What is the whole experience? Go back and have some tea.

CHIH-MEN

THE SELF

Chih-men was asked, "What is my self?"
  He replied, "Who is asking?"
  The questioner said, "Please help me more."
  Chih-men said, "The robber is a coward at heart."

ZEN MASTERS

Zen masters must clearly understand themselves, must have discriminating perception of objective truth, and call on teachers everywhere before they can determine the religious heritage of the Zen school and see where water and milk part ways.

TUNG-SHAN

TRUE NATURE

The real nature of ignorance is the Buddha-nature; the ephemeral body is the body of teachings. If you can trust in this, you will inevitably save energy.

This could refer to the story of Sudhana entering the tower of Maitreya, where infinite doors of truth were everywhere; he attained universal nonresistance, and realized the nonorigination of phenomena.

This is called acceptance of phenomena as nonoriginated. Infinite realms and objects, subjective and objective, are on a hair tip without obstruction; the ten times, ancient and modern, are never apart from the immediate moment of consciousness.

But I ask you, what is the immediate moment of consciousness? The very essence of your ignorance is actually the intangible luminous nature of your fundamental awakeness.

It is because you do not realize the root source of birth and death that you cling to the false as real. Under the influence of falsehood, you fall into repetitious routines and suffer all sorts of misery.

If you can turn attention around and look back, you will realize the original true nature is unborn and imperishable, and this is why it is said that the real nature of ignorance is the Buddha-nature, and the ephemeral body is the body of teachings.

The impure elemental body has no ultimate reality at all. It is like a dream, like an illusion, like a reflection, like an echo. For infinite eons it has drifted along in the waves of birth and death, compelled by craving, never at rest for a moment, going from one state to another, piling up a mountain of bones, drinking oceans of milk.

Why? Because you have no insight and do not realize the five clusters are fundamentally empty, without any substantial reality at all; you pursue falsehood, you are subject to birth, caught up in greedy desire, unable to be free. This is why the Buddha said, "Of the causes of all miseries, greed is fundamental; if you extinguish greed, they have no basis."

If you can realize that the ephemeral body is unreal and conditional, fundamentally empty and inert, these views will not arise. There is no self, person, being, or life.

All phenomena are thus; that is why it is said that the ephemeral body is the body of teachings. When awakened, there is no thing to the body of teaching; there is only the ungraspable, mysterious universal way, listening to truth and expounding truth, the true religion with no fixations.

This is why it is said, "The essence of the root source is the natural real Buddha."

SHIH-SHUANG

MUSTER YOUR SPIRIT

You should muster your spirit to penetrate the root source. Here you cannot speak of enlightenment, nirvana, thusness, liberation, transcendence, immanence, sitting in meditation, entering concentration, building bridges, or digging public wells.

Get it?

Even so, it won't do to say nothing.

When I set out on my journey, I didn't have the right intention to study Zen and learn the way; I just wanted to go to the eastern capital to listen to one or two scriptures and treatises to sustain me for everyday life.

I didn't expect that I'd wind up traveling around until I happened to meet the Zen master Shou-shan. Getting stuck by him, I simply ran with sweat.

At that time, I unconsciously bowed, but I've never gotten over my regret.

What do I regret? I regret not having dragged him off his Zen chair and given him a thrashing.

Even so, "Officially, nothing so much as even a needle is admitted; privately, even a horse and carriage can get through."

SHEN-TING

HOST AND GUEST

Ch'eng-t'ien was asked, "What is host within guest?"

He replied, "Unrecognized when met."

Then he was asked, "What is guest within host?"

Ch'eng-t'ien replied, "Poverty at home is not yet poverty; poverty on the road saddens people to death."

Finally he was asked, "What is host within host?"

Ch'eng-t'ien replied, "The words of the monarch are like strands, their dissemination is like strings."

STUDYING ZEN

Do you want to study Zen? You must let go.

Let go of what? Let go of the four elements and five clusters, let go of consciousness conditioned over incalculable time.

Focus on right where you stand and try to figure out what the reason is.

Keep on pondering, and suddenly the flower of mind will bloom with enlightenment, illuminating the whole universe.

This can be called getting it in the mind, responding to it in action. Thereupon you can turn the earth into gold and churn the rivers into cream. Wouldn't that make life exhilarating?

Do not just memorize sayings, recite words, and discuss Zen and the way based on books. The Zen way is not in books.

Even if you can recite the teachings of the whole canon and all the masters and philosophers, they are just useless words of no avail when you are facing death.

The ancients sought illumined guides only after they themselves had awakened and understood, in order to pick out the rubble and completely purify their realization of truth.

When they could measure pounds and ounces accurately, they were like people opening variety stores carrying all sorts of goods.

CHIEN-JU

AVOID DRIFTING OFF

If you really want to deal with birth and death, just avoid drifting off under any circumstances, whether you are dressing or eating, attending the calls of nature, walking, standing, sitting, or lying down.

Be like someone who sees a ferocious tiger, totally engrossed in getting away and escaping with his life.

Or be like someone on a battle front, who only wants to kill the leader of a rebellion: only when he has taken the leader's head can he rest.

Why bother with grasping and rejection, purity and defilement, profane and sacred, right and wrong, and so on?

Otherwise, it's all a waste of effort—when will peace ever be attained?

If you work in this way, it has some relevance to birth and death; otherwise, it's all contrivance, without benefit on the way. A former teacher said, "Don't get stuck in small successes, you must reach the state of the ancients before you attain freedom in life and death." Otherwise it is all something on the shore of birth and death; there's really no end in sight.

CHIEN-JU

The Experience of Zen Study

The experience of studying Zen is like hiding your body in fire: even if you have iron guts and a brass heart, here they will surely melt and flux.

Even so, space must shatter to smithereens and earth sink away before you will have a way to turn around. Only at such a time should you get a thrashing.

Chien-ju

Other Things

Studying Zen, learning the way, is originally for the sake of birth and death, no other thing.

What do I mean by other things? Arousing the mind and stirring thoughts right now; having contrivance and artificiality; having grasping and rejecting; having practice and realization; having purity and defilement; having sacred and profane; having Buddhas and sentient beings; writing verses and songs, composing poems and odes; discoursing on Zen and the way; discoursing on right and wrong; discoursing on past and present.

These various activities are not relevant to the issue of birth and death; they are all "other things."

Chien-ju

Virtue and Enlightenment

Cultivating blessings without cultivating the way has been scorned by Zen masters as delusive; practicing charity with the wrong attitude is pointed out in scripture as demonic activity.

From this point of view, the foremost blessing is not comparable to the teaching of the mind ground. If you do not know the mind, it will certainly be hard to eliminate the seeds of greed, wrath, and folly: even if you have heavenly blessings, after having risen you will sink again, like a bird with its feet tethered flying up in vain.

Therefore cultivating blessings is not as good for students of the way as is seeing essential nature. If you can see essential nature, then blessings are no longer limited.

TA-TU

THE QUEST

The quest of real followers of the path is just to oppose birth and death; they do not look for it in the sayings found in various sources in ancient and modern books. They just step back into themselves and bring it to mind, coolly yet keenly, at the very root and stem.

Suddenly their hands slip, they lose their footing, and they're lost: this is graduation from the study of a lifetime. Perceiving independently, like a solitary lamp, for the first time they are manifestly empowered.

They are like mountains; how could the fears of life and death shake them any more?

YING-AN

UNMINDING

If you want to understand readily, just be unminding at all times and all places, and you will naturally harmonize with the path.

Once you are in harmony with the path, then inside, outside, and in between are ultimately ungraspable; immediately empty yet solid, you are far beyond dependency.

This is what ancient worthies called "each state of mind not touching on things, each step not positioned anywhere."

YING-AN

THE KEY TO SPIRITUAL EFFECT

The reason the ancients had spiritual effect in learning the way was that the thieving mind had died completely. If the thieving mind does not die entirely away, there is no way you will ever attain self-fulfillment.

Speaking in simple terms, if you kill off a tenth of the thieving mind, you've learned a tenth of the way; if you kill off five tenths of the thieving mind, you've learned five tenths of the way. When the thieving mind is entirely gone, everything is the way.

MING-PEN

SWIFTER AND SLOWER WAYS

Worldly afflictions are as extensive as an ocean, noisy and clamorous; but they all arise from the thoughts in your own mind. When not a single thought is conceived, you are liberated from them all.

Since it depends on one's own self, how hard could it be? Attaining Buddhahood shouldn't take even a finger snap.

Viewed in this way, it seems very easy; but even so, you must be the one to do it. An ancient also said, "The moment you produce a thought, it is an object; just don't have a single thought, and objects disappear, so mind dies out spontaneously, and there is nothing more to pursue."

Those who already have good roots will understand this kind of talk the moment they hear it. Those who may be slower should look into it over and over—ultimately what principle is this?

TA-TU

KNOW YOUR OWN MIND

You really have to know your own fundamental mind before you can stop and rest.

If you know your mind and arrive at the fundamental, that is like space merging with space.

TA-TU

EMPTINESS

Bodhisattvas in the beginning stage first realize that all is empty. After that, they realize that all is not empty.

This is nondiscriminatory wisdom. It is what is meant by the saying that "form itself is emptiness."

It is not emptiness as annihilation of form; the very essence of form is empty.

The practice of bodhisattvas has emptiness as its realization. When beginners see emptiness, this is seeing emptiness; it is not real emptiness. Those who cultivate the way and attain real emptiness do not see emptiness or nonemptiness; they have no views.

TAO-HSIN

OBJECTIVE REALITY

If objective reality is not manifest, what awakening at all is there to talk about? It is all escapism and reality-avoidance. What do you call this? It is like putting a stone on grass; when you remove the stone, habit energies are still there as before.

You must understand wherever you are; you must be master of the objective world, avoiding compulsion by sense objects. It is very, very difficult; there are a thousand difficulties, myriad difficulties.

TA-SUI

PRACTICE

Just detach from all sound and form, but do not dwell in detachment, and do not dwell in intellectual interpretation—this is practice.

As for reading scriptures and studying the doctrines, according to worldly conventions it is a good thing, but from the perspective of one who is aware of inner truth, it chokes people. Even those in the tenth stage cannot escape completely; they flow into the river of birth and death.

PAI-CHANG

ALONG THE WAY

Ta-sui was asked, "What is the point to concentrate on along the way?"

He replied, "Don't be self-conceited."

IMMATURITY

As soon as you get some sense of contact, you want to be teachers of others. This is a big mistake.

TA-SUI

The First Point

Ta-sui was asked, "What is the very first point?"
He replied, "Don't think falsely."

Sincerity

The worthies of past ages all sought the truth and did not deceive themselves. They were not like moths throwing themselves into flames, destroying themselves in the process.

Ta-sui

Everywhere

Ta-sui was asked, "Buddha's truth is everywhere; so where do you teach students to plant their feet?"
He replied, "The vast ocean lets fish leap freely; the endless sky lets birds fly freely."

Foresight and Diagnosis

You must discern the result in the cause, and discern the cause in the result.

Ta-sui

What and Who

A student asked T'ou-tzu, "What is 'turning the wheel of the teaching in fire'?"
T'ou-tzu said, "Understood everywhere."
The student asked, "What about after understanding?"
T'ou-tzu said, "No wheel of teaching to turn."
The student asked, "What should be done about temporary lapses in presence?"
T'ou-tzu said, "Who informs you about them?"

No Mistake

Someone asked T'ou-tzu, "How is it when there is no mistake moment to moment?"

T'ou-tzu said, "Bragging."

The Obstruction of Nonobstruction

A student asked T'ou-tzu, "What is the one expression of Nonobstruction?"

T'ou-tzu said, " 'Thus.' "

The student said, "This is still an obstruction."

T'ou-tzu said, "Yes, it is."

Mind and Matter

Resistance does not mean walls and fences, nonresistance does not mean open space. If you can understand in this way, mind and matter are fundamentally the same.

TSU-HSIN

The Eye

In the teachings it says that all compounded things are like dreams, illusions, bubbles, and shadows; they are like dew and like lightning, and should be seen in this way.

What eye do you see with? When you have fully attained this eye, you will see the mountains, rivers, and earth do not ruin or adulterate yourselves, nor do yourselves ruin or adulterate the mountains, rivers, and earth. There is no more sacred doctrine therein to make for understanding or obstruction. And there is no ordinary convention to make for understanding or obstruction.

But can you believe it? If you can believe it, then consciousness conditioned by ignorance turns into endless meditation. If you can't believe, endless meditation turns into consciousness conditioned by ignorance.

TSU-HSIN

INDEPENDENCE

To know by thinking is secondary; to know without thinking is tertiary. It is essential for the individual to directly bear responsibility and put down the two extremes of clarity and unclarity from your learning hitherto; when you reach the state of cleanness and nakedness, then you must go on over to the Beyond, where you kill Buddhas when you see Buddhas, kill Zen masters when you see Zen masters.

In Zen, this is still the work of servants. Independent people should not seek Zen or Tao or mystery or marvel from the mouths of old monks sitting on the corners of meditation seats and stuff that into stinking skinbags, considering it the ultimate principle. Isn't this a mistake?

YING-AN

UNDERSTANDING ZEN

In reading scriptures and studying the doctrines, you should turn all words right around and apply them to yourself.

All the verbal teachings point to the inherent nature of the immediate mirroring awareness. As long as this is not affected by anything, existent or otherwise, it is your guide. It can shine through all realms, whether they exist or not.

This is adamantine wisdom, wherein you have your share of freedom and independence. If you cannot understand in this way, then even if you could recite the whole canon and all its branches of knowledge, that would only make you conceited. Paradoxically, it shows contempt for Buddha; it is not true practice.

PAI-CHANG

FALSE TEACHERS

Even if you seek tranquillity, delight in goodness, and search for the source, if you don't meet someone with genuine true knowledge and understanding, it will turn instead into major error. The fault lies in false teachers.

P'U-AN

Cleaning House

If you want to cut off the path of birth and death, you should throw away everything you have always treasured in your mind. Then your six senses will naturally be clean and naked. One day you will have a flash of insight and no longer worry that the road of birth and death will not be cut off.

If you do not make real application basic, and instead desire lots of knowledge and intellectual understanding, considering this the subtlety of self-realization, then you will be blown by the wind of knowledge and intellectual understanding, making you colder and hotter, constantly occurring to you, so that your nose is stuffed up and your head is unclear, day in and day out. This is a calamity you bring on yourself—it is not the fault of another.

Ying-An

Verbal Teachings

The verbal teachings of Buddhas and Zen masters that have come down from the past are like bits of tile used to knock on a door; it is a matter of expediency that we use them as entrances into truth.

For some years now, students have not been getting to the root of the aim of Zen, instead taking the verbal teachings of Buddhas and Zen masters to be the ultimate rule. That is like ignoring a hundred thousand pure clear oceans and only focusing attention on a single bubble.

Ying-An

The Way of Buddhas and Zen Masters

The way of Buddhas and Zen masters is open as cosmic space, vast as the ocean—how can careless mediocrities tell of it? And how can it be measured like feet and inches, or calculated like thatch?

Only those of great faculties, great capacity, and great power, exerting great intensity, stomp right through where not a single thought has arisen, not a single bubble has emerged, after that sitting and reclining on the heads of the Buddhas and Zen masters. Only then do they have a little bit of realization.

HSUEH-YEN

ACT ON REALITY

In learning this path, it is only important to walk on the real ground, to act on the basis of reality. The slightest phoniness, and you fall into the realm of demons.

If your vision is perfectly clear and you are not confused by objects twenty-four hours a day, then you gain power. If your vision does not penetrate freely, how can you do what is beyond measure?

An ancient said, "Even if there is anything beyond nirvana, I say it too is like a dream illusion." If your own eyes are not yet open, how can you understand?

The conduct of those transcendent people is like diamond flames, like a raging fire—there is no way for you to get near. It is not forcibly contrived; it is so by nature.

LIAO-AN

ACQUIESCENCE

Every point you find impenetrable in the realm of work on the way is just your own mind making obstacles. If this mind would acquiesce completely, you would arrive at the stage of Buddhas and Zen masters immediately, and there would be nothing supposedly obstructing you any more.

The right attitude for studying the way is just complete spontaneous acquiescence. Who cares whether it takes twenty or thirty years—you'll be naturally at peace, without the slightest bit of doubt or confusion. How can there be any obstruction again after spontaneous acquiescence? How can anyone arrive by way of externals?

MING-PEN

ONE SOURCE, SAME AIM

Ultimately, why should people who brush aside the weeds looking for the *way* necessarily be concerned with the cycle of birth and death? It

is essential to clarify the one actuality that is prior to "sentient beings" and "Buddhas."

If you try to look for it in quietude, it goes and crouches in clamor;
if you look for it in clamor, then it stands in quietude. If you want to
place it in the realm of nothingness, yet it is a living thing.

How can you get it? If you let action and stillness flow from one
source, and apply the ancient and the modern to the same aim, polishing and refining over and over, without getting hung up over the
time it may take, then naturally the autumn water will become still,
and the golden waves will suddenly appear, shining through the
mountains, rivers, and earth, the myriad distinctions and thousands
of differences.

It is only because temperaments are not the same that there are
differences in quickness and slowness.

CHUEH-AN

Two Ailments

In learning the way there are not more than two kinds of sickness:
either lingering in clear stillness, or staying in the midst of confusion
and disturbance. Those who are fierce and intense will sharply reject
both of these and leap through and beyond the Other Side in one
bound: not only do other and self, sound and form, subject and object
all vanish at once; no sign of birth and death can be found at all.

Only then can you be called an uncontrived free wayfarer with
nothing more to learn, having attained the great cessation, great rest,
and great bliss. But when you get to such a state, you can only be said
to have realized yourself and understood yourself; if you talk about
the thirty-six rivers of Shu, there are yet great difficulties ahead.

WU-CHUN

Complete Potential

Complete potential responds universally; perception is before activation of potential. Leaving aside perception for the moment, what
about the aftermath of response?

If you do not make your steps broad and pay close attention, you
will fall into stagnant water, with no hope of getting out.

If you can turn around and look at your shadow, this is already being slow about it.

When I talk like this, does it seem like my tongue is dragging on the ground? This is why in the *Lankavatara-sutra* Buddha says that mind is the source and emptiness is the door to the truth.

All the different speech of the world, mundane and transmundane, is an immense state of liberation.

Is this not what Buddha said, that only mind is the source? Where do you still worry you will not penetrate? What place is not your self?

If, however, you get the gist immediately in this way, I already know you will have understood it dogmatically. Let those with the adamantine eye discern!

HUAI-T'ANG

EVERYWHERE

Everywhere is where followers of the way lay down their lives. Everywhere is where followers of the way tune their minds.

Everywhere is the treasury of endless capacities of followers of the way. Everywhere is not everywhere; it is called everywhere.

I often see students who are narrow-minded, who gain a little bit in a limited context, with a limited perspective, and consider this enough, immediately insisting on stopping and resting. Eating their fill and sleeping, not taking care of anything at all, they consider themselves lively, but they are destitute ghosts.

HUI-K'UNG

AWARENESS

When aware that the content of awareness is empty, empty awareness is complete. When hearing the content of hearing is finite, finite hearing does not remain.

Even if you can see in this way, you are already involved in process. Has it not been said, "If feelings retain notions of the holy, this is still involvement in external objects; if the idea of self is not forgotten, it's the same as leaking."

How could it be possible to suppose that discoursing on mind and nature and lecturing on Zen and the path are effective vehicles to the source?

WU-CHIEN

PROGRESSIVE REALIZATION

Each form, each particle, is a Buddha. One form is all Buddhas. All forms, all particles, are all Buddhas. All forms, sounds, scents, feelings, and phenomena are also like this, each filling all fields.

This is the gross within the subtle; this is a good realm. This is the cognition and perception of all those in progress; this is the exit in life and entrance in death of all those in progress, crossing over everything, existent and nonexistent.

This is what is spoken of by those in progress. This is the nirvana of those in progress. This is the unexcelled Way. This is the spell that is peer to the peerless. This is the foremost teaching, considered the most profound of all teachings. No human being can reach it, but all enlightened ones keep it in mind, like pure waves able to express the purity and pollution of all waters, their deep flow and expansive function.

All enlightened ones keep this in mind. If you can be like this all the time, no matter what you are doing, then the body of pure clear light will be revealed to you.

PAI-CHANG

DETAILED INSTRUCTIONS

If we are to discuss the conditions of this great matter, although it is originally inherent in everyone, actually complete in each individual, lacking nothing at all, nevertheless for beginningless ages the seeds of the root of attachment, subjective ideas, and emotional thinking have become so deeply ingrained as habits that they block and cover the subtle light and thwart its real true function. Living totally within the shadows of subjective ideas of body, mind, and the world, you therefore flow in the waves of birth and death.

When Buddhas and Zen masters appear in the world, everything they say, all their various techniques, expounding Zen and the teachings, are without exception tools for breaking attachments according to the situation; basically there is no real doctrine to give people. So-called cultivation is just clearing away the reflections of force of habit and false thinking, according to ones own mind; insofar as effort is applied to this, it is called cultivation.

If false thinking suddenly stops for an instant, and you see through your own mind, the vastness of its original perfect light, the purity of its original state, no thing in it at all, this is called awakening. There is nothing to be awakened or cultivated other than this mind.

Because the substance of mind is like a mirror, the reflections of subjective thinking climbing around on objects are just dust and dirt on the true mind. That is why it is said, "The forms of thoughts are dust, the feelings of consciousness are dirt." If false thoughts are melted down, the original substance itself appears: it is just like polishing a mirror—when the dirt is cleaned off, clarity appears.

It is naturally like this, but we humans have accumulated eons of ingrained habits that have become hard and fast; the roots of self-love are deep and hard to pull out.

In the present life, if we have the fortune to know for ourselves what is intrinsic through the inner influence of inherent insight outwardly inspired by good friends, so we aspire to understand and shed birth and death, to tear out the very root of immeasurable ages of birth and death all at once, how could this be a small matter?

If you are not a person of great power and capacity who can bear it alone and plunge right in with a single sword, it is truly the most difficult thing there is. When an ancient said that it is like opposing ten thousand people all alone, he wasn't fooling!

On the whole, in this final age of the teaching, there are many practitioners, but few who succeed in genuine appreciation and application; there are many who waste power and few who attain power. Why is this? Generally because they have not taken a direct approach; they just use their subjective feelings to evaluate things based on previously learned opinions, intellectual interpretations, and verbal expressions. Suppressing random thoughts, they work at the gateway of shadows of a light. First they take mysterious words and marvelous sayings of ancient people and store them in their chests, making them out to be real doctrines, taking them for their own knowledge and vision, not knowing that it is utterly useless in this context.

That is precisely what is meant by the saying, "Reliance on others for understanding blocks the gateway of one's own awakening."

Now if you are going to do the work, first you must set aside intellectual interpretations and just work precisely on one thought, certain faith in the original purity of your own mind. Completely untrammeled, round and bright, it fills the universe. Originally there is no body, mind, or world, and no false ideas or emotional thinking. This one thought, itself originally unconceived, manifests all sorts of objects, all illusory, unreal—they are only reflections appearing in the true mind.

When you see through them in this way, then in the emergence and disappearance of wandering thoughts you can see for sure at a glance where thoughts arise and where they pass away. Focus your effort in this way, and no matter what wandering thought may occur, the moment you confront them they shatter, melt, and crumble away. Do not go along with them, and don't continue them. This is what Yung-chia meant when he said "It is essential to cut off the continuing mind."

After all, the insubstantial drifting mind is fundamentally rootless; under no circumstances should you make it out to be something real lying in your chest. The moment it appears, repudiate it; once you repudiate it, then it vanishes. Don't try to suppress it, for you will go along with it, making it like a gourd bobbing on water.

You just need to set body, mind, and the world to one side, and bring up this one thought, simply and precisely, like a precious sword across the sky—whether Buddha or devil, you cut them off equally, like cutting through tangled threads, pushing them to the side to move ahead—so-called direct, straightforward mindfulness of reality as such. Straightforward mindfulness involves no thought; if you can observe without thought, you can be said to be heading for the wisdom of Buddhas.

The very first inspiration to practice requires certain faith in the teaching of mind alone. Buddha said the triple world is only mind, myriad things are only consciousness. So many Buddhist teachings only explain this saying, clearly enabling every individual to believe in it. The two main roads of the ordinary mortal and the sage are simply the two routes of confusion and awakening within one's own mind. All good and bad causes and effects are totally ungraspable outside this mind.

Our subtle essence is natural; originally it is not in the domain of realization, so how can it get lost? Now when we say it is lost, that just means one does not understand there is originally not a single thing in one's own mind, and one has not realized the original emptiness of body, mind, and world; being obstructed by them, it is said to be lost. Operating only with the fluctuating mind thinking subjectively, taking that for truth, people therefore take all sorts of illusions associated with objects of the six senses to be realities.

Now when you aspire to go against the current and attain transcendence, it is totally essential to shed your previous knowledge and understanding completely. No knowledge or technique is applicable—it is just a matter of seeing right through your own present body, mind, and world: all are illusory reflections of ephemeral light manifested in your own mind, like images in a mirror, like the moon reflected in water.

Look upon all sounds as like wind passing through the trees; look upon all objects as like clouds floating through the sky, all of them illusory, unreal things. Not only are externals like this: your own mind's subjective notions and emotional thinking, the seeds of the roots of all attachments, forces of habit, and psychological afflictions, are empty, ephemeral, illusory, unreal.

Looking deeply in this way, whenever a thought arises be sure to check where it's going. Don't let it go too easily, and don't be deceived or deluded by it. When you work in this way, you are approaching true attentiveness. Other than this, if you spread out mysteries and marvels, knowledge and views, techniques and methods to linger over, you are completely out of touch.

So the fact is that explaining how to do the work is also just an expedient. It is like the use of military force: weapons, being instruments of ill omen, are only to be used when it cannot be avoided. Similarly, when the ancients spoke of bringing up sayings to study Zen, it was all because they could not help but do so.

Although there are many *kung-an*, the saying "Find out who is really invoking the name of Buddha" is the one with which it is most easy to attain power in the midst of worldly toils. While it is easy to attain power with it, nevertheless it is like a piece of tile used to knock on a door; in the end it is to be discarded, though not without putting it to use once.

To employ this to do work right now, you must trust it completely, rely on it steadily, and persevere in it continuously. Be sure not to vacillate; it won't do to be like this today and like that tomorrow, worrying you won't get enlightened, or disliking this as not mysterious or marvelous—these thoughts and calculations are all obstructions. It is necessary to explain them away first, so doubts and worries do not arise on specific occasions.

When you have done the work to the point where you have attained some power, and external objects do not enter in, but there are afflictions inside the mind arising arbitrarily in unruly ways—it may be desirous thoughts coming out, or psychological turmoil, or hangups of all sorts, tiring your mind and sapping your energy, beyond your control—these are seeds of forces of habit, stored in your repository consciousness over incalculable ages, now coming out under the pressure of the work.

It is absolutely necessary that this point be distinctly clear. You must see through these phenomena to begin with and pass right through them. Be sure not to be trapped by them, be sure not to fiddle around with them, and be sure not to take them for realities. Just clarify your spirit, exert yourself, and pluck up your courage: take up the saying you are looking into, and use it to chase away these thoughts when they arise. There are originally no such things in us— ask where they come from, and ultimately what they are; be sure to see what they come down to.

Keep on pushing like this, and you'll simply make spirits and ghosts weep; you'll obliterate tracks and traces. Strive to drive them all into extinction, not leaving any at all. Apply effort in this way, and you'll naturally see some good news. The moment you push all the way through, all errant thoughts will fall away at once, like the shadows of flowers in the sky dropping, like the waves of a mirage settling.

Once you've gone through this, you'll gain immeasurable ease and comfort, immeasurable freedom. This is the beginner's empowerment; it is not considered a mysterious marvel.

Now when you reach ease and freedom, still do not become joyful. If you become joyful, the demon of joy will stick to your mind and add yet another kind of obstacle.

If you come to forces of habit and seeds of the root of attachment that are so firmly rooted deep in the unconscious that a saying can exert no effect on them, then look into where the mind's perception cannot reach.

If you can't do anything yourself, then perform prostrations before

Buddhas, recite scriptures, and practice repentance. You also need to inwardly hold the essence of sacred spells, relying on the esoteric symbols of Buddha to dispel these obstacles. Because the esoteric spells are all impressions of the indestructible mind of Buddhas, when we use them it is like wielding a diamond club, smashing everything into atomic particles. The secret of the mind seal of the Buddhas and Zen masters since high antiquity is not beyond this. Therefore it is said that the Buddhas of the ten directions hold the essence of spells, attaining unexcelled universal true enlightenment.

In the schools of the Zen masters, it was feared that this would fall into common emotion, so it was kept secret and not spoken of; it's not that it wasn't used. This should be done on a regular daily basis; over a long period of time it becomes pure and mature, and very much power is gained. Just refrain from wanting or seeking spiritual experiences.

HAN-SHAN

DIRECT REALIZATION

The matter of Zen is only realized directly by people of superior faculties; those of mediocre and lesser potential have no part in it. Without opening any doors or setting out any pathways, it presents the whole right to your face, to be personally realized and personally attained, without any further how or why.

Speaking in extreme terms, the statement, "This very mind is Buddha" says it all. This statement, however, is still in the realm of inducement. If you actually understand it, every breath is cut off, all conceptions are cut off—you just silently accord, that's all. Otherwise, you are mistaking your consciousness for the master.

TA-TU

THE POISON SEA

If Zen students have not shed their stage of vision and have not forgotten their knowledge of principle, they fall into the poison sea of liberation. Their emotionalized perception is not yet erased, their objectivized perceptions are not empty: they are totally a mass of ignorance, composed of conditioned consciousness.

As long as the mass of ignorance composed of conditioned consciousness is not broken up, and the poison sea of liberation is not dried up, this is precisely the root of birth and death.

CH'IH-CHUEH

UNIVERSAL GOOD

Buddha said to the bodhisattva Universal Eye, "Is there anyone who can tell the whereabouts of the various illusory appearances in magical writings?" He answered, "No."

Buddha said to Universal Eye, "Since even the illusory appearances in illusions cannot be explained, how about the esoteric physical realm of the Universally Good bodhisattva, the esoteric verbal realm of the Universally Good bodhisattva, the esoteric mental realm of the Universally Good bodhisattva? Yet if you enter into them, you can penetrate and can see."

It is bright in the mind's eye, radiant in material form; don't call the silver world a temporary silver citadel.

PEI-CHIEN

NO SEPARATION

One moon appears everywhere in all bodies of water; the moons in all bodies of water are contained in one moon. This is a metaphor for one mind producing myriad things and myriad things producing one mind. This refers to dream illusions, flowers in the sky, half-seeming, half empty.

What if drifting clouds cover the sky; where is the clear light in the waters? Here, if you open up the eye of true insight, you will see that the moon has never not been there, the light has never disappeared—light and dark are as one, death and life have no separation.

HSUEH-YEN

NO

When you look into the word "No," it is only essential to arouse a feeling of doubt about the word "no" and look into it. Ask yourself, why did Chao-chou say the word "No"? Look into it this way twenty-four hours a day.

When you are looking into it, don't ask whether there is thinking going on or not; thinking and not thinking are both in the realm of illusion.

At present it is only necessary for you to keep up the feeling of doubt at the saying you're looking into. You do not need to think about anything at all; any thought you conceive apart from the saying you're looking into, no matter whether it is a thought of Buddha or a thought of the teaching, is not right mindfulness, but a seed of birth and death.

People who are really and truly doing the work are intent on it twenty-four hours a day, as intent as if they were saving their heads from burning, as if they were facing ten thousand adversaries single-handed. When would they find the leisure time to be obsessed with their personal lives or worldly conditions? And what leisure do they have to seek edification from others? What idle time, furthermore, do they have to question others, to look for sayings and statements, to seek interpretation and understanding?

Some people are at a loss and helpless if they don't get instruction from someone for three days. They are all in a whirl, chasing illusions; they are not doing the work.

In general terms, people doing the work are like thieves intent on stealing others' valuables. When they are walking, they are walking intent on stealing; and when they are sitting they are sitting intent on stealing. When at leisure they are intent on stealing at leisure, and when in a hurry they are intent on stealing in a hurry. Why would they willingly reveal their intention of stealing, so others could see? The keener their intent to steal, the more they keep it a hidden secret. If you can be like this in every state of mind, in every moment of thought, and continue thus unremittingly for a long time, surely you will reach the stage of the ancients.

This is not like those who are unable to be the master steadily twenty-four hours a day, but just want to forcibly be the master while going along with the whirl of random thoughts, rushing to their cushions to imitate a posture while frantically seeking, thought after thought, unwilling to stop and rest. How can they ever find accord?

MING-PEN

SAMENESS AND DIFFERENCE

In the Zen school there is a type of brilliant people who start out by attaining a semblance of understanding at teachers' words, then take it at that. At that time, if the teachers have no leisure to question whether they are enlightened or not enlightened, they let them go for the while.

At this point they teach their own insight to others; now they don't want anyone to doubt sayings, they only value ready-made understanding. Thus they drag each other down into a web of intellectual views. When they talk it seems like Zen, but their actions are totally unconnected.

There is a kind of beginner who is ignorant and slow, who hears that to study Zen one should look into a saying and arouse a great feeling of doubt, after which one may suddenly awaken insight, and then spends twenty or thirty years firmly relying on a saying for contemplation, continuously from beginning and end, unwilling to let it go. Eventually illusions suddenly vanish completely and they awaken.

After that, whenever learners ask them for help, they invariably want to have people look into sayings, arouse a feeling of doubt, and make concentrated effort. With teachers like this, while it is hard to make progress to insight, nevertheless they do not wind up ruining people's natures.

Ever since there have been Zen schools, although they speak of simply pointing to the human mind, they have employed countless different methods. Relying on the one principle of simple pointing, the teachers have guided differently in accord with people's dispositions as well as their own personal experience of enlightenment; yet in every case the supreme principle and the ultimate end were the same, the great matter of understanding and shedding birth and death, nothing else.

People's mentalities have many differences, and they cannot just "crap once and be done." There are statements to the effect that one should also see others after awakening, and there are statements to the effect that one still needs practice after attaining insight: these are for cases where awakening has not been thorough, and people still have different attachments and cannot remove sticking points and untie bonds for others.

Thus there are recommendations to see others or practice more, but for those who are enlightened once and for all there are no such teachings.

Although the ancients did not look into model stories and arouse the feeling of doubt, it must be remembered that their attitude before enlightenment was thoroughly dissimilar from that of people today. If you taught people today not to make concentrated effort, every one of them would sit inside a web of delusions.

An ancient said, "Relying on others to formulate understanding blocks the door of your own awakening." The *Scripture of Complete Enlightenment* says, "If people in the degenerate age want to attain the way, don't make them seek enlightenment, for they will only increase their formal learning, which will inflate their idea of themselves."

MING-PEN

BUDDHA'S TREASURY OF LIGHT

I observe the Buddha's treasury of light producing all oceans of lights: whether sage or ordinary mortal, animate or inanimate being, none are not endowed with this body of light and openly demonstrating the function of this light. Root and branches are completely included, withdrawal and expansiveness are uninhibited, self-help and helping others are inexhaustible.

It is like the sun rising in the sky, shining on all without discrimination. The illuminator and the illumined are both empty and silent, while all sentient beings benefit from the light, accomplishing their individual tasks. They never know each other, and don't rely on each other: no one knows why it is as it is, but that does not diminish the illumination provided by the sunshine. This is like the inherent spiritual light; it is not gotten from another, yet those who are blind to it do not awaken.

Are they blind to the end? If they can return to the light in an instant, it will be the same as having been there all along. So it is said, "The path is not far from people; it is realized in this very mind." Is that not so?

LIAO-AN

The Pure Land

The Pure Land is only mind; there is no land outside of mind. In this land that is only mind, there is no east in the east, no west in the west—all directions are contained in it.

The so-called Buddha-lands numerous as atoms in the ten directions are all realms within one's own Pure Land; the Buddhas of past, present, and future numerous as grains of sand in the Ganges River are Buddhas in one's own Pure Land.

Even Amitabha Buddha of the world of Bliss is simply one Buddha of one realm of one's own Pure Land.

WEI-TSE

The Sword of Zen

Of old it has been said, "There are basically no words for the way, but we use words to illustrate the way." It is also said, "If speech does not avoid cliché, how can it get you out of bondage?"

If powerful people are like long swords against the sky, cold and stern, inviolable, then they will finally have some freedom.

The expedients of Zen masters are like bonfires: get close to them, and you lose your life. If you understand by thinking and know by pondering, you're a thousand miles away.

WU-CHIEN

The Great Way

The Great Way is always present, but though it's present, it's hard to see. If you want to understand the true essence of the way, do not get rid of sound and form, words and speech; words and speech are themselves the Great Way.

You do not need to remove afflictions; afflictions are originally empty and null. Arbitrary feelings may wrap you up, but all are like shadows, like echoes; who knows what is bad, what good?

If you consciously grasp forms as real, your insight into essence will surely be imperfect. If you deliberately perform works seeking Buddhahood, these works are major evidences of birth and death.

While works of birth and death always follow you, you remain unawakened in a pitch dark hell. Once you have realized the principle, there has never been a difference; after awakening, who is late, who early?

The realm of reality is as vast as cosmic space; it is the knowing mind of sentient beings that is small. Just as long as you do not become egotistic and selfish, you will be ever sated with the spiritual food of nirvana.

PAO-CHIH

THE STRAIGHT PATH

I announce the straight path to all people: nonbeing is in fact not nonexistence. Nonbeing and non-nonexistence are not two; why should we talk about voidness in contrast to being? Being and nonexistence are names set up by confused minds; when one is refuted, the other does not remain.

Both names are made by your feelings; when there are no feelings, there is basic reality as such. If you want to seek Buddha but keep your feelings, you are hauling a net up a mountain to snare fish: it is a useless waste of effort, without benefit. How long will you misuse your time?

If you do not understand that mind itself is Buddha, you are as if riding a donkey in search of a donkey. If you do not hate or love anything, this affliction should disappear.

To get rid of this, you must detach from the body; when detached from the body, there is no Buddha, no cause. When no Buddha or cause can be grasped, there is naturally no doctrine or person.

PAO-CHIH

THE INGREDIENTS

It is laughable how slovenly people are, each holding onto a different view. They just want to stand by the pan, expecting a pancake; they do not know how to go back to the root and see the flour. The flour is the root of right and wrong; it changes in a hundred ways, depending on how people prepare it.

What is needed is to free the intellect in all ways, not to become partial or obsessed. Freedom from attachment is itself liberation; if you seek anything, you will again meet a snare. With a loving heart, be evenhanded to all, and the enlightenment of reality as such will spontaneously appear; if you keep a dualistic consciousness of others and self, you will not see the face of Buddha right in front of you.

PAO-CHIH

THE NONDUALITY OF MATTER AND EMPTINESS

The nature of things fundamentally has no color, but people idly create adornments. If you interpret cessation and contemplation through your ego, your own mind is in turmoil, unbalanced, mad.

If you do not know the subtle principle of complete penetration, when will you attain understanding of real eternity?

If you cannot cure your own sickness, and yet teach medicinal prescriptions to others, outwardly this may seem to be good, but inwardly you are like a rapacious beast.

The ignorant fear hell, but the wise consider it no different from heaven. If the mind is never aroused toward objects, then wherever you walk is the site of enlightenment.

Buddhas are not separate from people, but people create disparity themselves. If you want to get rid of the three poisons, you will never leave the conflagration; the wise know that mind is Buddha, while the ignorant wish for paradise.

PAO-CHIH

NATURALNESS

What is coming from nowhere? It means not depending on any practices.

What is going nowhere? It means not grasping any doctrine.

What is detachment from past existence? It means not dwelling on traces of the past, detaching from labels, and not intellectualizing anything.

What is detachment from present existence? It means the present mind is unaffected by the duality of being and nonbeing.

What is detachment from future existence? It means the mind does not grasp the future, but realizes the naturalness of things.

FU SHAN-HUI

VIRTUE AND KNOWLEDGE

As long as you are bound by all sorts of things, existent and nonexistent, you cannot be free. This is because you first possess virtue and knowledge before being firmly established in inner truth, so you are ridden by virtue and knowledge. It is like menials employing a noble.

It is better to settle the inner truth first, and then afterwards gain virtue and knowledge. Then if you need virtue and knowledge, as the occasion appears you will be able to turn gold into earth and earth into gold, change sea water into buttermilk, smash the polar mountain into dust, and place the waters of the four oceans into a single pore. You create unlimited meanings within one meaning, and make one meaning of unlimited meanings.

PAI-CHANG

KNOWING AND BEING

There are people in the world who constantly lecture on scriptures and ethics, who know what is wrong and what is not wrong, what is sinful and what is not sinful, what is offensive and what is not offensive. They are outwardly proper in their bearing, but have not stopped bad patterns in their inner minds; are they able to attain liberation from miseries?

Suppose someone inwardly has full knowledge of cause and effect, and the various conditions for misery and happiness, and he is also proper and mannerly in outward appearance, yet cannot take care of himself, and keeps five hundred iron barbs inside his clothes—do you think this person can be free of pain? If people who study the way now are outwardly proper but inwardly do not stop bad patterns in their minds, they will be like this.

FU SHAN-HUI

INSIGHT

It has been asked, "The principle and knowledge of the subtle truth of suchness is mysterious and profound: how can those of shallow perceptions gain insight?"

One should not misrepresent Buddha—Buddha did not speak in

this way. All things are neither deep nor shallow in themselves—it is just that you yourself don't see, and think that means extreme profundity.

When you have insight, everything you see is subtle; why put the bodhisattvas on a pedestal, or particularly set up sages? As Master Sheng said, 'It's not that knowledge is deep—things are deeper than knowledge.' This is just an expression of lament that knowledge cannot reach things.

Don't be discriminatory, don't keep a grasping and rejecting attitude. For this reason it is said, "Truth has no comparison, because it is not relative to anything."

The scriptures have body and mind for their meanings: the *Flower Ornament Scripture* says, "The body is the treasury of truths, the mind is the unobstructed lamp. Illuminating the emptiness of all things is called liberating people."

HUI-CHUNG

IMAGES AND RELICS

If you think you can become enlightened just by worshipping images and relics, this is a mistaken view. This is actually possession by the poisonous serpent of temptation.

DOGEN

DISCIPLINE

If you insist upon disciplinary regulations and vegetarianism as fundamental, make them established practices, and think you can attain enlightenment that way, you are wrong.

DOGEN

OVERCOMING GREED

If you would be free of greed, first you have to leave egotism behind. The best mental exercise for relinquishing egotism is contemplating impermanence.

DOGEN

TACT

When you see others' errors and you want to guide them because you think they are wrong and you feel compassion for them, you should employ tact to avoid angering them, and contrive to appear as if you were talking about something else.

DOGEN

EMOTIONAL VIEWS

Students of recent times cling to their own emotional views and go by their own subjective opinions, thinking Buddhism must be as they think it is, and denying it could be any different. As long as they are wandering in illusion seeking something resembling their own emotional judgments, most of them will make no progress on the way of enlightenment.

DOGEN

APPEARANCE AND REALITY

- Most people of the world want others to know when they have done something good, and want others not to know when they have done something bad.
- If you refrain from doing something because people would think ill of it, or if you try to do good so others will look upon you as a true Buddhist, these are still worldly feelings.
- If you have compassion and are imbued with the spirit of the Way, it is of no consequence to be criticized, even reviled, by the ignorant. But if you lack the spirit of the Way, you should be wary of being thought of by others as having the Way.
- What you think in your own mind to be good, or what people of the world think is good, is not necessarily good.
- If people who keep up appearances and are attached to themselves gather together to study, not one of them will emerge with an awakened mind.
- You should not be esteemed by others if you have no real inner virtue. People here in Japan esteem others on the basis of outward appearances, without knowing anything about real inner

virtue; so students lacking the spirit of the Way are dragged
down into bad habits and become subject to temptation.

DOGEN

PRACTICING TRUTH

- If you study a lot because you are worried that others will think
  badly of you for being ignorant and you'll feel stupid, this is a
  serious mistake.
- People of the world cannot necessarily be considered good—let
  them think whatever they will.
- To "leave the world" means that you do not let the feelings of
  worldly people hang on your mind.
- You should not do what is bad just because no one will see it or
  know of it.
- You should think about the fact that you will surely die. This
  truth is indisputable.
- Even if you don't think about the inevitability of death, you
  should determine not to pass your time in vain.
- Our lives are only here for now.
- One should not differentiate good and bad on the basis of taste.
- One need not necessarily depend on the words of the ancients,
  but must only think of what is really true.
- If you want to travel the Way of Buddhas and Zen masters, then
  expect nothing, seek nothing, and grasp nothing.

DOGEN

MORALS

- The ancients thought it shameful to seek advancement or to
  want to be the head of something, or the chief or senior.
- No one should torment people or break their hearts.
- Just regard people's virtues, don't be obsessed with their faults.
- People should cultivate secret virtue.
- No matter how bad a state of mind you may get into, if you keep
  strong and hold out, eventually the floating clouds must vanish
  and the withering wind must cease.

- Do not be so proud as to hope to equal the great sages; do not be so mean as to hope to equal the ignoble.
- If one pursued selfish schemes to stay alive, there would be no end to it.
- There is fundamentally no good or bad in the human mind; good and bad arise according to circumstances.
- Though a nobleman's power is greater than that of an ox, he does not contend with an ox.
- To plow deep but plant shallow is a way to natural disaster; if you help yourself but harm others, how could there be no consequences?

DOGEN

UNDERSTANDING

- Don't cling to your own understanding. Even if you do understand something, you should ask yourself if there might be something you have not fully resolved, or if there may be some higher meaning yet.
- Although a suspicious mind is bad, still it is wrong to cling to what you shouldn't believe in, or to fail to ask about a truth you should seek.
- Even if you have thoroughly studied the stories of the ancients and you sit constantly like iron or stone, as long as you are attached to yourself you cannot find the Way of the enlightened, ever.
- Although the Way is complete in everyone, realization of the Way depends on a combination of conditions.
- Tenacious opinionation is not transmitted by your parents; it is just that you have tacitly come to believe in opinions for no reason other than that over time you have picked up what people say.
- Whether or not beginners are imbued with the spirit of the Way, they should carefully read and study the sagacious teachings of the scriptures and treatises.
- Once having understood, you should read the teachings of the sages many times.
- Truth is not greater or lesser, but people are shallow or deep.

DOGEN

ATTITUDE

- ' Even if you are in a high place, don't forget you may fall. Even if you are safe, don't forget danger. Even though you are alive today, don't assume you will be alive tomorrow.
- ' The mind has no fixed characteristics; depending on circumstances, it may turn out any way at all.
- ' Even if it is painful and lonely, associate with worthy companions.
- ' Consider how you will travel the path, without taking notice of slander from others, without heeding resentment from others.
- ' Do not think of studying Buddhism in order to gain some advantage as a reward for practicing Buddhism.
- ' Everyone has great faults, and pride is the greatest fault.
- ' Prefer to be defeated in the presence of the wise than to excel among fools.
- ' If the mentality that seeks honor and advantage does not cease, you will be ill at ease all your life.
- ' Students of the Way must individually examine their own selves. To examine yourself means to reflect upon how you should carry yourself, mentally and physically.
- ' If the heart is not empty, it will not admit truthful words.

DOGEN

PRESENCE

- ' If you don't understand the Way as it meets your eyes, how can you know the Path as you walk?
- ' Progress is not a matter of far or near.
- ' All things have their function; it is a matter of use in the appropriate situation.
- ' Don't waste time.

SHIH-T'OU

CULTISM

How could it be permissible to form a cult, gather followers and cronies, dash off writings, and toil in pursuit of objects for love of honor and advantage?

TUNG-SHAN

CLARITY

- If you can forget both clamor and silence, you will surely understand the simultaneous realization of the absolute and the relative.
- Buy afterwards; try first.
- All obstructions due to actions come from false conceptions.
- Only a clear mind knows itself.

LIN-CH'UAN

WAKING UP

- The body of Buddha fills the cosmos, manifest to all sentient beings everywhere.
- The peak experience lights up the heavens and covers the earth, illumines past and present.
- The great cause of the Buddhas is not apart from your daily affairs.
- Look with intense concentration at the state before any forms are distinguished, before any illustration is evident.
- The sphere of perfect communion is clear everywhere—why are people in such a hurry?

DAIO

MIND MATTERS

If you misunderstand your mind, you are an ordinary mortal; if you understand your mind, you are a sage.

In this it makes no difference whether you are a male or female, old or young, smart or simple.

JAKUSHITSU

ZEN IN ACTION

If you wish to understand yourself, you must succeed in doing so in the midst of all kinds of confusions and upsets. Don't make the mistake of sitting dead in the cold ashes of a withered tree.

EMYO

GETTING IT RIGHT

> - What is the benefit of exerting mental effort in the wrong way?
> - Realization without making sure of right and wrong is of dubious benefit.

GUON

REALIZATION

> - Zen is not a conception—if you set up an idea of it, you turn away from the source.
> - The Way is beyond cultivated effects; if you set up accomplishment, you lose the essence.
> - After having killed all, you see that mountains are mountains, rivers are rivers.
> - Let go over a mile-high precipice, and appear with your whole body throughout the universe.
> - Sitting peacefully on a cushion day and night seeking to attain Buddhahood, rejecting life and death in hopes of realizing enlightenment, is all like a monkey grasping at the moon reflected in the water.
> - See for yourself.
> - Plunge boldly into the Beyond, then be free wherever you are.
> - Letting go of all objects and letting all things rest is the foremost technique, but if you stick to this technique it is not right.
> - Those with higher knowledge and keen faculties penetrate through to great realization without needing explanations, devices, or objectives.

SHOITSU

EVERYDAY ZEN

> - People see others in terms of themselves. If you are ambitious, that is the way you see others. If you are greedy, you see others in terms of desire.
> - It is easy to keep things at a distance. It is harder to be aloof of them.
> - When you are deluded, you are used by your body. When you are enlightened, you use your body.

- If there is any judgment in your heart, it will be blocked by the judgment.
- There is no Buddha outside your heart. Always keep a pure, clean heart.
- It is only necessary to see and hear directly.
- If you actually manage to see your basic mind, you must treat it as if you were raising an infant.

BUNAN

OBSERVATIONS

- The poor suffer from want, the rich suffer from possessions. The upper classes suffer from their high status, the lower classes suffer from their low status.
- When you die, you go alone. Who goes with you? What can you take along with you?
- Although their fundamental essence is the same, awakened people turn inward while emotional and intellectual people pursue externals.
- If you want to realize the essence that is the same as all Buddhas, first you must clearly understand the root of ignorance.
- When people seeking enlightenment see forms, they question what it is that sees. When they hear, they question what it is that hears. When they feel, they question what it is that feels. When they know something, they question what it is that knows.
- When you walk, practice while walking. When you rest, practice while resting. When you speak, practice while speaking.
- When you're busy and easily distracted, question what it is that gets distracted.
- In a single day an ordinary person "transmigrates" countless times, rarely keeping a human mind, much less roam in heavenly states.

TOREI

ZEN PROVERBS

- What is appropriate provisionally does not suit the real.
- Unless the medicine stuns you, it won't cure the disease.

- If you want both eyes to be perfectly clear, you must not dwell on mental or physical elements, and not get entangled in objects.
- Flowing water doesn't go stale.
- Whoever receives a salary without doing any service is uneasy sleeping and eating.
- Not being present, even temporarily, is like being dead.
- Who can be master in any place and meet the source in everything?
- You too can be host within the world, and also come as a guest from outside creation.
- It is not gotten from another.
- A petty officer often thinks of the rules; a seasoned general doesn't talk of soldiering.
- The hungry will eat anything; the thirsty will drink anything.
- Government officials are easily tested, but that doesn't finish the matter.
- Not falling into causality is forced denial; not being blind to causality is finding the wondrous along with the flow.
- Just do good; don't ask about the road ahead.
- Strictly executing the absolute imperative is still but half the issue.
- When your heart is crooked, you don't realize your tongue is forked.
- If you have a reason, you don't need to shout.
- Outwardly, do not react; inwardly, do not dwell in emptiness. Outwardly, do not pursue ramifications; inwardly, do not remain in trance.
- Sweeping away tracks makes traces, all the more evident the more you try to hide.
- Suspicion in the mind makes ghosts in the dark.
- Are there any elephant tusks in a rat's mouth?
- The nobility of the ancients was no more than purity and serenity—what need for bushels of emblems?
- Don't brag so much.
- When the house is rich, the children are haughty.
- Overindulging people is folly.

ZEN LETTERS
Teachings of Yuanwu

TRANSLATED WITH J. C. CLEARY

TRANSLATORS' INTRODUCTION

These letters were written by the Zen teacher known as Yuanwu to various friends, disciples, and associates—to women as well as to men, to people with families and worldly careers as well as to monks and nuns, to advanced adepts as well as to beginning seekers.

Yuanwu is best known as the author of the single most famous Zen book, *The Blue Cliff Record*, a collection of meditation cases with prose and verse comments. *The Blue Cliff Record* is an intricate web of Zen lore with endless subtleties. Here in these letters, Yuanwu delivers the Zen message in a more accessible form, in direct person-to-person lessons.

Yuanwu was a public spokesman for a tradition of wisdom that he saw coming down from time immemorial. In Yuanwu's Zen tradition, the man usually considered the historic founder of Buddhism was seen as just one buddha in a long line of enlightened ones extending back before history as we know it. In fact, Mahayana Buddhist texts regularly speak of "all the buddhas of the past, present, and future." Mahayana sutras like *The Flower Ornament Scripture* depict a vast universal process of enlightening teaching taking place in all worlds in all times through an infinite variety of forms.

The enlightened ones appeared in the world as teachers to alert people to the unsuspected fact that all of us possess an inherent potential for objective wisdom and unselfish compassion called buddha nature. These teachers meant to enable us to become aware of our buddha nature and to gain the use of it in our everyday life. Zen Buddhism, like all other branches of Mahayana Buddhism, maintains that it is the true destiny of every person to become enlightened.

From the perspective of Zen Buddhism, emotional allegiances, dogma, mechanical ritual, clerical careerism, and sectarian institutions must be seen as the enemies of true religion. True religion is by nature multiform; it consists of whatever practices and techniques and perspectives are effective in awakening the people of particular times and places and restoring their awareness of reality-in-itself, an absolute reality that contains all relative realities, without their getting trapped in any of their limited perspectives. No particular technique is worshipped as a panacea; all techniques are no more than expedient means employed by expert teachers to meet the specific needs of specific seekers.

The practice of Zen consists of a collection of liberative techniques that rest on a profound analysis of human perception and conditioning. In common with the seers of the other equivalent traditions around the world, the Zen adepts observed that ordinarily people are encased in a shell of emotion-laden conditioned perceptions that shape their motivations and limit their experience to a narrow range of standardized perspectives. Ordinarily people reify the concepts they have been unwittingly conditioned to believe in and to project upon the world—they see them as objectively true realities "out there," rather than as the arbitrary cultural constructs they are. Thus the Zen teachers actively worked to "untie the bonds and melt the sticking points" that were keeping their students' minds tied to habitual routines and conventional perceptions.

The Zen tradition, like all of Mahayana Buddhism, is invincibly optimistic about human possibilities—our true identity, our inherent buddha nature, can never be destroyed. It is our basic essence, and it is with us always, waiting to be activated and brought to life. "The sword that kills is the sword that brings life," runs an old Zen saying. The sword of wisdom that cuts away the conditioning and contrived activities that make up our false personality is what frees us and brings our enlightened potential out into the open.

The Mahayana seers did not agree with the modern materialists that we are basically animals forced by the demands of civilization to pit our feeble rationality and precarious moral sense against our submerged yet implacable instinctual drives. Nor did the Mahayana teachers follow the dualistic religions in seeing earthly life as an arena of sin and temptation where humankind is tested to qualify for a heavenly afterlife.

From the Mahayana point of view, once the human mind is washed clean of its conditioning and stripped of its delusions, the ordinary world is the site of enlightenment, suffused with the light of the

Source, where liberated humans can wander at play, naked and free, living the life of wisdom and compassion.

Needless to say, Yuanwu (who was born in 1063 and died in 1135 CE) lived in a world in many ways very different from our own. In Yuanwu's time, Manhattan Island was a leafy forest crisscrossed with streams of clear water. The great cities of Mexico and Peru had not fallen to conquerors from across the sea. The Americas, Africa, Australia, and Oceania were home to a mosaic of diverse cultures, each a symbolic world unto itself, with its own rich history and tradition and way of life.

The Old World of Eurasia and North Africa had already seen empires come and go for millennia: armies, taxes, bureaucracies, castes of nobles and warriors vying for power, ancient traditions of scholarship and learning, populations of peasants and herders eking out a living. The West European onslaught against the rest of the world had not yet begun, and the world was home to immeasurably greater cultural diversity than it is today. No one had yet dared to assert that military superiority was the same thing as cultural superiority.

China in Yuanwu's time was dotted with giant urban centers that were the focal points of administration, commerce, and high culture. A network of officially recognized Buddhist institutions existed throughout the country. The ancient political philosophy of Confucianism had been revived and reworked under Buddhist influences. Taoism, too, was taking on new forms strikingly parallel to Zen. Chinese art and literature in the Song dynasty reached an unprecedented level of clarity and elegance.

But there were severe problems as well. Sporadic peasant uprisings broke out to challenge the growing inequality of wealth. A reform-minded faction in the imperial bureaucracy aroused the bitter opposition of the bulk of the landlord elite and went down to defeat. Though adequate to the task of keeping the peasantry in check, the bloated military establishment was about to go down to crushing defeat at the hands of a relative handful of barbarian invaders. Whatever its glories, the world of Song dynasty China was anything but the serene homeland of "the wisdom of the East" that some modern Westerners like to imagine.

Given the vast historical distance that separates us today from Song dynasty China, it is all the more remarkable how directly Yuanwu's letters communicate with us about the universal issues of the life of wisdom.

Maybe we mistakenly overestimate the differences between ourselves and the people of other times and places. The differences in the technological environments are obvious. But then, as now, people were caught up in their conditioning, driven on by their hopes and fears, eager to live up to socially defined goals and pursue images of the good life. Aren't the perceptions of most of us today still structured in terms of self and others, gain and loss, love and hate, desire and aversion? Don't we automatically assume that these dualities reflect an objective reality that leaves us no choice in the matter?

If so, then the message of Yuanwu's writings still holds something of great value for us. That message is multidimensional and unfolds more fully in the translation below. But for now, just a taste of the timeless wisdom:

> If you can cut off outward clinging to objects and inwardly forget your false ideas of self, things themselves are the true self, and the true self itself is things: things and true self are One Suchness, opening through to infinity.
>
> If you are attached to perception, then this is a perception—it is not the arriving at the Truth. Those who arrive at Truth transcend perception, but they manage to use perception without dwelling in perception. When you pass directly through perception and get free of it, it is all the fundamental Truth.

Zen Letters

Ever since antiquity, with excellence beyond measure, the saints and sages have experienced this Great Cause alone, as if planting great potential and capacity. By the power of their vows of compassion, they have brought forth direct indications of the One Thing that is most profound and most recondite, the common essence of all the myriad forms of being.

Without setting up stages, they abruptly transcend to realize this essence alone. Since before the time when nothing existed, this essence has been ever still and unmoved, determining the basis of all conscious beings. It permeates all times and is beyond all thought. It is beyond holy and ordinary and transcends all knowledge and views. It has never fluctuated or wavered: it is there, pure and naked and full of life. All beings, both animate and inanimate, have it complete within them.

That is why when Shakyamuni Buddha was first born, he immediately pointed to the heavens and to the earth and with a great lion's roar brought it right out in front. Then after he had left home and sought enlightenment for six years, he awakened at the sight of the morning star. In the end, on Vulture Peak, he initiated the Zen transmission by holding up a flower. All that was important is that we should possess the comprehension of this True Eye.

From the time of Shakyamuni, the True Eye was secretly transmitted through the twenty-eight Indian Patriarchs and the six Chinese Patriarchs. Those who did not know of the existence of the True Eye of enlightened perception thought that there was some kind of supernatural power or magical ability involved, and just spoke of going along with the waves and pursuing the current, never searching out the root of the transmission. If you discover its ultimate import, there is no need to poke into it.

In olden times, when Marquis Li met Zen master Shimen, Shimen said to him: "This is the business of a truly great man, not something that can be done by mere generals and high officials." Li understood right away, and expressed himself in verse:

> To study the Way you must be an iron man
> Lay hold of the mind and act decisively

Heading directly for unexcelled enlightenment
Paying no attention to any affirmation or denial

In general, when superior wisdom, excellent capacity, and natural potential are already there, it is just a matter of working to penetrate through surely and truly. When you put it to use, you command Great Potential and unfurl Great Function, moving even before any impulse to action, operating free of things.

Yantou said: "Spurning things is superior, following things is inferior. If we talk about battle, each one's strength is in the turning point."

If you can turn fast on top of things, then everything will submit to you, and everything will be in your grasp. Capturing and releasing, rolling up and rolling out—all can be transformed. At all times you remain peaceful and tranquil, without having anything whatsoever hanging on your mind. In action you accord with the situation and its potential, holding the means of discernment within yourself. Shifting and changing and successfully adapting, you attain Great Freedom—all things and all circumstances open up before your blade, like bamboo splitting, all "bending down with the wind."

Therefore, if where you stand is reality, then your actions have power. Needless to say, leading brave heroes, commanding fierce warriors, routing powerful bandits, comforting the farmers, pacifying the nation, and assisting the work of restoring social harmony and cultural florescence all depend on this one revelation.

Turning the topmost key, achieving something that cannot be taken away in ten thousand generations, you see and hear the same as the ancient buddhas and share the same knowledge and functioning.

The Fourth Patriarch said: "If not for mind, there's no question of buddha."

Deshan said: "A buddha is just someone with no concerns."

Yongjia said: "It is not apart from *here*, always profoundly clear and still. If you search for it, you know you cannot see it."

Linji said: "The real being, with no status, is always going in and out through the doors of your face."

This is the substance of all these sayings.

REAL TEACHING AND REAL LEARNING

Since high antiquity, the source vehicle has been transcendence and direct realization, with teachers and apprentices joined in understanding, with nothing haphazard about it.

This is why the man who was to become the Second Zen Patriarch stood in the snow and cut off his arm to prove his sincerity to Bodhidharma, the First Patriarch. This is why the Sixth Patriarch worked pounding rice in the Fifth Patriarch's community at Huangmei. This is why other Zen adepts worked diligently for twenty or thirty years. How could the seal of approval be given lightly?

In general, genuine Zen teachers set forth their teachings only after observing the learners' situation and potential. Real teachers smelt and refine their students hundreds and thousands of times. Whenever the learner has any biased attachments or feelings of doubt, the teacher resolves them and breaks through them and causes the learner to penetrate through to the depths and let go of everything, so that the learner can realize equanimity and peace while in action. Real teachers transform learners so that they reach the stage where one cannot be broken, like a leather bag that can withstand any impact.

Only after this does the Zen teacher let the transformed student go forth to deal with people and help them. This is no small matter. If the student is incomplete in any respect, then the model is not right, and the unripe student comes out all uneven and full of excesses and deficiencies, and appears ridiculous to real adepts.

Therefore, in order to teach the Dharma, the ancient worthies worked for completeness and correctness, and clarity in all facets. This means inwardly having one's own practice as pure as ice and jade, and outwardly having a complete and well-rounded mastery of techniques, a perspicacious view of all conscious beings, and skill in interchange.

When such adepts met with potential learners, they examined each and every point in terms of the Fundamental. When the learners finally did understand, then the teachers employed techniques to polish and refine them. It was like transferring the water from one vessel into another vessel, with the utmost care not to spill a drop.

Among the methods the adepts employed, we see *driving off the plowman's ox* or *taking away the hungry man's food*. Unfathomable to spirits or ghosts, the genuine Zen adepts relied solely on the one great liberation. They didn't reveal the typical deformities of pretenders to enlightenment and "grow the horns characteristic of other species." At ease, without striving at contrived activity, they were true saints of discipline and virtue who had left behind the dusts of sensory attachments.

There is a saying by Bodhidharma: "Those whose actions and understanding were in accord we call *spiritual ancestors.*"

What Is a Zen Teacher?

Going on pilgrimages in search of enlightened teachers, going beyond convention—basically, this is done because of the importance of *the great matter of birth and death.*

Contacting people to help them is being a good spiritual friend. Bringing to light the causal conditions of the great matter operates on the principle of mutual seeking and mutual aid.

Ever since ancient times, it is only those who are able to bear the responsibility of being a vessel of the Great Dharma who have been able to undertake the role of a Zen teacher and *stand like a wall a mile high.* These people have been tempered and refined in the blast furnace of the teachers of the Source, taking shape under the impact of their hammers and tongs, until they become real and true from beginning to end. Otherwise, they do not appear in the world as teachers. If they do appear, they are sure to startle the crowd and move the people. Because their own realization and acceptance of the responsibility of communicating Truth was not hasty and haphazard, when they passed it on to others they were not rushed or careless.

We all know the classic examples. Master Rang staying with the Sixth Patriarch at Caoqi for eight years. Mazu at Guanyin Temple. Deshan and Longtan. Yangshan and Guishan. Linji and Huangbo. In every case it took at least ten or twenty years of close association between teacher and pupil before the pupil was fully prepared to become a teacher himself.

That is why, with the genuine Zen teachers, every word and every phrase, every act and every state resonated with the music of gold and jade.

Virtually no one in the latter generations has been able to see into what they were doing. You will only be able to see where they were really at when you achieve transcendental realization and reach the stage that all the enlightened ones share in common.

I recall this story from olden times. Mazu asked Xitang, "Have you ever read the scriptural teachings?" Xitang said, "Are the scriptural teachings any different?" Mazu asked, "If you haven't read the scriptures, how will you be able to explain for people in various ways?"

Xitang said, "I must care for my own sickness—how could I dare try to help other people?" Mazu said, "In your later years, you are sure to rise to greatness in the world." And that's the way it turned out later.

As we carefully consider the ancients, did they not achieve great penetration and great enlightenment toward the one great causal condition leading to transcendence? They cut off words and imagery and divorced themselves from the confusion of conditioned discrimination; they just knew for themselves, enjoying peace and freedom alone in a state of rest.

Yet Mazu still spurred Xitang on sternly like this, wanting him to achieve complete mastery of adaptive transformation, without sticking to one corner or getting bogged down in one place.

We must fully comprehend all times past and present and practice harmonious integration, merging into wholeness with no boundaries. It is important in the course of helping people, and receiving oncomers from all sides, that we fish out at least one or two "burnt tails" with the potential to become vessels of the Dharma from within the cave of weeds, people fit to become seedlings of the life of wisdom. Isn't this the work of using expedient means to repay the benevolence and virtue of the buddhas and ancestral teachers?

You must master your spirit, so that whenever you impart some expedient teachings you have the ability in every move to come out with the body of enlightenment and avoid blinding people's eyes. You will do no good if you misunderstand the result and are wrong about the causal basis. This is the most essential path for spiritual friends and teachers.

The great Zen teacher Huinan of Huanglong Temple once said: "The job of the teacher is to sit upright in the abbot's room and receive all comers with the Fundamental Matter. The other minor business should be entrusted to administrator-monks. Then everything will be accomplished."

How true these words are! When as a Zen teacher you employ people as administrative assistants, you must take great care in entrusting them with appropriate responsibilities, so that affairs will not be mishandled.

Zhenru of Dagui Temple said: "There is no special trick to being a Zen teacher and guiding a community of learners; all that's important is to be skillful in employing people."

Please think this over.

A proverb says: "Cleverness is not as good as a reliable model." Baizhang established a set of guidelines for Zen communities, and no one has ever been able to overthrow them.

Now you should just follow these guidelines conscientiously and take the lead in observing them yourself and do not violate Baizhang's elegant standards. Then everyone in your congregation will follow them too.

In the final breakthrough, a patch-robed monk penetrates through to freedom from death and birth. To succeed at this, you must know the move that a thousand sages cannot trap, the move that cuts off the root of life.

The ancient worthies greatly imbued with the Tao could skillfully capture or release, could skillfully kill or bring life. All the teachers who had attained great liberation used these techniques.

It is not difficult to know about such methods. Whether or not you have mastered them shows up in how you do things. When you can cut through decisively and make them work instantaneously in the situation—only then do you attain power in the long run.

Our ancestral teacher Yangqi spoke of *the diamond cage* and *the thicket of thorns* and used them to distinguish dragons and snakes and capture tigers and rhinos. If you are a genuine descendant of his family, then you will bring them forth at ease and cut off the tongues of Zen monks.

THE TRUE SCHOOL OF LINJI

The true school of Linji opened its great potential from Linji's great predecessors Mazu and Huangbo, unfurling its great function, escaping all cages, leaving all nests. Charging like tigers and galloping like dragons, flying like shooting stars, striking like lightning, the adepts of the Linji school rolled up and rolled out, captured and released, always employing expedient means based on the Fundamental, always continuous and accurate. When it came to Fengxue and Xinghua, the teaching of the school became more and more lofty, and its workings more and more steep. "West River sports with a lion, frost flowers energize the Diamond King."

No one could have a clue what the Linji school was all about without entering deeply into the inner sanctum and personally receiving the seal and promise of enlightenment. Uninitiated observers just gave their own arbitrary names and descriptions to what they thought they saw, only adding to the foolish word play.

Even having the mettle to storm heaven, and upholding the truth outside conventions, even defeating people's weapons without fighting and killing people without batting an eye—even this does not quite resemble what the Linji school is getting at. Nor for that matter does switching around the constellations and turning the pivot of heaven and the axis of the earth.

Therefore, Linji and his successors taught using such devices as the *three mysteries* and the *three essentials* and the *four perspectives*, and the *four levels of guest and host*, and *the Diamond King's precious sword*, and *the lion crouched to spring*, and *the shout not acting as a shout*, and *the probing pole and the reed shade*, and *distinguishing guest and host and illumination and action in a single shout*. They used so many lines at once! So many scholars have tried to assess these techniques and add explanations, without realizing in the least that their assessments are totally unfounded, because "there is no such blade in our sovereign's armory."

When the adepts of the Linji school bring forth some device for you to see, it happens in the blink of an eye. You must be the superior type of learner who has achieved realization and experiential recognition of the Zen message. Receiving it straight on and bringing it up from the side, you must be a true seedling of the school—how could you depend on intermediaries?

When Baoshou first appeared in his teaching hall, Sansheng pushed a monk forward, and Baoshou immediately hit him. Sansheng said, "If you help people like this, not only have you blinded this monk, but you have blinded the eyes of everyone in the whole city." Baoshou threw down the teacher's staff and returned to his quarters.

Once when Xinghua saw a fellow student approaching, he immediately shouted. The other monk also shouted. Xinghua shouted again. The other monk also shouted again. Xinghua said, "Look at this blind man!" Then he drove him out of the teaching hall with blows. One of his attendants asked, "What was this monk's offense?" Xinghua said, "He had both the provisional and the real, but I made two passes at him right in front of his face, and yet he didn't understand. If I don't beat a blind guy like this one, when would I ever beat anyone?"

Please observe the true style of the Linji school as it is displayed in these stories. It is absolutely transcendent and does not value any particular strategy. The correctness of one's eye for the Truth is the only thing it considers important.

If you want to uphold the true school and maintain the eye of the Source, you must be completely liberated from head to foot, with a liberation that penetrates the bone and penetrates the marrow and is not entangled with anything whatsoever. Only then can you truly succeed to the Linji school. Only then can you set up the great banner of this teaching and light the great lamp of this teaching. Only then can you continue the work of Mazu and Baizhang and Shoushan and Yangqi without being a usurper.

TRANSMITTING WISDOM

For Buddha's pure transmission on Spirit Peak, for Bodhidharma's secret bequest on Few Houses Mountain, you must stand out beyond categories and apart from conventions and test it in the movements of the windblown dust and grasses.

With your eyes shining bright, you penetrate through obscurities and recognize what is happening on the other side of the mountain. You swallow your sound and eliminate your traces, without leaving behind anything whatsoever. Yet you can set in motion waves that go against the current and employ the ability that cuts off the flow. You go right up to people and nip them. You are swift as a falcon that gets mistaken for a shadow as it soars into the air with its back to the deep blue sky. In the blink of an eye, it's gone. Point to it and it comes. Press it and it goes. It is unstoppably lofty and pure.

This is the way this true source is put into circulation, to serve as a model and standard for later generations. All those who would communicate the message of the source must be able to kill a person's false personality without blinking an eye—only then can they enter into it actively.

One example was old man Huangbo. He knew of this state innately. When he was on his travels, he came to Mount Tiantai, where he saw a saint walking across the waves, cutting off a torrent—Huangbo immediately wanted to strike him dead. When he reached Baizhang and heard the story about how a single shout from Mazu had left Baizhang deaf for three days, he drew back and stuck out his tongue. We know this was the action of Huangbo's great potential.

How could those with simplistic opinions and shallow learning form any opinion of it?

Later on Huangbo taught our ancestral teacher Linji and used the whole essence of this. By not holding back his compassion, Huangbo formed Linji into a capable successor who was to give shelter to everyone in the world.

People with the will to reach the Truth must be fully developed and thoroughly polished to make them go beyond conventions and transcend sects. After this they will have the means to *take away the hungry man's food* and *drive off the plowman's ox,* so they can continue the traditional guidance function and not mistake *turning toward* and *turning away.* They can only be seedlings of transcendence when at the subtle level they can see through every drop, and at the expansive level even the thousand sages cannot find them.

Old master Zufeng used to say, "Even Shakyamuni Buddha and Maitreya Buddha are *His* servants. Ultimately, who is *He?*"

How can this admit of arbitrary and confused probing? You will only get anywhere if you know He exists.

In general, when as a Zen teacher you would energize the indomitable spirit of a great person in your disciples and make them move ahead into the superior stream, you must set to work and make them so they cannot be trapped and cannot be called back.

As you help people and respond to their potential, it should all be clear and free. You mustn't roll around in the nest of weeds or play with your spirit in the ghost cave. If the supposed teacher uses contrived concepts of "mysteries" and "marvels" and "the essence of truth," if he cocks his eyebrows and puts a gleam in his eye and cavorts around uttering apt sayings and thereby binds the sons and daughters of other people's families with doctrines he claims are absolute realities, then he is just one blind man leading a crowd of blind people—how can this produce any genuine expedient teachings?

Since you already occupy the position of being called a teacher, you certainly cannot take it lightly. For your own part, you must be impeccable, aloof, and transcendent, like a lion on the prowl, with a spirit that frightens the crowd. You must always be unfathomable as you appear and disappear and release and capture. Suddenly, the lion crouches down and springs forward, and all the other animals scatter in a panic. Isn't this especially extraordinary?

If you are such a person, then you have already discerned the outline of this from three thousand miles away. That is why Yantou said: "An enlightened teacher is like a gourd on the water, floating free and at ease, who cannot be reined in or tied down."

When you make contact with Truth, then it covers heaven and earth. Always nurturing it and putting it into practice, you arrive at this stage. Only then do you have a share in the one line that comes from Spirit Peak and Few Houses Mountain. Only then can you take turns as guest and host with Huangbo, Linji, Yantou, and Xuefeng. Only then will your teaching be effective, so that "when the wind moves, the grasses bend down"—and you will not have appeared in the world as a Zen teacher in vain.

Uphold and disseminate the Dharma for twenty or thirty years, and then among the others there will naturally be those who can share in the stream of this realization with you, people of learning and perception who will join you in protecting it.

Who says that no one perceives "the priceless pearl"? I say the black dragon's pearl shines forth wherever it is.

PREPARING SUCCESSORS

The buddhas and ancestral teachers transmitted mind by mind. In this transmission, teacher and disciple were both supremely enlightened. Both had penetrated through to liberation, and so they acted like two mirrors reflecting each other. This is not something that words and images can capture.

When you far transcend all patterns and assessments, and the arrow points meet, without ever having any objective other than Truth, then you receive the marvel of the Way, become a successor of the ancestral teachers, and continue the transmission of the Lamp. You cut off the path of ideation and go beyond thinking and escape from emotional consciousness, to reach a clear, open state of freedom that sweeps all before it.

When it comes time to select people to whom you will impart the bequest, it is necessary to pick those of unique spirit whose enlightened perception is fully mature. Then they will not let the family reputation decline, and they will attain the teeth and claws that have always marked the Zen school since time immemorial. Only then will they be in accord with and truly assist in the transmission of Truth by Truth.

It is by this means that the Zen transmission has continued for many centuries, becoming more and more illustrious the longer it lasts. As the saying goes, "When the source is deep, the stream is long."

Nowadays many have lost the old way, and many try to usurp the style of Zen, setting up their own sects, keeping to clichés, and concocting standardized formulas and slogans. Since they themselves are not out of the rut, when they try to help other people, it is like a rat going into a hollow horn that grows narrower and narrower until the rat is trapped in a total impasse. Under such circumstances, how can the universal teaching not decline?

In the old days, when I first met my teacher Wuzu, I blurted out my realization and presented it to him. It was all words and phrases and intellectual points, all empty talk of "buddhadharma" and "essence of mind" and "mystic marvels."

What I got in return was my old teacher citing a couple of dry phrases: "The verbal and the nonverbal are like vines clinging to a tree." At first I shook this saying back and forth, using my verbal cleverness. Then I began to theorize and expound principles. There were no lengths to which I did not go in the end, as I tried to escape the dilemma he had posed: everything I brought up was included in it. Eventually I began to weep without realizing it. Still, I was never able to get into this saying at all. Again and again I earnestly tried to concentrate on it.

At that point my teacher told me, "You should just put an end to all your arbitrary views and understandings and judgments. When you have cleansed them away all at once, you will naturally gain insight." Then he said, "I have already explained it all for you. Now go."

I sat in my place and investigated the matter thoroughly until there was no seam or gap. Then I went into my teacher's room, and I spoke freely in a confused way. So he scolded me, saying, "Why are you babbling?" At that point I admitted to myself that a man whose eyes were truly clear was seeing into what was in my heart.

In the end, I wasn't able to enter into it, so I left the mountain. Two years later I returned.

Finally, "the bottom fell out of the bucket" for me as I was contemplating the saying: "She calls to her maid again and again, though there's nothing the matter, because she wants her lover to hear her voice." Then at last I saw that what my teacher had told me before was real medicine. It's just that I was deluded at the time and could not penetrate into it.

So I know that the real truth is like Liangsui's saying: "I know everything that you people know, but you people do not know what I know." How true these words are!

Xuefeng asked Deshan, "Do I have any part in the business of the vehicle of the school that has come down from antiquity?" Deshan hit him with his staff and said, "What are you saying?" Later Xuefeng said, "When I was at Deshan's, at a blow from his staff it seemed as if I had stripped off a thousand layers of sweat-soaked shirts clinging to my flesh."

Linji got hit three times by Huangbo and went to Dayu to ask if he was at fault or not. Dayu told him, "Huangbo was so kind to you, but you still come looking for fault." Linji had a powerful realization and unconsciously said, "After all, there's not much to Huangbo's Buddhism."

Both Xuefeng and Linji were outstanding members of the Zen community, and both were enlightened under the impact of a blow from the teacher's staff. Later on they both greatly energized the Zen school and made a ladder and a boat for the salvation of the world. Zen students today should think back on them: were they crude and shallow?

Yet in recent times some people say that using the staff to deal with people is *falling into device and object.* They claim that to enter into the subtle refinements it is necessary to investigate the true nature of mind thoroughly, to discuss mysteries and marvels exhaustively, to be consistent and meticulous at all times, and to pick up every stitch.

But what about all the schools of Buddhism that interpret the scriptural teachings, with their minute analyses, their revelations of hidden aspects, their discovery of ultimate reality and penetration of the true nature of buddhahood? Are these not subtle refinements? If this were all there is to it, then what was the need for the ancestral teacher of Zen to come from the West?

It is evident that since the stream of the Teaching has gone on so long, many divergent views have cropped up. Since they do not get the true transmission, they make the ambrosia of the Buddhist teachings into poison. Is this the fault of Deshan and Xuefeng and Huangbo and Linji?

A proverb says: "If the rope is short, it will not reach far enough to draw water from a deep spring."

ADEPTS IN ACTION

The Ultimate Path is simple and easy, yet profound and abstruse. From the start it does not set up steps. Standing like a wall miles high, it is called *the fundamental sustenance*.

Thus in Magadha the Buddha carried out the true imperative by shutting his door and staying in seclusion. At Vaishali, Vimalakirta revealed the fundamental principle by keeping his mouth shut and refusing to speak.

Even so, there are adepts who will not forgive them for these displays. How much less would they forgive getting involved with marvels and delving into mysteries, discoursing upon the true nature of mind, and having a sweaty shirt stuck to their skin and being unable to strip it off! That would appear even more broken down and decrepit.

From Bodhidharma to Huineng, the example set by the Zen patriarchs was exceptionally outstanding. The practical strategies of adepts like Linji and Deshan were immediately liberating. When the great Zen masters went into action, they were like dragons galloping and tigers charging: heaven and earth turned, and nothing could stop their revivifying people. They never dragged through the muddy water of emotionalism and intellectualism. Since time immemorial, as soon as they had certain penetration of the ultimate, those with great realization and enlightenment have been like swift falcons and hawks—riding the wind, dazzling in the sun, with the blue sky at their backs.

They penetrated directly through and made themselves completely unobstructed twenty-four hours a day, with their realization pervading everything in all directions, rolling up and rolling out, capturing and releasing. They did not even dwell in the station of sage, so how could they have been willing to remain in the ordinary current? Their hearts were washed clean, and they encompassed both present and past. Picking up a blade of grass, they used it as the golden body of buddha, and picking up the golden body of buddha, they used it as a blade of grass.

For them there was never any such thing as better or worse or grasping and rejecting. They were just vibrantly alive meeting the situation. Sometimes in guiding learners they took away the person but not the world, sometimes they took away the world but not the person, sometimes they took away both, and sometimes they took away neither. They moved beyond conventions and sectarian limits and were totally clear and free. How could they have had any interest in trapping people, in pulling the wool over their eyes, in manipulating them, in bending them out of shape?

It is necessary to get to the reality and reveal to learners the thing in each one of them that is the fundamental matter of great liberation, without dependencies, without contrived activities, without concerns.

This is how the ancients were aware in advance of the dust blowing in the wind and the grasses moving. As soon as any obstructive illusions sprouted, they would immediately mow them down. Still, they could hardly find anybody willing and able to share in the life of wisdom.

How could the genuine Zen teachers be compared with those phonies who roll around in the weeds together, pulling each other along, dragging each other into intellectual and verbal judgments and arbitrary choices, creating clichés to bury the sons and daughters of other people's families? It is obvious that such people are "wetting the bed with their eyes open." Those clear-eyed Zen adepts would never have put on such a display!

The will and energy of the truly great astounds the common herd. You must aim to be their true successor of the genuine school of Linji. With a shout and a blow, an act and a state, face reality and annihilate falsity. Haven't you seen this saying: "Having used the razor-sharp sword of wisdom, be quick to hone it again"?

MOVE WITH A MIGHTY FLOW

When your vision penetrates through and your use of it is clear, you are spontaneously able to turn without freezing up or getting stuck amid all kinds of lightning-fast changes and complex interactions and interlocking intricacies. You do not establish any views or keep to any mental states; you move with a mighty flow, so that "when the wind moves, the grasses bend down."

When you enter into enlightenment right where you are, you penetrate to the profoundest source. You cultivate this realization till you attain freedom of mind, harboring nothing in your heart. Here there is no "understanding" to be found, much less "not understanding."

You go on like this twenty-four hours a day, unfettered, free from all bonds. Since from the first you do not keep to subject and object or self and others, how could there be any "buddhadharma"? This is the realm of no mind, no contrived activity, and no concerns. How can this be judged with mere worldly intelligence and knowledge and discrimination and learning, if the fundamental basis is lacking?

Did Bodhidharma actually bring this teaching when he came from the West? All he did was to point out the true nature that each and every person inherently possesses, to enable people to thoroughly emerge clear and pure from the orbit of delusion and not be stained and defiled by all their erroneous knowledge and consciousness and false thoughts and judgments.

"Study must be true study." When you find a genuine teacher of the Way, he will not lead you into a den of weeds; he will cut through directly so you can meet with realization. He will strip off the sweaty shirt that is clinging to your flesh, to enable your heart to become empty and open, without the slightest sense of ordinary and holy, and without any external seeking, so that you become profoundly clear and still and genuine and true. Then even the thousand sages cannot place you. You attain a state that is unified and pure and naked, and pass through to *the other side of the empty aeon*. There even the Primordial Buddha is your descendant, so how could you seek any more from others?

Ever since the ancestral teachers, all the true adepts have been like this. Take the example of the Sixth Patriarch. He was a man from a frontier area in the south who sold firewood for a living, an illiterate. When he met the Fifth Patriarch face to face, he opened his heart and openly passed through to freedom.

The saints and sages live mixed in among the ordinary people, but even so, it is necessary to use appropriate means to reveal this matter that makes no separation between the worthy and the ignorant and is already inherent in all people.

Once you merge your tracks into the stream of Zen, you spend your days silencing your mind and studying with your whole being. You realize that this Great Cause is not obtained from anyone else but is just a matter of taking up the task boldly and strongly, and making constant progress. Day by day you shed your delusions, and day by day you enhance your clarity of mind. Your potential for enlightened perception is like fine gold that is to be refined hundreds and thousands of times. What is essential for getting out of the dusts, what is basic for helping living creatures, is that you must penetrate through freely in all directions and arrive at peace and security free from doubt and attain the stage of great potential and great function.

This work is located precisely in your own inner actions. It is just a matter of being in the midst of the interplay of the myriad causal conditions every day, in the confusion of the red dusts, amid favorable and adverse circumstances and gain and loss, appearing and disappearing in their midst, without being affected and "turned around" by them, but on the contrary, being able to transform them and "turn them around."

When you are leaping with life and water cannot wet you, this is your own measure of power. You reach an empty, solidified silence, but there is no duality between emptiness and form or silence and noise. You equalize all sorts of wondrous sayings and perilous devices and absolute perceptions; ultimately there is no gain or loss, and it is all your own to use.

When you go on "grinding and polishing" like this for a long time, you are liberated right in the midst of birth and death, and you look upon the world's useless reputation and ruinous profit as mere dust in the wind, as a dream, as a magical apparition, as an optical illusion. Set free, you pass through the world. Isn't this what it means to be a great saint who has emerged from the dusts of sensory attachments?

Don't Mix Poison with Your Food

Zhaozhou said, "During my thirty years in the south, the only times I mixed mundane concerns into my mental activity were during the morning and noon meals."

From this we should realize that in carrying out this matter, the ancient worthies did not take it as a casual thing. On the contrary, they took it seriously and treated it with respect. That's how they persevered in their practice and attained insight. That's how they reached thoroughgoing clarity and never fell into empty vanity in action or speech. Thus they managed to unify worldly phenomena and enlightened truth.

In the present time, those who want to draw near to reality must boldly mobilize their energies and transform what is within them. You must not cling to wrong knowledge and wrong views. You must not mix poison into your food. You must be uniformly pure and true and clean and wondrously illuminated to step directly into *the scenery of the fundamental ground* and reach the peaceful and secure stage of great liberation.

Then you stand aloof and alone, so that wind cannot blow in and water cannot wet you. The true essence becomes manifest, and in your daily activities you have a measure of power. As you hear sounds and see forms, you don't give rise to grasping or rejecting. With every move you have a road to get out on.

Haven't you read this story? A monk asked Jiufeng, "I have heard tell that you met Yanshou in person—is this true?" Jiufeng said, "Is the wheat in front of the mountain ripe yet or not?"

If you can recognize what Jiufeng was getting at on the intimate level, you will behold the ability of a true patch-robed monk, what is known as *the sword that kills, the sword that brings life.* Please always keep your eye on this. When you get beyond conventions, then you will naturally know where it's really at.

WHAT IS IT?

Zhaozhou said, "I don't like to hear the word *buddha.*"

Tell me, why was he like this? Was it because *buddha* means "omniscient person" that he didn't want to hear the word? Clearly, this was not the reason. Since it wasn't this, then why didn't he want to hear the word? If you are a clear-eyed person, then you'll know where it's really at as soon as you hear of this. Let me ask you: Where is it really at, what does it really mean? Try to divulge what you think about this so I can see.

When Luzu saw a monk coming, he would face the wall—was this helping people or not? Where is the proper proportion? If you want to act in accord with him, what approach should you take?

Every time Baizhang went to the hall, when he had finished expounding the Dharma, and the assembly was dispersing, he would call to them again. When they turned around he would say, "What is it?"

Yaoshan said, "Tell me about what Baizhang used to say as everyone was leaving the hall: whom was it used to contact, and how could insight be attained from it?"

STEP BACK AND TURN TO REALITY

Gao the patch-robed one,* with his fearless and sharp nature, traveled all over the country visiting the expert craftsmen of the Zen school. The former prime minister and Zen master Zhang Wujin came to know of him and respected him deeply as a vessel of the teaching.

Since Gao had an extraordinary spirit, he was not content to follow small understanding. After demonstrating his sincerity, he became one of my associates. We reached accord at a single word, and he shed the halter that had hitherto bridled him. Though he had still not reached total comprehension, he was a robust and lively fellow whom nobody could suppress or rein in.

When we trace back where this came from, after all it was due to Master Wujin inspiring him. Subsequently Gao braved the freezing cold and came for a while to visit me at Xianping. When he came to announce his departure, he asked for some words of teaching, which I accordingly gave him. This is what I told him:

"Those who wear the patched robe of a Zen wayfarer should be completely serious about taking death and birth as their business. You should work to melt away the obstructions caused by conditioned knowledge and views and interpretive understanding, and penetrate through to a realization of the great causal condition communicated and bequeathed by the buddhas and ancestral teachers. Don't covet name and fame. Step back and turn to reality, until your practical understanding and virtue are fully actualized.

"When there is real attainment, the more you try to hide it, the more it cannot be concealed. All the sages and the *devas* and *nagas* will try to push a person of real attainment forward, especially after years of cultivation and refinement. Wait until you are like a bell sounding when struck or a valley returning an echo. Wait until you are like pure gold coming forth from a forge where it has been smelted and refined ten thousand times, so that it will not change in ten thousand generations, so that it is *ten thousand years in a single moment.*

*This was Dahui Zonggao, one of Yuanwu's most illustrious successors, whose own letters and lectures are translated by J.C. Cleary in *Swampland Flowers* (New York: Grove Press, 1978).

"When the grip of transcendence is in your hand, when the grasses bend down as the wind blows, then won't you be expansive and generous with resources to spare?

"Remember, what is important in practice is perseverance and consistency."

KINDLING THE INEXHAUSTIBLE LAMP

By even speaking a phrase to you, I have already doused you with dirty water. It would be even worse for me to put a twinkle in my eye and raise my eyebrow to you, or rap on the meditation seat or hold up a whisk, or demand, "What is this?" As for shouting and hitting, it's obvious that this is just a pile of bones on level ground.

There are also the type who don't know good from bad and ask questions about Buddha and Dharma and Zen and the Tao. They ask to be helped, they beg to be received, they seek knowledge and sayings and theories relating to the Buddhist teaching and to transcending the world and to accommodating the world. This is washing dirt in mud and washing mud in dirt—when will they ever manage to clear it away?

Some people hear this kind of talk and jump to conclusions, claiming, "I understand! Fundamentally there is nothing to Buddhism—it's there in everybody. As I spend my days eating food and wearing clothes, has there ever been anything lacking?" Then they settle down in the realm of unconcerned ordinariness, far from realizing that nothing like this has ever been part of the real practice of Buddhism.

So we know that you must be someone genuinely within the tradition before you can be fully familiar with the fundamental portion of the vehicle of the school that has come down from time immemorial. If you really have an entry into enlightenment, then you know when to start and when to stop, when to advance and when to withdraw, and you can distinguish what is permissible from what is not.

Leaving behind all leakages, day by day you get closer to the truth and more familiar with it. As you go further, you change like a panther who no longer sticks to its den—you leap out of the corral. Then you no longer doubt all the sayings of the world's enlightened teachers—you are like cast iron. This is precisely the time to apply effort and cultivate practice and nourish your realization.

After that you can kindle the inexhaustible Lamp and travel the unobstructed Path. You relinquish your body and your life to rescue living beings. You enable them to come out of their cages and eliminate their attachments and bonds. You cure them of the diseases of being attached to being enlightened, so that having emerged from the deep pit of liberation, they can become uncontrived, unencumbered, joyfully alive people of the Path.

So then, when you yourself have crossed over, you must not abandon the carrying out of your bodhisattva vows. You must be mindful of saving all beings, and steadfastly endure the attendant hardship and toil, in order to serve as a boat on the ocean of all-knowledge. Only then will you have some accord with the Path.

Don't be a brittle pillar or a feeble lamp. Don't bat around your little clean ball of inner mystical experience. You may have understood for yourself, but what good does it do?

Therefore the ancient worthies necessarily urged people to travel the one road of the bodhisattva path, so they would be able to requite the unrequitable benevolence of our enlightened predecessors who communicated the Dharma to the world.

Nowadays there are many bright Zen monks in various localities who want to pass through directly. Some seek too much and want to understand easily. As soon as they know a little bit about the aim of the Path and how to proceed, they immediately want to show themselves as adepts. Yet they have already missed it and gone wrong. Some don't come forth even when they are pushed to do so, but they too are not yet completely enlightened.

You are a master of Buddhist teaching methods only when you can recognize junctures of times and patterns of causal conditions and manage not to miss real teaching opportunities.

HIDDEN TREASURE

Brave-spirited wearers of the patched robe possess an outstanding, extraordinary aspect. With great determination they give up conventional society. They look upon worldly status and evanescent fame as dust in the wind, as clouds floating by, as echoes in a valley.

Since they already have great faculties and great capacity from the past, they know that this level exists, and they transcend birth and death and move beyond holy and ordinary. This is the indestructible true essence that all the enlightened ones of all times witness, the wondrous mind that alone the generations of enlightened teachers have communicated.

To tread this unique path, to be a fragrant elephant or a giant, golden-winged bird, it is necessary to charge past the millions of categories and types and fly above them, to cut off the flow and brush against the heavens. How could the enlightened willingly be petty creatures, confined within distinctions of high and low and victory and defeat, trying futilely to make comparative judgments of instantaneous experience, and being utterly turned around by gain and loss?

For this reason, in olden times the people of great enlightenment did not pay attention to trivial matters and did not aspire to the shallow and easily accessible. They aroused their determination to transcend the buddhas and patriarchs. They wanted to bear the heavy responsibility that no one can fully take up, to rescue all living beings, to remove suffering and bring peace, to smash the ignorance and blindness that obstructs the Way. They wanted to break the poisonous arrows of ignorant folly and extract the thorns of arbitrary views from the eye of reality. They wanted to make the scenery of the fundamental ground clear and reveal the original face before the empty aeon.

You should train your mind and value actual practice wholeheartedly, exerting all your power, not shrinking from the cold or the heat. Go to the spot where you meditate and kill your mental monkey and slay your intellectual horse. Make yourself like a dead tree, like a withered stump.

Suddenly you penetrate through—how could it be attained from anyone else? You discover the hidden treasure, you light the lamp in the dark room, you launch the boat across the center of the ford. You experience great liberation, and without producing a single thought, you immediately attain true awakening. Having passed through the gate into the inner truth, you ascend to *the site of universal light*. Then you sit in the impeccably pure supreme seat of the emptiness of all things.

Moving into action as an enlightened teacher, with rolling waves in the ocean of speech, you unleash the skills of unobstructed understanding and eloquence. With chosen pupils you set up a situation or utter a saying to reveal extraordinary perceptions. You cause all beings, whether ordinary or sage, whether sentient or insentient, to look up to the awesome light and receive its protection.

But this is not yet the stage of effortless achievement. You must go further beyond, to where the thousand sages cannot trap you, the myriad conscious beings have no way to look up to you, the gods have no way to offer you flowers, and the demons and outsiders cannot spy on you. You must cast off knowledge and views, discard mysteries and marvels, and abandon all contrived actions. You simply eat when hungry and drink when thirsty, and that's all.

At this stage you are never aware of having mind or not having mind, of gaining mindfulness or losing mindfulness. So how could you still be attached to what you have previously learned and understood, to "mysteries" and "marvels" and analyses of essential nature, to the fetters of names and forms and arbitrary opinions? How could you still be attached to views of "Buddha" and views of "Dharma" or to earth-shaking worldly knowledge and intellect? You would be tying and binding yourself, you would be counting the grains of sand in the ocean—what would there be to rely on?

All those who are truly great must strive to overcome the obstacles of delusion and ignorance. They must strive to jolt the multitudes out of their complacency and to fulfill their own fundamental intent and vows. Only if you do this are you a true person of the Path, without contrived activity and without concerns, a genuine Wayfarer of great mind and great vision and great liberation.

A LOTUS IN FIRE

I wouldn't say that those in recent times who study the Way do not try hard, but often they just memorize Zen stories and try to pass judgment on the ancient and modern Zen masters, picking and choosing among words and phrases, creating complicated rationalizations and learning stale slogans. When will they ever be done with this? If you study Zen like this, all you will get is a collection of worn-out antiques and curios.

When you "seek the source and investigate the fundamental" in this fashion, after all you are just climbing up the pole of your own intellect and imagination. If you don't encounter an adept, if you don't have indomitable will yourself, if you have never stepped back into yourself and worked on your spirit, if you have not cast off all

your former and subsequent knowledge and views of surpassing wonder, if you have not directly gotten free of all this and comprehended
the causal conditions of *the fundamental great matter*—then that is
why you are still only halfway there and are falling behind and cannot
distinguish or understand clearly. If you just go on like this, then even
if you struggle diligently all your life, you still won't see the fundamental source even in a dream.

This is why the man of old said: "Enlightenment is apart from verbal explanations—there has never been any attainer."

Deshan said: "Our school has no verbal expressions and not a single thing or teaching to give to people."

Zhaozhou said: "I don't like to hear the word *buddha*."

Look at how, in verbally disavowing verbal explanations, they had
already scattered dirt and messed people up. If you go on looking for
mysteries and marvels in the Zen masters' blows and shouts and fa-
cial gestures and glaring looks and physical movements, you will fall
even further into the wild foxes' den.

All that is important in this school is that enlightenment be clear
and thorough, like *the silver mountain and the iron wall*, towering
up solitary and steep, many miles high. Since this realization is as
sudden as sparks and lightning, whether or not you try to figure it
out, you immediately fall into a pit. That is why since time immemorial the adepts have guarded this one revelation, and all arrived together at the same realization.

Here there is nowhere for you to take hold. Once you can clear up
your mind and you are able to abandon all entanglements, and you
are cultivating practice relying on an enlightened spiritual friend, it
would be really too bad if you weren't patient enough to get to the
level where the countless difficulties cannot get near you, and to lay
down your body and your mind there and investigate till you penetrate through all the way.

Over thousands of lifetimes and hundreds of aeons up until now,
has there ever been any discontinuity in the fundamental reality or
not? Since there has been no discontinuity, what birth and death and
going and coming is there for you to be in doubt about? Obviously
these things belong to the province of causal conditions and have absolutely no connection to the fundamental matter.

My teacher Wuzu often said, "I have been here for five decades,
and I have seen thousands and thousands of Zen followers come up

to the corner of my meditation seat. They were all just seeking to become buddhas and to expound Buddhism. I have never seen a single genuine wearer of the patched robe."

How true this is! As we observe the present time, even those who expound Buddhism are hard to find—much less any genuine people. The age is in decline and the sages are further and further distant. In the whole great land of China, the lineage of Buddha is dying out right before our very eyes. We may find one person or half a person who is putting the Dharma into practice, but we would not dare to expect them to be like the great exemplars of enlightenment, the "dragons and elephants" of yore.

Nevertheless, if you simply know the procedures and aims of practical application of the Dharma and carry on correctly from beginning to end, you are already producing a lotus from within the fire.

You must put aside all the conditioning that entangles you. Then you will be able to perceive the inner content of the great enlightenment that has come down since ancient times. Be at rest wherever you are, and carry on the secret, closely continuous, intimate-level practice. The *devas* will have no road to strew flowers on, and demons and outsiders will not be able to find your tracks. This is what it means to truly leave home and thoroughly understand oneself.

If, after you have reached this level, circumstances arise as the result of merit that lead you to come forth and extend a hand to communicate enlightenment to others, this would not be inappropriate. As Buddha said, "Just acquiesce in the truth; you surely won't be deceived."

But even for me to speak this way is another case of a man from bandit-land seeing off a thief.

Bringing Out the Family Treasure

If you want to attain Intimacy, the first thing is, don't seek it. If you attain through seeking, you have already fallen into interpretive understanding.

This is especially true because this great treasury extends through all times, clearly evident, empty and bright. Since time without beginning it has been your own basic root: you depend on its power entirely in all your actions.

You will only pass through to freedom when you cease and desist to the point that not even a single thought is born. Then you penetrate through without falling into sense and matter and without dwelling in conceptualizations and mental images.

When you absolutely transcend these, then the whole world does not hide it. Everywhere everything becomes its Great Function, and every single thing flows forth from your own breast. The ancients called this *bringing out the family treasure*. Once this is attained, it is attained forever. How could it ever be used up?

Just be wary that your investigation does not rest on a firm footing, and that you will not be able to penetrate through to realization. You must bravely cut off all entanglements, so there is not the slightest dependence or reliance. Relinquish your body and give up your life and directly accept the suchness that faces you; there is no other. Then even if the thousand sages came forth it wouldn't change you at all. Leaving it to the flow at all times, eating food and wearing clothes, you nurture the embryo of sagehood to maturity, not keeping to intellectual understanding. Isn't this an especially excellent teaching and a most essential shortcut?

A BOATLOAD OF MOONLIGHT

The early sages lived with utmost frugality, and the ancient worthies overcame hardships and lived austerely. They purified their *will* in this, forgetting food and sleep. They studied with total concentration and accurate focus, seeking true realization. How could they have been making plans for abundant food and fine clothes and luxurious housing and fancy medicines?

When it gets to the point where the path is not as good as in ancient times, then there is criticism that the wheel of the Dharma is not turning and that the wheel of food is taking precedence. Because of this the Zen monasteries call their chief elders "meal-chiefs." Isn't this completely opposite from the ancient way?

Nevertheless, in the gate of *changing along with conditions*, we also carry out the secondary level. "On the northern mountain welcoming wayfarers from all directions, we look to the southern fields."

This fall it happens that there is a big crop. We have asked you to oversee the harvest, and now that you are about to go, you have asked for some words of instruction, so I have told you about the foregoing set of circumstances.

What is important is to respect the root and extend it to the branches. This will benefit both root and branches and also illuminate the legitimate and fundamental task of people of complete enlightenment and comprehensive mastery. If you work hard to carry this out, you will surely improve.

In general, to study the Path and seek out the Mystery, you must have a great basis in faith. You use this faith to believe in a deep sense that *this matter* does not lie in words or in any of the myriad experiential states. In fact, in truth, the Path is right where you stand.

Put aside the crazy and false mind that has been concocting your knowledge and understanding, and make it so that nothing whatsoever is weighing on your mind. Fully take up *this matter* in your perfect, wondrous, inherent nature, which is fundamentally pure and quiescent. Subject and object are both forgotten, and the road of words and thoughts is cut off. You open through and clearly see your original face. Make it so that once found, it is found forever and remains solid and unmoving.

After that you can change your step and transform your personal existence. You can say things and put forth energy without falling into the realms of the delusions of form, sensation, conception, evaluation, and consciousness. Then all the phenomena of enlightenment will appear before you in regular array. You will reach the state where everything you do while walking and sitting is all Zen. You will shed the root of birth and death and forever leave behind all that covers and binds you. You will become a free and untrammeled wayfarer without concerns—why would you need to search the pages for someone else's dead words?

"There are ancestral teachers on the tips of the hundred grasses." With these words Jiashan pointed it out so people could become acquainted with it.

Kuanping said, "The great meaning is there in the fields."

Baizhang extended his hands, wanting to let people know.

If you can become round and complete as a ripe grain of rice, this is the transmission of the mind-seal. If you still long for a peaceful existence, this will make you experience the first noble truth that suffering exists. But how will you say something about coming out of the weeds? "A boatload of bright moonlight carries it back."

TRUTH AND PERCEPTION

The present perception is the Truth, but the Truth is beyond this perception. If you are attached to perception, then this is a perception—it is not the arriving at the Truth. Those who arrive at Truth transcend perception, but they manage to use perception without dwelling in perception. When you pass directly through perception and get free of it, it is all the fundamental Truth.

This Truth is not being or nonbeing. It is not speech or silence. Yet it can manifest both being and nonbeing, both speech and silence. It is forever constant and unchanging.

Therefore Yunmen said, "It cannot be existent when you speak of it and nonexistent when you don't, or existent when you think of it and nonexistent when you don't."

You must subtly arrive at this Truth and get its great function. Always let transcendent wisdom appear whether you are speaking or silent, whatever you are doing. Is there any need to say that it is close at hand when you are in your teacher's presence and far away when you are in the countryside? As you go directly forward, naturally you will encounter it wherever you are.

All the enlightened ones and ancestral teachers take *this one true thing* very seriously. It is spread among beings of all potentials, high and low, noble and lowly, without any preferences or aversions. It is in all the myriad kinds of action, naturally real, clear and complete.

If you make a special thing out of your views of "buddhadharma" and "mystic marvels," then there is a lack. But if you are able to refrain from creating arbitrary views, and are clean and naked like this, then it is completely revealed.

If this matter were in words, then it should be definable in a single statement, with no further change. Why would there be thousands and thousands of sayings imparted by enlightened adepts, with no end to them? From this we know that it is not within words, but we need to use words to illustrate this matter. Sharp-spirited people should directly comprehend this idea.

Those who realize transcendence pass through words and phrases and can make them come to life. They can use one saying as a hundred thousand sayings or use a hundred thousand sayings as one saying. Why should you have any more doubts about famous Zen sayings like these: "Mind itself is buddha"; "It's not mind, not buddha"; "It's not mind, not buddha, not a thing"; "Mind is not buddha, knowledge is not the Way"; "East Mountain walks on the water"; "Strike the midnight bell at noon"; "A donkey is eating grass in the backyard"; "Hide your body in the Northern Dipper"? All these sayings are strung on one thread.

The venerable Yanyang asked Zhaozhou, "When one doesn't bring a single thing, then what?" Zhaozhou said, "Put it down." Yanyang asked, "If I don't bring a single thing, what should I put down?" Zhaozhou said, "I see you cannot put it down." At these words, Yanyang was greatly enlightened.

Later Huanglong wrote a verse to go with this story:

> Not bringing a single thing
> He can't lift it even using both arms
> A clear-eyed man like Zhaozhou is hard to find
> At a word, Yanyang realized his error
> If he stepped back, he'd fall into a deep pit
> In his heart was boundless joy
> Like that of a pauper finding a jewel
> Once the poison is forgotten, there's no connection
> Snakes and tigers became his intimate friends
> Different species, equally understood
> Over the lonely centuries,
> The Pure Wind has never stopped.

If you discuss Zhaozhou's answer, "Put it down," from the standpoint of common sense, Yanyang said he wasn't bringing a single thing, so how could Zhaozhou tell him to put it down?

From this we know that the eye of objective reality illuminates the finest subtleties: Zhaozhou exposed the serious disease of carrying one's conditioned perceptions around everywhere, to make Yanyang begin to feel shame. But Yanyang still did not realize what Zhaozhou meant, so he persisted with his question. Zhaozhou again pointed out his error, at which point Yanyang dissolved and at last was thoroughly set free. Later on Yanyang got to the point that he could tame wild tigers and poisonous snakes. Isn't this a case of inner feeling and outward response?

Layman Pang was with his whole family sitting around the fire. Layman Pang suddenly said, "Difficult, difficult—ten bushels of oil hemp spread out on a tree." Mrs. Pang said, "Easy, easy—on the tips of the hundred grasses, the meaning of Zen." Their daughter Lingzhao said, "Not difficult, not easy—eating when hungry, sleeping when tired."

Usually when I relate this story to people, most of them prefer Lingzhao's remark for saving energy, and dislike what Old Man Pang and Old Lady Pang said about difficult and easy. This is nothing but "making interpretations by following the words." People who think like this are far from getting to the root of the fundamental design.

That is why "the arising of the tracks of words is the origin of paths that deviate from Truth."

Only if you can *forget the words and embody the meaning* will you see how these three Zen teachers each put forth a hand and together held up the bottomless basket, how they strained out mussels and clams. You will see how in every move they had the ability to kill people's false selves and conditioned perceptions, and how in every place they had a road to get out on.

DIRECT POINTING

When Bodhidharma came from the West bringing the Zen transmission to China, he didn't set up written or spoken formulations—he only pointed directly to the human mind.

If we speak of *direct pointing*, this just refers to what is inherent in everyone: the whole essence appears responsively from within the shell of ignorance. This is no different in ordinary people than in all the sages since time immemorial. It is what we call the natural, real, inherent nature, fundamentally pure, luminous and sublime. It swallows up and spits out all of space. It is a single solid realm that stands out alone, free of the senses and their objects.

Just detach from thoughts and cut off sentiments and transcend the ordinary conventions. Use your own inherent power and take up its great capacity and great wisdom right where you are. It is like letting go when you are hanging from a mile-high cliff, releasing your body and not relying on anything anymore.

Totally shed the obstructions of views and understanding, so that you are like a person who has *died the great death.* Your breath is cut off, and you arrive at great cessation and great rest on the fundamental ground. Your sense faculties have no inkling of this, and your consciousness and perceptions and sentiments and thoughts do not reach this far.

After that, in the cold ashes of the dead fire, it is clear everywhere, and among the stumps of the dead trees everything is illuminated. Then you merge with solitary transcendence and reach unapproachable heights. You don't have to seek mind or seek buddha anymore: you bump into them wherever you go, and they do not come from outside.

The hundreds and thousands of aspects and facets of enlightenment since time immemorial are just this. This is mind: there is no need to go on seeking mind. This is buddha: why keep struggling to seek buddha?

If you make slogans based on words and sprout interpretations based on objects, then you fall into the bag of antique curios, and you will never be able to find this true realm of absolute awareness beyond sentiments.

At this stage you are free to go forward in the wild field without choosing, picking up whatever comes to hand: the meaning of the ancestral teachers is clear in all that grows there. What's more, the thickets of green bamboo and the masses of yellow flowers and the fences and walls and tiles and pebbles are inanimate things teaching the Dharma. The water birds and the groves of trees expound the truths of suffering, emptiness, and selflessness. Based on the one true reality, they extend objectless compassion, and from the great jewel light of nirvana they reveal uncontrived, surpassingly wondrous powers.

Changqing said, "When you meet a companion on the Path, stand shoulder to shoulder and go on: then your lifetime task of learning will be completed."

ENLIGHTENED REALITY AND WORLDLY PHENOMENA

All things are set on a nonabiding basis. The nonabiding basis is based on nonabiding. If you can reach a thorough realization of this, then all things are One Suchness, and you cannot find even the slightest sign of abiding.

The whole of your present activities and behavior is nonabiding.

Once the basis is clear to you, it will be like having eyes: the sun is shining brightly, and you can see all kinds of colors and forms. Isn't this the mainspring of transcendent wisdom?

Yongjia said: "Without leaving wherever you are, there is constant clarity." No words come closer to the truth than these. If you start seeking, then we know that you are unable to see. Just cut off any duality between "wherever you are" and "constant clarity," and make yourself peaceful and serene. Avoid concocting intellectual understanding and seeking. As soon as you seek, it is like grasping at shadows.

Layman Pang asked Mazu, "Who is it that does not keep company with the myriad things?" I say to you: Turn the light around and reflect back on yourself and see.

Mazu replied, "When you drink up all the water in West River in one swallow, then I'll tell you." This answer was like an eight-cornered mortar running through space.

If you can come to grips with this and penetrate through, then what you see before your eyes will reach equilibrium, and the illusions that have afflicted you since time without beginning will be washed away.

Deshan beckoned with a fan from across the river, and someone immediately understood. The Bird's Nest Monk blew on a blanket and someone was enlightened. Doesn't this show that when the time for this Great Cause arrives, the roots and sprouts grow of themselves? Doesn't this confirm that there is space for the teacher's action and the learner's reaction to reach accord? Doesn't this prove that when the people involved have been practicing inwardly, without interruption, they can be activated by a genuine teacher?

When you have complete trust in the mind and you see through to its true nature, then there is not the least bit of leakage in daily activities. The totality of worldly phenomena is the buddhadharma, and the totality of the buddhadharma is worldly phenomena—they are equally One Suchness.

How could it be there when you speak of it and not there when you don't, or there when you think of it and not there when you don't? If that is so, then you are right there in the midst of false imagination and emotional interpretations—when have you ever experienced penetrating realization?

When there is continuous awareness from mind-moment to mind-moment that does not leave anything out, and mundane reality and enlightened reality are not separate, then you will naturally become pure and fully ripe and meet the Source on all sides. If anyone asks questions, you answer according to the question, and if there are no questions, you remain clear and still. Isn't this the essential guideline for really passing through birth and death to freedom?

When you have passed through the Last Word, then you won't even need to "see through" speech and no-speech, transcendence and accommodation, provisional and real, illumination and function, giving and taking away. Who recognizes the mastery of a great Zen teacher like Zhaozhou? To do this, you must be a seedling of our house.

THIS GREAT CAUSE

In the olden days, whenever teachers and students met, it was for the sake of *this Great Cause,* and they never failed to use it to inspire and uplift. Even when they were eating or sleeping or at leisure, they were always concentrating their minds on this.

That is why they were able to experience a meeting of potentials in a word or a phrase, a blow or a shout, or any momentary event or activity. This was because with sincerity and concentrated focus, and without so much defilement by wrong ideas and perceptions, they were able to take it up directly, and it didn't seem difficult.

These days the brethren are errant and dull and all mixed up with miscellaneous concerns. Even if they study with an enlightened teacher and are exposed to his influences for a long time, they still vacillate and waver and cannot proceed directly to penetrating realization. The problem is the lack of purity and focus over the long term.

If you can work hard on the Way day and night heedless of food and sleep, have no worries that you will not equal the ancients.

MEET THE SOURCE ON ALL SIDES

Those who are determined to practice the Way practice self-awareness and self-understanding twenty-four hours a day. They think of this and focus on this. They know that *the one Great Cause* is there right where they stand, that it is in sages without being augmented and in ordinary people without being diminished. They know that it stands alone free of senses and sense objects, and that it far transcends material things.

Wayfarers don't set up fixed locations in anything they do. They are clear and tranquil, with solid concentration, and the myriad changes and transformations never disturb them. They appear in response to conditions and go into action as they encounter events, leaving nothing incomplete.

You should just be empty and quiet, transcending everything. Once the main basis is clear, all obscurities are illuminated. *"Ten thousand years—a single thought. A single thought—ten thousand years."* Passing through from the heights to the depths, the great function of the whole potential is in operation. It is like when a strong man flexes his arm: he doesn't depend on anyone else's strength. Then the illusory blinders of birth and death vanish forever, and the true essence indestructible as a diamond is all that shows. Once realized, it is realized forever—there is no interruption.

All that the enlightened teachers, ancient and modern, have said and done—the scriptural teachings, the enlightenment stories, the meditation stories, the question-and-answer sessions, all their teaching functions—all of this illuminates this true essence alone.

If you can be free and clear in actual practice for a long time, naturally you will come to meet the Source on all sides and become unified and whole.

Haven't you seen Fadeng's verse?

> Going into a wild field, not choosing,
> Picking up whatever plant comes to hand,
> Rootless but finding life,
> Apart from the ground but not falling.

Right before your eyes, it has always been there. Facing the situation, why don't you speak?

If you don't know it in your daily life, where then will you look for it? Better find out.

TRULY GENUINE

Right now if students are in fact truly genuine, source teachers can contact their potential and activate it with a single word or phrase, or a single act or scene. What could be difficult about that?

The only problem is when your faculties are unstable and your consciousness shallow, whirled around and around like the wind in the treetops. True reality is shown to you thousands and thousands of times, but you still cannot mesh with it.

Even worse are those who are still wrapped up in making emotional interpretations and claim that there is no such thing as entry into enlightenment. If you think like this, then even in a blue moon you will never even dream of true reality.

Therefore, in learning the Way, what is most valuable is being true and sincere.

SERENE AND FREE

People who study the Way begin by having the faith to turn toward it. They are fed up with the vexations and filth of the world and are always afraid they will not be able to find a road of entry into the Way.

Once you have been directed by a teacher or else discovered on your own the *originally inherently complete real mind*, then no matter what situations or circumstances you encounter, you know for yourself where it's really at.

But then if you hold fast to that real mind, the problem is you cannot get out, and it becomes a nest. You set up "illumination" and "function" in acts and states, snort and clap and glare and raise your eyebrows, deliberately putting on a scene.

When you meet a genuine expert of the school again, he removes all this knowledge and understanding for you, so you can merge directly with realization of the original uncontrived, unpreoccupied, unminding state. After this you will feel shame and repentance and know to cease and desist. You will proceed to vanish utterly, so that not even the sages can find you arising anywhere, much less anyone else.

That is why Yantou said, "Those people who actually realize it just keep serene and free at all times, without cravings, without dependence." Isn't this the door to peace and happiness?

In olden times Guanxi went to Moshan. Moshan asked him, "Where have you just come from?" Guanxi said, "From the mouth of the road." Moshan said, "Why didn't you cover it?" Guanxi had no reply.

The next day Guanxi asked, "What is the realm of Mount Moshan like?" Moshan said, "The peak doesn't show." Guanxi asked: "What is the man on the mountain like?" Moshan said, "Not any characteristics like male or female." Guanxi said, "Why don't you transform?" Moshan said, "I'm not a spirit or a ghost—what would I transform?"

Weren't the Zen adepts in these stories treading on the ground of reality and reaching the level where one stands like a wall miles high?

Thus it is said: "At the Last Word, you finally reach the impenetrable barrier. Holding the essential crossing, you let neither holy nor ordinary pass."

Since the ancients were like this, how can it be that we modern people are lacking?

Luckily, there is the indestructible diamond sword of wisdom. You must meet someone who knows it intimately, and then you can bring it out.

ACTIVE MEDITATION

The ancients worked hard for the sake of *the one Great Cause*. Their determination is indeed worthy of respect, and they served as an everlasting example for later generations.

When you set your body on the meditation bench, it is no more than silencing and emptying the mind and investigating with your whole being. Just make your mind and thoughts clarify and become still. A fine place to do active meditation work is amid confusion and disturbances. When you do active meditation, you must penetrate through the heights and the depths, without omitting anything. The whole essential being appears ready-made before you, and it no longer arises from anywhere else. It is just this *one Great Potential*, turning smoothly and steadily. Why talk any more about "worldly phenomena" and "enlightened truth"? If you maintain a uniform equilibrium over months and years, naturally your stand will be true and solid.

You will experience realization, like water being poured into water, like gold being traded for gold. Everything will be equalized in One Suchness, profoundly clear, real, and pure. This is knowing how to live.

Just do not give birth to a single thought: let go and become crystal clear. As soon as any notions of right and wrong and self and others and gain and loss are present, do not follow them off. Then you will be personally studying with your own true enlightened teacher.

If you do that, what worry is there that this work will not be accomplished? You must see for yourself!

HOW TO BE A HOUSEHOLDER-BODHISATTVA

This affair is a matter of people of sharp faculties and superior wisdom who do not consider it difficult to understand a thousand when hearing one. It requires a stand that is solid and true and faith that is thoroughgoing.

Then you can hold fast and act the master and take all sorts of adverse and favorable situations and differing circumstances and fuse them into one whole—a whole that is like empty space, without the least obstruction, profoundly clear and empty and illuminated, never changing even in a hundred aeons or a thousand lifetimes, unitary from beginning to end. Only then do you find peace and tranquillity.

I have seen many people who are intellectually brilliant but whose faculties are unstable and whose practice is shallow. They think they witness transformation in verbal statements, and they assume that there is no way to go beyond the worldly. Thus they increase the thorns of arbitrary opinion as they show off their ability and understanding. They take advantage of their verbal agility and think that the buddhadharma is like this. When situations are born from causal conditions, they cannot pass through to freedom, so they wind up vacillating back and forth. This is really a great pity!

This is why the ancients went through all sorts of experiences and faced all sorts of demons and difficulties. They might be cut to pieces, but they never gave it a thought; they took charge of their minds all the way along and made them as strong as iron or stone. Thus when it came to passing through birth and death, they didn't waste any effort. Isn't this where the special strength and generosity beyond emotionalism that truly great people possess lies?

When bodhisattvas who live a householder's life cultivate the practices of home-leavers, it is like a lotus blooming in fire. It will always be hard to tame the will for fame and rank and power and position, not to mention all the myriad starting points of vexation and turmoil associated with the burning house of worldly existence. The only way

is for you yourself to realize your fundamental, real, wondrous wholeness and reach the stage of great calm and stability and rest.

It would be best if you managed to cast off everything and be empty
and ordinary. Thoroughly experience the absence of conditioned
mind, and observe that all phenomena are like dreams and magical
illusions. Be empty all the way through, and continue on clearing out
your mind according to the time and the situation. Then you will
have the same correct foundation as all the great enlightened laymen
in Buddhist tradition.

According to your own measure of power, you will transform those
not yet enlightened so you can enter together into the uncontrived,
uncluttered ocean of true nature. Then your life here on this earth
will not be a loss.

IT DOESN'T COME FROM OUTSIDE

The essential thing in studying the Way is to make the roots deep and
the stem strong. Be aware of where you really are twenty-four hours
a day. You must be most attentive. When nothing at all gets on your
mind, it all merges harmoniously, without boundaries—the whole
thing is empty and still, and there is no more doubt or hesitation in
anything you do. This is called the fundamental matter appearing
ready-made.

As soon as you give rise to the slightest bit of dualistic perception
or arbitrary understanding and you want to take charge of this fundamental matter and act the master, then you immediately fall into the
realm of the clusters of form, sensation, conception, value synthesis,
and consciousness. You are entrapped by seeing, hearing, feeling, and
knowing, by gain and loss and right and wrong. You are half drunk
and half sober and unable to clean all this up.

Frankly speaking, you simply must manage to keep concentrating
even in the midst of clamor and tumult, acting as though there were
not a single thing happening, penetrating all the way through from
the heights to the depths. You must become perfectly complete, without any shapes or forms at all, without wasting effort, yet not inhibited from acting. Whether you speak or stay silent, whether you get
up or lie down, it is never anyone else.

If you become aware of getting at all stuck or blocked, this is all
false thought at work. Make yourself completely untrammeled, like

empty space, like a clear mirror on its stand, like the rising sun lighting up the sky. Moving or still, going or coming, it doesn't come from outside. Let go and make yourself independent and free, not being bound by things and not seeking to escape from things. From beginning to end, fuse everything into one whole. Where has there ever been any separate worldly phenomenon apart from the buddhadharma, or any separate buddhadharma apart from worldly phenomena?

This is why the founder of Zen pointed directly to the human mind. This is why *The Diamond Sutra* taught the importance of human beings detaching from forms. When a strong man moves his arm, he does not depend on someone else's strength—that's what it's like to be detached from forms.

To develop this essential insight, it is best to spend a long time going back into yourself and investigating with your whole being, so that you can arrive at the stage of the genuine experience of enlightenment. This is what it means to study with boundless, infinite enlightened teachers everywhere in every moment.

Strive sincerely for true faith, and apply yourself diligently to your meditation work. This is the best course for you.

ABANDONING ENTANGLEMENTS

Yantou said, "Abandoning things is superior, pursuing things is inferior." If your own state is empty and tranquil, perfectly illuminated and silently shining, then you will be able to confront whatever circumstances impinge on you with the indestructible sword of wisdom and cut everything off—everything from the myriad entangling objects to the verbal teachings of the past and present. Then your awesome, chilling spirit cuts off everything, and everything retreats of itself without having to be pushed away. Isn't this what it means to be well endowed and have plenty to spare?

If the basis you establish is not clear, if you are the least bit bogged down in hesitation and doubt, then you will be dragged off by entangling conditions, and obviously you will not be able to separate yourself from them. How can you avoid being turned around by other things? When you are following other things, you will never have any freedom.

The Ultimate Path is simple and easy—it is just a matter of

whether you abandon things or pursue them. Those who would experience the Path should think deeply on this.

People in ancient times gave up their whole bodies for the sake of this one matter. They stood out in the snow, worked as rice pounders, sold off their hearts and livers, burned their arms, threw themselves into roaring fires, got dismembered and cut to pieces, fed themselves to tigers and birds of prey, gave away their heads and eyes, endured a thousand kinds of pain and suffering.

In sum, if you do not suffer hardship, you will not arrive at deep realization. Those with the will for the Path must certainly consider the ancients as their comrades and aspire to equal their standard.

MEETING IT WHEREVER YOU TOUCH

Round and clear, empty and still—such is the essence of the Way. Extending and withdrawing, killing and bringing life—such is its marvelous function.

When you are able to travel on the sword's edge, when you are able to persevere and hold on, when you are like a pearl rolling around in a bowl, like a bowl rolling a pearl around inside it, when you never fall into empty vanity even for an instant, when you never divide worldly phenomena from the buddhadharma but fuse them into one whole—this is called *meeting it wherever you touch.* You appear and disappear and move freely in all directions, and there is never anything external. You are clean and naked, turning smoothly, sealing everything with the fundamental. It is clear everywhere, complete in everything—when has there ever been gain and loss or affirmation and denial or good and evil or long and short?

Your only fear should be that your own correct eye is not yet perfectly clear. This will cause you to fall into duality, and then you will lose touch with reality. Haven't you read what Yongjia said? "The top-flight people have one decisive realization and comprehend all. With people of the middling and lower sort, the more they hear, the more they don't believe."

WORDS AND TRUTH

The verbal teachings of the buddhas and ancestral teachers are just a snare and a trap. They are used as a means of entry into truth. Once you have opened through into clear enlightenment and taken it up, then in the true essence, everything is complete. Then you look upon all the verbal teachings of the buddhas and ancestral teachers as belonging to the realm of shadows and echoes, so you never carry them around in your head.

Many students in recent times do not get to the basis of the fundamental design of the Zen school. They just hold onto the words and phrases, trying to choose among them, discussing how close or how far away they are from the truth, and distinguishing gain and loss. They interpret fleeting provisional teachings as real doctrines and boast about how many koans they have been able to sift through and how well they can ask questions about the sayings of the Five Houses of Zen. They are totally sunk in emotional consciousness, and they have lost the true essence in their delusions. This is truly a pitiful situation!

A genuine Zen teacher would use any means necessary to warn them of their error and enable them to get away from all such wrong knowledge and wrong views. But they would reject this—they would call it contrived mental activity to turn people around and shake them up and refine them. Thus they enter ever more deeply into the forest of thorns of erroneous views.

As the saying goes, "In the end, if you do not meet an adept, as you get older you will just become a fossil."

You must not depend on either the pure or the impure. Having mind and having no mind, having views and having no views—both alternatives vanish like a snowflake put on a red-hot stove. Twenty-four hours a day, from top to bottom, you are free and untrammeled as you wander this road that the thousand sages do not share. Just bring this to complete purity and ripeness and you will naturally become a real person, beyond study and free from contrived activity, a real person whom thousands and tens of thousands of people cannot trap or cage.

THE GATE BEYOND

Where is it that you are walking? If you knew all about the currents as you sailed the boat and could tell the waves apart as you plied the oars, then what need would there be to go to such lengths to admonish and instruct you? You could reach complete comprehension at one stroke.

Thus, the wind blows and lightning flashes—if you hesitate, you are a thousand miles away. This Zen teaching is only for receiving the swift, not for the ignorant. That is why in Zen we say, "We cast our hook into the four oceans, just to catch fierce dragons. The mysterious device beyond conventions is just to seek out those who know."

Once you have arrived in Zen, as you observe all in the world and beyond the world, there has never been any change: you see through everything from top to bottom. Then you know how to relinquish your body and your life, and in the midst of all kinds of different situations, you will be calm and unmoved. You will always be equanimous, even if you meet the power of the wind of objects, and you will always be at ease, even if you are doused with poison.

If you do not continue to practice and nurture and develop this for a long time, then how can you hold up the sun and the moon of the buddhadharma with great insight and great illumination, appearing and disappearing freely? There has never been any turning toward or turning away with this stage: you must open up the gate beyond.

WALKING ON THE GROUND OF REALITY

For the sake of this Great Teaching, the ancients gave up their bodies and their lives and endured endless immeasurable hardship and toil, until they thoroughly clarified its profound essential message. They treasured it like a precious jewel and guarded it like their eyes. They worked on it assiduously and never let it be taken lightly or defiled.

As soon as the slightest trace of special understanding arises, it is like clouds casting a pall over a clear sky, like dust obscuring the surface of a mirror.

Thus Zhaozhou said, "When I was in the south, for thirty years, except at mealtimes, I never used my mind in a way that mixed in worldly concerns."

Caoshan instructed people to guard this matter as carefully as if they were passing through a village with poisoned wells and could not let a single drop of the poisoned water touch them.

By forgetting conditioned mind and cutting off conditioned awareness, you arrive in practice at the true realm of Thusness. There is nothing on your mind and no mind on things: you are equanimous and free from contrived actions, transcendent as you move on alone.

Only when you yourself walk upon the ground of reality can you help people by dissolving sticking points and removing bonds. You liberate everyone, even though there is really no one to liberate.

You must put the Last Word to use—then you will have a way out everywhere in everything.

ALWAYS MINDFUL

The ancients were always mindful of *this matter*. Whether deep in the mountain valleys or in the bustling villages and towns, they never turned their backs on it for an instant. Whatever scenes or circumstances they encountered, amidst sound and form, in the course of movement and action, they invariably turned around and focused back on their own true selves. The practice of all the adepts since time immemorial who completely penetrated through was none other than this.

Thus, with their fundamental basis firm and strong, they were not blown around following the wind of objects. They were serene and at peace and did not fall into the scope of feelings of holy and ordinary. They came directly to great cessation and great rest: they "found the seat and put on the robe."

Now you are returning to your home village, able to see as the ancients saw. If you can make it continuous and unbroken, how will it be any different than when you were in the monastery being guided by the abbot and doing your meditation work? If you turn your back on it at all, and there is some break in the continuity, then you will lose contact.

We are about to part, so remember these words. Another time in the future, don't look back and blame me for not admonishing you.

BE UNDEFINABLE

For students of mystic wisdom, seeing the real nature of things and awakening to the true pattern and treading in the steps of the buddhas is everyday food and drink.

You should realize that on the crown of the heads of the buddhas and enlightened adepts there is a wondrous way of "changing the bones" and transforming your existence. Only then can you get beyond conventional categories and sectarian limits and act like a transcendent person, so that even great Zen masters like Linji and Deshan would have no way to apply their blows and shouts to you.

At all times just remain free and uninvolved. Never make any displays of clever tricks—be like a stolid simpleton in a village of three families. Then the gods will have no road on which to offer you flowers, and demons and outsiders will not be able to spy on you.

Be undefinable, and do not reveal any conspicuous signs of your special attainment. It should be as if you are there among myriad precious goods locked up securely and deeply hidden in a treasure house. With your face smeared with mud and ashes, join in the work of the common laborers, neither speaking out nor thinking.

Live your whole life so that no one can figure you out, while your spirit and mind are at peace. Isn't this what it is to be imbued with the Way without any contrived or forced actions, a genuinely unconcerned person?

Among the enlightened adepts, being able to speak the Truth has nothing to do with the tongue, and being able to talk about the Dharma is not a matter of words.

Clearly we know that the words spoken by the ancients were not meant to be passively depended on. Anything the ancients said was intended only so that people would directly experience the fundamental reality. Thus, the teachings of the sutras are like a finger pointing to the moon, and the sayings of the Zen masters are like a piece of tile used to knock on a door.

If you know this, then rest. If your practice is continuous and meticulous and your application broad and all-pervading, and you do not deviate from this over the years, then you will mature in your ability to handle the teachings, to gather up and to release, and you will be able to see through petty things and cut them off without leaving a trace.

Then when you come to the juncture of death and birth, where all the lines intersect, you won't get mixed up. You will be clear and immovable, and you will be set free as you leave this life behind. This is deathbed Zen, for the last day of your life.

COMPLETING THE TASK

Awakening on your own without a teacher, *before the Primordial Buddha,* you proceed straight to transcendent realization, on the same road as the thousand sages. You are able to let go and act freely, able to hold fast and be absolutely still, able to act the master. The Whole appears before you in all its completeness—without needing to be refined, it naturally becomes pure and ripe.

When it comes to *after the Primordial Buddha,* though you have your own independence which you directly accept to arrive at the stage where there is no doubt, you still should rely on a teacher to make sure and to approve your enlightenment and make you into a vessel of the Teaching. Otherwise, there are sure to be demons who will malevolently ruin the correct basis.

For this reason, ever since the ancestral teachers, the apprentice receives and the teacher transmits, and the teacher's teaching is of the utmost value. This is especially true with *this matter,* which is not something that can be comprehended by worldly intelligence or confined within perception and knowledge.

Unless you have the bold, fierce spirit of a person of power, and manage to select a genuine enlightened teacher as your spiritual friend, how can you cut off the flow of birth and death and break out of the shell of ignorance?

If you investigate and inquire diligently for a long time with single-minded concentration, the time of fruition will come—suddenly the bottom drops out of the bucket and you will empty out and awaken to enlightenment. After that, you work wholeheartedly to weed out what's wrong and make sure of what's right, for experiential proof of your realization. Then it will naturally be like a boat going downstream—no need to work at rowing. This is the true meeting of teacher and disciple.

Once you have attained the essential gist of the teaching, concentrate continuously so there are no breaks or interruptions, to enable the embryo of sagehood to grow and mature. Then even if you encounter bad conditions, you will be able to melt them away with true insight and the power of concentration, and fuse everything into one whole, so the great changes of birth and death will not be enough to disturb your heart.

Nurturing your enlightenment over many years, you become a

greatly liberated person who is free from contrived actions and obsessive concerns. Isn't this what it is to have accomplished what was to be done and completed the task of travel?

OUT AND BACK

This matter lies in the swiftness and sharpness of the person involved. Once you have taken it up and put it into practice, and you know you have your own place to stand, you should be aloof and independent—stand alone and go alone. You should cut off sentiments and detach from perception and make yourself empty and silent so there is not a single thing that can be grasped. Cut off the myriad entanglements, and make yourself free and untrammeled, and reach the stage of great peace. When this is closely continuous without any leaks, this is what is called standing like a wall miles high, lofty and steep.

After that you come back to the world and respond to beings. Since there is never any sense of self, how could there be any realms of sound and form, of adversity and ease, of delusion and enlightenment?

What is most difficult is to be perfectly at rest, not activating the conceptual faculty. If you are suddenly dragged off by it, you have leaked and tarried. You must continue to concentrate so that your mind does not wander off. After a long time it will fuse into one whole. This at last is where you find rest.

From here you must still go on to master transcendent action. An ancient worthy said, "Find the seat and put on the robe, and afterward see for yourself."

WASHED CLEAN

In visiting enlightened teachers and questioning them, you must see real nature and awaken to truth. As you directly forget feelings and put an end to views, you are inwardly washed clean. You become like a simpleton, not calculating gain and loss, not contending for superiority. Favorable or adverse, you cut everything off and don't let it continue. After a long time at this, you naturally arrive at the stage where there are no contrived activities and no concerns.

As soon as you have the slightest wish to be unconcerned, a concern has already arisen. Once one wave goes into motion, myriad waves follow—when will it ever stop? When death comes upon you in that condition, you will be frantic and confused, simply because you are not free and clear.

Just make this work sure and true, and naturally even in a noisy marketplace it will be silent and still as water. Why worry then that you will not accomplish your task?

"As soon as there is affirmation and negation, the mind is lost in confusion." How many people have been started by this statement into making judgments and arguments! If you cut them off at the start, you penetrate through to the other side of the Primordial Buddha. If you follow these words along, you'll be even more confused. To get it, you have to turn your own light around and look back.

SELF AND THINGS

All the myriad things are neither opposed to nor contrary to your true self. Directly pass through to freedom and they make one whole. It has been this way from time without beginning.

The only problem is when people put themselves in opposition to it and spurn it and impose orientations of grasping or rejecting, creating a concern where there is none. This is precisely why they are not joyfully alive.

If you can cut off outward clinging to objects and inwardly forget your false ideas of self, things themselves are the true self, and the true self itself is things: things and true self are one suchness, opening through to infinity.

Then at all times, whatever you may be doing, it stands like a mile-high wall—where is all the trouble and disturbance?

Time and again I see longtime Zen students who have been freezing their spirits and letting their perception settle out and clarify for a long time. Though they have entered the Way, they immediately accepted a single device or a single state, and now they rigidly hold to it and won't allow it to be stripped away. This is truly a serious disease.

To succeed it is necessary to melt and let go and spontaneously attain a state of great rest.

THE SECRET SEAL

Here at my place there is no Zen to explain and no Path to transmit. Though five hundred patch-robed ones are gathered together here, I just use *the diamond trap* and *the thicket of thorns*. Those who leap out of the diamond trap make an effort to leap out, those who swallow the thicket of thorns swallow it with care. Don't be surprised that they have no flavor or that they are dangerous and steep.

If you suddenly attain realization, it is like returning to your native village in broad daylight dressed in brocade: everyone will look up to you in admiration.

In essence, you cannot find where this one comes from: it's called the fundamental matter that is inherent in everyone. As soon as you deliberately intend to accept it or take it up, this is already not the fundamental anymore. Just get the myriad impulses to cease, so even the thousand sages do not accompany you—then how could there still be any dependency?

You should put everything aside right away and penetrate through to freedom on that side. That is why it is said, "Even the slightest thing is dust—as soon as you rouse your intellect you are assailed by the demons of delusion."

Forming all things just depends on *that*; destroying all things also just depends on *that*.

What should be formed and perfected? The causal conditions of special excellence, the treasury of merits and virtues countless as the sands, the countless wondrous adornments and world-transcending rarities.

What should be destroyed and obliterated? Greed and anger and jealousy, emotional consciousness and attachments, contrived actions and defiled actions, filth and confusion, names and forms and the interpretive route, arbitrary views and knowledge and false sentiments.

That can transform all things, but nothing can transform *that*. Though it has no shape or visage, it contains all of space. It contains the ordinary and nurtures the holy. If you try to grasp it through forms, then in grasping at it you fall into the thorns of views, and you will never ever find it.

It was just this wondrous mind that the buddhas revealed and the ancestral teachers directly pointed out. When you take it up directly, without producing a single thought, and penetrate from the heights to the depths, everything appears ready-made. Here where it appears ready-made, you do not exert any mental effort: you go along freely with the natural flow, without any grasping or rejecting. This is the real esoteric seal.

Bearing this esoteric seal is like carrying a lamp hidden in the darkness as you roam through the world without longing or fear—it is all the realm of your own great liberation, continuing forever without interruption.

That is why it is said that the sixteen-foot golden body of buddha functions as a blade of grass, and a blade of grass functions as the sixteen-foot golden body of buddha. How could there be anything else?

THIS SIDE AND THAT SIDE

You came to my room and asked about the issues you have doubts about. You said, "In this one matter, why do Zen teachers often speak to people of 'this side' and 'That Side'?" So I spoke to you about this.

Cutting directly through based on the fundamental, how could there be any such plurality? Yet the Zen teachers imparted various expedient teachings and provisional techniques for the purpose of helping people enter into the experience of the Way. Thus they imposed this division into "this side" and "That Side," though there is actually no duality.

Haven't you seen this story? A monk asked Caoshan, "The ancients upheld 'That Side.' How would you have me approach it?" Caoshan said, "Step back to your true self and you won't miss anything." On hearing this, the monk had an insight.

This is what is called *recognizing the intent on the hook* that the teacher uses to "fish" for the student's true potential and *not accepting the marks on the scale* of a provisional definition as an absolute standard.

You must reach the limit of the present time, then you can take up the transcendent matter. But how will you manage to reach the limit of the present time? You yourself must be quick to apply your energies, slough off entangling sense objects, and make your heat free and clear. Not establishing anything, you penetrate through from top to bottom and become open and empty and still. Don't try to interpret this as some extraordinary experience. Just wait till you reach accord with the fundamental, and you will naturally realize enlightenment on your own and reach the realm of great peace.

How can this be conveyed in words on paper? Please try to see it with your own eyes.

TOTAL PEACE

The wondrous path of the enlightened ones is straight and direct. They just pointed directly to the human mind so we would work to see its true nature and achieve enlightenment.

This mind-source is originally empty and peaceful, clear and wondrous, and free from the slightest obstruction. But we screen it off with false thoughts and give rise to defilements and blockages in this unobstructed one. We turn our backs on the fundamental and pursue the trivial and foolishly revolve in the cycle of routine.

If you have great capacity, you won't seek outside anymore. Right where you stand you will come forth in independent realization. When the transitory blinders of false perception have been dissolved away, the original correct perception is complete and wondrous. This is called the identity of mind and buddha.

From this, once realized, it is realized forever. It is like the bottom falling out of a bucket: you open through and merge with the Way, and there is nothing occupying your mind. Beholding the essence, pure and still, you receive the use of it and have no more doubts. Then when one is comprehended, all are comprehended.

When you hear it said that "it is not mind, not buddha," when you encounter situations favorable or unfavorable, good or bad, you seal it fast with one seal. How could there be any self or others, any same or different? How could there be so many kinds of mixed-up knowledge and views?

Thus the ancient worthies achieved sincerity and entered truth with every act and every state, with every word and every silence. A thousand methods, ten thousand doors—ultimately there is no difference. It is like hundreds and thousands of different streams all returning to the great ocean.

Once you spontaneously abide at peace in this, and can put it to use in a thoroughgoing, penetrating way, then you are a person of the

Path who has nothing more to learn, free from contrived activities and obsessive concerns. Twenty-four hours a day you do not engender any other states of mind or give rise to any divergent views. You eat and drink and dress according to the occasion. You are empty and solid in all situations, and you will never waver, even in a thousand years.

When you are in this state of great concentration, isn't this inconceivable great liberation? Just let it continue for a long time without interruption. Do not fall into "inner" and "outer" and "in-between." Do not fall into being and nothingness, into defiled and pure. Cease and desist straightaway. When you see buddhas and sentient beings as equal and no different, this at last is the stage of total peace and bliss.

Now that you have the right orientation, it is just a matter of nurturing it and making it pure and ripe. Keep on refining and perfecting it. Only when you are like fine gold that has been smelted a hundred times can you become a great vessel of the Teaching.

ENTERING THE PATH

The Tao is originally without words, but we use words to reveal the Tao. People who truly embody the Tao penetrate it in the mind and clarify it at its very basis. They strip off thousands and thousands of layers of sweaty shirts sticking to their skin and open through to awaken to the real, true, immutable essence, which is just as it is: originally real and pure and luminous and wondrous, wholly empty and utterly silent.

When you reach the point where not a single thought is born and before and after are cut off, you walk upon the scenery of the fundamental ground. All the wrong perceptions and wrong views of self and others and "is" and "is not" that make up the defiled mind of birth and death are no longer there. You are completely cleansed and purified, and you have complete certainty. Then you are no different from all the other enlightened people since time immemorial.

You are at peace, not fabricating anything, not clinging to anything, freely pervading everything by being empty, perfectly fused with everything, without boundaries. You eat and dress according to the time and season and have the integral realization of true normality. This is what it means to be a true nondoing, unaffected Wayfarer.

In sum, it depends on the fundamental basis being illuminated and the six sense faculties being pure and still. Knowledge and truth merge, and mind and objects join. There is no profundity to be considered deep and no marvel to be considered wondrous. When it comes to practical application, you naturally know how to harmonize with everything. This is called "finding the seat and putting on the robe."

After this you see on your own. You never consent to bury yourself at the verbal level in the public cases of the ancients or to make your living in the ghost cave or under the black mountain. The only thing you consider essential is enlightenment and deep realization. You naturally arrive at the stage of unaffected ordinariness, which is the ultimate in simplicity and ease. But you never agree to sit there as though dead, falling into the realm of nothingness and unconcern.

This is why, in all the teaching methods they employed, the enlightened adepts since antiquity thought the only important thing was for the people being taught to stand out alive and independent, so that ten thousand people couldn't trap them, and to realize that the vehicle of the school of transcendence does actually exist.

The enlightened adepts never ever made rigid dogmatic definitions, thereby digging pitfalls to bury people in. Anyone who does anything like this is certainly playing with mud pies—he is not someone who has boldly passed through to freedom, not someone who truly has the enlightened eye.

Therefore, we do not eat other people's leftovers by accepting stale formulas and worn-out clichés, for to do so would mean being tied up to a hitching post for donkeys. Not only would this bury the Zen style; it would also mean being unable to penetrate through birth and death oneself. Even worse would be to hand on slogans and clichés and subjective interpretations to future students and to become one blind person leading a crowd of blind people and proceeding together into a fiery pit.

Do you think this would be only a minor calamity? It would cause the true religion to weaken and fade, and make the comprehensive teaching design of the enlightened ancestors collapse. How painful that would be!

Therefore, in studying the Tao, the first requirement is to select a teacher with true knowledge and correct insight. After that, you put down your baggage and, without any question of how long it will take, you work continuously and carefully on this task. Don't be afraid that it is difficult and painful and hard to get into. Just keep boring in—you must penetrate through completely.

Haven't you seen Muzhou's saying? "If you haven't gained entry, you must gain entry. Once you have gained entry, don't turn your back on your old teacher."

When you manage to work sincerely and preserve your wholeness for a long time, and you go through a tremendous process of smelting and forging and refining and polishing in the furnace of a true teacher, you grow nearer and more familiar day by day, and your state becomes secure and continuous.

Keep working like this, maintaining your focus for a long time still, to make your realization of enlightenment unbroken from beginning to end. The things of the world and the buddhadharma are fused into one whole. Everywhere in everything you have a way out—you do not fall into objects and states or get turned around by anything.

At a bustling crossroads in the marketplace, amid the endless waves of life—this is exactly the right place to exert effort.

JOYOUSLY ALIVE

The essential requirement in studying Zen is concentrated focus. You don't engage in any forced actions: you just keep to the Fundamental. Right where you stand, you must pass through to freedom. You must see the original face and walk through the scenery of the fundamental ground. You do not change your ordinary actions, yet outside and inside are One Suchness. You act according to the natural flow and do not set up anything as particularly special—you are no different from an ordinary person.

This is called being a Wayfarer who is free and at peace, beyond learning, free from contrived actions. Being in this stage, you do not reveal any traces of mind—there is no road for the gods to offer you flowers, and no way for demons and outsiders to spy on you. This at last is simple unadorned reality.

Keep on nurturing this for a long time, and worldly phenomena and the buddhadharma fuse into one whole, merging without boundaries. Power functions ready-made, so what is so difficult about penetrating through birth and death to freedom?

The only worry is that your initial realization will not be accurate and true. If there is anything in your breast, then you're hung up and blocked. If you want to *reach accord* quickly, you must dissolve everything as soon as it happens, like a snowflake placed on a red-hot stove. Then you will naturally open through and become peaceful and still and attain great liberation.

Step back yourself and examine this. You have associated with a teacher for quite a while already, so ask yourself if your practice is reaching the right outcome or not. If it is coming down in the right place, then what are you still in doubt about?

From now on, do not give rise to a single thought, and accept true reality with your whole body. If you are real in one place, then how could it be any different in a thousand or ten thousand places?

The ancestral teachers just wanted people to see their true nature. All the enlightened ones came forth to enable people to awaken to mind. Once you arrive at the reality of mind and its true nature, and it is pure and unified and unmixed with deluded perceptions, then the four elements that make up your physical body, and the five clusters of form, sensation, conception, evaluative synthesis, and consciousness, and the six sense faculties and the six sense objects, and all the myriad forms of being together comprise the place where you relinquish your body and your life.

When you are at peace and washed clean, it is like the sun shining everywhere, like the infinite expanse of space. How can you confine yourself to your limited body and mind and keep yourself from being joyously alive?

People of olden times would spend ten or twenty years studying just to penetrate through. And after they penetrated through, they knew how to live.

Are people these days lacking anything to keep them from proceeding along the same path? Just don't give rise to any feelings of wanting or needing anything, or engender any clingings or attachments. Then, according to your power as you encounter situations, you will not fail to penetrate through.

All that's important is concentrated focus, purity, and stillness. Even when you are engaged in doing things, this is not something external. Take hold of them and return them to your true self—this is what *wondrous function* is. The eighty thousand sensory afflictions are immediately transformed into eighty thousand means of transcendence, and there is no more need to make a special point of studying with teachers. In your daily activities you deliver countless numbers of sentient beings and accomplish countless enlightening works and pass through countless gates of the Dharma. It all flows out from within your own breast—how could there be any other?

As the saying goes: "From atop the hundred-foot-high pole, you must take a step forward—then the universe in all its multiplicity reveals the whole body of reality."

NOW IS THE TIME

To study the Path you should step back and study with your whole being. Make birth and death your only thought. The worldly truth is impermanent, this body is not everlasting. Once you stop breathing, then it's already another lifetime. In another birth you may sink into nonhuman species, and then you might go on for thousands of lifetimes through countless ages without emerging.

Luckily, at present you still have plenty of time. Now is the time to apply effort to turn toward the Path every moment, without your mind wavering or your attention faltering. Catch sight of it right where you are. When you reach the point where not a single thought is born and before and after are cut off, you will suddenly penetrate through to freedom. It's like the bottom falling out of a bucket. Then you experience joy.

You investigate into the ultimate depths until you walk in *the scenery of the fundamental ground* and clearly see *the original face.* Then you will have no more doubts about what the Zen masters have said. You will be able to cut everything off and hold everything still, nurturing it by having no conditioned mind and no contrived effort and no particular concerns. Then twenty-four hours a day, there will be no more wasted effort. Your mind does not touch upon things and your steps are beyond location.

At this point you are a true Zen monk who has understood things and completed the work. You do not aim to get famous or play false to grasp at profit. You stand like a wall miles high—impeccable, with "each drop of water a drop of ice." You work on your own mission of getting beyond birth and death and pay no attention to anything else. Not disturbing anything in the realm of sound and form, not startling the everyday people, you go freely into independent liberation and become a true saint who has gone beyond the dusts.

You must have faith in this and put it into practice.

LEAPING OUT OF THE PIT

Since ancient times we have only esteemed forgetting thoughts and feelings and finding independent realization. Once getting this realization, we do not set up the idea of self, and we do not congratulate ourselves or put on lofty airs. We just go along freely according to the natural flow, like know-nothings, like simpletons. Only this can be called the practice of a nonstriving, unconcerned person of the Path.

If you can go on like this for three or four or five decades without changing or deviating, then it will also be *thus*, being as it is, for a thousand lifetimes and ten thousand aeons. As the saying goes, "Hardest of all to find are people who will persevere forever." If you go on consistently like this, fully believing, completely penetrating through, have no worries that you will be unable to cross over the world and leap out of the pit of the afflictions of birth and death.

It is just a matter of the person concerned having faculties that are bold and sharp—then it wouldn't be considered difficult even to transcend the cosmic buddha Vairocana or go beyond all the generations of ancestral teachers. This is the real gate of great liberation.

When Bodhidharma passed on the Zen teaching to his successor Huike, was he bogged down in so many verbal explanations?

You must comprehend directly, penetrating from the heights to the depths without the slightest deviation, so that apparent reality cannot break you and the myriad impulses cannot get to you. After that you let everything flow forth from the nonabiding basis in unhindered harmony. All activities are just one's own wondrous function. Wherever you are, you pull out nails and extract wedges for people and enable each of them to become peaceful and secure. Isn't this what's most essential?

One day Xuansha saw some men carrying a corpse. He pointed to this and said to his companions, "Four dead men are carrying one live one." According to the conventional view, Xuansha got it backward. If you use the true eye of transcendence to detach from subjective views and go beyond conventional sentiments, then you will know that Xuansha was being extremely kind in helping people.

Therefore, to pass through to freedom, you must get beyond the nexus of form, sensation, conception, motivational synthesis, and consciousness.

Haven't you read the ancient worthy's saying? "The white clouds are clear and still, and the rivers flow into the blue sea. The myriad things are originally peaceful, but people make trouble for themselves."

After all, this statement is completely accurate and true. If you know what it means as soon as you hear it mentioned, you can use it to pass through birth and death to freedom and no longer be obstructed by the psycho-physical nexus. You will be like a bird getting out of a cage—independent and free. With a single stroke you put a stop to all other actions and talk, and you no longer fall into secondary views.

ENLIGHTENMENT RIGHT WHERE YOU STAND

Among the marvels of Buddhism, nothing surpasses the Zen school for experiencing direct surpassing realization and reaching quick accord with transcendent wisdom. This is the pure, clean Zen of the supreme vehicle of those who come from Thusness.

It has been specially carried on outside of doctrine ever since Shakyamuni Buddha held up a flower on Spirit Peak and Mahakashyapa smiled—Shakyamuni entrusted to him the wondrous mind of nirvana, the treasury of the eye of the correct teaching. The pure transmission of the mind-seal continued through twenty-seven generations in India, until bodhidharma came from the West to bring it to China. He pointed directly to the human mind, to enable people to see their true nature and become enlightened, regardless of whether they are ordinary or sagely or far or near.

When the basic capacity is attuned, you pass through to freedom in an instant. It doesn't take three incalculable aeons: you immediately witness the original buddha, which is perfect and complete and pure and wondrous.

Therefore, to travel in the Zen school, you need a great capacity for the Dharma. You must establish your determination from the start and set out: then you must come forth transcendent. This is what is called realizing buddhahood right where you stand. Reining in your thoughts and concentrating your awareness for a while, you no longer set up "before" and "after"—you experience the unborn.

This is not obtained from anyone else. It is just a matter of bold and sharp practice on your own part. It is like cutting through a skein of thread: when one thread is cut, they are all cut. Your inherent spiritual awareness is instantly liberated: one moment you're an ordinary person, and the next moment you're a sage. Whether you intend it or not, the ordinary and the sagely are One Suchness, embracing all of space, with no more direction or location.

Yongjia said: "How can you draw any comparisons to the uncreated state of absolute reality? Transcend directly to enter into the stage of those who realize Thusness."

At the assembly where Buddha preached *The Lotus Sutra,* a *naga* girl offered a pearl and immediately achieved true awakening. Isn't this immediate realization of the wondrous fruit of enlightenment in the turn of a thought?

This reality cannot be covered by the skies or held up by the earth. Space cannot contain it. It abides within all sentient beings and is the support on which all of them rest. It has always been clean and naked. There is nowhere it does not pervade.

People are unable to experience this true essence simply because they are hemmed in by emotional consciousness and separated from it by hearing and seeing, and because they falsely accept the perceived reflections of objects for mind itself and the gross physical elements as the real body.

That is why the sages, with the power of their vows of compassion, have pointed out this true essence to people, to enable all people with the basic capacity to turn the light around and reflect back, so they can pick it out and witness it in its pure form.

How about the "pearl" that the *naga* girl offered to Buddha—where is it right now? If you can take it up as soon as it's mentioned, then you will never go to the words to construct an understanding, or make a nest in mental maneuvers and conceptual thoughts. Then it will be no different from the undefiled world of Spirit Peak.

Since time immemorial we in the Zen school have only valued the very first mental moment, the very first statement. Before thought is born, before sound comes forth, cut through directly—all at once cut off the spiritual workings of the thousand sages and the spiritual talisman of the myriad sentient beings. Isn't this the essential wondrous realm of liberation and freedom, where you achieve great independence?

Layman Pang asked Mazu, "Who is the one who does not keep company with the myriad things?" Mazu said, "When you can swallow all the water in West River in one gulp, I'll tell you."

Many are the people who make verbal evaluations of this public case, interpreting it in terms of mind and environment, but they are far from accepting the design of Zen.

You have to be made of cast iron: only then can you go against the flow and experience transcendent realization. Then you will capsize the iron boat of Layman Pang and Mazu. When you arrive at last at *towering up like a wall miles high*, you will finally know that there aren't so many things.

TIME WAITS FOR NO ONE

All those with conditioned minds are as far apart from true reality as the sky is from the earth. Right now, if you cannot pass through the barrier, it is obviously because your mind has many serious attachments. If you can clear these away and reach the realm where there is no conditioned mind, all delusions and defilements and emotional habits will end, and all the obstructions created by conditioned knowledge and arbitrary views and intellectual understanding will be dissolved away—what else is there?

This is why Nanquan said that, once freed from its conditioning, the ordinary mind is the Way. But as soon as you produce a thought seeking to be "ordinary," you have already turned away and missed it. This is the point that is most subtle and hardest to approach. Even immeasurably great people falter and hesitate when they get here— how much the more so for those still in the stage of learning.

You must strive with all your might to bite through here and cut off conditioned habits of mind. Be like a person who has *died the great death:* after your breath is cut off, then you come back to life. Only then do you realize that it is as open as empty space. Only then do you reach the point where your feet are walking on the ground of reality.

When you experience profound realization of this matter, you become thoroughly clear, and your faith becomes complete. You are free and at ease and clean clear through—not knowing anything, not understanding anything. As soon as anything touches you, you turn freely, with no more constraints, and without getting put anywhere. When you want to act, you act, and when you want to go, you go. There is no more gain or loss or affirmation or denial. You encompass everything from top to bottom all at once.

How could it be easy to carry into practice or even to approach this realm where there is no conditioned mind? You must be a suitable person to do so. If you are not yet like this, you must put aside mind and body and immerse yourself in silent reflection until you are free from the slightest dependency. Keep watching, watching, as you come and go. After a long time you will naturally come to cover heaven and earth, so that true reality appears ready-made wherever you touch.

Before there was a natural-born Shakyamuni Buddha, before there was a spontaneously so Maitreya Buddha, who was it who understood while still in the womb? You must be quick to focus your energy. Time does not wait for people. Suddenly, in one bite, you will bite through, and nobody will be able to do anything about you. To succeed at this, a truly great person must reach the realm of self-realization, independence, and freedom.

MAKE ENLIGHTENMENT YOUR STANDARD

Fundamentally, this great light is there with each and every person right where they stand—empty clear through, spiritually aware, all-pervasive, it is called *the scenery of the fundamental ground.*

Sentient beings and buddhas are both inherently equipped with it. It is perfectly fluid and boundless, fusing everything within it. It is within your own heart and is the basis of your physical body and of the five clusters of form, sensation, conception, motivational synthesis, and consciousness. It has never been defiled or stained, and its fundamental nature is still and silent.

False thoughts suddenly arise and cover it over and block it off and confine it within the six sense faculties and sense objects. Sense faculties and sense objects are paired off, and you get stuck and begin clinging and getting attached. You grasp at all the various objects and scenes, and produce all sorts of false thoughts, and sink down into the toils of birth and death, unable to gain liberation.

All the buddhas and ancestral teachers awakened to this true source and penetrated clear through to the fundamental basis. They took pity on all the sentient beings sunk in the cycle of birth and death and were inspired by great compassion, so they appeared in the world precisely for this reason. It was also for this reason that Bodhidharma came from the West with the special practice outside of doctrine.

The most important thing is for people of great faculties and sharp wisdom to turn the light of mind around and shine back and clearly awaken to this mind before a single thought is born. This mind can produce all world-transcending and worldly phenomena. When it is forever stamped with enlightenment, your inner heart is independent and transcendent and brimming over with life. As soon as you rouse your conditioned mind and set errant thoughts moving, then you have obscured this fundamental clarity.

If you want to pass through easily and directly right now, just let your body and mind become thoroughly empty, so it is vacant and silent yet aware and luminous. Inwardly, forget all your conceptions of self, and outwardly, cut off all sensory defilements. When inside and outside are clear all the way through, there is just one true reality. Then eyes, ears, nose, tongue, body, and conceptual mind, form, sound, smell, flavor, touch, and conceptualized phenomena—all of these are established based on that one reality. This one reality stands free of and transcends all the myriad entangling phenomena. The myriad phenomena have never had any fixed characteristics—they are all transformations based on this light.

If you can trust in this oneness, then with one comprehended, all are comprehended, and with one illuminated, all are illuminated. Then in whatever you do, it can all be the indestructible true essence of great liberation from top to bottom.

You must awaken to this mind first, and afterward cultivate all forms of good. Haven't you seen this story? The renowned poet Bo Juyi asked the Bird's Nest Monk, "What is the Way?" The Bird's Nest Monk said, "Don't do any evils, do all forms of good." Bo Juyi said, "Even a three-year-old could say this." The Bird's Nest Monk said, "Though a three-year-old might be able to say it, an eighty-year-old might not be able to carry it out."

Thus we must search out our faults and cultivate practice; this is like the eyes and the feet depending on each other. If you are able to refrain from doing any evil and refine your practice of the many forms of good, even if you only uphold the elementary forms of discipline and virtue, you will be able to avoid sinking down to the levels of animals, hungry ghosts, and hell-beings. This is even more true if you first awaken to the indestructible essence of the wondrous, illuminated true mind and after that cultivate practice to the best of your ability and carry out all the forms of virtuous conduct.

Let no one be deluded about cause and effect. You must realize that the causal basis of hell and heaven is all formed by your own inherent mind.

You must keep this mind balanced and equanimous, without deluded ideas of self and others, without arbitrary loves and hates, without grasping or rejecting, without notions of gain and loss. Go on gradually nurturing this for a long time, perhaps twenty or thirty years. Whether you encounter favorable or adverse conditions, do not retreat or regress—then when you come to the juncture between life and death, you will naturally be set free and not be afraid. As the saying goes, "Truth requires sudden awakening, but the phenomenal level calls for gradual cultivation."

I often see those who are trying to study Buddhism just use their worldly intelligence to sift among the verbal teachings of the buddhas and ancestral teachers, trying to pick out especially wondrous sayings to use as conversation pieces to display their ability and understanding. This is not the correct view of the matter. You must abandon your worldly mentality and sit quietly with mind silent. Forget entangling causes and investigate with your whole being. When you are thoroughly clear, then whatever you bring forth from your own inexhaustible treasury of priceless jewels is sure to be genuine and real.

So first you must awaken to the Fundamental and clearly see the true essence where mind equals buddha. Detach from all false entanglements and become free and clean. After that, respectfully practice all forms of good, and arouse great compassion to bring benefits to all sentient beings. In all that you do, be even and balanced and attuned to the inherent equality of all things—be selfless and have no attachments. When wondrous wisdom manifests itself and you penetrate through to the basic essence, all your deeds will be wonder-working. Thus it is said, "Just manage to accept the truth—you won't be deceived."

Make enlightenment your standard, and don't feel bad if it is slow in coming. Take care!

THE ORIGINAL PERSON

The Great Teaching is basically quite ordinary. It is easy to enter for those with sharp faculties and quick wits and broad penetration who don't use their intellectual brilliance to try to comprehend it.

The usual problem is if you are overloaded with conditioned knowledge and arbitrary views. Then when you try to approach this source, the more you delve into it, the farther away you get, and you are completely unable to penetrate through.

If you are equanimous toward everything, including the ultimate ungraspability of mind itself, and your conditioned mind fades away and spontaneously comes to an end, then the perfect illumination of inherent nature appears whole without needing any contrived efforts to make it. You cut off the flow and experience profound realization. When you neither go too far nor fail to go far enough, then you arrive at the naturally real working essence of the mind. This is what is meant by the saying, "Set to work on mind, and the matter is decided." If you always let this naturally real essence appear amidst your daily activities, then how can you not be settled and secure?

When the ancients awakened to mind, they awakened to this mind. When they activated its working potential, they activated this working potential. They were able to stay free and at ease for ten thousand generations without changing. They stood forth transcendent, in independent realization, and no longer placed themselves in opposition to anything.

If you are in opposition to anything, then this creates duality. Then you are stuck with self and others and gain and loss, and you are unable to walk upon the ground of reality.

If you take a step further, not a single thing is established—after that you are quiet and properly attuned, and you clearly see the original person. You get rid of all the concerns in your breast and the mental moment that's before your eyes, so that your whole being is liberated and at peace. You are forever beyond any possibility of retreating or regressing. You attain fearlessness, and with expedient means based on this fearlessness, you can rescue sentient beings.

You must continue this way without interruption forever—this is the best.

WITNESSING THE TAO

This Tao is deep and remote. Beyond the time before heaven and earth had taken shape and sentient beings and buddhas were separated, it was profoundly clear, solid and still, as the root of the myriad transformations. From the beginning it was never existent or nonexistent and never fell into the dusty realm of sensory objects. This Tao shines and glitters, and none can fathom its limits. It has no reality that can be considered real and no wonder that can be considered wondrous. It is absolutely transcendent and lies beyond the scope of concepts and images. There is nothing that can be used to compare it with.

Therefore, the perfected people witness it independently and come forth liberated. They are annihilated and totally cleansed, and they penetrate through to this primal source.

By the power of expedient means, these perfected people bring it up directly in its pure form, to receive students of the highest potential without establishing any steps or stages. This is why their teaching is called *the vehicle of the source*, and *the special practice outside doctrines*. They seal qualified disciples with this one seal. In turning the key of transcendence, there is no room for hesitation in thought.

In all the methods and gestures they use, the enlightened teachers leave behind the nests of cliché and theory and verbal sloganeering. They are like sparks struck from stone, like flashes of lightning—instantaneous, swift. They produce thousands of changes and transformations without ever depending on anything. From top to bottom they cut through the net that traps people. They sanction only the outstanding students and disregard the dullards.

To be a legitimate Zen teacher, you must have the spirit to kill a person's false personality in the blink of an eye. Understanding one, you understand all; illuminating one, you illuminate all. After that you arrive at the far-seeing perception and lofty consciousness that comes with getting beyond birth and death and transcending ordinary life and entering into the bequest of the sages. You live in an ordinary way and do not reveal your sharp point. When you suddenly come forth free and at ease, you startle the multitude and move the crowd.

In sum, your roots are deep and your stem is strong. You see that *before the Primordial Buddha* and *the other side of the empty aeon* are no different from your functioning here and now. Once your practice has power, you are able to bear the heavy responsibility of teaching the Dharma and achieve far-reaching effects—you achieve great mastery. Then compressing three aeons into a single moment or stretching out seven days into a whole age is just minor action—to say nothing of taking the galaxy and hurling it beyond space, or putting the polar mountain into a mustard seed. This is your everyday food and drink.

In the past there were many examples of enlightened lay people who combined worldly achievement with profound mystic realization. It wasn't so hard—all they did was directly comprehend this one Great Cause. Once they had this Tao as their foundation, they were able to disregard other people's conventional judgments and mobilize their own courage and boldness. When interacting with people, they focused the eye of enlightenment and set in motion their quick potential and sharp wisdom to turn all the myriad forms of being around, back into their own grasp. They rolled out and they rolled up, they released and they captured. Thus they were no different from all the people of great attainment down through the ages whose practice was pure and ripe and who held within them the virtues and power of the Tao.

Just make the transmission continue without a break from source to source, and then you will be a joyously alive person on the road of eternal life.

The ancestral teacher said: "Mind turns following the myriad objects. If you can really reach the hidden depths of this turning and recognize true nature going along with the flow, then there is no joy and no sorrow." As soon as you can find the deep meaning in this transformation process, you will penetrate through the moving flow and see inherent true nature. When you move beyond duality and do not abide in the middle path, how can there still be any such things as adverse and favorable, sorrow and joy, or love and hate to block your free functioning?

To transmit mind by means of mind, to seal true nature with true nature—this is like water being poured into water, like trading gold for gold. Joyous, easy, ordinary, without contrived activity, without concerns—as you meet situations and circumstances, they are not worth a push.

Are the direct teaching methods of the classic Zen masters so remote? Just do not let yourself be transformed by following your emotions. Get above form and ride upon sound. Transcend ancient and modern. Move quickly on the razor's edge amidst the multiplicity.

Thus it is said, "Push open the passageway to transcendence, and all the thousand sages are downwind of you."

RIGHT IN YOUR OWN LIFE

This thing is there with everyone right where they stand. But only if you have planted deep and strong roots in the past will you have the strength in the midst of the worldly truth to be able to push entangling objects away.

You must constantly step back from conventional perceptions and worldly entanglements to move along on your own and reflect with an independent awareness. Cleanse and purify your karma of mind, body, and mouth, sit upright and investigate reality, until you arrive at subtle insight and clear liberation.

Right in your own life, detach from conditioned views and cut off sentiments. Stand like a wall a mile high. Abandon the deep-seated conditioning and the erroneous perception that has been with you since time without beginning. Smash the mountain of self to pieces, dry up views based on craving, and directly take up the truth. The thousand sages cannot alter it, and the myriad forms cannot cover it or hide it. It lights up the heaven and the earth.

The buddhas and ancestral teachers pointed directly to this indestructible, inherent true essence, which is wondrous, immaculate, and pure. Set your eyes on it amid the thousands of intricate complexities that are impossible to analyze. Apply your blade where the interlocking crosscurrents cannot be split apart.

Your potential operates prior to things, and your words go beyond the scope of concepts. You are free and unbound, pure and still. You turn independently, with your powerful functioning alive and liberated. You share the same attainment and the same functioning with all the outstanding adepts since antiquity who have achieved this realization—you are not different, not separate. Unoccupied and at ease, you just preserve stillness and silence and never show your sharp point. You seem like a simpleton, totally abandoned and relaxed, eating when hungry and drinking when thirsty, no different than usual. This is what is called secretly manifesting the great function and activating the great potential without startling the crowd.

When you have done this for a long time and arrived at the stage where you are pure and ripe and at peace and genuine, is there any more old bric-a-brac like affliction and birth and death that can tie you down?

Therefore, those among the ancients who were adept in the Way and its powers directed people who had already freed themselves from sensory entanglements to extend the esoteric seal.

You should spend twenty or thirty years doing dispassionate and tranquil meditation work, sweeping away any conditioned knowledge and interpretive understanding as soon as it arises, and not letting the traces of the sweeping itself remain either. Let go on That Side, abandon your whole body, and go on rigorously correcting yourself until you attain great joyous life. The only fear is that in knowing about this strategy, the very act of knowing will lead to disaster. Only when you proceed like this will it be real and genuine practice.

Haven't you read of all the Zen masters who emphatically praised the state where there is no conditioned mind? They really wanted future learners to proceed like this. If you make a display of your cleverness and verbal analyses and intellectual understanding, you are polluting the mind ground, and you will never be able to enter the stream of the Way. Many people have tried to spin out rationales to explain why Buddha held up the flower on Spirit Peak and why Bodhidharma sat facing a wall at Shaolin, but they do not rely on the fundamental. They are far from realizing that searching for the meaning of the mind-to-mind transmission through verbal categories and sound and form is like sticking your head into a bowl of glue.

As for the outstanding type, they certainly do not act like this. They are able to delve into it on their own and are sure to get the sense of the great and far-reaching acts of the classic teachers. They discover the real truth by engaging with it. That is why people of attainment do not even have any spare time to wipe their noses.

But tell me, where were the ancestral teachers of Zen operating? It's evident that the unique transmission outside of doctrine was not a hurried undertaking. They looked to the void and traced its outline: each and every one penetrated through from the heights to the depths and covered heaven and earth. They were like lions roaming at ease, sovereign and free. When they were empty and open, they really were empty and open, and when they were close and continuous, they really were close and continuous.

Although it is just this one thing that we all stand on, ultimately you yourself must mobilize and focus your energy. Only then will you really receive the use of it.

ENTERING THE PATH

The subtle wondrous Path of the buddhas and enlightened teachers is nowhere else but in the fundamental basis of each and every person. It is really not apart from the fundamentally pure, wondrously illuminated, uncontrived, unconcerned mind.

If you have sincerely devoted yourself to it for a long time, yet are still not able to become really genuine, it is because you have been trying to approach it via your intellectual nature and its many machinations.

You should simply make this mind empty and unoccupied and quiet and still. If you continue in a state of profound stillness and harmony with reality as it is for a long time without changing or shifting, there is sure to come a day when you enjoy total peace and bliss.

What you should worry about is that you will be unable to stop and will go on seeking outside yourself with your intellect. Little do you realize that the real nature you inherently possess is hard and solid as a diamond, secure and everlasting. It is just a matter of never letting there be even a moment's interruption in your awareness of your real nature.

If you put your conditioned intellect to rest for a long time, suddenly it will be like the bottom falling out of a bucket—then you will naturally be happy and at peace. If you seek teachers and insist on memorizing a lot of their instructions, you are even further off. What you must do is use your bold basic nature and boldly cut off and abandon your conditioned mind—you are sure to experience the Path and know it for yourself.

After you know you have entered the Path, you do not set up even this "knowing"—then you arrive at last at the realm of true purity.

THE INEXHAUSTIBLE TREASURY

Devas and humans and all sentient beings, including the enlightened ones, all depend on the awesome power of this thing.

But although ordinary sentient beings have this within them, they are in the dark about it, and so they become wrongly subject to sinking down into the cycle of birth and death and affliction.

The enlightened ones, on the other hand, arrive at the awesome power of this thing and thus experience transcendent realization.

Though delusion and enlightenment differ, their underlying inconceivable reality is one and the same.

That is why the buddhas and ancestral teachers gave instructions and pointed directly to this reality. They always directed sentient beings to comprehend for themselves their own inherent, fundamental, perfect, wondrously illuminated true mind and to dispense with all the false thoughts and schemes and knowledge and views associated with sensory afflictions and troubles.

Go directly to your personal existence in the field of the five clusters of form, sensation, conception, motivational synthesis, and consciousness, turn the light around and reflect back. Your true nature is clear and still and as-is—empty through and accept it. When you clearly see this true nature, this true nature *is* mind, and this mind *is* true nature. All activities, all the myriad changes and transformations in the sensory realm, have never shaken it. That is why it is called the ever-abiding fundamental source.

If you reach this basic root, whatever you do in your empowered functioning will penetrate through. What is necessary is to cut off the flow of your conditioned mind and witness it. If you hesitate in thought, then you are out of touch. If a person's root nature has been pure and still and settled for a long time, it is very easy to be empowered—just reflect back a bit, and penetrate through, and then you can witness it and experience entry.

The ancients called this *the inexhaustible treasury* and also *the wish-granting jewel* and also *the indestructible precious sword.* You must have deep roots of faith and believe that this is not gotten from anyone else.

Whether you are walking, standing, sitting, or lying down, concentrate your spirit and silently reflect. Be pure and naked, without interruptions and without breaks, so that naturally no subjective views arise, and you will merge with this true essence. It is neither born nor destroyed, neither existent nor nonexistent. It is neither solid nor empty; it is apart from names and forms. This is the scenery of your own fundamental ground, your own original face.

When the ancients employed all their hundreds and thousands and millions of expedient teaching devices, it was always to enable people to go toward this and penetrate through to freedom. As soon as you penetrate through, then you penetrate through deeply to the source. You cast aside the tile that was used to knock at the gate, the provisional means that were used to get you there, and there is absolutely nothing occupying your feelings.

Actually practice at this level for twenty or thirty years and cut off all the verbal demonstrations and creeping vines and useless devices and states, until you are set free from conditioned mind. Then this will be the place of peace and bliss where you stop and rest.

Thus it is said: "If you are stopping now, then stop. If you seek a time when you finish, there will never be a time when you finish."

SIMPLE AND EASY

"The wonders of the Path are as simple and easy as can be." How true these words are! But those who have not reached the source think that the Path is extremely abstruse and mysterious. They think that the ultimate reality of the Path lies before the empty aeon, before the differentiation of the primeval chaos, before heaven and earth were formed. They think it is something silent and dark and vague, something impossible to fully fathom or investigate or probe, and that only the sages can experience or know it. Thus they know the words of the sages, but they do not know their meaning. How can we talk to them about this matter?

People who think like this are far from realizing that the Path is perfect and complete right under everyone's feet, that it is pure and naked in the midst of everyday activities. It encompasses all mental moments and is omnipresent in all places. There is no dark place it does not illuminate and no time it is not in operation.

It is just that people have been running off in the opposite direction for a long time, branching off in aberrant ways, unwilling to believe in their own buddha nature, always seeking externally—that is why the more they seek, the further away they get from the Path.

This is why Bodhidharma came from the West and just pointed directly to the human mind. This mind is the unconcerned mind in its normal equilibrium. Its natural potential spontaneously extends forth, without constraints and without clinging, without abiding anywhere or getting attached to anything. It shares in the powers of heaven and earth and merges with the light of the sun and moon.

There is no room here to set up arbitrary opinions. You flood out into great comprehension and merge into a state free from conditioned mind and its contrived actions and obsessive concerns. If you set up the slightest trace of dualism between subject and object and self and others, then you are blocked off and obstructed, and you will never penetrate through to it.

As the saying goes: "The real nature of ignorance is buddha nature, and the empty body of illusory transformation is the buddha's body of reality." If you can witness real nature within the shell of ignorance, then instantaneously the essence underlying ignorance is brought into play. If you can see the body of reality within the shell of the physical body, then instantaneously the essence underlying the empty body is wholly illuminated. The only fear is that you will contrive actions and set up views within the empty body of ignorance—then you lose contact with the essential reality.

Once you have penetrated through to this true essence and you have discovered that the empty body of ignorance is not separate from it, then none of the myriad forms of being is outside it. When your state is genuine and true, then it is totally inclusive at all times, leaving nothing outside of it, and you can put down your body and mind anywhere. Haven't you seen the ancients say that along with sensory affliction come the seeds of enlightenment?

When you reach this level, observing the reality of physical existence is the same as observing buddha. Then worldly phenomena and the buddhadharma are fused into one single whole. You are completely free and at ease as you eat food and put on clothes—this *is* "Great Potential and Great Function." How could you have any more doubts about all the various teaching methods and gestures and acts and states of the Zen masters?

When you arrive at these ultimately simple, ultimately easy wonders of the Path that are right under your feet, the infinite gates to reality open up and appear before you all at once. You penetrate through birth and death to liberation, and you attain the supremely wondrous fruit of enlightenment. How could this be hard?

Don't Pass Your Life in Vain

Ever since ancient times, people with the will for the Path have traveled around from region to region seeking instruction from adept Wayfarers. They truly did not let their lives in this world go by in vain. Thus they did their best to put their conditioned minds to rest and picked out teachers who genuinely possessed the enlightened eye. When they encountered such teachers, they put down their baggage and stayed for as long as necessary, relying on these adept teachers to help them complete the work. When we observe the paths they followed, we see that they were real "dragons and elephants."

Right now, if you have within you the will to proceed toward the Great Cause, you must put all your strength into concentrating your focus on it and making your concentration solid and sure. Forget about eating and sleeping, do not shrink from strenuous efforts, work hard and endure the pain. If you investigate it with your whole being, after a long time you will naturally achieve certainty and enter the Path.

This one Great Cause has been perfectly complete right within you since the beginning. It has never been lacking in you—it is in you no different than in the buddhas and enlightened teachers. You cannot directly experience it as it really is, simply because you give rise to erroneous knowledge and views, impose arbitrary separations, and occupy yourself with emotional attachments and empty falsehoods.

If you have planted the basis for a root nature that is quick and sharp, then when not a single thought is born, you will suddenly transcend all forms of being and experience perfect realization of your own inherent wondrous nature that is as it is. You will no longer give birth to any ideas of subject and object or self and others. You will empty through in great comprehension—holy and ordinary are equal, self and others are Thusness.

Being a buddha, you will no longer seek buddhahood; being present with mind, you will never again look for mind. Here there is no duality between buddha and mind—wherever you go, they appear ready-made. You no longer fall into empty falsity at any time of the day or night.

This then is walking on the ground of reality, opening up your own treasury, and bringing out the family jewels. However you activate your potential, you go beyond sectarian conventions. You penetrate through to the level where you are genuine and true and leaping with life.

As the saying goes, "A lot of falsity is not as good as a little reality." Just let your initial aspiration for enlightenment keep its original boldness, and continue on until you penetrate all the way through—don't worry that you will not accomplish your work on the Path.

A truly great person must completely master transcendent Great Potential and Great Functioning. When you are at peace and full of joy, you are finally drawing near to it. Do not be content with a little bit of comprehension. You must go on working hard for a long time, until you spontaneously get it. Isn't this liberation?

TEACHING ZEN

Surely you have seen this saying: "The one road to transcendence is not transmitted by the thousand sages." If you have directly experienced the meaning that is not transmitted by the sages, then you have indeed finished the work of the Path.

If we directly discuss this matter, there is no place for you to use your mental machinations and no place for you to approach and settle in. That is why Zen adepts ever since ancient times have only taught via direct pointing—they wanted people to reach mystic awakening outside conventional categories. They did not want people to slog through muddy water or fall into sensory entanglements.

Thus it is said, "The superior type get up and carry it out as soon as they hear it mentioned. A thousand devices cannot take them in, and a thousand sages cannot trap them."

To be a genuine Zen teacher, it is necessary to study like this and experience entry into the Path like this, and it is necessary to propagate the Path like this and to extol the Path like this. How could this be a matter for dullards? Every true teacher must have eyes like shooting stars and be able to kill a person's false self without blinking an eye—only then is there accord with the Path. If you hesitate and get hung up, you have missed it by a thousand miles.

Only when you are at the stage where you possess this ultimate treasure can you set up myriad distinctions. If you have really reached such a stage, you will never concoct strange things or impose arbitrary forms or create rigid models or rote patterns. You just keep open and free, and even this cannot be grasped. When you establish yourself and penetrate through to freedom and dissolve the sticking points and remove the bonds to help other people, it is always done according to the place and time.

Linji said: "What I see, I want all people to know."

How could this be something that crude worldly thinking can assess? You must gather together all your false thoughts and calculations and attachments to sentiments and sensations and judgmental views, and cut them off with one stroke—explaining and distinguishing "true nature" and the "true pattern" will never be the Fundamental. You must get free of all this and get your own realization.

Then all the objects in all the worlds of the ten directions are contained in the space of the tip of a single hair. Then your whole function is buddha, and the whole buddha is your functioning. A blow, a shout, a statement, a device—there are no clichés here. Everything is sealed with genuine realization. It is like the philosopher's stone turning iron into gold. Everything flows out from the true self.

After you have been studying for a long time, and you have created a lot of subjective views and interpretations, this only makes you more learned—it is not the real thing. You must get so that when you stop one, you stop all, and when you comprehend one, you comprehend all. You must see this original face and reach the scenery of this fundamental ground.

After this, when you act, everything is ready-made, and it no longer depends on any mental effort. It is as the proverb says: "When the wind blows, the grasses bend down." Though the mountains and forests and cities and towns are still there, there is no duality. This is called being able to hold fast and act the master. The scale to weigh the lifeline of sentient beings is in your own hand, and you judge them according to what their minds do.

This is called the uncontrived Path. Isn't this the most essential, utterly peaceful and secure, great liberation?

LEARNING ZEN

Fundamentally the Path is wordless, and the Truth is birthless. Wordless words are used to reveal the birthless Truth. There is no second thing. As soon as you try to pursue and catch hold of the wordless Path and the birthless Truth, you have already stumbled past it.

That is why when the ancestral teacher of Zen came from the West, he only propagated this thing. He only valued personal apprehension outside of words and direct comprehension outside of mental maneuvers. Apart from those of the highest potential and capacity, who could take it up immediately?

If you have set your will on this, you do not calculate how long the journey will take. In establishing your will, you must be independent and deadly serious, and succeed in cutting clear through. With bold and sharp body and mind, put down your baggage and take refuge with a teacher whose techniques are as deadly as a dog biting a boar. Wholeheartedly set before him the knowledge and opinions that are sticking to your flesh, all the explanations and theories you have accumulated in your previous studies. Make your breast completely empty, so that your egotism does not reveal itself and you don't do a single thing—then you will be able to experience the realization that penetrates to the depths. Do not deviate one bit from the precedent established by all the enlightened ones since time immemorial.

When you can be like this, you still need to realize that there is such a thing as the strategy of the transcendent teachers. Thus, when the ancients were asked about buddhas and transcendence, they answered, "It is not buddha," or they answered, "Provisionally it is called buddha." So even talk of "seeing true nature and becoming buddha" is a snare to capture the attention of learners. What did the ancients intend when they pointed to the east and called it the west?

You must achieve intimate, level accord with the Truth. Once you are able to sustain this on your own, then you can be totally free. What further talk is there of realizing nirvana or understanding birth and death—these are extraneous words. Even so, this is just me talking like this: you shouldn't take it as an absolute standard, if you are going to avoid the sickness of reifying the concepts of "buddha" and "enlightened teacher."

When quality people plan to investigate mind, how can they set a rigid time limit? Just achieve deep faith and consistently go forward. You are sure to walk upon the ground of reality if you renew yourself day by day and strip away your illusions day by day. Step back all the way, and it is *this;* when you reach the point that even *this* is not established, this is precisely the place to do the work.

SHŌBŌGENZŌ
Zen Essays by Dōgen

FOREWORD

The thirteenth-century Japanese Zen teacher Dōgen Kigen is widely respected as a religious reformer, an accomplished Buddhist adept, a profound thinker, and a brilliant writer. His master work, *Shōbo-genzō*, written in a complex, innovative style, appreciated in recent times not only for its philosophical achievements but even for its literary excellence, is among the most demanding of Zen texts. Acting forcefully on the inertia of routine thought, the *Shōbōgenzō* demonstrates how the mind is used in working Zen, and how literature can be used to foster and direct the Zen use of the mind. This volume presents translations of thirteen chapters of the *Shōbōgenzō*, selected for their emphasis on perennial issues in Buddhist learning and action.

INTRODUCTION

Zen Master Dōgen is revered as the founder of the Sōtō Zen school in Japan, but in modern times his reputation as an exceptionally advanced intellect has reached far beyond sectarian bounds. Largely kept hidden for centuries, Dōgen's *Shōbōgenzō*, a remarkable collection of essays, has lately attracted widespread attention from scholars and others within and without Zen circles. Much admired for its linguistic artistry and metaphysical subtlety, the *Shōbōgenzō* is a classic of such status and magnitude that entire careers have been devoted to its study and exegesis.

According to the *Kenzeiki*, a medieval biography of Dōgen,[1] the master was born in the year 1200 C.E. to a noble family in Kyoto, the imperial capital and cultural center of Japan. While still a small child he began to receive the rigorous education considered proper for his status and expectations, learning classical Chinese, the language of philosophy and government in old Japan. At the age of seven he was already reading the ancient Chinese classics *Tso Chuan* and *Mao Shih* and was considered a prodigy by Confucian scholars of the time.

When Dōgen was eight his mother died. This event is said to have awakened him to the impermanence of life and provoked in him a desire to leave secular society and become a monk. Later, when he finally left home and abandoned his future at court, he revealed that his dying mother had herself urged him to become a monk. He began to add Buddhist lore to the enormous stock of book learning which he accumulated over the years, and is said to have been reading intricate Buddhist *abhidharma*, analytic philosophy, by the age of nine.

About this time, Dōgen was adopted by the imperial regent, a distinguished scholar and statesman, and was taught political science as it was known at that time, with a view to making him a member of the court. Dōgen, however, had no desire for a secular career and at the age of thirteen ran away to become a monk. He sought out an uncle who was a high priest of the Tendai school of Buddhism, and prevailed upon him to accept his decision to leave home and help him to attain his wish to pursue a religious life.

At fourteen Dōgen was formally ordained and "studied the way of the Tendai school, including the secret teachings from south India, the principles of the greater and lesser vehicles, and the inner meanings of the exoteric and esoteric doctrines." When he was fifteen he went to see the Zen master Eisai and heard about the teachings of the Rinzai school of Zen; the following year Eisai died, and Dōgen continued to consult his successor Myōzen, seeing the latter on and off for several years until he finally became his disciple formally when he was eighteen years old. During this time Dōgen also continued his canonical studies and is said to have read through the whole of the voluminous Buddhist canon twice while still in his teens.

Dōgen is said to have been encouraged to study Zen by a high priest of the Tendai school to whom he applied with his question of why Buddhas aspire to and practice the way of enlightenment if the reality of enlightenment is inherent. According to *Denkōroku*, another medieval Sōtō text, Dōgen under Myōzen's tutelage studied not only Zen but also ethical precepts, the Tendai meditation methods known as "stopping and seeing" (*shi-kan*), and esoteric rites, in the manner of Eisai's syncretic school. When Dōgen was twenty-one he was given recognition as Myōzen's Zen successor, and was thus considered a tenth-generation heir of the Ōryū branch of Rinzai Zen, which Eisai had introduced from China.

By his own account, Dōgen studied with Myōzen for nine years. At the age of twenty-four he went to China with Myōzen for further inquiry. The political conditions in China at that time made it impractical, if not impossible, to travel widely, but Dōgen was able to meet several Zen teachers in eastern China. After fruitless contact with seven Zen teachers, however, he felt he had nothing to learn from any of them and decided to return to Japan. He was urged, however, to see the redoubtable Nyojō, who had just replaced the late abbot of a famous public monastery. In 1225 Dōgen met the man who was to be his last teacher.

Absorbed in learning and meditating, Dōgen spent nearly two years in the congregation of Nyojō without ever lying down to sleep. Finally, one morning in the early hours he heard the teacher scold a dozing monk with the words, "Zen study requires the shedding of body and mind," and at that moment Dōgen was greatly awakened. Subsequently his realization was recognized by Nyojō, and he was formally designated a successor. In 1227, having, in his own words, "finished his life's study," Dōgen returned to Japan.

In Japan Dōgen did not hasten to set himself up as a teacher. He stayed for a time at Kenninji, the monastery in Kyoto founded by Eisai at which he had studied with Eisai's successor Myōzen. According to *Denkōroku*, over the next few years Dōgen spent time at thirteen different places offered to him by patrons, but none of them suited him. In 1234 he settled down at Kōshō Hōrin temple outside Kyoto and began to teach. The *Denkōroku* states that more than fifty students gathered here, including Koun Ejō, who was to become Dōgen's first successor.

In 1235 Ejō was formally installed as the assembly leader and recognized as Dōgen's heir and teaching assistant. That same year Dōgen began to solicit funds to build a monks' hall (*sōdō*), used for communal meditation and residence in a traditional Zen monastery. Dōgen was the first Japanese Zen teacher to base his organization on the observances of Chinese Zen without the admixture of rites from the esoteric branch of Tendai Buddhism that had characterized the organization of Eisai and Myōzen.

Something of the historical sense that Dōgen had of his transmission of Zen to Japan can be glimpsed in a 1242 conversation with a nobleman who asked if the Zen school had been transmitted to Japan in past times. Dōgen replied:

> In our country literal and formal Buddhism has been transmitted, and it has been somewhat more than four hundred years that the terms and forms of Buddhism have been heard of here. And now the Buddha-mind school (Zen) is becoming current: and it should be at precisely this time.
>
> In China literal and formal Buddhism was first transmitted between 58 and 76 C.E.; from then to the year 520 (when Bodhidharma brought Zen from India to China) is somewhat more than four hundred years. It was at that time that the way of the adepts, direct pointing, brought from the West (India), first became current. Six generations later was Sokei (the sixth patriarch of Zen in China), and after (his disciples) Seigen and Nangaku it branched into five schools.

In our country nominal Buddhism was first heard of in the sixth century C.E., after which the sacred doctrines transmitted from Korea filled the land. But there have not yet been adepts at transmitting mind by mind—there has only been a succession of nation-protecting and wonder-working monks.[2]

Since it was more than four hundred years between the time of the first introduction of Buddhism into Japan and Dōgen's bringing of Zen from China, it is likely that Dōgen's reckoning refers to the founding of the Tendai and Shingon schools in the early ninth century, which would be four centuries before Dōgen brought Zen, referred to here by the traditional terms "direct pointing," "the way of the adepts," and "transmitting mind by mind." So-called "nation-protecting and wonder-working monks" refers to the practice of rites for the protection of the state and production of magical effects, known to be prevalent in Japanese Buddhism of the time. Basically, Dōgen relates the transmission of Zen by analogy to Chinese Buddhist history, suggesting that the time in Japan was finally ripe to progress from the externals of Buddhism, the names and forms, to the internal, mind-to-mind transmission. Although Dōgen declined to use the term "Zen sect," emphasizing the essential unity of Buddhism, the evidence suggests that he was aware of initiating something new in the history of Japanese Buddhism.

In 1242, one of his most prolific years in terms of the composition of *Shōbōgenzō*, Dōgen formally designated his second successor, Gi'in. In the same year, the monk Shinchi Kakushin came to Dōgen and received the Mahayana Buddhist precepts from him. This monk later went to China and succeeded to the teaching of Mumon Ekai, author of the popular Zen classic *Mumonkan;* he eventually returned to Japan, beginning his own Zen school, and was given the honorific title Lamp of Religion, Teacher of the Nation. Also in 1242, the recorded sayings of Dōgen's teacher Nyojō arrived from China.

During his decade or so at Kōshō temple, Dōgen had many contacts with the nobility of Kyoto and initiated over two thousand people into the bodhisattva precepts. Finally he came to desire a more quiet and undisturbed setting. The *Kenzeiki* records that he was offered twelve different places by patrons, none of which suited him—a possible reference to the same process mentioned in *Denkōroku*, which says that Dōgen was offered thirteen places from the time he came back to Japan until the time he settled at Kōshō. In any case, Dōgen was finally offered an old temple site in the province of Echizen, modern Fukui prefecture, by the provincial governor at whose residence Dōgen had delivered the *Shōbōgenzō* essay *Zenki* in 1242. Dōgen accepted this offer and in 1243 took up residence in Echizen. In 1244 he formally opened his new monastery, then called Daibutsuji; in 1246 its name was changed to Eiheiji, as it is known today.

During the 1240s Dōgen was given a robe and title of honor by the emperor Gosaga. This period was most productive. He wrote nearly eighty of the ninety-five essays of the *Shōbōgenzō* between 1239 and 1246, the majority of them between 1240 and 1243.

In 1247, invited by the regent of the military government, Hōjō Tokiyori, an earnest Zen student, and also urged by his patron the governor of Echizen, Dōgen went to Kamakura in eastern Japan, the seat of the shogunate. Tokiyori wanted Dōgen to stay in Kamakura and offered him the position of founding abbot of the new Kenchōji monastery, but Dōgen refused and returned to Eiheiji after six months in Kamakura. Upon his return he said these words in a speech to his disciples:

> Last year on the third day of the eighth month I left the mountain and went to Kamakura and expounded the Teaching for a patron lay disciple. This year, this month, yesterday, I returned, and this morning I have come before you to speak. Some people may be suspicious about this event. I crossed so many mountains and rivers to expound the Teaching for a lay disciple—this seems like esteeming a layman more than monks. Also some may wonder if there is a teaching I have not explained here, a teaching you have not heard. But there is no teaching I have not explained here, none you have not heard. I only explained to him that those who do good rise while those who do evil fall. Cultivating cause, effect is experienced.[3]

He ended the speech with the remark that his love of the mountains was even greater than before, and this theme of retreat and seclusion from secular society, which appears elsewhere in his works, gains increasing emphasis toward the end of Dōgen's life.

In the same year, 1247, Dōgen also exchanged correspondence with Zen Master Daikaku (Rankei Dōryū), a Chinese Zen monk in Kamakura who received the post of abbot at Kenchōji which Dōgen is said to have declined. This seems to be the only clear record of contact between Dōgen and another Zen school in Japan, apart from the school founded by Eisai and the Bodhidharma sect, a native Japanese Zen movement.

In 1253 Dōgen's successor Ejō was installed as the second abbot of Eiheiji. Dōgen himself, terminally ill, went to Kyoto for medical care. Staying in the house of a lay disciple in Kyoto, Dōgen passed away in the eighth month of the same year.

Dōgen's magnum opus *Shōbōgenzō*, "Treasury of the Eye of True Teaching," is the first major Buddhist text to have been composed in the Japanese language, written in a time when classical Chinese was considered the preferred medium for religious literature in Japan, much in the same way that Latin and Arabic were the standard languages for philosophical discourse in medieval Europe. *Shōbōgenzō* contains many passages and phrases in Chinese embedded in the Japanese matrix of the text and manipulated with striking effect, producing an intense style which demands a great deal of concentration on the part of the reader. It may be said that the form as well as the content of the compositions in *Shōbōgenzō* is instrumental, in that it provokes definite effects on the attention and stream of consciousness of the reader.

Insofar as it deals with both topical and perennial matters, *Shōbogenzō* contains material which is primarily relevant to thirteenth-century Japanese Buddhism, particularly in its monastic forms, and also material which is timeless, presenting insights that not only permeate spiritual teachings found all over the world but also anticipate modern scientific realizations about the nature of knowledge. While in certain respects Dōgen's presentations in *Shōbōgenzō* differ in manner from other Zen teachings, he also uses traditional strategies in his handling of Zen and Buddhist lore.

One characteristic which *Shōbōgenzō* shares with other Zen writing is the way Dōgen draws freely from Buddhist literature without concern for any context but that in which he is presently handling a story, saying, or technical term. This freedom includes the practice of partial quotation, using only so much of a given story or speech as is useful in conveying the intended message or impact of the moment. This practice seems to reflect the general Zen view of literature as being instrumental rather than sacred writ, allowing for a flexible exercise of possibilities in association and imagery.

Another feature of Dōgen's treatment of sayings and stories which is also to be found throughout Zen literature as an important device is referred to by Dōgen himself, and in earlier Zen writing such as the *Blue Cliff Record,* as "presenting sideways and using upside down." This is the practice of using a story, saying, term, or symbol in a way that departs from the obvious or the stereotyped, traditional view. This practice is exercised, according to Zen writing on the subject, to help break up the "nest of cliché" which Zen teaching often cites as both a symptom and a cause of mental stagnation. Apart from clichéd understanding acquired at second hand, however, even understanding which is valid at a given level of personal development inhibits deeper realization if it is held fast to as ultimate. In Buddhism this is technically called "the barrier of knowledge," and the fact that Dōgen's disciples already had considerable learning is likely reason for Dōgen's striking use of verbal shock techniques such as this one.

A particular aspect of the barrier of knowledge which another feature of Zen literature is designed to counter is the overestimation of conceptual understanding at the expense of practical understanding. According to Zen teaching, the study of Zen requires actual participation, because it is only through participation that the transformation of the individual can take place. Zen literature does not merely state this principle, however; it enforces it, so to speak, by presenting material that is impenetrable without the exercise of qualities essential to Zen work, such as patience, concentration, and ability to suspend automatic thought.

Confucius, the great educator of ancient China, reportedly said that if he pointed out one corner of a matter and the student could not come back with the other three, he would not repeat himself. This statement by Confucius is cited in classic Zen writing to indicate that the capacity to "understand three when one is raised" is also essential in Zen students. The principle of "not saying everything" or "not explaining thoroughly" *(fuseppa)* so as to provoke the student to the necessary levels of effort is found explicitly and implicitly in many forms in Zen literature, and is also applied by Dōgen in *Shōbogenzō.* One of Dōgen's characteristic devices is to present a number of views, often generating them from variations on themes from stories and sayings, then leaving the audience to work through them.

Sometimes this is done in the form of a series of questions which Dōgen then tells his hearers to think over.

Emphasis on concentration techniques is a common feature of the three "new" or "reform" movements of Japanese Buddhism in Dogen's time—the Nichiren, Pure Land, and Zen schools. Close study of the literature of each of these forms of Buddhism reveals a demand for concentration in conjunction with special attention patterns, concrete methods of developing concentration, and a wealth of concealed meanings which are only accessible in the light of structured concentration. Concentration is deemed necessary to empower the teachings, to validate them experientially, because existing mental habits, which form boundaries inhibiting the potential of consciousness of the conditioned person, go back to "beginningless time"—that is, to subconscious sociopersonal history—and have become ingrained or "naturalized" into the fabric of the person's views of reality. Conceptual exercise alone is held to be too shallow and ephemeral to exert the force necessary to break through deeply established mental conditionings. The "doubt feeling" (gijō), deliberately produced by certain Zen verbal devices frustrating linear thought, is one way in which such force is accumulated and directed in order to pierce this veil of inertia.

Much of Dōgen's writing in Shōbōgenzō dealing with perennial issues may be read on both philosophical and experiential planes, as indeed these planes mirror one another. The actual integration of these realms of understanding, however, takes place after the Zen initiatory experience (nissho), which uproots the fixation of views and makes possible the more subtle perceptions and integrations with which more advanced Zen practice works. In systematic Zen kōan study, at least as it is represented in the writings of Sung dynasty Chinese teachers and Japanese teachers, simple kōan which focus the attention off of discriminating consciousness on to totality are dealt with first, to break conceptual habits. After gross fixations of conditioned thought are shed and a measure of flexibility is retrieved, more complex kōan are taken up in order to integrate holistic and differentiating awareness. A great deal of Dōgen's writings for contemplation in Shōbōgenzō would fall into the general category of complex kōan, and can be used with great effect in aiding the mind in the practice of fluid integration of multiple perspectives.

To appreciate this quality of Shōbōgenzō, it is helpful to have a glimpse of the practical core of which the *Shōbōgenzō* meditations are refinements. Observation of certain fundamentals of Zen meditation will also afford a rough comparison of Dōgen's approaches with those of other teachers.

Certain basic patterns can be discerned in expressions of Zen meditation techniques designed to bring about transformation of consciousness. For example, a recurrent image in Zen literature is that of death and rebirth, referring to the process of stripping away the accretions of conditioning and then returning to the ordinary world purified and free. An analogy may be drawn with the famous line of scripture which says "form is empty, emptiness is form"; experientially, "form is empty" corresponds to detachment from appearances, while "emptiness is form" corresponds to the fullness of the field of perception accessible to the opened mind. This twin aspect of enlightenment experience is also referred to by such terms as "the heart of nirvana and the knowledge of differentiation," "silence and illumination," "dismantling and constructing," and a host of similarly structured metaphors.

Sōzan, one of the early masters of the Sōtō Zen tradition, expresses this process in the following terms: "As a beginner, knowing there is something fundamental in oneself, when one turns the light around (shifts attention from sense experience to the essence of mind) one ejects form, sound, smell, flavor, touch, and phenomena, and attains tranquility. Then, after fully accomplishing this, one does not grasp the sense data but descends among them without being blinded, letting them be, without interference."[4]

Dōgen's teacher Nyojō provides a vivid description along similar lines:

> You should "gouge out" your eyes and see nothing at all—after that there will be nothing you don't see; only then can it be called seeing. . . . You should "block off" your ears and hear nothing at all—after that there will be nothing you don't hear; only then can it be called hearing. . . . You should "knock off" your nose and not distinguish smells—after that there will be none you can't distinguish; only then can it be called smelling. . . . You should "pull out" your tongue, so that the world is silent—after that your ebullience will be uninterrupted; only then can it be called speaking. . . . You should "slough off" the

physical elements and be completely independent—after that you manifest forms adapting to various types; only then can it be called person. . . . You should permanently stop clinging thought, so the incalculable ages are empty—after that arising and vanishing continue unceasing; only then can it be called consciousness.[5]

In the early treatise on *zazen*, Dōgen says, "You should stop the intellectual practice of pursuing words and learn the 'stepping back' of 'turning the light around and shining back'; mind and body will naturally 'drop off,' and the 'original face' will appear." The Zen "art" of looking into the mind source instead of pursuing thoughts or external stimuli is called *ekō henshō*, "turning the light around and shining (or looking) back." In this same treatise, and in *Shōbōgenzō*, Dōgen uses the following story to illustrate the method of this practice, which he calls the essential art of *zazen*. As the Zen master Yakuzan was sitting, a monk asked, "What are you thinking of, so still and intent." Yakuzan said, "I am thinking of that which is not thinking." The monk said, "How can one think of that which is not thinking." Yakuzan said, "It isn't thought."[6] In his *Zazenshin* essay in *Shōbōgenzō*, Dōgen writes, "In thinking of *what isn't think-ing*, one always uses *nonthought*. In *nonthought* is 'who'—'who' carries 'I'."[7]

The word "who," or some phrase like "who is carrying around this corpse?" is also one of the "words" *(watō)* that have been traditionally used in Zen meditation (particularly since the late Sung dynasty) to evoke the "doubt feeling" *(gijō)* of looking into the innermost self. There are numerous sayings and stories in the records of the classical Zen masters alluding to this practice of "looking back." A monk once asked Master Isan, "What is the Path?" Isan said, "No-mind is the Path." The monk said, "I don't understand." Isan said, "You should understand that which doesn't understand." The monk asked, "What is that which doesn't understand?" Isan said, "Just you are it. It is not someone else." Isan continued, "People of the present time should just directly realize that which doesn't understand. This indeed is your mind, this indeed is your Buddha. If you externally get a piece of knowledge, a piece of understanding, and consider that the path of Zen, you're out of touch. This is called carrying excrement in—it is not called taking excrement out. It defiles your mind-field, so I say it is not the Path."[8]

Goȳzan asked Isan, "What is the abode of the real Buddha?" Isan said, "With the subtlety of thinking of no thought, think back to the endlessness of the spiritual flame. When thought is exhausted, you return to the source; essence and characteristics always abide, phenomena and noumenon are not two—the real Buddha is thusness as is."[9]

A monk asked the adept Shijō, "Whenever I sit at night, my thoughts are in a flurry, and I don't know how to subdue them. Please give me some guidance." Shijō said:

> When you sit still at night and your thoughts are in a flurry, then use the flurried mind to investigate the place of the flurry. Investigating this thoroughly, you find there is no place—then how can the flurry of thoughts remain? Then turn back to investigate the investigating mind—then where is the mind which can investigate? Furthermore, the perceiving knowledge is fundamentally empty, so the object focused on is also quiescent. Quiescent yet not quiescent, because there is no stilling person; perceiving yet not perceiving, because there is no perceived object. When object and knowledge are both quiescent, mind and thought are at rest. Outwardly not pursuing ramifications, inwardly not dwelling in concentration, both roads having disappeared, the one nature is tranquil. This is the essential path of returning to the source.[10]

This technique is also part of the battery of meditation practices of Tendai Buddhism. For example, one meditation manual says, "Since we know observation comes from mind, or from analyzing objects, this is not merging with the fundamental source: so one should turn back to observe the observing mind."[11] This type of introspection is also found in the technical literature of the Pure Land school in China:

> Outwardly not clinging to objects, inwardly not dwelling in concentration, "turn the light around" and observe once—inside and outside are both quiescent. After that subtly invoke the name of Amitabhā Buddha three to five times. Turn the light around and introspect—"it is said that seeing nature one realizes buddhahood; ultimately, what is my inherent Amitabhā Buddha?" Then also watch and observe that which has just brought

this up—"where does one thought come from?" Seeing through this one thought, then see through this seer—who is it?[12]

A useful Zen story illustrating the technique of "turning the light around and looking back"—its application and limitations—is found in the *Book of Serenity* (in Japanese, *Shōyōroku*), a classic collection of Zen lore compiled and expounded by outstanding Chinese Sōtō Zen masters. The master Gyōzan asked a monk, "Where do you come from?" The monk said, "From Yun-chou." Gyōzan said, "Do you think of that place?" The monk said, "I always think of it." Gyōzan said, "That which thinks is mind, that which is thought of is object. In that place are various things—mountains, rivers, land, buildings, houses, people, animals. Think back to the mind which thinks—are there so many things in there?" The monk said, "When I get here, I do not see their existence at all." Gyōzan said, "This is right for the stage of faith, but not yet for the stage of person."

Basically, in this technique the exercise is to turn away from the preoccupations of the mind and back to the mind itself. Since mind or awareness as an object in itself cannot be grasped, the exercise of focus on an ungraspable object, or objectless focus, has a particular effect. The teacher says that the monk's state of disentanglement from objects and absorption in the objectless mind is right for the stage of "faith." In Zen literature, the expression "entry by faith" appears occasionally in reference to an initial stage of enlightenment. Faith here does not mean belief in an idea or object; rather it has the sense of acquiescence. The Zen master Rinzai refers to insufficient faith or "trust" in oneself as the reason for restless external search and the consequent failure to realize intrinsic enlightenment.

In the aforementioned treatise on meditation, Dōgen also writes, "Even if one can boast of understanding, is rich in enlightenment, gains a glimpse of penetrating knowledge, attains the Way, clarifies the mind, and becomes very high spirited, yet even though one roams freely within the bounds of 'entry,' one may lack the living road of manifestation in being." Here what is referred to as "entry," a common Zen term for initiation into enlightened consciousness, might be equated with what Gyōzan refers to as the "stage of faith" in the foregoing story, while Gyōzan's stage of "person" might be equated with what Dōgen refers to, using a familiar Zen expression, as the "living road of manifestation in being," a step beyond preliminary disentanglement from objects.

The story goes on. The monk asked, "Do you have any other particular directions?" Gyōzan said, "To say there is something particular or not would not be accurate. Based on your view, you only get one mystery. You get the seat and wear the robe—after this, see on your own." If one applies the model of the "seat," "robe," and "room" of Buddha according to the *Hokke (Saddharmapuṇḍarīka)* scripture, the "seat" is the emptiness of all phenomena, the "robe" is forbearance. These fit the story rather well, considering that the effect of the exercise of looking into the mind is disentanglement. The "room" of a Buddha is compassion, and this is the essence of being in the world, of active expression; this also fits the story as well as Dōgen's admonition, representing the next stage of development.

The poem recorded in the *Book of Serenity* illustrating this story, composed by Wanshi, acknowledged as one of the great masters of Sōtō Zen, clarifies these points most beautifully: "Containing without omission, penetrating without obstruction. Gates and walls high and steep, barrier locks doubled and redoubled. The wine always sweet, it lays out the guests; though the meal is filling, it ruins the farmers. The wind supports the condor's wings as it bursts out in space; thunder accompanies the dragon as it treads over the ocean."

"Containing without omission, penetrating without obstruction" characterizes the mind; "gates and walls high and steep, barrier locks doubled and redoubled" characterizes objects. "The wine always sweet, it lays out the guests; though the meal is filling, it ruins the farmers"—this refers to absorption in mind-introspection; total indulgence in this at the expense of participation in the world produces a lopsided, partial development. In Buddhist scriptures concentration is sometimes referred to as "wine," meditation as "food"—indulgence in "intoxication" and "tasting" is forbidden to the bodhisattvas, who are to balance detachment and identification, transcendence and being in the world. Here being in the world, the active personality, is symbolized by "guest" and "farmer," and this is seen as a necessary part of the total balance of the whole being.

"The wind supports the condor's wings as it bursts out in space; thunder accompanies the dragon as it treads over the ocean." Here the "condor" and "dragon" represent the awakened person; the "wind" and "thunder" refer to the world, which becomes a vehicle for the awakened. The phrase "bursts out in space," which can be taken to refer to emancipation, emptying, can also be read "bursts out of empty space," suggesting going beyond the stage of emptiness. The phrase "treads over the ocean" is literally "treads on and turns over the ocean," conveying a similar sense of going beyond the oceanic realm of pure consciousness. So in the end the exercise of "turning the light around and looking back" can be seen as a means of "entry," to be replaced by a more comprehensive realization of integration. An ancient teacher said, "If you haven't attained entry, first attain entry; if you have attained entry, don't turn your back on me," suggesting again that there is more to learn after awakening.

Accordingly, Dōgen describes this technique as "the essential art of *zazen*" but does not refer to it as the whole art of *zazen*. Clearly, there is more content in the total program of meditation in Zen schools, and a function of the teacher's contact with the students is to provide material for contemplation. Dōgen's *Shōbōgenzō* provides numerous examples of outlines for meditations presented to his disciples to work through, and he repeatedly urges them to ponder his questions and statements carefully.

It is well known that in the Rinzai Zen schools *kōan*, Zen stories, are commonly used in meditation, with pressure being put on the student to "answer" or illustrate the *kōan* as part of the method. Since there are many cases in Dōgen's written and spoken works where he deals with traditional *kōan*, and also evidence of his own use of *kōan* as a testing device, there can be no doubt that the *kōan* was an integral part of his teaching method. Nevertheless, it is questionable whether Dōgen gave the *kōan* the same kind of stress as Rinzai Zen teachers ordinarily did, or similarly demanded answers in a graded system. In a record of some of his early teaching, he seems to play down the value of such a method:

> In the study of the Way, the prime essential is sitting meditation *(zazen)*. The attainment of the Way by numerous people in China is due in each case to the power of sitting meditation. Even ignorant people with no talent, who do not understand a single letter, if they sit wholeheartedly in meditation, then by the accomplishment of meditative stability they will surpass even brilliant people who have studied for a long time. Thus, students should only be concerned with the act of sitting—do not get involved with other things. The Way of Buddhas is just sitting meditation; one should not follow other concerns.

(Ejō asked,) In practicing both sitting and reading, when looking at the recorded sayings (of Zen masters) and *kōan*, it happens that one may understand somewhat one out of a hundred or a thousand. In the case of sitting meditation, there is no particular experiential proof such as this. Yet should we still be devoted to sitting meditation?

(Dōgen replied), When looking at the words of the public cases, though one may seem to have some perception, that is a factor which causes estrangement from the Way of Buddhas. If you spend your time sitting straight without attaining anything or understanding anything, then it would be the Way of Buddhas. Although even the ancients encouraged both reading and just sitting, they still encouraged sitting wholeheartedly. And though there have been people whose awakening was opened by words, those too were situations in which the opening of awakening was due to the accomplishment in sitting. The true attainment is due to the sitting.[13]

However, in the same record there is also evidence that contemplating sayings was practiced in Dōgen's school:

It is said, "Even a thousand acres of clear fields is not as good as a bit of skill that you can take around with you." "Benevolence does not hope for reward; having given to someone, do not regret it." "If you keep your mouth as silent as your nose, you will avoid ten thousand calamities." "A person whose action is firm is naturally admired; but someone of outstanding ability will naturally be brought down." "To plow deep but plant shallow is the way to a natural disaster. When you help yourself and harm others, how could there be no consequences?" When students of the Way are looking at sayings, you must exert your power to the utmost and examine them very very closely.[14]

It is interesting to note that the specific examples of Dōgen mentions in this speech are not of the type usually associated with *kōan* meditation, but rather appear on the surface as advice for living. In other works of Dōgen there are *kōan* with his comments in prose and poetry in traditional Zen style.

In connection with practice, Dōgen is noted for asserting the unity of practice and realization. In one of his early essays, *Bendōwa*, he writes:

To think practice and realization are not one is a heretical view. In Buddhism, practice and realization are one equivalence. Even now, because it is practice based on realization, the beginner's practice of the Way is the whole of the fundamental realization. For this reason, even in presenting the orientation of practice, the teaching is to not anticipate realization outside of practice; this must be because it is the fundamental realization, directly pointed to. Being the realization of practice, there is no boundary of realization; being the practice of realization, there is no beginning of practice. . . . Since there is practice which is not apart from realization, the beginner's practice of the Way, in which we are fortunate to simply transmit one portion of subtle practice, is precisely attainment of one portion of fundamental realization in the state of nonstriving. You should know that the enlightened ones repeatedly teach that practice should not be relaxed, so that realization which is not apart from practice will not be defiled. When you put down subtle practice, fundamental realization fills your hands; when you express fundamental realization bodily, subtle practice is carried out through your whole body.[15]

This approach of presenting practice as "practice of realization" and realization as "realization of practice" may be further clarified in terms of the Tendai doctrine of the six aspects of identity between conscious beings and Buddha—identity in respect to essence, doctrine, meditation practice, conformity, partial realization, and ultimate realization. As Dōgen says, practice is practice of realization, so it must first of all be based on the essence, the intrinsic buddhanature; recollecting this essence and cultivating its expression in action, however, generally depend on teaching to point the way. Insofar as meditation practice is attuned to the true essence by way of teaching and correct application, it can develop into conformity with the essence. By purification of the senses and conformity with the essence, the veil of ignorance—the habit energy of the ego—is removed, and the essence, the buddha-nature or original mind, then takes over the consciousness and ultimately becomes fully awakened and manifest in life. From the beginning the essence is the same, while the depth of realization of it on the part of the person corresponds to the degree of purity and perfection of practical conformity with it and expression of it.

Dōgen's presentation of *zazen* practice is at times also reminiscent of the teaching of esoteric Buddhism of the Shingon school and the esoteric branch of the Tendai school, according to which the unity of the cosmic Buddha and all existence is realized and expressed in people through the medium of certain physical, verbal, and mental actions. In the case of the esoteric rites, these would be the various *mudrā* (symbolic gestures or signs), *mantra* or *dhāraṇī* (mystic incantations), and *samādhi* (concentration, absorption in specific visualizations and thoughts). In *Bendōwa* Dōgen writes, "If someone, even for one period of time, shows the Buddha-seal in physical, verbal, and mental action, and sits straight in concentration, the whole cosmos becomes the Buddha-seal, all of space becomes enlightenment."[16]

There is, however, a stipulation: the ego must be overcome. In the *Genjōkōan* essay in *Shōbōgenzō* Dōgen writes that ego-laden practice and realization are delusion; as long as there is egotism—attachment to the idea of the self—practice and realization cannot be practice and realization of enlightenment. In one of his early talks Dōgen makes this clear, and also recommends a traditional method for overcoming this barrier:

> The foremost concern of a student is first to detach from the notion of self. To detach from the notion of self means that we must not cling to this body. Even if you have thoroughly studied the stories of the ancients and sit constantly like iron or stone, if you are attached to your body and do not detach from it, you could not find the Way of Buddhas even in ten thousand eons, in a thousand lifetimes. Though you may say you have understood the temporary and true doctrines and the true exoteric and esoteric teachings, if you do not leave off your feeling of attachment to your body, you are idly counting the treasures of others without having a halfpenny of your own. I only ask that students sit quietly and look into the beginning and end of this body as it truly is. The body, limbs, hair, and skin come from the sperm and ovum; when the breath ceases, they separate and decay in the mountains and fields, eventually turning into mud and earth. What do you have to cling to as your body? This is all the more apparent when we look at it from the point of view of the elements; in the conjunction and dispersal of the elements, what elements can you definitely consider as your own body?

Whether it is within the teachings (i.e. doctrinal schools) or outside the teachings (i.e. Zen schools), the fact is the same—that
neither beginning nor end of one's body can be grasped is the
essential point to be aware of in practicing the Way. If you have
first arrived at this truth, the real Buddha Way is something that
is obviously so.[17]

Attachment to self also has more subtle manifestations, and
Dōgen distinguishes the *zazen* of non-Buddhists and Buddhists aiming for individual salvation from the *zazen* of Buddhas in terms of
characteristic flaws which are related to some sense of self. Quoting
the great Buddhist master Nāgārjuna, Dōgen says that the *zazen* of
non-Buddhists has the flaw of attachment to experiences and wrong
views, while the *zazen* of Buddhists in quest of individual salvation
has the flaw of aspiration for self-tranquilization and aiming for extinction.[18] A similar sense of clinging being a barrier to true realization is expressed in the *Sandhinirmocana* scripture in explaining the
relationship between practices and ultimate truth.

According to the argument of this scripture, if ultimate truth and
practices were entirely the same, then everyone, regardless of what
they do, would have seen the truth and would have attained nirvana
or enlightenment; but since not everyone has actually seen the truth
and attained nirvana or enlightenment, it cannot be said that ultimate truth and practices are entirely the same.

Furthermore, it explains, if there were no difference at all between
ultimate truth and practices, then since practices are susceptible to
degeneration, so also would ultimate truth be susceptible to degeneration; but whatever is subject to degeneration cannot be ultimate
truth. Moreover, whereas forms of practice are differentiated, ultimate truth is undifferentiated, inasmuch as what varies is not ultimate. So again it cannot be said that ultimate truth and practices are
no different.

On the other hand, the scripture continues, if ultimate truth and
practices were totally different, then those who see the truth would
not be able to do away with the forms of practice and would still be
in bondage to form, since realization of truth would have no effect on
a totally different realm. However, those who see the truth are in fact
able to do away with the forms of practice, these being conditional
and not absolute, and they are indeed freed from bondage to form.

The common characteristic of practices is ultimate truth, the emptiness or nonabsoluteness of forms. Viewing it from another angle, the scripture says that practices being the manifestations of selflessness is itself the characteristic of ultimate truth. Thus practices and ultimate truth cannot be said to be completely different, just as they cannot be said to be no different.

This scripture illustrates how, on the one hand, it can be said that practice and realization are one, yet on the other hand some people are said to become enlightened and others not, and some practice and realization is said to be delusion while other practice and realization is said to be enlightenment. Dōgen's critical stipulation of detachment from self is reflected in the scripture's statement that practice being a manifestation of selflessness is the characteristic of ultimate truth—under this condition they are one. Furthermore, as noted, attachment to self can mean clinging not only to the idea and feeling of self as a physical entity, but also to the experiences and aims and thoughts of the self. Here again Dōgen differentiates the enlightened and the unenlightened within fundamental realization in terms of the presence or absence of barriers such as clinging to concepts. In *Bendōwa* he writes, "The Buddhas, always herein as maintainers, do not leave conceptual knowledge on its several particular aspects; as common beings eternally function herein, its aspects do not appear in their several particular conceptual knowledges."[19] Accordingly, in another talk on *zazen*, Dōgen speaks of it as beyond any formulation or notion or experience, in conformity with the nonduality of ultimate truth and practice as described in the scripture:

> The *zazen* of the Buddhas is not motion or stillness, not practice or realization. It has nothing to do with mind or body, it doesn't depend on delusion or enlightenment. It doesn't empty mental objects, it doesn't cling to any realm of sense. It doesn't value form, sensation, conception, conditionings, or discriminating consciousness. Study of the Way doesn't use form, sensation, conception, conditionings, or discriminating consciousness—if you act on form, sensation, conception, conditionings, or discriminating consciousness, this is form, sensation, conception, conditions, and discriminating consciousness, not study of the Way.[20]

Nonetheless, as seen in the teaching of the middle way, complete realization embraces both absolute and relative truth. Since ancient times Buddhism has noted that extremism is a characteristic disease of human thought and action, and in Zen lore it is pointed out that effort to transcend form can lapse into nihilism. Nāgārjuna wrote, "Emptiness has been said by the Conquerors (Buddhas) to be the relinquishment of views; but they have said that those who hold to the view of emptiness are incurable."[21] In a similar vein, Dōgen says, "Originally the various 'emptinesses' were needed to break through existence. Once/Since there are no existents, what 'emptiness' is needed?"[22] The principles of emptiness and meditation on emptiness are used to break through reification of phenomena as subjectively viewed; when it is actually realized that there is nothing in the world that can be grasped as permanent, definite, or absolute, and clinging to objects is ended, then "emptiness" has fulfilled its function. The fourth patriarch of Zen said, "The practice of bodhisattvas has emptiness as its realization: when beginning students see emptiness, this is seeing emptiness, it is not real emptiness. Those who cultivate the Way and attain real emptiness do not see emptiness or nonemptiness; they have no views."[23]

In spite of the clarity of such statements by Nāgārjuna and others regarding the meaning of emptiness and its function as a doctrine and a focus of meditation, there is a persistent tendency, noted in Buddhist texts over the ages, for both observers and participants to exaggerate emptiness into nihilism. Zen writings of the Sung dynasty particularly mention this as a prevalent form of immaturity or degeneracy in Zen, a typical symptom of which is denial or ignorance of cause and effect relations. Dōgen, having studied in Sung China, and working in Japan during the early period of transplantation of Sung Zen traditions, also addresses this issue in emphatic terms from a number of angles; it may even be possible to see this as a major theme of the Shōbōgenzō, recurring in various forms.

Dōgen's famous paraphrase of the scriptural line "all beings have buddha-nature" into "all being is buddha-nature" might be taken as representative of this effort to resolve unintegrated dualities. In his essay on buddha-nature, Busshō, he complains that portraying the "moon disc," which conventionally represents buddha-nature, as an empty circle is misleading, because in fact all forms and appearances are themselves the "moon disc." Here he addresses the philosophical and meditative error of imagining buddha-nature as like a soul or spirit separate from the body and distinct from the total field of experience, a realm of clarity divorced from the everyday world. Such a realm of clarity is a mental object, a state cultivated by concentration, and whatever its value as a temporary tool may be, it is not true realization of the all-embracing awareness of enlightenment.

Perhaps nowhere is Dōgen's counterbalancing of negative extremism more concisely typified than in a passage in his *Sesshin-sesshō* essay where he mentions the famous image of the "true person with no position" used by the ancestors of Rinzai Zen to refer to the free human being without vain imaginings, and adds that this alone is incomplete because it leaves unexpressed the "true person that has position." In the following pages of translations from *Shōbōgenzō*, the subtle interweaving of emptiness and existence is described in great detail in Dōgen's own words.

The texts from *Shōbōgenzō* presented here have been translated with a view to preserving form as well as content, on the premise that both are functional parts of the original design, which is arresting and demands close attention. Accordingly, passages and phrases which the original text keeps in Chinese, as well as certain technical terms which seem to stand out for emphasis, have been italicized in the English translation. Exceptions to this practice have been made in certain instances, such as in the case of technical terms in common parlance. For convenience, proper names have been rendered in their Japanese pronunciations.

Needless to say, the incommensurability of languages makes translation an affair which is incomplete and imperfect by its very nature. Even modern Japanese translations of *Shōbōgenzō* are pale indeed in comparison with the original. As with any literature of this caliber, there is actually no way to fully appreciate *Shōbōgenzō* except in the original. But insofar as language compromises experience in any event, there is no reason to reject further compromise of language. Similarly, the brief introductions and annotations which have been added to the each of the following essays from *Shōbōgenzō* should be regarded as a compromise between the projected needs of a general contemporary audience and the demands of Zen literature as an instrument with specific functions. They are not intended to be definitive or exhaustive in any sense, but rather to be merely suggestive of some of the potentials of *Shōbōgenzō*.

Notes

1. The following account, based mainly on *Kenzeiki*, is not intended to be an exhaustive or critical account of Dōgen's life, but merely to show how Dōgen's career is basically seen in Zen lore; accordingly, theoretical problems such as whether or not Dōgen really met Eisai and what all his motives were for leaving the Kyoto area will not be dealt with, being in any event of little or no significance to those of Dōgen's writings which are herein presented. The *Kenzeiki* is at times clearly sectarian and hagiographic, but it is a useful compilation of various available sources; the parts presented here are those which basically accord with earlier sources. Ages are given as in the text, which means that they are counted according to the number of new years, not birthdays.

2. A note in the text of *Kenzeiki* says that the available record of this conversation is in the hand of a sixth-generation Sōtō monk.

3. *Eihei Kōroku*, scroll 3.

4. Taishō Shinshū Daizōkyō (hereafter TT), vol. 47, p. 534a.

5. Ibid., vol. 48, p. 130a.

6. From *Fukanzazengi*. "Thinking about that which is not thinking" can read "thinking about who isn't thinking" or "thinking about what doesn't think." The particle after "not thinking" in the original story makes it attributive, and by convention refers to the unexpressed subject modified by the attributive verbal expression; thus it means contemplating the mind source, the technique of "turning the light around and looking back" (*ekō henshō*), which Dōgen states he is recommending in this treatise as the essential art of *zazen*. The story goes on further to point out that the contemplation which is done in *ekō henshō* is not thinking; that is to say, it is not conceptual or discursive thought. Besides the stories quoted in the text following, there are many such pointers to be found in Zen lore, using terms such as "before any traces appear," "before a single thought arises," "before the Buddha appears in the world," "before the universe is differentiated," and so on, to orient the mind in the *ekō henshō* technique.

7. *Shōbōgenzō Zazenshin* (Iwanami edition), vol. 1, p. 397.

8. TT, vol. 47, p. 550a.

9. *Ching-te Chuan-teng lu*, scroll 11.

10. Ibid., scroll 21.

11. TT, vol. 46, p. 550a.

12. Ibid., vol. 47, pp. 311c–312a.

13. *Shōbōgenzō Zuimonki*, trans. T. Cleary, *Record of Things Heard from the Treasury of the Eye of the True Teaching* (Boulder, 1980), p. 109.

14. Ibid., p. 105.

15. *Shōbōgenzō Bendōwa*, vol. 1, pp. 65–66.

16. Ibid., p. 57.

17. Cleary, *Record of Things Heard*, pp. 71–72.

18. *Eihei Kōroku*, scroll 2.

19. *Shōbōgenzō Bendōwa*, vol. 1, p. 55.

20. *Eihei Kōroku*, scroll 4.

21. *Mūlamadhyamakakārikā*, saṃskāra parīkṣā, verse 8.

22. *Eihei Kōroku*, scroll 6.

23. T. Cleary, *The Sayings and Doings of Pai Chang* (Los Angeles, 1979), p. 11.

Shōbōgenzō: Zen Essays by Dōgen

GREAT TRANSCENDENT WISDOM
(Makahannyaharamitsu)

The subject of this essay, *mahāprajñāpāramitā* in Sanskrit, is the general title and essential theme of one of the major groups of Buddhist scriptures, and is one of the most important issues in Buddhism. Sanskrit *mahā*, meaning "great," conveys the notion of universality. *Prajñā*, often translated as "wisdom," might be rendered as *intense knowledge*; it is commonly described as knowledge of the true nature of things, as being "empty" or lacking absolute, independent existence. *Pāramitā* means "reached the other shore" or "reached the ultimate," and connotes transcendence of mundane limitations, the "other shore" referring to liberation of the mind.

Thus "great transcendent wisdom," as we read it here, means transcendence by universal intense knowledge. The *Treatise on Great Transcendent Wisdom*, a classic work on this teaching, says, "All things are subject to causes and conditions, none are independent. . . . All are born from causes and conditions, and because of this they have no intrinsic nature of their own. Because of having no intrinsic nature, they are ultimately empty. Not clinging to them because they are ultimately empty is called transcendent wisdom."

From this it can be seen that knowledge of "emptiness" is knowledge of conditionality: emptiness, being the absence of independence or own being of conditional things, is not apart from the conditional. This includes all things, whether concrete or abstract, even the items of the Buddhist teachings. Hence transcendent wisdom is that whereby the world, including even the doctrines and means of Buddhism, is transcended, so that there is no clinging to anything. According to Buddhist philosophy, clinging is a prime source of delusion, whether that clinging be to "profane" or "sacred" things. Therefore realization of the relativity, or nonabsoluteness, of all things is at the core of freedom and enlightenment as proposed by Mahayana Buddhism.

However, if it is because of relativity, or conditionality, that all things are "empty," it is equally true that by the very same conditionality they do exist dependently. The tendency to misinterpret "emptiness" nihilistically, whether by intellectual misunderstanding or by mistaking concentration states for insight, is well known and often mentioned in Buddhist texts, especially texts of the Zen schools, where, perhaps due in part to overemphasis on concentration, it seems to have been a not uncommon problem. A thorough reading of Dōgen's *Shōbōgenzō* will reveal that correcting or preventing the tendency toward nihilistic interpretation of emptiness is a major concern of Dōgen's teaching. In this essay, Dōgen identifies phenomena themselves with transcendent wisdom, emphasizing that within so-called nothing or emptiness all things are found, including the facilities, or means, of the Buddhist teachings.

The image Dōgen uses for the realization of wisdom is that of space. As Dōgen says, "Learning wisdom is space, space is learning wisdom." As a common Zen metaphor for the open mind, space may be said to contain all things without being affected by them. The spacelike mind thus is to be distinguished from the mind which is, as it were, *in* space, the former being the nongrasping, nonrejecting openness traditionally preached by Zen, the latter being a concentration state, often practiced by those who seek tranquility and detachment alone. Dōgen here presents the "middle way" in which the emptiness and existence of all things are simultaneously realized, the center-point, the balance, of Mahayana Buddhism.

Much of the essay consists of extracts from Buddhist scripture, and a number of technical terms are brought up. It is not imperative to know exactly what these terms refer to in order to understand the essence of the message, for they refer to Buddhist doctrines, practices, and descriptions as part of the totality of phenomena which all exist yet are empty, are empty yet exist. For the sake of convenience, definitions are provided in a glossary appended to the essay.

GREAT TRANSCENDENT WISDOM

The time when the Independent Seer practices profound transcendent wisdom is the whole body's clear vision that the five clusters are all empty. The five clusters are physical form, sensations, perceptions, conditionings, and consciousness. They are five layers of wisdom. *Clear vision* is wisdom.

In expounding and manifesting this fundamental message, we would say form is empty, emptiness is form, form is form, emptiness is empty. It is *the hundred grasses,* it is myriad forms.

Twelve layers of wisdom are the twelve sense-media. There is also eighteen-layer wisdom—eye, ear, nose, tongue, body, intellect, form, sound, smell, taste, touch, phenomena, as well as the consciousness of the eye, ear, nose, tongue, body, and intellect. There is also four layered wisdom, which is suffering, its accumulation, its extinction, and the path to its extinction. Also there is six-layered wisdom, which is charity, morality, forbearance, vigor, meditation, and wisdom. There is also one-layer wisdom, which is manifest in the immediate present, which is unexcelled complete perfect enlightenment. There are also three layers of wisdom, which are past, present, and future. There are also six layers of wisdom, which are earth, water, fire, air, space, and consciousness. Also, four-layered wisdom is constantly being carried out—it is walking, standing, sitting, and reclining.

> In the assembly of Shakyamuni Buddha was a monk who thought to himself, "I should pay obeisance to most profound transcendent wisdom. Though there is no origination or extinction of phenomena herein, yet there are available facilities of bodies of precepts, meditation, wisdom, liberation, and knowledge and insight of liberation. Also there are available facilities of the fruit of the stream-enterer, the fruit of the once-returner, the fruit of the nonreturner, and the fruit of the saint. Also there are available facilities of self-enlightenment and enlightening beings. Also there is the available facility of unexcelled true enlightenment. Also there are the available facilities of the Buddha, Teaching, and Community. Also there are the available facilities of the turning of the wheel of the sublime teaching and liberating living beings." The Buddha, knowing what he was thinking, said to the monk, "It is so, it is so. Most profound transcendent wisdom is extremely subtle and hard to fathom."

As for the present monk's *thinking to himself,* where all phenomena are respected, wisdom which still *has no origination or extinction* is *paying obeisance.* Precisely at the time of their obeisance, accordingly wisdom with *available facilities* has become manifest: that is what is referred to as precepts, meditation, wisdom, and so on, up to the liberation of living beings. This is called nothing. The facilities of *nothing* are available in this way. This is transcendent wisdom which is most profound, extremely subtle, and hard to fathom.

> The king of gods asked the honorable Subhūti, "O Great Worthy, if great bodhisattvas want to learn most profound transcendent wisdom, how should they learn it?" Subhūti answered, "If great bodhisattvas want to learn most profound transcendent wisdom, they should learn it like space."

So learning wisdom is space, space is learning wisdom.

> The king of gods also said to the Buddha, "World Honored One, if good men and women accept and hold this most profound transcendent wisdom you have explained, repeat it, reflect upon it in truth, and expound it to others, how should I offer protection?" Then Subhūti said to the king of gods, "Do you see that there is something to protect?" The king said, "No, I do not see that there is anything to protect." Subhūti said, "If good men and women live according to most profound transcendent wisdom as they are taught, that is protection. If good men and women abide in most profound transcendent wisdom as taught here, and never depart from it, no humans or nonhumans can find any way to harm them. If you want to protect the bodhisattvas who live in most profound transcendent wisdom as taught, this is no different from wanting to protect space."

We should know that receiving, holding, repeating, and reflecting reasonably are none other than protecting wisdom. Wanting to protect is receiving and holding and repeating and so on.

My late teacher said, "The whole body is like a mouth hung in space; without question of east, west, south, or north winds, it equally tells others of wisdom. Drop after drop freezes." This is the speaking of wisdom of the lineage of Buddhas and Zen adepts. It is whole body wisdom, whole other wisdom, whole self wisdom, whole east west south north wisdom.

> Shakyamuni Buddha said, "Shariputra, living beings should abide in this transcendent wisdom as Buddhas do. They should

make offerings, pay obeisance, and contemplate transcendent wisdom just as they make offerings and pay obeisance to the Blessed Buddha. Why? Because transcendent wisdom is not different from the Blessed Buddha, the Blessed Buddha is not different from transcendent wisdom. Transcendent wisdom *is* Buddha, Buddha *is* transcendent wisdom. Why? It is because all those who realize thusness, worthies, truly enlightened ones, appear due to transcendent wisdom. It is because all great bodhisattvas, self-enlightened people, saints, nonreturners, once-returners, stream-enterers, and so on, appear due to transcendent wisdom. It is because all manner of virtuous action in the world, the four meditations, four formless concentrations, and five spiritual powers all appear due to transcendent wisdom."

Therefore the Buddha, the Blessed One, is transcendent wisdom. Transcendent wisdom is all things. These "all things" are the characteristics of emptiness, unoriginated, imperishable, not defiled, not pure, not increasing, not decreasing. The manifestation of this transcendent wisdom is the manifestation of the Buddha. One should inquire into it, investigate it, honor and pay homage to it. This is attending and serving the Buddha, it is the Buddha of attendance and service.

1233

Glossary

CHARITY, MORALITY, FORBEARANCE, VIGOR, MEDITATION, WISDOM: These are the so-called six perfections, or ways of transcendence, one of the basic formulations of Mahayana Buddhism.

EARTH, WATER, FIRE, AIR, SPACE, CONSCIOUSNESS: These are the "six elements" of which the universe is composed, according to the Shingon school; these elements are said to be the cosmic Buddha itself as well as the substance of all beings, and this is taken as a basic sense in which Buddha and sentient beings are one.

ENLIGHTENING BEINGS: This refers to bodhisattvas, people dedicated to enlightenment for all.

FIVE CLUSTERS: According to the Buddhist description, these are basic components, or classes of components, of the body-mind.

STREAM-ENTERER, ONCE-RETURNER, NONRETURNER, SAINT: These are four stages of fruition of the way to nirvana—a stream-enterer is one who has begun to be disentangled from the world; a once-returner is one who comes back to the mundane once before attaining release; a nonreturner never comes back; a saint is one who has reached nirvana and is individually emancipated.

SUFFERING, ACCUMULATION, EXTINCTION, PATH TO EXTINCTION: These are the "four noble truths," or four main axioms, of pristine Buddhism—there is suffering, suffering has a cause, there is an end to suffering, and there is a way to end suffering.

TWELVE SENSE MEDIA: This refers to the sense faculties (eye, ear, nose, tongue, body, and mind) and their respective fields of data (form/color, sound, odor, flavor, tactile feelings, and phenomena).

The Issue at Hand
(Genjōkōan)

The term *genjōkōan* seems to appear first in ninth-century China and is often used in Japanese Sōtō Zen to refer to present being as the topic of meditation or the issue of Zen. *Gen* means "manifestation" or "present," *jō* means "become." *Genjō* means actuality—being as is, at hand, or accomplished, as of an accomplished fact. *Kōan* is a common Zen word which is often left untranslated, having to some extent become a naturalized English word. *Kō* means official, public, or open, as opposed to private or personal; *an* means a consideration, or a considered decision. A *kōan* in standard literary Chinese means an official report or an issue under consideration. The term was adopted in Zen with much the same meanings, only transported into the frame of reference of Zen tradition and experience.

Genjōkōan is one of the most popular and oft-quoted essays in *Shobōgenzō*. Written to a lay disciple, it contains a number of key points stated in a most concise fashion. The very first paragraph contains a complete outline of Zen, in a covert presentation of the so-called "five ranks" (*go i*) device of the original Chinese Sōtō Zen school. The scheme of the five ranks—relative within absolute, absolute within relative, coming from within the absolute, arriving in the relative, and simultaneous attainment in both relative and absolute—is not overtly used in Dōgen's work, perhaps because of the confusion surrounding it, but its structures are to be found throughout *Shōbōgenzō*.

Following this summary introduction, the essay proceeds to the discussion of enlightenment. Dōgen says the way to enlightenment is to forget the self. The self in this sense refers to an accumulation of habits, including the habit of attachment to this accumulation as a genuine personality. Dōgen calls this forgetting "shedding body and mind," an expression which is said to have galvanized his awareness as a young man and which he repeatedly uses to describe Zen study.

Commentators on Dōgen's lectures describe it in these terms: "Each moment of time is thoughtless; things do not provoke a second thought," and "This is the time when the whole mind and body attains great freedom."

This, however, is not the whole issue. In one of his lectures Dōgen says that "shedding body and mind" is the beginning of the effort, and in *Genjōkōan* he affirms that there is continuing progress in buddhahood, going beyond the attainment of enlightenment: "There is ceasing the traces of enlightenment, which causes one to forever leave the traces of enlightenment which is cessation." In the *Hokke* scripture Buddha reveals to his liberated disciples that nirvana, cessation of afflictive habits, which had been expediently represented as the goal, is as it were a resting place on an infinite path.

In the essay *The Business of Progress (or transcendence) of Buddha,* also in *Shōbōgenzō,* Dōgen wrote, "To go on informing the Buddha of today it is not only today is called the business of progress of Buddha." The celebrated Zen master Hakuin said, "Without cultivation and practice after enlightenment, many who have seen the essence miss the boat"; and Hakuin's assistant Tōrei said, "Lesser enlightenment turns out to be a hindrance to great enlightenment. If you give up lesser enlightenments and don't cling to them, great enlightenment will surely be realized." Dōgen says that there are differences in depth and breadth of the realization of enlightenment, and speaks here of enlightenment as being enlightened by all things. This leads to the issue of perspective.

Dōen states that delusion is a matter of experiencing things with the burden of the self—the bundle of mental habits, ingrained views, which is identified with the self. This is a basic issue of all Buddhist thought. The condition of the self, with its set of conditioned perceptions and views, is implicitly taken as a kind of absolute or veritable point of reference, if one takes one's experience as conceived to be reality. In order to overcome hidden prejudice in the form of unquestioned views, Dōgen says that introspection is necessary, to see that things have no absolute identity, that they are not necessarily or totally as one may view them.

But then Dōgen goes on to point out the absoluteness, so to speak, of relative identity. Logically, if particular things exist, or are defined, relative to one another and therefore lack absolute identity, yet that absolute identitylessness still depends on their relative identity. The approach Dōgen takes, however, is not that of deduction but of direct witness (*genryō*), which he refers to, in classic Zen terminology, as the realms of before and after being disconnected. Thus Dōgen explains the traditional "characteristics of emptiness" called birthlessness and nonperishing in terms of the noncoexistence of before and after, or the nonconcurrence of a state with its own nonexistence. Dōgen's emphasis here seems to be not on discursive understanding of this point of logic, but on presence of mind in the most thoroughgoing sense, direct experience of the present.

Dōgen also speaks of enlightenment in terms of the universal being reflected in the individual; this "merging" of universe and individual does not, however, obliterate the individual or restrict the universal. This leads to the apparent paradox of life being at once finite and infinite. One life, or one sphere of experience, contains everything that is within its scope and nothing that is beyond its range. At every moment we reach, or are at, the full extent of our experience; and yet this never limits the potential of experience in itself. Each moment is complete, hence infinite, in itself, though it be finite as a point of comparison with past or future. In the Kegon philosophy, this interpenetration of the finite and the infinite is represented by the figure of "arriving in one step," each moment of awareness being the focal point of the whole nexus of existence. Again Dōgen drives at the full experience of the present without conceptually delineating it.

Finally Dōgen quotes a classic Zen story alluding to the necessity of practical application even though truth, or enlightenment, is inherent in everyone. A monk asks his teacher why he uses a fan if the nature of wind is eternal and omnipresent; the teacher replies that the student knows the nature of eternity but not the principle of omnipresence, and to illustrate this principle the teacher just fans himself. As one of the Kegon philosophers said, "If not for practice flowing from reality, there is no means to merge with reality."

The Issue at Hand

When all things are Buddha-teachings, then there is delusion and enlightenment, there is cultivation of practice, there is birth, there is death, there are Buddhas, there are sentient beings. When myriad things are all not self, there is no delusion, no enlightenment, no Buddhas, no sentient beings, no birth, no death. Because the Buddha Way originally sprang forth from abundance and paucity, there is birth and death, delusion and enlightenment, sentient beings and Buddhas. Moreover, though this is so, flowers fall when we cling to them, and weeds only grow when we dislike them.

Acting on and witnessing myriad things with the burden of oneself is "delusion." Acting on and witnessing oneself in the advent of myriad things is enlightenment. Great enlightenment about delusion is Buddhas; great delusion about enlightenment in sentient beings. There are also those who attain enlightenment on top of enlightenment, and there are those who are further deluded in the midst of delusion. When the Buddhas are indeed the Buddhas, there is no need to be self-conscious of being Buddhas; nevertheless it is realizing buddhahood—Buddhas go on realizing.

In seeing forms with the whole body-mind, hearing sound with the whole body-mind, though one intimately understands, it isn't like reflecting images in a mirror, it's not like water and the moon—when you witness one side, one side is obscure.

Studying the Buddha Way is studying oneself. Studying oneself is forgetting oneself. Forgetting oneself is being enlightened by all things. Being enlightened by all things is causing the body-mind of oneself and the body-mind of others to be shed. There is ceasing the traces of enlightenment, which causes one to forever leave the traces of enlightenment which is cessation.

When people first seek the Teaching, they are far from the bounds of the Teaching. Once the Teaching is properly conveyed in oneself, already one is the original human being.

When someone rides in a boat, as he looks at the shore he has the illusion that the shore is moving. When he looks at the boat under him, he realizes the boat is moving. In the same way, when one takes things for granted with confused ideas of body-mind, one has the illusion that one's own mind and own nature are permanent; but if one pays close attention to one's own actions, the truth that things are not self will be clear.

Kindling becomes ash, and cannot become kindling again. However, we should not see the ash as after and the kindling as before. Know that kindling abides in the normative state of kindling, and though it has a before and after, the realms of before and after are disconnected. Ash, in the normative state of ash, has before and after. Just as that kindling, after having become ash, does not again become kindling, so after dying a person does not become alive again. This being the case, not saying that life becomes death is an established custom in Buddhism—therefore it is called *unborn*. That death does not become life is an established teaching of the Buddha; therefore we say *imperishable*. Life is an individual temporal state, death is an individual temporal state. It is like winter and spring—we don't think winter becomes spring, we don't say spring becomes summer.

People's attaining enlightenment is like the moon reflected in water. The moon does not get wet, the water isn't broken. Though it is a vast expansive light, it rests in a little bit of water—even the whole moon, the whole sky, rests in a dewdrop on the grass, rests in even a single droplet of water. That enlightenment does not shatter people is like the moon not piercing the water. People's not obstructing enlightenment is like the drop of dew not obstructing the moon in the sky. The depth is proportionate to the height. As for the length and brevity of time, examining the great and small bodies of water, you should discern the breadth and narrowness of the moon in the sky.

Before one has studied the Teaching fully in body and mind, one feels one is already sufficient in the Teaching. If the body and mind are replete with the Teaching, in one respect one senses insufficiency. For example, when one rides a boat out onto the ocean where there are no mountains and looks around, it only appears round, and one can see no other, different characteristics. However, this ocean is not round, nor is it square—the remaining qualities of the ocean are inexhaustible. It is like a palace, it is like ornaments, yet as far as our eyes can see, it only seems round. It is the same with all things—in the realms of matter, beyond conceptualization, they include many aspects, but we see and comprehend only what the power of our eye of contemplative study reaches. If we inquire into the "family ways" of myriad things, the qualities of seas and mountains, beyond seeming square or round, are endlessly numerous. We should realize there exist worlds everywhere. It's not only thus in out of the way places—know that even a single drop right before us is also thus.

As a fish travels through water, there is no bound to the water no matter how far it goes; as a bird flies through the sky, there's no bound to the sky no matter how far it flies. While this is so, the fish and birds have never been apart from the water and the sky—it's just that when the need is large the use is large, and when the requirement is small the use is small. In this way, though the bounds are unfailingly reached everywhere and tread upon in every single place, the bird would instantly die if it left the sky and the fish would instantly

die if it left the water. Obviously, water is life; obviously the sky is
life. There is bird being life. There is fish being life. There is life being
bird, there is life being fish. There must be progress beyond this—
there is cultivation and realization, the existence of the living one
being like this. Under these circumstances, if there were birds or fish
who attempted to traverse the waters or the sky after having found
the limits of the water or sky, they wouldn't find a path in the water
or the sky—they won't find any place. When one finds this place, this
action accordingly manifests as the issue at hand; when one finds this
path, this action accordingly manifests as the issue at hand. This
path, this place, is not big or small, not self or other, not preexistent,
not now appearing—therefore it exists in this way. In this way, if
someone cultivates and realizes the Buddha Way, it is *attaining a
principle, mastering the principle;* it is *encountering a practice, cultivating the practice.* In this there is a place where the path has been
accomplished, hence the unknowability of the known boundary is
born together and studies along with the thorough investigation of
the Buddha Teaching of this knowing—therefore it is thus. Don't get
the idea that the attainment necessarily becomes one's own knowledge and view, that it would be known by discursive knowledge.
Though realizational comprehension already takes place, implicit
being is not necessarily obvious—*why necessarily* is there obvious
becoming?

Zen Master Hōtetsu of Mt. Mayoku was using a fan. A monk asked
him about this: "The nature of wind is eternal and all-pervasive—
why then do you use a fan?" The master said, "You only know the
nature of wind is eternal, but do not yet know the principle of its
omnipresence." The monk asked, "What is the principle of its omnipresence?" The master just fanned. The monk bowed.

The experience of the Buddha Teaching, the living road of right
transmission, is like this. To say that since (the nature of wind) is
permanent one should not use a fan, and that one should feel the
breeze even when not using a fan, is not knowing permanence and
not knowing the nature of the wind either. Because the nature of
wind is eternal, the wind of Buddhism causes the manifestation of
the earth's being gold and by participation develops the long river
into butter.

1233

The Nature of Things
(Hosshō)

The *nature of things* is a fundamental term of Mahayana Buddhism. It is defined as being the nature of *thusness, emptiness,* and *nirvana.* In pristine Buddhism, nirvana, or "extinction," refers to the attainment of dispassion, peace of mind, freedom from anxiety and mental afflictions. In Mahayana Buddhism, nirvana is commonly used in reference to things, with the meaning of "emptiness." In terms of the person, nirvana refers to the extinction of false description, of fixed views; this results in awareness of the "empty" or "open" nature of things. Emptiness means that things in themselves are indefinable; being dependent on relations, things are said to have no individual or absolute nature of their own. It is this nonabsoluteness which is called emptiness. Another way of expressing it is in terms of inconceivability. The descriptions by which things are defined, and even the experience of things, depend on the mind, and are not the supposed things in themselves. Thus the nature of things in themselves is said to be inconceivable, beyond description, or "empty."

Yet this "emptiness" has no existence of its own either, since it is nothing but the nature of things as relative and identityless. That is to say, the emptiness of things and the relative existence of things are not antithetical but identical in essence. The term *thusness* embraces both of these aspects of reality—the relative existence of things and the emptiness of absolute existence of particular things. These two perspectives are referred to as two facets of thusness—that which is unchanging (absolute emptiness) and that which accords with conditions (relative existence). The term *thusness* itself alludes to the simultaneous realization of emptiness and existence, experiencing directly and openly without fixed conceptual glosses, seeing everything as being simply "thus."

This essay by Dōgen clearly aims at countering the mistaken notion that the nature of things *qua* emptiness is opposed to or exclu-sive of the appearance of things, or relative existence. This erroneous notion posits the obliteration of appearances as the means of realizing the nature of things, something which Dōgen opposes throughout his works. Rather than trying to obliterate anything, Dōgen aims at breaking through the barrier of conception to realize the nature of things in everything, to realize the nature of things *is* everything.

The Nature of Things

In meditation study, whether following scripture or following a teacher, one *becomes enlightened alone without a teacher.* Becoming *enlightened alone without a teacher* is the activity of the nature of things. Even though one can be *born knowing,* one should seek a teacher to inquire about the Path. Even in the case of *knowledge of the birthless*[1] one should definitely direct effort to mastering the Path. Which individuals are not *born knowing?* Even up to enlighten-ment, the fruit of buddhahood, it is a matter of following scriptures and teachers. Know that encountering a scripture or a teacher and attaining *absorption in the nature of things* is called the *born know-ing* that attains *absorption in the nature of things* on encountering *absorption in the nature of things.* This is attaining knowledge of past lives, attaining the three superknowledges,[2] realizing unexcelled enlightenment, encountering inborn knowledge and learning inborn knowledge, encountering teacherless knowledge and spontaneous knowledge and correctly conveying teacherless knowledge and spon-taneous knowledge.

If one were not *born knowing,* even though might encounter scrip-tures and teachers one could not hear of the *nature of things,* one could not witness the *nature of things.* The *Great Path* is not the principle of *like someone drinking water knows for himself whether it's warm or cool.* All Buddhas as well as all bodhisattvas and all liv-ing beings clarify the Great Path of the nature of all things by the power of inborn knowledge. To clarify the *Great Path* of the *nature of things* following scriptures or teachers is called clarifying the *na-ture of things* by oneself. Scriptures are the nature of things, are one-

SHŌBŌGENZŌ: ZEN ESSAYS BY DŌGEN 283

self. Teachers are the *nature of things*, are oneself. The *nature of things* is the teacher, the *nature of things* is oneself. Because the *nature of things* is oneself, it is not the self misconceived by heretics and demons. In the *nature of things* there are no heretics or demons—it is only *eating breakfast, eating lunch, having a snack.* Even so, those who claim to have studied for a long time, for twenty or thirty years, pass their whole life in a daze when they read or hear talk of the *nature of things.* Those who claim to have fulfilled Zen study and assume the rank of teacher, while they hear the voice of the *nature of things* and see the forms of the *nature of things,* yet their body and mind, objective and subjective experience, always just rise and fall in the pit of confusion. What this is like is wrongly thinking that the *nature of things* will appear when the whole world we perceive is obliterated, that the *nature of things* is not the present totality of phenomena. The principle of the *nature of things* cannot be like this. This *totality of phenomena* and the *nature of things* are far beyond any question of sameness or difference, beyond talk of distinction or identity. It is not past, present, or future, not annihilation or eternity, not form, sensation, conception, conditioning, or consciousness—therefore it is the *nature of things.*

Zen Master Baso said, "All living beings, for infinite eons, have never left absorption in the nature of things: they are always within absorption in the nature of things, wearing clothes, eating, conversing—the functions of the six sense organs, and all activities, all are the nature of things."

The *nature of things* spoken of by Baso is the *nature of things* spoken of by the *nature of things.* It learns from the same source as Baso, is a fellow student of the *nature of things:* since hearing of it takes place, how could there not be speaking of it? The fact is that *the nature of things rides Baso;* it is *people eat food, food eats people.* Ever since the *nature of things,* it has never left *absorption in the nature of things.* It doesn't leave the *nature of things* after the *nature of things,* it doesn't leave the *nature of things* before the *nature of things.* The *nature of things,* along with *infinite eons,* is *absorption in the nature of things;* the *nature of things* is called *infinite eons.* Therefore the *here* of the immediate present is the *nature of things;* the *nature of things* is the *here* of the immediate present. *Wearing clothes and eating food is the wearing clothes and eating food of absorption in the nature of things.* It is the manifestation of the *na-*

ture of things of food, it is the manifestation of the *nature of things* of eating, it is the manifestation of the *nature of things* of clothing, it is the manifestation of the *nature of things* of wearing.³ If one does not dress or eat, does not talk or answer, does not use the senses, does not act at all, it is not the *nature of things*, is is *not entering the nature of things*.

The manifestation of the Path of the immediate present was transmitted by the Buddhas, reaching Shakyamuni Buddha; correctly conveyed by the Zen adepts, it reached Baso. Buddha to Buddha, adept to adept, correctly conveyed and handed on, it has been correctly communicated in *absorption in the nature of things*. Buddhas and Zen adepts, *not entering*, enliven the *nature of things*.⁴ Though externalist scholars may have the term *nature of things*, it is not the *nature of things* spoken of by Baso. Though the power to propose that *living beings* who *don't leave the nature of things* are not the *nature of things* may achieve something, this is three or four new layers of the *nature of things*. To speak, reply, function, and act as if it were not the *nature of things* must be the *nature of things*. The days and months of *infinite eons* are the passage of the *nature of things*. The same is so of past, present, and future. If you take the limit of body and mind as the limit of body and mind and think it is far from the *nature of things*, this thinking still is the *nature of things*. If you don't consider the limit of body and mind as the limit of body and mind and think it is not the *nature of beings*, this thought too is the *nature of things*. Thinking and not thinking are both the *nature of things*. To learn that since we have said *nature* (it means that) water must not flow and trees must not bloom and wither, is heretical.

Shakyamuni Buddha said, "Such characteristics, such nature." So *flowers blooming* and *leaves falling* are *such nature*. Yet ignorant people think that there could not be *flowers blooming and leaves falling* in the realm of the *nature of things*. For the time being one should not question another. You should model your doubt on verbal expression. Bringing it up as others have said it, you should investigate it over and over again—there will be escape from before.⁵ The aforementioned thoughts are not wrong thinking, they are just thoughts while not yet having understood. It is not that this thinking will be caused to disappear when one understands. Flowers blooming and leaves falling are of themselves flowers blooming and leaves falling. The thinking that is thought that there can't be flowers blooming or leaves falling in the *nature of things* is the *nature of things*. It is thought which has fallen out according to a pattern; therefore it is thought of the *nature of things*. The whole thinking of thinking of the *nature of things* is such an appearance.

Although Baso's statement *all is the nature of things* is truly an *eighty or ninety percent* statement, there are many points which Baso has not expressed. That is to say, he doesn't say *the natures of all things do not leave the nature of things*,[6] he doesn't say *the natures of all things are all the nature of things*.[6] He doesn't say *all living beings do not leave living beings*,[7] he doesn't say *all living beings are a little bit of the nature of things*, he doesn't say *all living beings are a little bit of all living beings*,[8] he doesn't say *the natures of all things are a little bit of living beings*.[9] He doesn't say *half a living being is half the nature of things*.[10] He doesn't say *nonexistence of living beings is the nature of things*,[11] he doesn't say *the nature of things is not living beings*,[11] he doesn't say *the nature of things exudes the nature of things*, he doesn't say *living beings shed living beings*. We only hear that living beings do not leave absorption in the nature of things—he doesn't say that the nature of things cannot leave absorption in living beings, there is no statement of absorption in the nature of things exiting and entering absorption in living beings. Needless to say, we don't hear of the attainment of buddhahood of the *nature of things*, we don't hear *living beings realize the nature of things*, we don't hear *the nature of things* realizes the nature of things, there is no statement of how *inanimate beings don't leave the nature of things*. Now one should ask Baso, what do you call "living beings"? If you call the *nature of things* living beings, it is *what thing comes thus?* If you call living beings living beings, it is *if you speak of it as something, you miss it*. Speak quickly, speak quickly!

1243

Notes

1. "The birthless" means emptiness, also immediate experience without comparison of before and after. This line could read "Even if one be without inborn knowledge . . . ," but in Buddhism the term conventionally refers to knowledge of the uncreated.

2. The three superknowledges are paranormal perceptions of saints and

Buddhas: knowledge of the features of birth and death of beings in the past, knowledge of the features of birth and death of beings in the future, and knowledge of extinguishing mental contaminations. In Zen all three are sometimes interpreted in reference to insight into the fundamental mind, which is in essence the same in all times and has no inherent contamination.

3. Var, lect. "Clothing is the manifestation of the nature of things, food is the manifestation of the nature of things, eating is the manifestation of the nature of things, wearing is the manifestation of the nature of things."

4. Here "not entering" means that the nature of things is not something external to be entered; rather it is something ominpresent to be lived.

5. This passage seems to point to *kōan* practice, specifically the use of *kosoku kōan* or ancient model *kōan*, Zen sayings or stories used to focus awareness in certain ways. "There will be escape from before" refers to the shedding of former views or states of mind.

6. The (individual) natures of things are not apart from the (universal) nature of things, because individual natures are relative, hence empty of absolute identity—this emptiness itself is the universal nature of things.

7. Living beings *qua* living beings—that is, in terms of relative identity or conditional existence—are always such, by definition.

8. "All living beings" as seen from one point of view (such as that of human perception) are a small part of "all living beings" as seen or experienced from all possible points of reference. This is reminiscent of the Kegon teaching of the infinite interreflection of interdependent existences, and the Tendai teaching of all realms of being mutually containing one another. According to the Tendai doctrine, the totality of living beings is defined in terms of ten realms or universes, but as each contains the potential of all the others, this makes one hundred realms. The Kegon doctrine takes this further and says that each of the latent or potential realms in each realm also contains the latent potential of every other realm, so they are, in terms of their endless interrelation, multiplied and remultiplied infinitely.

9. In terms of the doctrine of the interdependence of everything in the cosmos, as exemplified by the Kegon teaching, all things are a part of the existence of each and every thing and being.

10. Essence (emptiness of absolute identity) and characteristics (existence of relative identity) may be likened to two "halves" of the totality of all existence and the nature of things.

11. "Nonexistence of living beings" as emptiness of an absolute nature of "living beings" is the nature of things *qua* emptiness.

THE WHOLE WORKS
(Zenki)

This essay is strongly reminiscent of the central teaching of the philosophy of the Kegon school: interdependent origination, and its corollaries dealing with the interpenetration of existence and emptiness, unity and multiplicity.

The word *zenki* consists of two elements: *zen* means "whole" or total or complete; *ki* has many meanings, those relevent to this case including "works" in the sense of machinery, potential, impetus, pivot or vital point, and the flux of nature. *Ki* therefore refers to phenomena in respect to their dynamic aspect, and to the dynamic or vital point itself which underlies, and is revealed by, the active coexistence of phenomena. In Kegon terms, *ki* includes both senses of phenomena and principle, phenomena being interdependent things, the principle being that of interdependence itself. *Zen* refers to the inclusiveness and pervasiveness of *ki* in both senses. We translate *zenki* as "the whole works" to convey by the colloquial sense of this expression the notion of inclusion of the totality of existence, and by the standard sense the notion of the total dynamic underlying the manifestations of existence.

In the Zen classic *Blue Cliff Record*, the sixty-first case says, "If a single atom is set up, the nation flourishes; if a single atom is not set up, the nation perishes." This essay of Dōgen's may be said to center around a restatement of this theme: "In life the whole works is manifest; in death the whole works is manifest," or, to render the same passage another way, "Life is the manifestation of the whole works; death too is the manifestation of the whole works."

In terms of the existence-emptiness equation, from the point of view of existence (represented by the terms "set up" and "life") all that is exists, while from the point of view of emptiness ("not set up," "death") all is empty. The concurrence of existence and emptiness is not as separate entities, but as different aspects or perspectives on the same totality. To borrow Kegon terms again, life as the manifestation of the whole works illustrates *ki* as phenomena, while death as the manifestation of the whole works illustrates *ki* as nounemon.

The passage from the *Blue Cliff Record* alludes to the Kegon doctrine that phenomena do not exist individually but interdependently, that the manifold depends on the unit and the unit on the manifold. A refinement of this principle in Kegon philosophy is called the mystery of principal and satellites: this means that every element in a conditional nexus can be looked upon as the hub, or "principal," whereupon all the other elements become the cooperative conditions, or "satellites"—hence all elements are at once "principal" and "satellite" to all other elements. It is the mutuality, the complementarity, of the elements which makes them functionally what they are. Dōgen presents this idea by likening life to riding in a boat—one is naught without the boat, yet it is one's riding in it that makes it in effect a "boat." Furthermore, "the boat is the world—even the sky, the water, and the shore are circumstances of the boat. . . . The whole earth and all of space are workings of the boat."

The distinction of existence and emptiness, the noncontradiction and mutual interpenetration of existence and emptiness, and thereby the transcendence of existence and emptiness—these are traditional steps of Mahayana Buddhist dialectic. In this essay they are presented by Dōgen in his subtle, almost covert way, evidently to induce the reader to search out these insights by personal contemplation. The ultimate vision of totality, in which the whole and the individuals foster one another—the crown of Kegon Buddhist metaphysics—is one of the fundamental themes of Dōgen's philosophical writings, to be met with time and again in various guises. In this essay it is conveyed in a most succinct manner, worthy of representing Zen Buddhist philosophy.

THE WHOLE WORKS

The Great Path of the Buddhas, in its consummation, is passage to freedom, is actualization. That passage to freedom, in one sense, is that life passes through life to freedom, and death too passes through death to freedom. Therefore, there is leaving life and death, there is entering life and death; both are the Great Path of consummation. There is abandoning life and death, there is crossing over life and death; both are the Great Path of consummation.

Actualization is life, life is actualization. When that actualization is taking place, it is without exception the complete actualization of life, it is the complete actualization of death. This pivotal working can cause life and cause death. At the precise moment of the actualization of this working, it is not necessarily great, not necessarily small, not all-pervasive, not limited, not extensive, not brief.

The present life is in this working, this working is in the present life. Life is not coming, not going, not present, not becoming. Nevertheless, life is the manifestation of the whole works, death is the manifestation of the whole works. Know that among the infinite things in oneself, there is life and there is death. One should calmly think: is this present life, along with the myriad things concomitant with life, together with life or not? There is nothing at all, not so much as one time or one phenomenon, that is not together with life. Even be it a single thing, a single mind, none is not together with life.

Life is like when one rides in a boat: though in this boat one works the sail, the rudder, and the pole, the boat carries one, and one is naught without the boat. Riding in the boat, one even causes the boat to be a boat. One should meditate on this precise point. At this very moment, the boat is the world—even the sky, the water, and the shore all have become circumstances of the boat, unlike circumstances which are not the boat. For this reason life is our causing to live; it is life's causing us to be ourselves. When riding in a boat, the mind and body, object and subject, are all workings of the boat; the whole earth and all of space are both workings of the boat. We that are life, life that is we, are the same way.

Zen Master Engo Kokugon said, "In life the whole works appears; in death the whole works appears." One should thoroughly investigate and understand this saying. What thorough investigation means is that the principle of *in the whole works appears* has nothing to do with beginning and end; though it is the whole earth and all space, not only does it not block *the appearance of the whole works in life*, it doesn't block *the appearance of the whole works in death* either. When *the whole works appears in death*, though it is the whole earth and all space, not only does it not block *the appearance of the whole works in death*, it doesn't block *the appearance of the whole works in life* either. For this reason, life doesn't obstruct death, death doesn't obstruct life. The whole earth and all space are in life and in death too. However, it is not fulfilling the potential of one whole earth and one whole space in life and fulfilling their potential in death too. Though they are not one, they are not different; though they are not different, they are not identical; though they are not identical, they are not multiple. Therefore, in life there are myriad phenomena of the appearance of the whole works, and in death too there are myriad phenomena of the apperance of the whole works. There is also the manifestation of the whole works in what is neither life nor death.

In the manifestation of the whole works there is life and there is death. Therefore, the whole works of life and death must be like a man bending and straightening his arm. Herein there are so many spiritual powers and lights which are manifest. At the moment of manifestation, because it is completely activated by manifestation, one sees and understands that there is no manifestation before manifestation. However, prior to this manifestation is previous manifestation of the whole works. Although there is previous manifestation of the whole works, it is does not block the present manifestation of the whole works. For this reason, such a vision and understanding vigorously appears.

1242

SUCH
(Immo)

This essay begins with a saying of an ancient master: "To attain such a thing, you must be such a person; since you are such a person, why trouble about such a thing?" This is an extract from a longer speech describing the Zen adept, in the course of which the master said, "One who has comprehended has a mind like a fan in winter, has a mouth growing moldy (from disuse). This is not something you force—it is naturally so. If you want to attain such a thing, you must be such a person. Since (or, Once) you are such a person, why trouble about such a thing?"

The word used here for "such," *immo* in Sino-Japanese, is a colloquial word which is equivalent to a classical word used in Buddhism for the term *thusness,* being-as-is, the all-inclusive reality. A lesson that might be drawn from this saying is that thusness, or *suchness,* is arrived at by merging with it; it is not something obtained externally—since you are *thus,* or once you realize you are *thus,* why worry about *thusness* as something to attain? This is basic Zen teaching. That which obstructs the consciousness from realizing oneness with *thusness* is arbitrary conception and false description projected by the mind; hence the saying that one who comprehends has a mind (unused) like a fan in winter and a mouth growing mold (from disuse) might be interpreted as meaning realization of thusness is a matter of not obscuring it by mental construction and fixed labels. Cessation of compulsive mental habits and silencing of the mind are a means of accomplishing this.

Dōgen returns to this theme of being *such* or *thus* throughout the essay. He illustrates the fundamental and all-embracing nature of suchness by the traditional saying "If one falls on the ground, one must rise from the ground." Understanding suchness as the "ground" of being leads to the insight that both illusion and enlightenment are

based on this ground and have no existence apart from it. In characteristic fashion, Dōgen proceeds to vary this statement, now using
the metaphor of "sky" for emptiness and "ground" for existence, to
illustrate the countering of one-sided clinging.

Subsequently Dōgen brings up two stories from the lore of the Zen
patriarchs which appear to say that the events of the environment are
objectifications of mind. This is a familiar Buddhist concept, but here
Dōgen aims at doing away with the misinterpretation that the world
of sense exists because of mind or is in the mind. What Dōgen indicates is that, to use a classic statement, while things are empty in
themselves, yet they exist inconceivably; the product of the mind
is not things in themselves but the subjective description. It is this
description which separates subject and object and interferes with
pure awareness of being as *such*. The essay concludes with two Zen
stories illustrating the inapplicability of concepts—even that of
"suchness"—to *suchness* as it really is, and two aspects of Zen
"method"—nongrasping and observation without conceptualization.

SUCH

Master Ungo was the heir of Tōzan, a thirty-ninth generation religious descendant of Shakyamuni Buddha, and a principal ancestor of
the Tōzan school. One day he said to the congregation, "If you want
to attain such a thing, you must be such a person. Since you are such
a person, why trouble about such a thing?" That is to say, to consider
attaining *such a thing*, one must be *such a person*; already being *such
a person*, why trouble about *such a thing?* The basic message of this
is *directly proceeding toward unexcelled enlightenment* is for the
moment called *such*. As for what this unexcelled enlightenment is
like, even *all worlds in the ten directions* are a little bit of unexcelled
enlightenment; the extent of enlightenment must be even more than
all worlds. We too are all equipment within those worlds of the ten
directions.

Whereby do we know *suchness* exists? It is as if to say body and
mind together appear in the whole world, and because they are not

self, we know they are *thus.* Since the body is not oneself, life is borne along by the passage of time, hardly to be kept for even a moment. Rosy cheeks have gone away somewhere—as they vanish, there are no trances. When we look carefully, there are many things gone which we can never see again. The red heart doesn't stay either—it comes and goes bit by bit. Though we might say there is truth, it is not something that lingers in the region of ego and self.

There are those who, being *such,* are inspired spontaneously. Once this inspiration occurs, they give up what they had hitherto been fascinated with, hope to learn what they haven't yet learned, and seek to realize what they haven't realized—this is totally not the doing of the self. Know that one is thus because one is *such a person.* How do we know one is *such a person?* We know one is *such a person* because one wants to attain *such a thing.* Since one has the face of *such a person,* one shouldn't trouble about this *such a thing.* Because troubling too is *such a thing,* it is not trouble. Also one should not be surprised at *such a thing's* being *such.* Even if there is *suchness* which seems strange, this too is *such*—there is the *suchness* of "one should not be surprised." This is not to be measured simply by the measure of Buddha, it is not to be measured by the measure of mind, it is not to be measured by the measure of the realm of pehnomena and principles, it is not to be measured by the measure of the whole world—it can only be *since you are such a person, why trouble about such a thing?*

Therefore, the *suchness* of sound and form must be *such;* the *suchness* of body and mind must be *such;* the *suchness* of the Buddhas must be *such.* For example, in *understanding of such* the time of *falling on the ground* as being *such,* at one time of the *suchness* of *necessarily rising from the ground,* one does not think *falling on the ground* strange. There is a statement that has been made from antiquity, that has been made from India, that has been made from heaven: *if one falls on the ground, one rises from the ground; there is no way to rise apart from the ground.* What this is saying is that one who falls on the ground must get up from the ground, and cannot hope to rise except by way of the ground. It has been considered excellent to become greatly enlightened when this is brought up, and considered a path to liberate body and mind as well. Therefore, if one asks what the principle of enlightenment of the Buddhas is, it is said to be like someone fallen on the ground rising from the ground. One should investigate this and pass through the past to freedom, should pass through the future to freedom, should pass through the present *suchness* to freedom.

Greatly enlightened, not becoming enlightened, returning to delusion, losing delusion, being blocked by enlightenment, being blocked by delusion are all the principle of one fallen on the ground rising from the ground. This is a saying of heaven and earth, of India and China, of past, present, and future, of ancient Buddhas and new Buddhas. This saying has left nothing unsaid, it has no lack. However, if one only understands *so* and has no understanding of *not so*, it is as though one has not thoroughly investigated this saying.

Even though the saying of the ancient Buddhas has come down *thus*, if one would go on to hear the ancient Buddhas' saying as an ancient Buddha, one must have hearing beyond this. Though it hasn't been said in India or in the heavens, there is a further principle to express. That is, if one fallen to the ground tries to arise from the ground, one can never ever rise. In truth, one manages to arise from a *living road.* That is to say, one fallen to the ground must arise from the sky, and one fallen to the sky must arise from the ground. Otherwise one can never get up. All the Buddhas and Zen adepts were thus. If someone were to ask thus: "How far apart are sky and ground?" Thus asked, I would answer thus: sky and ground are one hundred and eight thousand miles apart.[1] *If one falls to the ground, one must arise from the sky; if one tries to arise apart from the sky, there will never be a way. If one falls to the sky one must arise from the ground; if one tries to arise apart from the ground, there will never be a way.* If one has not yet expressed it in this way, one does not yet know, does not yet see the measure of the *ground* and *sky* spoken of by Buddha.

The seventeenth-generation ancestral teacher of Buddhism was the honorable Sanghanandi; his religious successor was Gayashata. Once, hearing the chimes hung in a chamber ring when blown by the wind, he asked Gayashata, "Would you say the wind is ringing or the chimes ringing?" Gayashata said, "It is not the wind ringing or are the chimes ringing; it is my mind ringing." Sanghanandi said, "And what is the mind?" Gayashata said, "Both are silent." Sanghanandi said, "Good, good! Who but you could succeed to my way?" Subsequently he imparted the *treasury of the eye of true teaching* to him.

This is studying *my mind ringing* where it is not wind ringing, and studying *my mind ringing* when it is not chimes ringing. Though *my mind ringing* is *such*, yet *both are silent*. Transmitted from India to China, from ancient times to the present day, this story has been taken as a standard for study of the Way, yet there are many who misunderstand it. It is said that Gayashata's statement that it is not the wind ringing or the chimes ringing, but the mind ringing, means that at such a moment of the hearer thought arises, and this arising of thought is called mind; if this mental thought were not there, how could the mind focus on the sound of ringing—because hearing takes place due to this thought, it should be called the basis of hearing, and so it is called mind. This is a misinterpretation, all due to not having gotten the power of a true teacher. It is like the interpretation of linguistic philosophers.[2] This kind of interpretation is not the mystic study of the Buddha Way.

What one learns from a true heir of the Buddha Way is that the *treasury of the eye of true teaching* of unexcelled enlightenment is called *silent*,[3] is called *uncreated*, is called *samādhi*,[4] is called *dhāranī*.[5] The principle is that as soon as one thing is *silent*, myriad things are *silent*. Since the wind blowing is *silent*, the chimes ringing is *silent*. This is why he said *both are silent*. He is saying the *mind ringing* is not the *wind ringing*, the *mind ringing* is not the *chimes ringing*, the *mind ringing* is not the *mind ringing*. If we would closely investigate it as *such*, we should simply say further that it is the wind ringing, it is the chimes ringing, it is the blowing ringing, it is the ringing ringing—we could also say this. Because *why trouble over such a thing*, it is not existing as *such*;[6] since it is *why be concerned with such a thing*, it is *such*.[6]

When the thirty-third ancestor of Buddhism, the sixth patriarch of Zen, was lodging in Hosshō monastery in Canton before his ordination, there were two monks arguing, one saying it is the flag moving, one saying it is the wind moving. As they argued ceaselessly back and forth like this, the patriarch said, "It is the wind moving, it is not the flag moving—it is your minds moving." The two monks immediately accepted this.

Those two monks had come from India. So in this statement the patriarch says that the wind, the flag, and the movement are all the mind. In fact, though people now here this statement, they do not know it; much less are they able to express what the patriarch said. Why do I say so? Hearing the saying *your minds are moving*, to say *you minds are moving* while trying to say *your minds are moving* is not to see the patriarch, is not to be a descendant of the teaching of the patriarch. Now as descendants of the patriarch, saying what the patriarch said, saying it with the body and limbs, hair and skin of the patriarch, we should speak thus: be *your minds moving* as it may, we should say *you are moving*. Why do I say so? Because since *that which is moving is moving,* therefore *you are you.* Because of *already being such a person* one *speaks in such a way.*

This sixth patriarch of Zen used to be a woodcutter in south China. He knew the mountains and streams thoroughly. Though he worked under the green pines and cut through the roots, how could he know of the existence of ease inside a monastery and of ancient teachings which illumine the mind? From whom did he learn self-discipline and purification? He heard a scripture being recited in the market-place—this was not something he himself anticipated, nor was it enjoined upon him by another. He lost his father as a boy, and supported his mother when he grew up. He didn't know this jewel in his clothing[7] shone through heaven and earth. Once he was suddenly enlightened, he left his mother and sought a teacher—this is rare behavior among people. For whom are gratitude and love insignificant? He gave up sentiments because he considered the truth more important. This is the principle of how if people with wisdom hear *they can immediately believe and understand.* "Wisdom" is not learned in people, it doesn't arise of itself; wisdom is communicated to wisdom, wisdom seeks wisdom. In the case of the five hundred bats,[8] wisdom spontaneously consumed their bodies and they had no more body or mind. As for the ten thousand floundering fish,[9] wisdom itself was their bodies, so even though it wasn't condition or cause, when they heard the Teaching they immediately understood. It is not a matter of coming or entering. It's like the spirit of spring meeting the spring. Wisdom is not imbued with thought, wisdom is not devoid of thought; wisdom is not mindful, wisdom is not mindless—how much less has it to do with great or small, how much less is it a question of delusion or enlightenment. What we're saying is that (the sixth patriarch of Zen) didn't know anything about Buddhism, and since he hadn't heard about it before, he didn't admire or seek it, yet nevertheless when he heard the teaching, he neglected sentiment and forgot himself, all due to the fact that the body-mind with wisdom is already not oneself. This is called being *immediately able to believe and understand.*

Who knows how many cycles of birth and death we have gone through in vain sensual toils while having this wisdom. It is like a rock containing a jewel, the jewel not knowing it is enclosed in rock, and the rock not knowing it contains a jewel. People know of it and take it—this is not anticipated or awaited by the jewel or the rock, it doesn't depend on the rock's knowledge or insight, and it is not the thought of the jewel. So it is as if in spite of the fact that the person and wisdom do not know one another, the Way is surely heard by wisdom.

There is a saying: *lacking wisdom, doubt and suspicion then is an eternal loss.* Though wisdom is not necessarily existent, and not necessarily nonexistent, there is existence which is one time's *spring pines,* there is nonexistence which is *autumn chrysanthemums.* When there is no wisdom, perfect enlightenment all becomes *doubt and suspicion,* all things are *doubt and suspicion.* At this time *eternal loss then is.* The Way which is to be heard, the principle to be realized, then are *doubt and suspicion.*

The whole world, which is not self, has no hidden place; it is *a single rail of iron ten thousand miles long* which is not anyone. Even if branches sprout *thus,* the fact is that *in the Buddha lands of the ten directions there is only the teaching of one vehicle.* Even if leaves fall *thus,* the fact is that *these phenomena abide in their normal state—the features of the world are permanent.* Because it is already such a thing, having wisdom and not having wisdom are *sun face* and *moon face.*[10]

Because he was *such a person,* the sixth patriarch of Zen too was awakened. Subsequently he went to Mt. Ōbai and paid his respects to the Zen master Daiman, who sent him down to the workers' building. When he had been pounding rice day and night for a mere eight months, one night when it was very late Daiman himself stole into the millery and asked, "Is the rice polished yet?" He said, "It's polished but not sifted." Daiman struck the mortar thrice with his staff, whereupon the sixth patriarch sifted the rice in the sieve thrice. This is called the moment of the meshing of the path of teacher and apprentice. Though one doesn't know oneself and others do not understand, the *transmission of the teaching and the robe* is indeed the *precise time* of being *such.*

Master Sekitō was asked by Yakuzan, "I have a rough knowledge of the canonical teaching of Buddhism, but I've heard that in the

South they directly point to the human mind, see its nature, and attain buddhahood—I really do not understand this, and hope you will be so compassionate as to give me some indication of it." This is a question of Yakuzan, who originally was a lecturer. He had mastered the canonical Buddhist teachings, so it seemed there was nothing further about Buddhism that was not clear to him. In ancient times, before the separate schools had arisen, just to understand the canonical teachings was considered the way of doctrinal study. Nowadays many people, being stupid, set up individual schools and assess Buddhism this way, but this is not the rule of the Buddha Way. In reply to Yakuzan's question, Sekitō said, *It cannot be grasped as such, it cannot be grasped as not such—as such or not such, it cannot be grasped at all: what about you?* This is the great master's statement for Yakuzan. Truly, because it *cannot be grasped at all, as such or not such,* therefore *it cannot be grasped as such, it cannot be grasped as not such. Such* means *thus.* It is not limited needs for the way, it is not unlimited needs for the way. *Suchness* should be studied in *nongrasping,* and *nongrasping* should be sought in *suchness.* This *suchness* and *nongrasping* are not only confined to the measure of Buddha. It is *understanding not grasping;* it is *realizing not grasping.*[11]

The sixth patriarch of Zen said to Zen Master Daie of Nangaku, *What thing comes thus?* This saying is because *thus* is nondoubting, is nonunderstanding. Because it is *what thing is it,* myriad things must be investigated as being *what thing;* one thing must be investigated as being *what thing. What thing* is not doubting—it is *thus come.*

1242

Notes

1. 108,000 stands for all delusions or attachments: "sky" and "earth," or emptiness and existence, are in essence identical, and what stands between them, or what blocks realization of their unity, are subjective delusions or attachments to appearances.

2. Literally "the teachers" of 'relying on the principal' and 'association' "—these expressions refer to two kinds of Sanskrit compounds, *avyayībhāva* (indeclinable) and *tatpuruṣa* (determinative). The latter is described in Chinese as establishing the name of the dependent element based on the depended-upon element; the former is defined as establishing a name based on the dominant associated element.

3. "Silent" means "empty," referring to emptiness of absolute existence.

4. *Samādhi* means mental concentration or absorption, but in Zen literature it is often used loosely to refer to a spiritual state or realization.

5. A *dhāraṇī* is a mystical incantation in which teachings are concentrated; in Zen literature this term is sometimes used loosely to refer to spiritual realization.

6. It doesn't "exist" as such as an external thing to grasp—yet there would be no experience in the case of total nonexistence, so it must be *such.*

7. A metaphor for inherent Buddha-potential, from the *Hokke* scripture. While a traveler is intoxicated, a benefactor sews a priceless jewel in his robe. The traveler, unaware of the jewel, goes to another country and ekes out a living, suffering much hardship. Later he again meets his benefactor, who calls his attention to the jewel in his robe.

8. Five hundred bats were living in a tree. A group of traveling merchants stopped there and their campfire spread to the tree. Even while the tree they lived in burned, the bats did not flee but remained there to listen to one of the people reciting holy writ, and were consumed in the flames. Because of this the bats were reborn as humans and became sages.

9. As ten thousand fish were about to die in a dried-up lake, someone gave them food and water and also expounded Buddhism to them. The fish died and were reborn in heaven due to listening to the teaching.

10. Dōgen said, "Truly the Way has no obstruction—rich and poor, high and low, old and young, ignorant and slow, all travel on it. The glorious magnificence of buddhahood comes from the Way, and even evildoers have a part in it." Also, "Birth and death, desire for food and drink and warmth, growing up, anger and joy, gain and loss, going and returning, all are as such because there is one great Way without obstruction." (*Eihei Kōroku*)

11. Using Sung dynasty Chinese grammar, this could be read, "This cannot be understood, cannot be realized."

ONE BRIGHT JEWEL

(Ikka Myōju)

This essay emphasizes the total unity of being, a persistent theme of Dōgen's writings and sayings. It is based on a well-known saying of a famous teacher of ancient times, that the whole world, or all worlds, the whole universe, is "one bright jewel."

When a student asked that teacher how to understand this saying, he said, "What's it got to do with understanding?" or "Why do you want to understand?" or "What's the use of understanding?" Each of these points is worth reflecting upon, but an underlying message applying to any way we might read this reply seems to be that the unity of beings is so whether or not anyone consciously understands it; being is not made one by means of understanding. Furthermore, conceptual understanding, with its inherent discrimination, can obscure rather than reveal this unity, should one "miss the forest for the trees."

However, this does not mean that the only alternative is ignorance: in the story, when the student hands the teacher back the same answer on the following day, the teacher makes a remark suggesting that the student is clinging to nonunderstanding, or simply hanging on to a slogan in place of true understanding. Throughout this essay Dōgen shows how to avoid missing the whole for the parts while at the same time still appreciating the infinite variety of particulars as "adornments" of the whole, as "lights" of the "one jewel."

ONE BRIGHT JEWEL

The great master Gensha had the religious name Shibi; his lay surname was Sha. In lay life he enjoyed fishing and used to ply his boat on the Nandai river, following the ways of the fishermen. He must have had, *without exception,* the *golden fish* which *comes up by itself without being fished out.* At the beginning of the Kantsū era of the Tang dynasty (860–873), he suddenly wished to *leave the world;* he left his boat and went into the mountains. He was thirty years old at the time. Realizing the peril of the ephemeral world, he came to know the lofty value of the Buddha Way. Finally he climbed Snowy Peak Mountain, called on the great Zen master Seppō, and worked on the Way day and night.

One time, in order to make a thorough study of Zen as taught all over the country, he took his knapsack and headed out of the mountain, but on the way he stubbed his toe on a rock, and as it bled painfully, he suddenly had a powerful insight and said, *This body is not existent—where does pain come from?* So he then went back to Seppō. Seppō asked him, *Which one is the ascetic Shibi?* Gensha said, *I never dare fool people.* Seppō especially liked this saying, and said, "Who does not have this saying? Who can utter this saying?" Seppō asked further, "Ascetic Shibi, why don't you travel to study?" He replied, *Bodhidharma did not come to China, the second patriarch did not go to India.*[1] Seppō particularly praised him for this saying. Because he had up to then been a fisherman, he had never seen the various scriptures and treatises even in dreams, yet nevertheless because the depth of his aspiration was paramount, a determined spirit beyond others had appeared. Seppō thought him outstanding in the community and praised him as being a standard among his disciples. He dressed in plain muslin, and because he never replaced his one robe, it was all patched. He used paper for his underclothing, and also wore mugwort plants. He didn't call on any teacher except Seppō. Nevertheless, he had accomplished the power to inherit his teacher's way.

After he had finally attained the Way, he said to people, *The whole world in all ten directions is a single bright jewel.* Then a monk asked, *I hear you have a saying, that the whole world in all ten directions is one bright jewel—how can a student understand this?* The master said, *The whole world in all ten directions is one bright jewel—what does it have to do with understanding?* The next day the master asked that monk, *The whole world in all ten directions is one bright jewel—how do you understand?* The monk replied, *The whole world in all ten directions is one bright jewel—what does it have to do with understanding?* The master said, *I knew you were making a living in a ghost cave in the mountain of darkness.*[2]

This saying, the whole world in all ten directions is one bright jewel, began with Gensha. The essential message is that *the whole universe* is not *vast*, not *small*, not *round or square*, not *balanced and correct*, not *lively and active*, not *standing way out*. Because furthermore it is not *birth and death, coming and going*, it is *birth and death, coming and going*. Being thus, *having in the past gone from here*, it *now comes from here*. In making a thorough investigation someone must see through it as being weightless, someone must find out it is being single-minded.

All ten directions is the *nonceasing* of *pursuing things as oneself, pursuing oneself as things.* Expressing *when emotions arise wisdom is blocked* as blockage is *turning the head, changing the face*, it is *setting forth events, meeting the situation*. Because of *pursuing self as things*, it is the *all ten directions* which is *unceasing*. Because it is the principle of incipience, there is superabundance in the mastery of the pivot of function. *Is one bright jewel*, though not yet a name, is expression. This has come to be taken as a name. As for *one bright jewel*, it is *even ten thousand years*; as it *extends through antiquity, yet unfinished*, it *extends through the present, having arrived*. Though there is *the present of the body* and *the present of the mind*, it is *a bright jewel*. It is not the *plants and tree* of *here and there*, not the *mountains and rivers* of *heaven and earth*—it is *a bright jewel*.

How can a student understand? As for this saying, even if it seems that the monk was *sporting active consciousness*, it is *the great function manifesting being a great rule*. Going onward, one should cause *a foot of water, a foot of wave*[3] to stand out high. This is what is called *ten feet of jewel, ten feet of brightness*. To express what he meant to say, Gensha said, *The whole world in all ten directions is one bright jewel—what does it have to do with understanding?* This saying is an expression of Buddhas succeeding to Buddhas, Zen adepts succeeding to Zen adepts, Gensha succeeding to Gensha. In trying to escape succession, though it is not that there could be no place to escape, even if one clearly escapes for the time being, as long as there is the arising of expression, it is the covering of time by manifestation.

The next day Gensha asked that monk, "The whole world in all ten directions is one bright jewel—how do you understand?" This says, *yesterday I spoke a definite principle;* today, using a second layer, he *exudes energy⁴—today I speak the indefinite principle*—he is *pushing yesterday over, nodding and laughing.* The monk said, "The whole world in all ten directions is one bright jewel—what does understanding have to do with it?" We could call this *riding a thief's horse in pursuit of the thief.* In an ancient Buddha's explanation for you, it is *acting among different species.*⁵ For a time you should *turn the light around and introspect*—how many levels of *what has it to do with understanding* are there? In trying to say, though one may say it is *seven milk pancakes, five vegetable pancakes,* this is the teaching and practice of *south of Shō, north of Tan.*⁶

Gensha said, "I knew you were making a living in a ghost cave in the mountain of darkness." Know that *sun face, moon face⁷* has never changed since remote antiquity. *Sun face* comes out together with *sun face,* and *moon face* comes out together with *moon face,* so therefore *if the sixth month you say is just the right time, you cannot say your nature is mature.*⁸ Therefore the beginning or beginninglessness of this *bright jewel* has no point of reference—it is *the whole world in all ten directions is one bright jewel.* He doesn't say two or three—the *whole body* is one single *eye of truth,* the *whole body* is the *embodiment of reality,* the *whole body* is one phrase, the *whole body* is light, the *whole body* is the whole body. When being the *whole body,* the *whole body* has no obstruction—it is *perfectly round,* it *rolls smoothly.* Because the qualities of the *bright jewel* are thus manifest, there are the *Kannon and Miroku⁹* of the present *seeing form and hearing sound,* there are the *old Buddhas and new Buddhas who appear physically to expound the truth.* At *this precise time,* be it hung in the sky, or inside one's clothing, or under the jaw, or in the topknot, in each case it is *the whole world in all ten directions is one bright jewel.*

Hanging it inside the clothing is considered to be the way—don't say you'll hang it on the outside. Hanging it in the topknot or under the jaw is considered to be the way—don't try to sport it on the outside of the topknot or jaw. There is a close friend who gives the jewel to you while you're intoxicated with wine—to a close friend the jewel should be given. At the time when the jewel is hung, one is always intoxicated with wine. *Being thus is the one bright jewel which is the whole world in the ten directions.* This being so, then though it seems to go changing faces, turning or not turning, yet it is *a bright jewel.* It is precisely knowing that the jewel has all along been thus that is itself the *bright jewel.* The *bright jewel* has *sound and form* which sounds this way. In being *already at thusness,* as far as worrying that oneself is not the *bright jewel* is concerned, one should not suspect that that is not the jewel. Worrying and doubting, grasping and rejection, action and inaction are all but temporary views of small measure. What is more, it is merely causing resemblance to small measure. Isn't it lovely—such lusters and lights of the *bright jewel* are unlimited. Each flicker, each beam, of each luster, each light, is a quality of the whole world in all ten directions. Who can take them away? There is no one casting a tile in the marketplace.[10] Don't bother about *not falling into* or *not being blind to*[11] the cause and effect of mundane existences—the unclouded original bright jewel which is *true through and through* is the face; the *bright jewel* is the eyes.

However, for me and you both, the *thinking of everything, not thinking of anything* which doesn't know what is the *bright jewel* and what is not the *bright jewel* may have gathered fodder of clarity, but if we have, by way of Gensha's saying, also heard and known and understood what the body and mind which are the *bright jewel* are like, the mind is not oneself—as being who would we bother to grasp or reject becoming and extinction as being the *bright jewel* or not being the *bright jewel?* Even if we doubt and worry, that does not mean it is not that this is not the *bright jewel.* Since it is not action or thought caused by something existing which is not the *bright jewel,* the simple fact is that *forward steps and backward steps* in the *ghost cave in the mountain of darkness* are just *one bright jewel.*

1238

Notes

1. The implication of this is that reality is omnipresent.
2. "Ghost cave in the mountain of darkness" is usually used in Zen to refer to being sunk in quiescence, stillness, formless concentration, nonknowing. It is also called falling into one-sided emptiness or nihilistic emptiness. This is its usage in reference to meditation; it is also used to refer to clinging to stagnant, stereotyped concepts.
3. "Water" stands for essence, emptiness, noumenon; "waves" stands for characteristics, appearances, phenomena. "A foot of water, a foot of

wave" refers to perfect realization integration of emptiness and existence.

4. "Exude energy" or "show life" is used to refer to active function or flexibility, not being stuck in one position or cliche.

5. "Acting among different species" is a technical term in the Chinese
parent school of Sōtō Zen and basically means acting in the world in
whatever forms may be appropriate. Sōzan (Ts'ao shan), a progenitor of
the school, wrote, "Bodhisattvas' assimilation to different species
means first understanding oneself, then after that entering the different
kinds in birth and death to save others; having already realized nirvana,
they do not abandon creatures in birth and death—helping themselves
and others, they vow that all sentient beings shall attain buddhahood."
Sōzan discusses various types or aspects of "acting among different species," but in general "different species" means the world of differentiation, all kinds of different forms and states.

6. "Seven milk pancakes, five vegetable pancakes" means "everything,"
and "south of Shō, north of Tan," means "everywhere" (cf. *Blue Cliff
Record*, case 18). Everything is "the bright jewel," everything everywhere is *thusness*—specific understandings or descriptions have their
place and use, but are by nature fragmentary and do not capture the
whole. Yet since this principle extends to all specifics, as the Kegon
philosophy emphasizes, one is all and all are one. In Zen synecdoche,
any particular object can be used to represent all being.

7. Cf. *Blue Cliff Record*, case 3.

8. An ancient teacher said, "Every day is a good day." Cf. *Blue Cliff
Record*, case 6.

9. Kannon is Avalokiteśvara, the bodhisattva of compassion; Miroku is
Maitreya, the bodhisattva of kindness.

10. "Casting a tile" to draw a piece of jade means to give a little to get more;
someone once posted two lines of verse in a temple where a famous
poet was expected to visit, provoking the poet to complete the verse.
The lines added by the poet were superior, and the man who wrote the
first two lines was said to have thrown a tile and drawn a piece of jade.

11. In a well-known Zen story, an old man told the Zen master Hyakujō
that he had been a teacher in the past, but when a student asked if
someone who is highly cultivated in meditation falls into the province
of cause and effect, he denied it and became a "wild fox." Then the old
man posed the same question to Hyakujō, who answered that someone
who is highly cultivated "isn't blind to cause and effect."

FLOWERS IN THE SKY
(Kuge)

This essay is strongly colored with the Kegon doctrine of the inter-penetration of reality and illusion. Reality, in Kegon terms, means the interdependence of all things, which also means the "emptiness" of things in themselves. Particular emphasis is placed in this essay on counteracting nihilistic tendencies in the interpretation of emptiness and illusoriness: this may be noted time and again as one of Dōgen's persistent themes.

This point of emphasis is summed up in Dōgen's reversal of the focus of a traditional expression, "flowers in the sky." This term refers to that which is illusory or unreal; but where it conventionally had a negative connotation, Dōgen uses it here in a positive way. That is, instead of treating illusion as something to be annihilated, Dōgen points out that all is illusion, and being empty in its very essence is in that sense identical to absolute reality.

This is like saying that all existence is relative and therefore empty of absolutes, so to realize emptiness it is not necessary to annihilate existence. In fact, the very idea of annihilating presumes existence as something in itself real, hence is illusion within illusion. Dōgen points out that not only mundane things are "flowers in the sky," but so are the Buddhist teachings themselves. This might be said to be a fundamental point of departure of Mahayana Buddhism, as articulated by the great dialectician Nāgārjuna a millenium earlier.

The essay begins with a famous line attributed to Bodhidharma, the alleged founder of Zen in China: "One flower opens with five petals, forming a fruit of its own accord." The "five petals" are traditionally thought to refer to the five Chinese patriarchs of Zen, or to the five houses of Chinese Zen. Dōgen points out these are multifold aspects of one "flower," while the "one flower" is the unfolding of these various aspects. Elsewhere in *Shōbōgenzō*, Dōgen emphasizes that the five houses or schools of Zen are not to be thought of as representing divisions or fundamental differences, and that Buddhism should be viewed not in a fragmentary, sectarian way, but as a whole comprising many different facets. This notion of Buddhism as a whole which is unified though various, various though unified, is also characteristic of the idea of "one vehicle" in the Kegon and Hokke teachings. Also like the Kegon, Dōgen here in his introduction emphasizes practice, symbolized by the flower, naturally bearing the "fruit" of realization. The metaphor of the flower and petals also can be extended to refer to the unity and multiplicity of all phenomena.

Next Dōgen goes on to bring up the classic symbol of the udumbara flower. This is a flower that blooms but once in three thousand years, a standard symbol for Buddha. Dōgen quotes an ancient saying that the udumbara flower blooms in "fire," suggesting that buddhahood is realized in the world. This emphasis on nondualism, on the cultivation and realization of buddhahood as being nowhere but in this life, is also typical of Dōgen; he carries this logic through to illustrate the interdependence of awareness and existence, and the identity of Buddha and existence itself.

Subsequently the essay proceeds to its main theme, the unity of existence and emptiness. The word for "sky" in the expression "flowers in the sky" is the same in Sino-Japanese as the word for the Buddhist term "emptiness," so this expression could also be read from Chinese as "empty flowers" or "flowers of emptiness." Dōgen stresses that everything without exception is "flowers in the sky." The traditional saying that "flowers in the sky" are due to cataracts or obstructions in the eye is here presented positively, with "cataracts" being used to refer to compassion, or nonextinction, the acceptance and recognition of life as it is. This positive interpretation of "sickness" is also characteristic of the popular *Vimalakīrti* scripture, in which "sickness" represents the sage's compassion and adaptive being in the world. Like that scripture, this essay by Dōgen is aimed at cutting through the notion of nirvana as opposite to mundane life.

FLOWERS IN THE SKY

The founder of Zen said, "One flower opens, with five petals, forming a fruit which ripens of its own accord."

One should study the time of this flower's blooming, as well as its light and color. The multiplicity of one flower is five petals, the opening of five petals is one flower. Where the principle of one flower comes across is *I originally came to this land to communicate the Teaching and save deluded sentient beings.* Where the light and color are sought must be this meditative study. It is *the forming of the fruit is up to your forming of the fruit*—this is called *ripening of its own accord. Ripening of its own accord* means cultivating the cause and experiencing the result. There is cause in the realm of common experience, there is result in the realm of common experience. Cultivating this cause and effect in the realm of common experience, one experiences cause and effect in the realm of common experience. *Own* is the self, the self is definitely *you*—it means the four gross elements and five clusters.[1] Because of being able to employ the *true human with no position,*[2] it is not "I," it is not *who;* therefore being *not compulsory* is called *on its own. Accord* is permission. *Ripening of its own accord* is the time of the flower's opening and forming fruit, it is the time of *communicating the Teaching to save deluded sentient beings.*

For example, it is like the time and place of the udumbara flower's blooming being in fire, during fire. Drilling for fire and flaming fire are both the place and the time of blooming of the udumbara flower. If not for the time and place of the udumbara flower, not a single spark of fire comes into being, there is not a single spark of life. Know that in a single spark of fire are a hundred thousand udumbara flowers, blooming in the sky, blooming on the ground, blooming in the past, blooming in the present. To perceive the time and place of the fire's appearance is to perceive the udumbara flower. We should not miss perceiving the time and place of the udumbara flower.

An ancient said, *The udumbara flower blooms in fire.* So the udumbara flower always blooms in fire. If you want to know *fire,* it is where the udumbara flower blooms. You should not, by clinging to views of humanity or views of heaven, fail to learn about *in the fire.* If you would doubt it, you should also doubt that lotus flowers grow in water; you should also doubt that there are flowers on branches. Also, if you must doubt, you should doubt the structure of the material world. Even so, you don't doubt.

If one is not a Buddha or Zen adept, one does not know *when a flower blooms the world comes into being. A flower blooms* is *in* *front, three by three, in back, three by three.*³ In order to fulfill this number of members, all things are assembled and made grandiose. Invoking this principle, one can know the measure of spring and autumn.

But it's not that there are flowers and fruits in spring and autumn; *being time* always has flowers and fruit. Flowers and fruit together preserve time and season, time and season together preserve flowers and fruit. For this reason *the hundred plants*⁴ all have flowers and fruits, all trees have flowers and fruits. Gold, silver, copper, iron, coral, and jewel trees all have flowers and fruits; earth, water, fire, air, and space trees all have flowers and fruits. Human trees have flowers, human flowers have flowers, *withered trees*⁵ have flowers.

Among such as these existing, there are the *flowers in the sky* spoken of by the Buddha. However, those of little learning and little insight do not know what the colors, luster, leaves and blossoms of the *flowers in the sky* are like—they only hear of them as nonexistent flowers. Know that in the Buddha Way there is talk of *flowers in the sky*—outsiders don't know the talk about *flowers in the sky*, much less consciously understand it. Only Buddhas and Zen adepts alone know the blooming and falling of sky flowers and earth flowers, know the blooming and falling of world flowers, and so on, and know the sky flowers, earth flowers, world flowers, and so on are scriptures. This is the guideline for Buddhist study. Because that which Buddhas and Zen adepts ride on is *flowers in the sky*, the worlds of Buddhas as well as the teachings of the Buddhas are in fact *flowers in the sky*.

However, what ordinary ignoramuses think when they hear that the Buddha said what eyes with cataracts see are *flowers in the sky*, is that *eyes with cataracts* refers to the distorted eyes of sentient beings; they reason that since diseased eyes are distorted, they perceive nonexistent flowers in the clear sky. By clinging to this reasoning, they think it means falsely seeing as existent the nonexistent three worlds, six paths,⁶ existent Buddhas, nonexistent Buddhas. They make a living on the idea that this says that if the deluding cataracts in the eyes were gone, these flowers in the sky would not be seen, and so there are originally no flowers in the sky. It is a pity that people like this don't know the time and season and process of the *flowers in the sky* spoken of by Buddha. The principle of the *cataracts in the eye, flowers in the sky* spoken of by Buddhas is not yet apparent to ordinary people and outsiders. The Buddhas, enlightened ones, cultivating these *flowers in the sky*, thereby *acquire the robe, seat, and room*,[7] attain enlightenment and realize its fruition. *Holding up a flower and winking*[8] is a public case where *cataracts in the eye, flowers in the sky* manifest. The *treasury of the eye of true teaching, the ineffable mind of nirvana*, correctly transmitted to the present without lapse, is called *cataracts in the eye, flowers in the sky*. Enlightenment, nirvana, the body of reality, inherent nature, and so on are a few petals of the *opening five petals* of *flowers in the sky*.

Shakyamuni Buddha said, "It is like someone with cataracts seeing flowers in the sky: when the affliction of cataracts is removed, the flowers perish in the sky."

There has not yet been a scholar who has understood this statement. Because they don't know *the sky*, they don't know the *flowers in the sky*. Because they don't know the *flowers in the sky*, they don't know *the person with cataracts;* they do not see *the person with cataracts*, do not meet *the person with cataracts*, are not *the person with cataracts*. One should meet *the person with cataracts*, know *the sky*, and see *the flowers in the sky* too. After seeing the *flowers in the sky*, one should also see *the flowers perish in the sky*. To think that once the *flowers in the sky* cease they should not exist anymore is the view of a small vehicle.[9] If the *flowers in the sky* were not seen, what would they be? (Those with the view of the small vehicle) only know *flowers in the sky* as something to be abandoned, and do not know the *great matter* after the *flowers in the sky*—they do not know the planting, ripening, and shedding of the *flowers in the sky*.

Ordinary scholars today think that where the sun energy abides is *the sky*, that where the sun, moon, planets, and stars hang is *the sky*, and due to that they think that saying *flowers in the sky* means the appearance of forms like floating clouds in this clear air, flying flowers blown hither and thither in the wind rising and falling. They are far from knowing that the creating and created four gross elements, all the phenomena of the material world, as well as fundamental enlightenment, fundamental nature, and so on, are called *flowers in the sky*. Also they do not know that the creative four elements and so on exist due to phenomena; they do not know that the material world remains in its normal state due to phenomena. They only see phenomena as existing due to the material world. They only realize that there are *flowers in the sky* due to *cataracted eyes;* they do not realize the principle that *cataract eyes* are caused to exist by *flowers in the sky.* Know that the *person with cataracts* spoken of by the Buddha is the originally enlightened person, the ineffably enlightened person, the person of the Buddhas, the person of the three worlds, the person beyond Buddha. Do not ignorantly consider *cataracts* to be delusive factors and this study as if there were something else which is real—that would be a small view. If cataract flowers are delusions, the agent and action wrongly clinging to them as delusions would have to be delusions. If they are all delusions, there can be no logical reasoning. If there is no reason established, the fact that cataract flowers are delusions cannot be so.

In so far as enlightenment is a *cataract,* the myriad elements of enlightenment are all elements of a magnificent array of *cataracts,* the myriad elements of delusion are all elements of a grandiose array of *cataracts.* For now we should say that since *cataracted eyes* are equal, *flowers in the sky* are equal; since *cataracted eyes* are birthless,[10] *flowers in the sky* are birthless. Since all things are characteristics of reality, cataract flowers are characteristics of reality. It's not a question of past, present, and future, not a matter of beginning, middle, and end—because they are not blocked by origination and destruction, they are able to cause origination and destruction to be originated and destroyed. They originate in the sky and perish in the sky, originate in cataracts and perish in the cataracts, originate in flowers and perish in the flowers. All other times and places are also like this.

Study of *flowers in the sky* certainly has many grades. There is that which is seen by eyes with cataracts, there is that which is seen by clear eyes, there is that which is seen by the eyes of Buddhas, there is that which is seen by the eyes of Zen adepts, there is that which is seen by the eye of the Way, there is that which is seen by blind eyes. There is that which is seen for three thousand years, there is that which is seen for eight hundred years.[11] There is that which is seen for a hundred eons, there is that which is seen for measureless eons. Though these are all seeing *flowers in the sky,* since *sky* is of various kinds, *flowers* too are multifold.

You should know that *the sky is one plant.* This *sky* inevitably flowers, just as all plants flower. As an expression of this principle, the Buddha said there are originally no flowers in the sky. Although *there are originally no flowers,* where the fact that there are now flowers is concerned, the peaches and plums are thus, and the apricots and willows are also thus—it's like saying the *apricot trees yesterday had no flowers—the apricot trees in spring have flowers.* When the season arrives, flowers bloom—it must be the time of the flowers, it must be the arrival of the flowers. The precise moment of this arrival of the flowers has never been arbitrary. Apricot and willow flowers always bloom on apricots and willows—when you see the flowers you know they are apricots or willows; seeing apricots and willows, you can tell the flowers. Peach and plum flowers have never bloomed on apricots or willows—apricot and willow flowers blossom on apricot and willow trees, peach and plum flowers blossom on peach and plum trees.

The blooming of *flowers in the sky* is also like this—they don't bloom on any other plants or trees. Seeing the colors of the *flowers in the sky,* one assesses the inexhaustibility of the fruits in the sky. Seeing the blooming and falling of *flowers in the sky,* one should study the spring and autumn of the *flowers in the sky.* The spring of *flowers in the sky* and the spring of other flowers must be equal. Just as flowers in the sky are various, the time of spring must also be such. For this reason there exists spring and autumn of all time. To learn that *flowers in the sky* are not real but other flowers are real is ignorance of the Buddha's teaching. Hearing it said that there are originally no flowers in the sky, if one takes it to mean that *flowers in the sky* which were originally nonexistent now exist, it would be shallow thinking and small insight—one should go on to think in a more far-reaching way. A Zen adept said, "The flowers have never been born." The manifestation of this message is, for example, the principle of *the flowers have never been born, and never perish; the flowers have never been flowers, the sky has never been the sky.* There should be no inanity about existence or nonexistence confusing the context of the time of the flowers. It is like flowers always being imbued with colors: the colors are not necessarily limited to flowers, and the times also have colors such as green, yellow, red, and white. Spring brings on flowers, flowers bring on spring.

A certain scholar was a lay disciple of the Zen master Sekisō. He composed a verse on awakening to the Way which said:

> Light shines silently throughout infinity

This light has newly manifested the monks' hall, the buddha shrine, the pantry, and the monastery gate. *Throughout infinity* is the manifestation of the light, it is the light of manifestation.

All conscious beings, ordinary and wise, are my family

It is not that there are not ordinary folk and sages—but don't slander ordinary people and sages because of this.

A single thought unborn, the totality of being manifests

Each thought is individual; this is certainly unborn.[12] This is the totality of being, totally manifest. Therefore he expressed this as *a single thought unborn*.

As soon as the six sense faculties stir they are blocked by clouds

Though the six sense faculties are eye, ear, nose, tongue, body, and mind, they are not necessarily two times three—they must be *three by three, before and behind. Stirring* is like the polar mountain, it is like the earth, it is like the six senses, it is like *as soon as they stir.* Since *stirring* is like the polar mountain, not stirring is also like the poplar mountain. For example, it is making clouds and rain.

Removing afflictions doubly increases illness

It is not that there has been no illness hitherto; there is the illness of Buddha, the illness of Zen adepts. This knowledge and removal is doubling illness, increasing illness. At the very moment of removing, certainly that is affliction; they are simultaneous, they are not simultaneous. The fact is that afflictions always include the way to remove them.

Aiming for thusness is also wrong

Turning away from thusness is wrong, aiming for thusness is also wrong. *Thusness* is aiming for and turning away; in the individuality of each, aiming for and turning away, this is *thusness.*[13] Who would have known this *wrong* is also thusness!

Going along with the conditions of the world, without
  hindrance

Conditions of the world going along with conditions of the world, going along is a condition of the world when going along—this is called *without hindrance.* As for hindrance and nonhindrance, one must learn while hindered by the eye.[14]

Nirvana and life-death are flowers in the sky

Nirvana is unexcelled complete perfect enlightenment; the resting place of the Buddhas and Zen adepts as well as the disciples of Buddhas and Zen adepts is this. *Life and death* is the *real human body*. Though nirvana and life and death are these things, they are *flowers in the sky*. The roots and stems, branches and leaves, blossoms and fruits, luster and color of the *flowers in the sky* are all the blooming of the *flowers in the sky*. Sky flowers also produce sky fruits and give out sky seeds. Because the triple world we now perceive is the *five petals opening* of the *flowers in the sky*, it is *not as good as the triple world seeing the triple world*. It is this *true characteristic of all things*. It is this *flower characteristic of all things. All things, ultimately unfathomable*, are flowers and fruits in the sky. You should study them as equal to the apricots, willows, peaches, and plums.

Zen Master Reikun, when he first called on Zen Master Kisō, asked, "What is Buddha?" Kisō said, "If I tell you, will you believe?" Reikun said, "How dare I not believe the true words of the teacher?" Kisō said, "You are it." Reikun said, "How can I preserve it?" Kisō said, "When there is a single cataract in the eye, flowers in the sky shower every which way."

This saying of Kisō, *when there is a single cataract in the eye, flowers in the sky shower every which way*, is an expression of preserving Buddha. Therefore, know that the *showering every which way* of *cataract flowers* is the manifestation of Buddha. The flowers and fruits in the eye-sky are the preservation of the Buddhas. By means of *cataracts* the eye is caused to manifest; manifesting sky flowers in the eye, it manifests the eye in the sky flowers. It follows that *when there are sky flowers in the eye, one cataract showers every which way*, and *when one eye is in the sky, myriad cataracts shower every which way.* Because of this, *cataracts too are the manifestation of the whole works, the eye too is the manifestation of the whole works, the sky too is the manifestation of the whole works, the flowers too are the manifestation of the whole works. Showering every which way is a thousand eyes; it is eyes throughout the body.*[15] In whatever time and place there is an eye, there are inevitably *flowers in the sky*, there are *flowers in the eye*. Flowers in the eye are called flowers in the sky—the expression of flowers in the eye must be open and clear.

Great Master Kōshō said, "What a marvel! The Buddhas of the ten directions are basically flowers in the eye. If you want to know the flowers in the eye, they are basically the Buddhas of the ten directions. If you want to know the Buddhas of the ten directions, they are not the flowers in the eye; if you want to know the flowers in the eye, they are not the Buddhas of the ten directions. If you understand this, the fault is in the Buddhas of the ten directions. If you don't understand, a disciple does a dance, a self-awakened one puts on makeup."

You should know that it is not that the Buddhas of the ten directions are not real—they are basically *flowers in the eye*. The place where the Buddhas of the ten directions are in their position is *in the eye*. If it is not *in the eye* it is not the abode of the Buddhas. *Flowers in the eye* are not nonexistent, not existent, not void, not substantial—they are of themselves *the Buddhas of the ten directions*.

Now if you just want to know *the Buddhas of the ten directions*, it is not the *flowers in the eye*, and if you just want to know the *flowers in the eye*, it is not the *Buddhas of the ten directions*—this is how it is. Because it is this way, understanding and not understanding are both *flowers in the eye*, are *the Buddhas of the ten directions*. *Want to know* and *are not* are the marvel of manifestation, are a great marvel. The doctrine of sky flowers and earth flowers spoken by all Buddhas and Zen adepts is such a *flashing of style*. Though even teachers of the scriptures and treatises have heard of the name of *flowers in the sky*, when it comes to the life pulse of earth flowers there are no conditions for any but Buddhas and Zen adepts to see or hear of them. Knowledge of the life pulse of the earth flowers is captured in the sayings of the Buddhas and Zen adepts.

Zen Master Etetsu of Mt. Sekimon in China was an adept in the line of Ryōzan. A monk asked him, "What is the jewel in the mountain?" The point of this question is the same as asking, for example, what Buddha is; it is like asking what the Path is. The master said, "Sky flowers emerge from the earth; the whole country has no way to buy." This statement should not be considered on a par with others at all. Usually when Zen teachers talk about flowers in the sky, they only say they originate *in the sky* and then perish *in the sky*. None have yet known *from the sky*, much less *from the earth*—only Sekimon alone knew. "From the earth" is *beginning, middle, and end* ultimately *from the earth. Emerge* means *bloom.* At this precise time, they *emerge from the whole earth,* they *bloom from the whole earth. The whole country has no way to buy* doesn't mean that the whole country doesn't buy, it means that there is no way to buy. There are sky flowers that emerge from the earth, there is the whole earth that blooms from the flowers. Therefore know that *flowers in the sky* have the meaning of causing both earth and sky to bloom.

1243

Notes

1. "Four gross elements and five clusters" means the mental and physical elements of being.
2. "True human with no position" is a famous Zen expression referring to the ego-free human. See *Being Time,* note 8.
3. "In front, three by three, in back, three by three"—see *Blue Cliff Record,* case 35. Zen Master Hakuin says, "If you want to know how many this is, you must know the number of last night's stars, the number of the drops of this morning's rain." It may be taken as referring to the totality of experience, differentiated in terms of appearances, characteristics, while equal in terms of essence.
4. "A hundred plants" means all things.
5. "Withered tree" refers to dispassion, disillusion. Dōgen's spiritual ancestor Tōzan spoke of Zen as "flowers blooming on a withered tree," or being in the world but not of the world.
6. The three worlds, or triple world, are the realms of desire, form, and formlessness. The six paths are the conditions of "animals" (delusion), "ghosts" (greed), "titans" (anger), "hell" (delusion, greed, and anger), "humans" (social virtue), and "celestials" (abstract meditation). These terms are a way of summing the sphere of mundane, conditioned existence.
7. "Robe, seat, and room" is an expression from the *Hokke* scripture: the "robe" of Buddhas is conciliation and tolerance; the "seat" of Buddhas is the emptiness of all things; the "room" of Buddhas is compassion for all beings.
8. The Zen legend of the beginning of the Zen transmission is that once before an assembly Shakyamuni Buddha said nothing but held up a flower and winked—no one understood but the chief disciple Mahā-Kāśyapa, who smiled. Buddha said, "I have the treasury of the eye of true teaching, the ineffable mind of nirvana, the true form, which is formless—this I hand on to Mahā-Kāśyapa."

9. The "small vehicle" of Buddhism emphasizes individual liberation, and its realization is sometimes referred to as "extinguishing cognition and reducing the body to ashes." It is contrasted to the so-called great vehicle, which emphasizes universal liberation, in that it is aimed at annihilating illusion whereas the great vehicle holds that illusion and enlightenment are not separate, and tries to attain liberation through comprehending illusion in both form and essence.

10. "Birthless" is used to mean "empty" in the sense of having no independent existence; accordingly, it also refers to the notion of the beginningless, endless, inextricable interrelation of all phenomena.

11. "Eight hundred" and "three thousand" are a pair of numbers commonly used in Zen talk to refer to indefinite multiplicity.

12. The sense of "unborn" here means every moment is unique; from the point of view of the moment, considering the moment in itself, there is no before or after in the present moment itself.

13. Var. lect. "In each of the aiming for and turning away that have aiming for and turning away from thusness, this is thusness." Thusness is all-inclusive. Those who try to aim for it, or who turn away from it, miss it in terms of conscious realization, but nevertheless are still part of thusness, and so are their efforts.

14. "Hindered" here means existence; being "hindered" by the eye means experiencing through the eye.

15. See *The Ocean Seal Concentration*, note 9.

THE OCEAN SEAL CONCENTRATION

(Kai-in zammai)

The "ocean seal concentration," or, as it is sometimes rendered, the "oceanic reflection concentration," is said to be the concentration from which the Kegon scripture emerged, abruptly revealing the vast panorama of the Buddha's enlightenment. The treatise *Return to the Source Contemplation*, a Kegon work popular in Chinese Zen schools, says, "The 'ocean seal' is the fundamental awareness of true thusness. When delusion ends, the mind is clear and myriad forms simultaneously appear. It is like the ocean: due to wind there arise waves; if the wind stops the ocean water is calm and clear, and all images can reflect in it." Thus, in terms of mind, the ocean seal concentration may be said to refer to holistic, impartial awareness.

The twenty-fifth book of the *Ratnakūṭa* scripture says, "Just as all streams enter the ocean, all phenomena enter the seal of phenomena, hence the name oceanic seal." The "seal of phenomena," or "seal of law," refers to the treble seal of Buddhism. The twenty-second book of the *Treatise on Great Transcendent Wisdom* says, "The seal of law of Buddhism is threefold: first, all compounded things are born and perish from moment to moment, all are impermanent; second, all things are selfless; third is silent, extinct nirvana." The twentieth book of the same treatise says, "If one thinks in a discriminatory way, this is the net of the devil; not being moved and not remaining based on this is the seal of the law."

In this essay Dōgen introduces the ocean seal concentration by a paraphrase based on a passage from the scripture spoken by Vimalakı̄rti and the recorded sayings of the great master Baso. Following Baso, Dōgen cites the scripture in this way: "Only by the compounding of many elements (or phenomena) is this body made. At the time of its arising, only elements arise; at the time of its vanishing, only elements vanish." The strategy of analysis into elements is a traditional

Buddhist device to dissolve the notion of intrinsic identity of the body (and mind) as a self or person; it also counters the notion of inherent identity of any compounded form. At the same time, in its broad application, this passage refers to the "body" of the universe as being a single compound or nexus of elements, a typical Kegon view; as Dōgen makes clear later, this seeing of the whole nexus is the ocean seal concentration.

The scripture as quoted by Dōgen goes on to say that the elements do not announce their arising and vanishing. This is like saying that they have no intrinsic identity. The notion of phenomena arising and vanishing depends on discriminating thought. In the terms of the treatise *Awakening of Faith in the Mahayana*, popular in both Zen and Kegon schools, awareness has two aspects: awareness of thusness and awareness of birth and death. Delusion means being trapped in the latter, in discriminating thought, which singles out things as discrete entities and thus is a linear, sequential way of perceiving, marking beginnings and ends. This is called delusion when it is believed—implicitly or explicitly—to be all there is, to be the only way of seeing, to be the true description of reality. This kind of awareness is by nature restrictive and exclusive (and for that reason may be useful and practically necessary at times while being harmful and counterproductive at others); to put it in a wider perspective the awareness of *thusness* (being-as-is, without conceptual glosses) is cultivated in Buddhism. Ultimately, enlightenment includes both aspects, so that one is neither forced to feel that thought and discrimination reveal the whole of reality, nor rendered incapable of orderly perception and discursive reasoning.

The final portion of the scriptural passage hints at the method of arriving at this synthesis: "Prior moment, succeeding moment—each successive moment does not await the next: prior element, succeeding element—the elements do not await each other. This is called the ocean seal concentration." The word "moment" also can be rendered as "thought," and in Sanskrit texts the term "thought-moment" or "mental moment" is often found. The point, as it applies to Zen meditation, seems to be awareness of the flux of moments without clinging, without stopping to bind them mentally into fixed structures or images. Thus, without the attention being caught up or dwelling on anything conceptually specified, the holistic awareness remains free and unobscured while the flow of events is clearly and impartially reflected therein. In the latter part of the essay Dōgen goes on to bring up further quotations and allusions from scriptures and Zen lore to develop illustrations of awareness and ways of fostering meditation to arrive at consciousness of the immediate totality.

The Ocean Seal Concentration

In being Buddhas and Zen adepts, it is necessary to be the *ocean seal concentration.* In swimming in this concentration, there is a time of speaking, a time of experiencing, a time of acting. The virtue of traveling on the ocean involves travel on the very bottom; this is traveling on the ocean as being *travel on the bottom of the deepest ocean.* Hoping to return *flowing in the ways of birth and death* to the source is not *what mental action is this?*[1] Though the passing through barriers and breaking divisions hitherto is originally each of the Buddhas and Zen adepts, this is the oceanic reflection concentration returning to the source.

Buddha said that only by the compounding of many elements is this body made. At the time of its appearance, only elements arise; at the time of its disappearance, only elements vanish. At the time these elements arise, they do not say "I arise," and at the time these elements vanish, they do not say "I vanish." Prior moment, succeeding moment—each successive moment does not wait for the next: prior element, succeeding element—the elements do not await each other. This is called the ocean seal concentration.

One should examine and meditate on this statement of Buddha in detail. Attaining the Way and entering into realization doesn't necessarily depend on much learning or a lot of talk. Broad learning still attains the Way in four propositions,[2] while thorough study of innumerable doctrines after all enters realization in a single line or verse. How much the more so of this statement—it is not seeking fundamental enlightenment in the future, nor is it bringing up initial enlightenment within realization.[3] Though causing the likes of fundamental enlightenment to become manifest is the virtue of Buddhas and Zen adepts, that does not mean that the enlightenments such as fundamental enlightenment and initial enlightenment are considered the Buddhas and Zen adepts.

The time of the so-called ocean reflection concentration is precisely the time of *only by many elements*. It is the expression of *only by many elements*. This time is called *compounding to make this body*. The *single compounded form* which has compounded many elements is *this body*. This is not taking the body to be one compounded form—it is a *compound of many elements*; it is expressing *compounding to make this body* as *this body*.

When it arises, only elements arise—this *elements arise* never leaves behind arising: therefore arising is not cognitive awareness, not knowledge or perception—this is called *they don't say "I arise."*[4] In not saying "I arise," it isn't that others perceive or cognize, think or discern that these elements arise. When meeting transcendentally there is indeed loss of opportunity in meeting. Arising is necessarily the arrival of the time, because time is arising. What is arising? It must be "arisen." This is already arising which is time, causing *skin, flesh, bones and marrow* to all be *revealed alone*. Because arising is the arising of formation by compounding, it is *only by many elements* which is the *this body* of arising, which is the *"I arise"* of arising. It is not just seeing and hearing it as sound and form; it is the *many elements* of *"I arise,"* it is the unspoken "I arise." Not speaking is not not expressing, because expression is not verbalization. The time of arising is *these elements*, it is not the twenty-four hours. *These elements* are the time of arising, not the simultaneous arising of the three worlds.

In ancient times the Buddha said, "Suddenly fire arises." The independence of this arising is expressed as *fire arises*. An ancient illuminate said, "How is it when arising and vanishing don't stop?"[5] So this *arising and vanishing* is unceasing *as we arise, we vanish*. This statement of not stopping should be comprehended positively by leaving it to itself. It causes this *time when arising and vanishing don't stop* to cease and continue as the life pulse of the enlightened ones. *When arising and vanishing don't stop* is *whose arising and vanishing!* *Whose arising and vanishing is it* is *to those who may be liberated by this body* . . . , it is *then manifesting this body* . . . it is . . . *and teaching them*,[6] it is *the past mind cannot be found*,[7] it is *you have attained my marrow*, it is *you have attained my bones*[8]—because it is *whose arising and vanishing*.

"When these elements vanish, they don't say 'I vanish' "—indeed, the time of *they don't say "I vanish"* is *when these elements vanish.* Vanishing is the vanishing of elements; though it is vanishing, it must be elements. Because they are elements, they are not adventitious defilements; because they are not adventitious defilements, they don't defile. Precisely this nondefilement is the Buddhas and Zen adepts. *You too are thus,* (a Zen patriarch) says—who might not be you? This is because the preceding moment and the succeeding moment are both *I.* In this vanishing are arrayed many *hands and eyes*[9]—referred to as "unexcelled great nirvana," "this is called death," "clinging to it as annihilation," "being the dwelling place." That is to say, many such *hands and eyes* are, as they are, qualities of *vanishing.*[10] Though *not saying* at the time of vanishing being *I* and *not saying* at the time of arising being *I* have the *same birth* of *not saying,* they cannot be *not saying* having the *same death.*[11] Already it is the vanishing of the preceding elements, it is the vanishing of the succeeding elements, it is the preceding moment of the elements, it is the succeeding moment of the elements. They are elements preceding and succeeding momentary elements, they are the preceding and succeeding moments of the elements. *Not awaiting each other* are momentary elements, not relating to each other are elements. That which causes them not to be mutually relative and not to await one another is the expression of eighty or ninety percent. There is *letting go* and there is *gathering in* which make the four gross elements and five clusters of extinction into *hands and eyes.* There is progression and there is meeting which make the four gross elements and five clusters into the itinerary. At this time, *throughout the body is hands and eyes,* but yet it is not enough;[12] *all over the body is hands and eyes,* but yet it is not enough.[12] In general, extinction is a quality of Buddhas and Zen adepts. As for the fact that now there is this statement of nonrelation and nonawaiting, know that *arising* is arising in the beginning, middle, and end; it is a case of *officially not even a needle is admitted; privately, even a horse and carriage can pass.*[13] It is not making extinction await or relate to *beginning, middle, and end.* Even though elements suddenly arise where there has been extinction, this is not the arising of the extinct, it is the arising of elements. Because it is the arising of elements, they do not await each other.[14] Also it is not relating extinction to extinction. Extinction is also extinction of beginning, middle, and end. It is a case of *not bringing it forth when meeting, raising the idea you know it exists.* Even though there is suddenly extinction where there has been arising, it is not the extinction of arising, it is the extinction of elements. Though it may be the *this is* of extinction, though it may be the *this is* of arising, it is *just the ocean seal concentration being called myriad elements.* The cultivation and realization of *this is* is not nonexistent, it is *just this nondefilement is called the ocean seal concentration. Concentration* is actualization, it is expression, it is the nighttime when one *reaches back for the pillow.* The reaching for the pillow wherein the nighttime is *reaching back for the pillow* is not merely for billions and billions of eons—it is a case of *in the ocean I only expound the scripture of the lotus of the wonderful teaching eternally.*

Because it is *not saying "I arise,"* it is *I, in the ocean.* The preceding face is *eternally expounding,* which is *as soon as one wave moves, myriad waves follow;* the succeeding face is the *scripture of the lotus of the wonderful teaching* of *as soon as myriad waves move, one wave follows.*[15] Even though causing a thousand or ten thousand foot string to be rolled up and rolled out, what is to be regretted is its hanging straight down. The "preceding and succeeding faces" are *I, on the face of the ocean*—it is like saying the preceding point and the succeeding point. "The preceding point and the succeeding point" is *putting a head on top of the head. In the ocean* is not that there are people; *I, in the ocean* is not the abode of people of the world, it is not what sages love. *I alone am in the ocean*—this is the *expounding* of *only, eternally.* This *in the ocean* is not the province of in between, inside, or outside: it is *eternally expounding the scripture of the lotus of the wonderful teaching.* Though it is *not dwelling* in the east, west, south, or north, it is *the full boat empty, carrying the moon back.* This true return is *directly returning*[16]— who would say this is action lingering in the water? It is just manifesting actualization within the bounds of the Buddha Way, that is all. This is considered the seal that stamps water. Further, we say it is the seal that stamps mud. The seal that stamps water is not necessarily the seal that stamps the ocean; it must be the seal that stamps the ocean transcendentally. This is called the ocean seal, the water seal, the mud seal, the mind seal. Purely conveying the mind seal, it stamps water, stamps mud, stamps space.[17]

Master Sōzan was asked by a monk, "I understand that in the teachings it says the great ocean does not lodge a dead body—what is the ocean?" Sōzan said, "It contains all existents." The monk said, "Why doesn't it lodge a dead body?" Sōzan said, "One void of breath is not attached." The monk said, "Since it contains all existents, why isn't one void of breath attached?" Sōzan said, "It is not that myriad existents are void of breath in effect."[18]

This Sōzan was a spiritual brother of Ungo; here the essential message of Tōzan was truly accurate. This *I understand that in the teachings it says* refers to the true teachings of Buddhas and Zen adepts; it is not the teachings of ordinary or holy people, it is not the small teaching of transmitting Buddhist doctrines. *The great ocean does not retain a dead body*—this so-called *great ocean* is not an internal ocean or an external ocean, and cannot be like the eight oceans. These are not what the student is questioning. It is not only recognizing what is not an ocean as the ocean, it is recognizing what is an ocean as the ocean. Even though one insists they are oceans, they should not be called the *great ocean*. The *great ocean* is not necessarily a ninefold abyss with salt water or something. *Many elements* must *compound to form*. How could the *great ocean* necessarily be merely deep water? For this reason, to ask *what is the ocean* is speaking of the *great ocean* because the *great ocean* is as yet unknown to humans and celestials. As for *not retaining a dead body*, *not retaining* must be *when light comes, striking light; when darkness comes, striking darkness*.[19] The *dead body* is dead ashes; it is *how many times encountering the spring without change of mind*. The *dead body* is something nobody has ever yet seen—that is the reason for not knowing.

Sōzan's statement *it contains all existents* speaks of the ocean. This expression of the essential message doesn't say that the one thing which is *who* contains all existents; it is *containing all existents*. It is not saying that the *great ocean* contains all existents; to say *it contains all existents* is simply the *great ocean*. Even though not being known as something, for the time being it is *all existents*. When *containing*, though it be a mountain, it is not merely *standing atop the highest peak*; though it be water, it is not merely *walking on the bottom of the deepest ocean*. *Gathering in* must be like this, *letting go* must be like this. The *ocean of buddha-nature*, the *ocean of Vairocana's treasury*,[20] are only *all existents*.

Though the surface of the ocean is unseen, there is no doubt in the act of swimming along. For example, in Tafuku's speaking of a grove of bamboo, even if it is *one stem straight, two stems curved, three stems, four stems slanted*,[21] even if it is action causing *all existents* to be missed, why didn't he say it is a thousand curved, ten thousand curved, why didn't he say it is a thousand groves, ten thousand groves? We should not forget the principle that a single grove of bamboo exists in this way. Sōzan's saying *it contains all existents* is still *all existents*.[22]

As for the monk's saying, *Why is one void of breath not attached?*—while it is the face of mistakenly doubting, it must be *what mental activity is this?* When *I had hitherto doubted this fellow*, this is only meeting with *I had hitherto doubted this fellow*. In *what location?* is *why is one void of breath not attached*, it is *why doesn't it retain a dead body*. Here it is precisely *since it contains all existents, why doesn't it retain a dead body?* We should know that containing is not attachment; containing is *not retaining*. Even though all existents be a dead body, it must be the *simply requiring myriad years* of *not retaining*. It must be *the single expression of this old monk* of nonattachment. What Sōzan was trying to say with *it is not that myriad existents are void of breath in effect* is that whether all existents be void of breath or not, one must be unattached. Even though a dead body is a dead body, as long as there is practice which similarly learns from myriad existents, it must contain, it must be containing. The preceding process and the succeeding process, which are all existents, have their effect—this is not being void of breath. It is what is called one of the blind leading a group of the blind. The principle of one of the blind leading a group of the blind is, further, one of the blind leading one of the blind, it is a group of the blind leading a group of the blind. When it is a group of the blind leading a group of the blind, it is *containing all existents* being contained by *containing all existents*. In the Great Path one continues to travel on, if it is not all existents, its practice is not actualized—this is the ocean seal concentration.

1242

Notes

1. "What mental action is this?" is a Zen phrase which is often used to question apparently or actually arbitrary thought or action; or it may

be used to question an intention or expression of thought or action without any presupposition.

2. The "four propositions" are existence, nonexistence, both, neither. These are said to underlie all human conception and to have fallacies which make it impossible for any one of them to be unequivocally true. On the other hand, defining existence as relative existence or conditional existence and nonexistence as emptiness of absolute existence, Buddhist logic shows how all of them can be both true and untrue, summing up the foundations of philosophy therein.

3. "Fundamental enlightenment" refers to the inherent buddha-nature which is said to be in all conscious beings; "initial enlightenment" refers to the realization of this nature. Upon initial realization, the distinction between fundamental and initial enlightenment disappears.

4. "*Elements arise* never leave behind arising"—that is to say, each moment is new, becoming is continuous: "therefore arising is not cognitive awareness, not knowledge or perception"—the direct experience characterized by "not leaving behind arising," or continual renewal, cannot be said to be cognitive awareness, knowledge, or perception because these are after-the-fact organizations of data recollected from the preceding moment of the ongoing flux; also they are indicative of subject-object dichotomy, which does not pertain in direct experience. Thus the nonidentification of arising elements refers to the immediate experience without conceptualization or labeling.

5. A monk asked Razan, "How about when arising and vanishing don't cease?" Razan said, "Tch! Whose arising and vanishing is it?" (or, "Who is it arising and vanishing?") (*Book of Serenity*, case 43)

6. The *Hokke* scripture's book on the "All-Sided One" says the embodiment of universal compassion manifests such and such bodies to people who can be liberated by such and such bodies, in order to teach them; that is, the enlightening beings, the bodhisattvas, appear in different forms according to the mentalities and potentials of the people they teach. Also, in a general sense, "reality" appears differently depending on the perceiver. So Dōgen uses "whose arising and vanishing is it" in a sense as an allusion to the relativity of perceiver and perceived.

7. The *Kongō* scripture says, "The past mind cannot be found (or grasped); the present mind cannot be found; the future mind cannot be found." The question "who?" is commonly used in Zen meditation to focus the attention in such a way as to lead to the actual experience of "the mind cannot be found." The singling out of the "past mind" here seems to direct the attention to unidentified immediate awareness.

8. "You have attained my marrow, you have attained my bones": according to Zen legend, when the Zen founder Bodhidharma was about to

depart from China he called his four enlightened disciples together and had them reveal their understanding one by one. In responding to them, Bodhidharma said to the first, "You have attained my skin," to the second, "You have attained my flesh," to the third, "You have attained my bones," and to the last, "You have attained my marrow." The term *skin-flesh-bones-marrow* is often used by Dōgen, with the sense of the total being, the total experience or realization. Dōgen does not treat these four as different levels of understanding.

9. The bodhisattva, or enlightening being, personifying universal compassion is sometimes represented as having a thousand hands and eyes, to see and save all beings. Case 89 of the *Blue Cliff Record*, to which Dōgen repeatedly alludes in this essay, also is supposed to deal with totality: Ungan asked Dōgo, "What does the bodhisattva of great compassion do with so many hands and eyes?" Dōgo said, "It's like someone reaching back for the pillow in the night." Ungan said, "I understand." Dōgo said, "How?" Ungan said, "All over the body is hands and eyes." Dōgo said, "You've said quite a bit, but you've said only eighty percent." Ungan said, "What do you say?" Dōgo said, "Throughout the body are hands and eyes."

10. "Vanishing" is a word used for "extinction" and "nirvana." In the subsequent text "extinction" is used instead of "vanishing" for convenience.

11. Emptiness ("not saying") is the relativity or conditionality of phenomena, which arise and pass away; hence the temporarily existent and the no longer existent are the same in terms of emptiness *qua* relativity, but emptiness *qua* relativity is not the same as annihilation.

12. Instead of "not enough," there is a variant reading "not it." Emotional interpretations, or clinging to the side of existence, are not right. See the verse and commentary to case 89 of the *Blue Cliff Record*.

13. This means everything exists conditionally ("privately") while nothing exists absolutely ("officially"). It also means wisdom, seeing through everything, doesn't cling to anything, but compassion may use any appropriate means for enlightenment.

14. Var. lect. "They are not relative to the characteristic of awaiting." Nonrelation and nonawaiting refer in a way to both conventional and absolute reality: provisonally, things seem to be discrete; absolutely, there is nothing in essence to relate to or await, because there is no intrinsic reality in elements.

15. This passage can be interpreted in terms of both the Kegon and Hokke teachings. According to Kegon philosophy, the interrelation and independence of all things means that the unit implies the manifold and the manifold implies the unit—so "when one wave moves, myriad follow; when myriad waves move, one follows." Another interpretation

would be to take "one" in a totalistic sense: the one whole contains many elements, many elements make one whole. On this pattern, the first part (myriad following one) represents the Kegon teaching while the second (one following myriad) represents the Hokke. That is, the Kegon, which is represented as the eternal teaching of all Buddhas as manifestations of the cosmic Buddha, emphasizes many teachings emerging from the holistic realization of Buddha; the Hokke teaching, which is called "the lotus of the wonderful teaching," emphasizes many teachings leading into the total enlightenment of Buddha.

16. *Annals of the Empty Hall,* a Zen classic of the Chinese parent of the Sōtō school, says in case 17: "Turning around the light of awareness to illumine within, you directly return: clearly arriving at the spiritual root, it is not grasping or rejection."

17. "Stamping mud, water, space": according to the Sōtō teacher Tenkei Denson, "Though we divide it into three seals according to the potential of people with greater, middling, and lesser faculties, really it is the Great Way which has one stamp—there is nothing else at all. If you stamp space, there is no clue or trace; if you stamp water, there seems to be some clue; if you stamp mud, the pattern appears evident." (Hekiganroku Kōgi)

18. This translation is based on a truncated quotation as it appears in some texts of *Shōbōgenzō.* Other versions have a fuller quote, but this truncated version seems to be the form in which Dōgen intended to use it, to convey the notion that nonattachment does not mean annihilation. Cutting a quote to produce something quite different from the original is something Dōgen does at times when it fits his purpose.

19. This passage refers to eliminating attachments to differentiation and nondifferentiation, to being and nonbeing.

20. Vairocana is the main Buddha of the Kegon scripture, representing cosmic buddhahood; the ocean of Vairocana stands for the cosmos, as described in the Kegon scripture.

21. A monk asked Tafuku, "What is Tafuku's one grove of bamboo?" Tafuku said, "One stem, two stems, slanted." The monk said, "I don't understand." Tafuku said, "Three stems, four stems, curved." (*Transmission of the Lamp,* vol. 11)

22. Var. lect. "is still the great ocean."

The Scripture of Mountains and Waters

(Sansuikyō)

This essay presents an intricate, highly symbolic study of the inter-penetration of phenomenal existence and emptiness. It is characteristic of Zen writing that something may be used both as a metaphor and at face value in the same text, even in the same passage or the same word. In this essay, a most interesting pattern is revealed by taking "mountains" as a symbol of phenomena or existence, and "waters" as a symbol of noumenon or emptiness. These symbolic values, which have precedent in Chinese Zen literature, bring out the coherence of the essay. Because of the interpenetration, or interidentification, of existence and emptiness, the "mountains" and "waters," while primarily representing existence and emptiness respectively, each individually present both existence and emptiness as well.

The essay beings by stating that "mountains and waters" are the way of enlightenment; in essence both are beyond conception. It goes on to emphasize that the way to transcendence or liberation is none other than the "mountains"—this world. To counter the naive notion of phenomena as fixed entities, Dōgen then points out by means of Zen anecdote that while phenomenal existence abides, it is always in flux.

Attacking the limitations of fixed views, Dōgen contrasts the in-finity of reality with the restriction of discriminatory thought. Throughout this essay he demonstrates shifting of perspective, to focus on existence, emptiness, emptiness in existence, existence in emptiness, and their fundamental unity. While this is often thoroughly implicit and embedded in symbolic language, Dōgen also approaches the interpenetration of emptiness and existence more explicitly and analytically through examination of relativity among objects and between subject and object. The former approach is characteristic of the Sanron school of Buddhism, the latter of the Yuishiki school, while both are included in the Tendai and Kegon schools. In this connection Dōgen also pauses to denouce the contention that emptiness has no logic or reason, a view characteristic of immature or degenerate Zen theory.

In view of the length and complexity of this essay, specific explanations of significant transformations which may be obscure are provided in the notes. In general terms, Dōgen is concerned with dismissing the notion that things are just as one views them, the notion of emptiness as nothingness, the notion of permanence as constancy, and the notion of impermanence as annihilation. Thus dealing with the fundamental metaphysical bases of Mahayana Buddhism, the essay is aptly called a "scripture" in this sense as well as in the Kegon sense of "all things teach."

The Scripture of Mountains and Waters

The mountains and waters of the immediate present are the manifestation of the path of the ancient Buddhas. Together abiding in their normative state, they have consummated the qualities of thorough exhaustiveness. Because they are events *prior to the empty eon,*[1] they are the livelihood of the immediate present. Because they are the self *before the emergence of signs,*[1] they are the penetrating liberation of immediate actuality. By the height and breadth of the qualities of the mountains, the virtue of *riding the clouds*[2] is always mastered from the mountains and the subtle work of *following the wind*[2] as a rule penetrates through to liberation from the mountains.

Master Dōkai said to the congregation, *The green mountains are forever walking; a stone woman bears a child by night.*[3] Mountains lack none of the qualities proper to them. For this reason they *forever remain settled* and they *forever walk.* That quality of *walking* should be investigated in detail. Because the *walking* of mountains must be like the walking of people, don't doubt the *walking* of mountains just because it doesn't look the same as the walking of human beings. Now the teaching of the Buddhas and Zen adepts has already pointed out *walking*—this is the attainment of the fundamental. You should thoroughly examine and be sure about this indication to the congregation of *forever walking*—because of *walking*, it is *forever*. Though the *walking* of the *green mountains* is *fast as wind* and even faster, *people in the mountains* are *unaware, uncognizant*. *In the mountains* is *blooming of flowers* that is *inside the world*—and *people outside the mountains* are *unaware, uncognizant*. People who do not have the eyes to see the mountains do not notice, do not know, they do not see, do not hear—it is this principle.

If one doubts the *walking* of the mountains, one doesn't even yet know one's own walking either. It's not that one's own walking doesn't exist—it is that one does not yet know or understand one's own walking. If one knew one's own walking, one would know the walking of the green mountains. The green mountains are not animate, not inanimate; the self is not animate; not inanimate. One should not doubt this *walking* of the green mountains.

Who knows by the measure of how many phenomenal realms the *green mountains* may have perceived. The *walking* of the *green mountains* as well as the walking of oneself should be clearly examined. There should be examination both in *stepping back* and *stepping forward*.[4] *At the precise time* of *before signs*, as well as from *the other side of the king of emptiness*, in *stepping forward* and *stepping back*, *walking* never stops for a moment—this fact you should examine. If *walking* ever stopped, *Buddhas and Zen adepts would not appear*. If walking has a final end, *Buddhism wouldn't have reached the present*. *Stepping forward* has never stopped, *stepping back* has never stopped. When *stepping forward*, that doesn't oppose *stepping back*, and when *stepping back*, that doesn't oppose *stepping forward*. This quality is called the *mountains flowing*, it is called the *flowing mountains*. Because the *green mountains* too learn *walking*, and the *eastern mountains* learn *traveling on the water*, this *learning* is the *learning* of the mountains. This doesn't change the body and mind of the *mountain*—keeping the face of the *mountains*, they have *learned on a winding road*.

Don't repudiate this by saying that the green mountains cannot walk, that the eastern mountains cannot travel on the waters. It is because of the meanness of a low point of view that one doubts the saying *the green mountains are walking;* it is because of the incompetence of little learning that one is startled by the saying *flowing mountains.* While you don't even understand fully the words *flowing water* now, you are only sunk and drowning in small views and small learning.

So it is that the total bringing forth of amassed qualities is made into form and name, into the lifeline. There is *walking*, there is *flowing*. There is a time when mountains give birth to mountain children. Because of the principle of mountains becoming Buddhas and Zen adepts, Buddhas and Zen adepts emerge and appear in this way. Even when we may have eyes for the manifestation of *plants and trees, earth and stones, walls and fences,* we are not in doubt, not disturbed—this is not *total manifestation of being.* Even though a time may manifest when it is seen as *arrays of treasures,* this is not the true ultimate. Even if there is *manifestation of being* seen as the realm of the Buddhas' practice of the Way, it is not necessarily something to love. Even if we attain the summit of *seeing manifestation of being* as the inconceivable qualities of the Buddhas, reality as it is is not only like this. Individual views of being are individual objects and subjects. This is not to say that they are to be considered the *work on the Way* of Buddhas and Zen adepts—they are limited views of one corner. *Transforming the environment, transforming the mind* is something scorned by great sages; *speaking of mind, speaking of nature* is something not approved by Buddhas and Zen adepts; *seeing the mind, seeing nature* is the livelihood of heretics; *sticking to words and phrases* is not the expression of liberation. There is that which has passed through and shed such realms—that is *the green mountains are forever walking,* it is *the eastern mountains travel on the waters.* You should examine this thoroughly.

As for *a stone woman bearing a child by night,* the time when a stone woman bears a child is called *night.* Generally speaking, there are male stones and female stones, and there are stones neither male nor female;[5] they patch the sky and patch the earth. These are celestial stones and earth stones. Though this is a folk saying, it is rare for anyone to know it. You should know the principle of *bearing a child.* When *bearing a child,* do *parent and child emanate together?* Would you only approach the study of this in terms of child becoming parent being the actualization of *bearing a child?* You should study and penetrate how the time when parent becomes child is the *practice and realization* of *bearing a child.*[6]

Greater Master Ummon said, *The eastern mountains travel on the waters.* As for the essential meaning of this expression of being, all mountains are *the eastern mountains;* all *the eastern mountains* are *traveling on the waters.* For this reason the manifestation, the experience of the nine mountains, Mt. Sumeru,[7] and so on is called *the eastern mountains.* But how could Ummon pass freely through the *skin, flesh, bones, and marrow,* the *livelihood of cultivation and realization* of *the eastern mountains?*

Now in China there is a type of incompetent, the number of which has grown so large that it cannot be countered by the small number of the genuine. They say that such stories as the one about *the eastern mountains* and the story of Nansen's sickle[8] are *stories without rational understanding.* Their idea is that stories involved with thoughts are not the Zen stories of the enlightened ones, and that stories without rational understanding are the stories of the enlightened ones. Therefore Ōbaku's caning[9] as well as Rinzai's shouting,[10] being unreachable by rational understanding and having nothing to do with thoughts, they consider to be the great enlightenment which is *before the emergence of indications.* The techniques of the worthies of the past are said to often use phrases which cut off complications—this is nonrational understanding. Those who talk this way have never met a genuine teacher, do not have the eye of meditation study; they are little ignoramuses who are not worth talking about. For the last two or three hundred years in China, baldheaded devil troops like this have been numerous. What a pity—the great Way of the Buddhas and Zen adepts is dying out. The interpretation of these people is not even equal to the listeners of the small vehicle; it is more stupid even than heretics. They are not lay people, not monks, not humans, not celestials. They are stupider even than animals studying the Buddha Way. The *stories without rational understanding* these baldies speak of have no rational understanding for them alone—it is not so of the Buddhas and Zen adepts. Just because they are not rationally understood by you, that doesn't mean you shouldn't study the road of rational understanding of the Buddhas and Zen adepts. Even if it should be *ultimately without rational understanding,* the rational understanding you are voicing now cannot reach it. People like this are numerous in the various Zen centers in China—I saw them with my own eyes. What a pity—they don't know that thoughts are verbal expressions, they don't know that verbal expressions transcend thoughts. When I laughed at them in China, they had nothing to say—they didn't say anything. Nothing but this false idea of no rational understanding. Who taught you this? Even if there is no teacher of natural reality, this is the heretical view of naturalism.

You should know that *the eastern mountains travel on the waters* is the *bones and marrow* of the Buddhas and Zen adepts. The *waters* have become manifest at the feet of *the eastern mountains;* for this reason the mountains climb to the clouds and walk in the heavens. The *top of the head* of *the waters* is *the mountain; walking,* both *heading upwards* and *right down,* is *on the waters.* The points of the feet of *the mountains* walk on *the waters,* cause *the waters* to spurt forth; so the *walking* is uninhibited, it is *not that there is no cultivation and realization.*

Water is not strong or weak, nor wet or dry, not moving or still, not cool or warm, not existent or nonexistent, not delusion or enlightenment. When frozen, it is hard as diamond—who can break it? When melted, it is softer than whey—who can break it? Thus one cannot doubt the qualities it manifestly has.

For the time being you should study the time when you must look upon the waters of the ten directions in the ten directions. This is not the study of only when humans or celestials see water. There is the study of water seeing water. Because water *cultivates and realizes* water, there is the investigation of water expressing water. One should actualize the *way through* where self meets self. Ond should advance on the *living road* where other meets other, and should *leap out.*

Seeing mountains and waters has differences depending on the species. That is to say, there are those who see water as jewel necklaces; nevertheless, that is not seeing jewel necklaces as water. As what forms would we see that which they take to be water? Their jewel necklaces we see as water. There are those who see water as beautiful flowers; but they don't use flowers as water. Ghosts see water as raging fire, as pus and blood. Dragons and fish see palaces and pavilions. Some may see water as precious substances and jewels, or as forests and walls, or as the natural state of *pure liberation,* or as the *real human body,* or as the *characteristics of the body and nature of the mind.* People see it as water. It is an interdependency of killing and enlivening.[11]

It is established that what is seen differs according to the species. For the moment we should question this. Do you say that in viewing one object the views are varied? Do you say it is misapprehending multiple forms as one object? At the peak of effort one should exert further effort. Thus cultivation and experience, clarification of the Way, cannot be either one or dual; the ultimate sphere must be a thousandfold, ten thousandfold. In reflecting further on the basic meaning here, even though the types of water may be many, it is as if there were no basic water, as if there were no water of various kinds. However, the various waters according to the species (of perceiver) do not depend on mind, do not depend on body, are not born from actions, are not dependent on the eyes, do not depend on others—there is transcendence which *depends on water.*[12] Therefore *water* is not of the ranks of *earth-water-fire-air-space-consciousness,*[13] water is not blue, yellow, red, white, black, and so on, it is not form, sound, odor, flavor, feeling, phenomenon, and so on—yet nevertheless the water of *earth-water-fire-air-space-consciousness* is spontaneously manifested. Being so, one can hardly say for sure what the lands and dwellings of the present are producers or products of. To say they are resting in a sphere of space or an atmosphere is not the truth of self and not the truth of other—it is a proposal of the calculation of a small view. This statement comes from the idea that they cannot abide if they don't rest on anything.

Buddha said, *All things, ultimately liberated, have no abode.* You should know that although they are liberated and have no bondage, *all things dwell in their normative state.* This being so, when humans see water, there is a way of seeing it as flowing incessantly. That flowing has many kinds—this is one aspect of people's perception. It is said to flow through the earth, flow through the sky, flow upwards, flow downwards, flow through one bend, and flow in nine abyssal troughs. Rising, it becomes clouds; descending, it becomes pools.

In an old Confucian book it says, "The path of water is to become rain and dew when it goes up into the sky, to become rivers and streams when it descends to the earth." Even the saying of a worldly man was like this; for those who would claim to be descendants of the Buddhas and Zen founders to be more ignorant than a worldling would be most shameful. What this says is that while the path of water is not yet consciously known by water, yet water does actualize it; while it is not that water is unaware, water does actualize its course. The book says *ascending to the sky, it becomes rain and dew*—you should know that water ascends to any number of skies and upper regions and makes rain and dew. *Rain and dew* are various according to the world. To say there is somewhere water doesn't reach is the teaching of the listeners of the small vehicle. Or it is the wrong teaching of heretics. *Water* reaches even into the flames of fire, it reaches even into thoughts, contemplations, and discriminations, and it reaches into awareness of the buddha-nature.

Descending to the earth, it becomes rivers and streams: you should know that when water descends to the earth it makes rivers and streams. The spirit of rivers and streams becomes wise people. Now what ordinary fools and common types think is that *water* must be in rivers, streams, oceans. That is not so. Rivers and oceans are made within *water*, therefore there is *water* even in places where there are no rivers or seas; when water descends to the earth it performs the function of rivers and seas, that's all. Also, you shouldn't get the idea that in places where water has formed rivers or seas there can't be worlds or buddha-lands there. Even in one drop infinite buddha-lands are manifest. So it is not that there is *water* in buddha-lands, and it is not that there are buddha-lands in *water*. Where *water* is has no relation to past, present, or future, no relation to the elemental cosmos. Yet even so, it is the *issue* of the *manifestation of water*. Wherever there are Buddhas and Zen adepts, there must be *water*; wherever there is *water*, Buddhas and Zen adepts must appear. Because of this, Buddhas and Zen adepts always bring up *water* as their body and mind, as their meditation. Therefore to say *water* doesn't rise on high is not in accord with either Buddhist or non-Buddhist classics. The *path of water* is to permeate *above and below, vertically and horizontally.*

However, in Buddhist scriptures, fire and air rise above, earth and water descend below. This *above and below* has a point to study. That is to study the *above and below* of the Buddha Way. That is to say, where earth and water go is considered *below*—it is not that *below* is taken to be the place where earth and water go. Where fire and air go is *above*—it is not that *above* is taken to be where fire and air go. Though the elemental cosmos doesn't necessarily have anything to do with measurements of direction, nevertheless, based on the action of the four, five, and six major elements, we temporarily set up an elemental cosmos of locations and directions. It is not that *thoughtless heaven* is above and *uninterrupted hell* is below— *uninterrupted hell* is the whole cosmos, *thoughtless heaven* is the whole cosmos too. Thus, when dragons and fish see water as palaces, it must be like people seeing palaces. They cannot cognize or see them as flowing anymore. If a bystander should tell them, "Your palaces are flowing water," the dragons and fish would be surprised and doubtful, just as we are when we now hear it said that the mountains are flowing. Yet they might maintain that there is such an explanation of the balustrades, stairs, and pillars of the palaces and pavilions. You should quietly ponder this treatment of the matter.

If you do not learn to penetrate freely beyond these bounds, you have not been liberated from the body and mind of ordinary people, you have not thoroughly investigated the lands of Buddhas and Zen adepts. Nor have you thoroughly investigated the lands of ordinary people, and they have not thoroughly investigated the palaces of ordinary people. Though now in the human world they have deeply ingrained cognition of what is in the oceans and rivers as water, they do not yet know what dragons, fish, and so on perceive and know and use as water. Do not ignorantly assume that what you perceive and know as water is used as water by all other species too. One should not linger only in the human realm—one should go on to study the *water* of the Buddha Way. As what do we see the *water* used by Buddhas and Zen adepts—one should study this. One should also study whether there is or there is not *water* in the house of the Buddhas and Zen adepts.

Mountains have been the dwelling place of great sages since beyond the past and beyond the present. Wise people and holy people both have made mountains their inner sanctum, have made mountains their body and mind; due to the wise and holy people, mountains have become manifest. Though it seems that so many great saints and great sages have gone into the mountains and gathered there, after having entered the mountains, there is not a single person who has met a single person—it is only a manifestation of the livelihood of the mountains. There are no further traces even of having entered.

In the time of gazing at the mountains while being in the world, the *crown and eyes* are far different from the time of meeting the mountains in the mountains. The idea of not flowing, and the cognition and view of not flowing as well, could not be equal to the cognition and views of dragons and fish. Humans and celestials find palaces in their own worlds; other species doubt this, or may not even get to the point of doubting. Thus you should learn about the saying *mountains flow* from Buddhas and Zen adepts—you should not give free reign to surprise and doubt. *Bringing up one, it is flowing; bringing up one, it is not flowing: one time is flowing; one time is not flowing.*[14] Without this exhaustive study, it is not *the Buddha's wheel of true teaching.* An ancient Buddha said, *If you want to be able not to elicit hellish karma, don't repudiate the Buddha's wheel of true teaching.* You should engrave this statement on your *skin, flesh, bones, and marrow.* You should engrave it on *body and mind, object and subject;* you should engrave it on *emptiness,* engrave it on *form.* It is engraved on *trees and stones,* on *fields and hamlets.*

Though mountains belong to the territory of the nation, they are entrusted to people who love the mountains. When mountains definitely love the "owners," saints, sages, and those of exalted virtue are in the mountains. When saints and sages live in the mountains, because the mountains belong to them, *the trees and rocks are abundant, the birds and beasts are holy.* This is because the saints and sages affect them with their virtue. You should know that the fact exists that mountains like sages and saints.

Many rulers have gone to the mountains to pay respects to sages and ask questions of great saints—this is an excellent example for past and present. When they do so, they pay respect to the saints as teachers, without following the ordinary laws of society. In the sphere of influence of wise rulers, there is no compulsion of mountain sages at all. It should be obvious that the mountains are apart from human society. In remote antiquity a chieftain went on his knees kowtowing to call on a sage in the mountains. Shakyamuni Buddha left the palace of his father the raja and went into the mountains, but his father didn't resent the mountains, nor did he suspect the people in the mountains who taught his son. Most of the Buddha's twelve years of training were in the mountains. The beginning of his teaching was also in the mountains. Truly even a supreme ruler doesn't coerce the mountains. Know that the *mountains* are not the realm of human society, not the realm of heavens. One cannot know or see the *mountains* by the measurements of human thought. If they did not take the flowing of the human world as the standard of comparison, who would doubt the *flowing of the mountains* or the *nonflowing of the mountains?*

Then again, since ancient times there have occasionally been sages and saints who live on the water. While living on the water, they have caught fish, they have caught people, they have caught the Way. All of these are ancient traditions of life on the waters. Advancing further, there should be catching oneself, there should be catching catching, there should be being caught by catching, there should be being caught by the Way.

In olden times monk Tokujō one day left Yakuzan to live on the river. Then he found the sage of Flower Inn River. Why not catch fish, catch people, catch water, catch oneself? Someone's getting to see *virtue and sincerity* is virtue and sincerity; *virtue and sincerity* making contact with someone is meeting someone.[15]

It is not just that there is water in the world; there are worlds in the realm of water. And this is so not only in water—there are also worlds of sentient beings in clouds, there are worlds of sentient beings in wind, there are worlds of sentient beings in fire, there are worlds of sentient beings in earth, there are worlds of sentient beings in phenomena, there are worlds of sentient beings in a single blade of grass, there are worlds of sentient beings in a single staff.[16] Where there are worlds of sentient beings, there must be the world of Buddhas and Zen adepts[17]—you should meditate on this principle very thoroughly.

So water is the palace of the true dragon.[18] It is not flowing. If you recognize it only as flowing, the word *flow* slanders water. That is because it is like insisting that it doesn't flow. *Water* is just the *true form of thusness* of water. The fact is that *water is the quality of water.* It is not *flowing.* In investigating the flow of one body of water and investigating *not flowing*, the *completed investigation* of myriad phenomena suddenly becomes apparent.

In the case of mountains too, there are mountains concealed in jewels, there are mountains concealed in marshes, there are mountains concealed in the sky, there are mountains concealed in mountains. There is study which *conceals mountains in concealment.*

An ancient Buddha said, *Mountains are mountains, waters are waters.* This saying does not say that "mountains" are mountains; it says mountains are mountains. Therefore you should investigate the mountains. If you investigate the mountains; that is meditation in the mountains. Such mountains and waters of themselves make sages and saints.

1240

Notes

1. These are standard Zen phrases meaning before or beyond conceptualization.
2. These are Taoistic expressions, here used to refer to freedom or transcendence.
3. "Stone woman" means a barren woman, but the term is rendered literally here for the sake of subsequent metaphor, since it does not alter the meaning. A stone/barren woman bearing a child refers to conditions without inherent nature producing interdependent origination. That is to say, phenomena, being conditional, have no absolute own-being, are not existent as independent entities. As "not existent," they are represented by the term "barren woman," which cannot produce. Yet in terms of conditional relations, things do exist—this is the "child." This is what is referred to by the Zen terms "really empty yet inconceivably existing." "Night" symbolizes emptiness, which is the identity of relative existence and absolute emptiness. The "mountains walking" alludes to the continual flux of the phenomenal, which temporally exists, but not as something static and fixed. This saying of Dōkai sums up the teaching of emptiness within existence and existence within emptiness.
4. "Stepping back" and "stepping forward" may be interpreted as contemplation of "existence is empty" and "emptiness is existence," respectively. The famed Sandōkai of Sekitō, a Chinese classic of Sōtō Zen, says, "Light and darkness are relative, like forward and backward steps." Experientially, stepping back and stepping forward can also be interpreted as, respectively, introspection and merging with the world.
5. Commentaries often refer to folk beliefs, but the point Dōgen seems to be driving at is that emptiness does not mean nondifferentiation in terms of characteristics; there is differentiation, but the differentiations are not absolutes. Hence "stone" may refer to emptiness in essence, "male and female" to characteristics of forms. Again this points to the nonduality of emptiness and form. Also, based on the ancient Zen terminology of "like a stone," used to describe the nonattached mind, this can refer to the ability to be unattached yet still active and versatile, able to appear and act in different ways without that action disturbing fundamental transcendence.

6. Child becoming parent and parent becoming child refer to the relativity of cause and effect—"cause" cannot be "cause" without "effect," by definition, so in a sense "effect" creates "cause." Generally, things are produced by conditions, but since the conditions must be interdependent, they cannot exist as conditions outside of their interrelation—so the "child," the interrelation, or product, is in that sense parent to the "parent" conditions. This type of reasoning was articulated by the Buddhist philosopher Nāgārjuna, to show the inconceivability of simultaneous interdependent origination in terms of linear logic. The specific manifestation of relativity which is illustrated by "child and parent" in the literal sense of the words is of course also possible here.

7. The nine mountains and Mt. Sumeru allude to an ancient Indian image of the world which was incorporated into Buddhist lore.

8. Nansen was working on the mountainside when a monk stopped and asked him, without realizing who he was, the way to Master Nansen's place. Nansen held up his sickle and said, "I bought this sickle for thirty coins." The monk said, "I didn't ask about the sickle—which way is it to Nansen?" Nansen said, "I use it real fast."

9. Thrice Rinzai asked Ōbaku the meaning of Buddhism, and Ōbaku hit him each time. Later someone told Rinzai that Ōbaku was just trying to relieve him of his distress (by halting his seeking mind), and upon hearing this Rinzai was enlightened.

10. Rinzai was famous for using shouts in his teaching activity. He said sometimes his shout was like a probe, sometimes like a cutting sword, sometimes like a crouching lion, and sometimes not used as "a shout."

11. What something "is" or "is not" (appears to be or does not appear to be) in the terms of the perceiver is a dependent matter. "Killing" means denial or nonbeing, "enlivening" means affirmation or being. The phenomenon of seeing things in different ways denies the absoluteness or ineluctability of any particular way of perceiving, yet affirms the possibility of all perceptions there may be.

12. This refers to the emptiness of own-being of water in noumenal terms, approached by repudiating the own-being of various waters in relations. In terms of the doctrine of emptiness—conditionality, emptiness is not itself something relative to existence, so there is no "basic water," taking "water" as a symbol for emptiness—"emptiness" is not itself something that exists. Furthermore, conditions do not have absolute existence, so there are no "various waters." The particular relative or conditional existents are usually said to depend on mind, or perception, and so on, but that refers to characteristics—here Dōgen is talking about essence, the very absence of own-being or inherent nature; this is the "transcendence which depends on water (emptiness)." In terms of

Kegon philosophy, this is expressed by saying that form is empty (being relative), but the characteristics of form are not themselves the principle of emptiness.

13. These are the six major elements of the cosmos according to the description used in the Shingon school of Buddhism.

14. We may see the same actuality in terms of phenomenal characteristics (which flow) or noumenal emptiness (which does not flow).

15. I take this as a play on the name Tokujō, which literally means virtue and sincerity, saying that one can only see sincerity if one is sincere oneself, and contact with sincerity being what is called "meeting someone" in the Zen mind-to-mind sense of meeting. The fact that Dōgen uses the name Tokujō here instead of the nickname for this person—"The Boat Monk"—which is usually used, strengthens the case for taking it at its semantic value.

16. Each phenomenon is or contains various worlds according to the perception of various beings, the perception of each being in relation to the phenomenon being as it were a realm or a world.

17. According to the doctrine of Tendai Buddhism, the realm of buddhahood is latent in all realms of conscious beings.

18. "Dragons" are said to live in water, but here dragon is symbolic. The "dragon *samādhi*" represents being in the world and engaging in action without being fundamentally disturbed in mind; this can only be accomplished by realization of emptiness, because there is inevitably a limit to forced control.

BEING TIME
(Uji)

This essay has provoked the interest of most modern writers on Dōgen, presenting what seems to be his most original idea: the identity of being and time. This might be represented by the statement that time is a necessary factor of all manifestations of being. But Dōgen is less abstract. In effect, time here is seen as being concrete, being is seen as concrete, and the two are seen as inseparable in this concreteness.

Ordinary definitions of time, understood in terms of duration of objects or events, or as differentiations of velocity and distance, demand a concrete context, so the notion of the inseparability of being and time, arresting though it may be when expressed as *being-time*, is not especially difficult for the modern reader to acknowledge. What is more, Dōgen's idea of being time bears a degree of resemblance to the concept of space-time in the relativity theory of modern physics. In space-time, *time* is the fourth dimension, or fourth coordinate in terms of which, along with three spacelike coordinates, events are described.

One aspect of space-time is that the dimension of time is relative to the observer. In this essay Dōgen also shows how time may be seen in different ways—how, for example, "it passes from today to tomorrow, and passes from today to yesterday." That is, from the standpoint of looking forward and looking backward, time progresses from the present into the future, so that the passing present recedes into the past. This is the usual view of time. But then Dōgen goes on to say, "It passes from yesterday to today, it passes from today to today, it passes from tomorrow to tomorrow." The passage of time "from yesterday to today" is like its passage "from today to tomorrow" except that it refers to the future of the past instead of the future of the present. "From today to today" refers to the present of the present, each passing day being "today" from the vantage point of the day itself. "From tomorrow to tomorrow" refers to the future of the future, "tomorrow" as "the next day" never becoming today, but continuing to become "tomorrow."

This view of the relativity of time, one of the so-called ten mysteries of Kegon Buddhism, includes the notion of all things in all times always existing, in their respective times—that is, since their mutual relativity includes the relativity of their "time," they all exist at once without losing the order of their respective times. This view of the noninterference of linear time and "total" time is skillfully presented by Dōgen, and the essay demonstrates how particular manifestations of being are not only individual times but also part of the total fabric of the whole manifestation of being time. Thus all things and beings have their respective being times while simultaneously sharing in the being time of all existence.

While "being time" is one of the most, if not the most, striking and original presentations in Dōgen's thought, a survey of his entire work shows that he did not sloganize this expression or try to build a philosophy on this point per se. Rather, this essay on being time is another of Dōgen's versatile and lucid expressions of his more encompassing theme: the unity of being, and the misdirection of seeking or thinking of enlightenment outside the here and now.

BEING TIME

An ancient Buddha said, *At a time of being, standing on the summit of the highest peak; at a time of being, walking on the bottom of the deepest ocean; at a time of being, three-headed and eight-armed;*[1] *at a time of being, sixteen feet and eight feet;*[2] *at a time of being, staff and whisk; at a time of being, pillar and lamp;*[3] *at a time of being, the average man; at a time of being, earth and sky.*

So-called *time of being* means time is already being; all being is time. The *sixteen foot tall golden body* is time; because it is time, it has the adornments and radiance of time. You should study it in the twenty-four hours of the present. *Three-headed, eight-armed* is time; because it is time, it must be *one suchness* in the twenty-four hours of the present. The length and brevity of the twenty-four hours, though not as yet measured, is called twenty-four hours. Because the direction and course of their going and coming are obvious, people don't doubt them—yet though they don't doubt them, this is not to say that they know them. Because sentient beings' doubting of things which they don't know is not fixed, the future course of their doubting does not necessarily accord with their doubts of the present. It's just that doubting is for the moment *time*.

Self is arrayed as the whole world. You should perceive that each point, each thing of this *whole world* is an individual *time*. The mutual noninterference of things is like the mutual noninterference of *times*. For this reason there is *arousal of minds at the same time*, there is *arousal of times in the same mind*. Cultivating practice and achieving enlightenment are also like this. Arraying self, self sees this—such is the principle of *self* being *time*.

Because it is the principle of *being such*, there are *myriad forms, a hundred grasses*[4] on *the whole earth*. You should learn that each *single blade of grass*, each *single form*, is on *the whole earth*. Such *going and coming* is the starting point of cultivation of practice. When one reaches the state of *suchness*, it is *one blade of grass, one form*; it is *understanding forms, not understanding forms*, it is *understanding grasses, not understanding grasses*.[5] Because it is only *right at such a time*, therefore *being time* is all *the whole time*. *Being grass* and *being form* are both time. In the time of *time's time* there is *the whole of being, the whole world*. For a while try to visualize whether or not there is *the whole being, the whole world* apart from the present time.

In spite of this, when people are ordinary folk who have not studied the Buddha's teaching, the views they have are such that when they hear the expression *a time of being*, they think at some time one had become *three-headed and eight-armed*, at some time one had become *sixteen feet tall, eight feet seated*, like having crossed rivers and crossed mountains. They think, "Even though those mountains and rivers may exist still, I have passed them and am now in the vermillion tower of the jewel palace—the mountains and rivers and I are as far apart as sky and earth." However, the truth is not just this one line of reasoning alone. In the time one climbed the mountains and crossed the rivers, there was oneself. There must be *time* in oneself. Since oneself exists, *time* cannot leave. If time is not the appearances of going and coming, the time of climbing a mountain is the *immedi-*

ate present of *being time.* If time preserves the appearances of going and coming, there is in oneself the *immediate present* of *being time*—this is *being time.* Does not that *time* of *climbing mountains and crossing rivers* swallow up this *time* of the *vermillion tower of the jewel palace?* Does it not spew it forth?

Three-headed, eight-armed is yesterday's *time; sixteen feet, eight feet* is today's *time.* However, the principle of *yesterday and today* is just the time of directly entering the mountains and gazing out over the thousand peaks, the myriad peaks—it is not a matter of having passed. *Three-headed, eight-armed* too *transpires* as one's own *being time; sixteen feet, eight feet* too *transpires* as one's own *being time.* Though it seems to be elsewhere, it is *right now.* So pines are *time* too; bamboo is *time* too.

One should not understand time only as flying away; one should not only get the idea that flying away is the function of time. If time only were to fly, then there would be gaps. Not having heard of the path of *being time* is because of learning only that it has passed. To tell the gist of it, all existences in the whole world, while being lined up, are individual times. Because it is *being time*, it is *my being time.*

In *being time* there is the quality of passage. That is, it passes from today to tomorrow, it passes from today to yesterday, it passes from yesterday to today, it passes from today to today, it passes from tomorrow to tomorrow.

Because passage is a quality of time, past and present time doesn't pile up, doesn't accumulate in a row—nevertheless Seigen is *time,* Ōbaku too is *time,* Baso and Sekitō also are *time.*[6] Since self and others are *time,* cultivation and realization are times. *Going into the mud, going into the water*[7] is similarly *time.*

Though the present views and the conditions of views of ordinary people are what ordinary people see, they are not the norm of ordinary people. It is merely that the norm temporarily conditions ordinary people. Because of learning that this *time,* this *being,* are not the norm, they take the *sixteen foot tall golden body* as not themselves. Trying to escape by claiming that oneself is not the *sixteen foot tall golden body* is also itself bits of *being time;* it is the *looking* of those *who have not yet verified it.*[8]

Even causing the horses and sheep now arrayed in the world to exist is the *rising and falling, ups and downs* which are the *suchness of remaining in the normal position.*[9] The *rat* is time, the *tiger* is time too.[10] Living beings are time. Buddhas are time too. This *time* witnesses the whole world with *three heads and eight arms*, it witnesses the whole world with *the sixteen foot tall golden body.*

Now exhausting the limits of the whole world by means of the whole world is called investigating exhaustively. To actualize being *the sixteen foot golden body* by means of *the sixteen foot golden body* as determination, cultivating practice, enlightenment, and nirvana, is *being*, is *time*. Just investigating exhaustively *all time* as *all being*, there is nothing left over. Because leftovers are leftovers, even the *being time* of half-exhaustive investigation is the exhaustive investigation of half *being time.*[11]

Even forms which seem to slip by are *being*. Furthermore, if you leave it at that, being the period of manifestation of *slipping by*, it is the *abiding in position* of *being time*. Don't stir it as nonexistence, don't insist on it as existence. Only conceiving of time as passing one way, one doesn't understand it as not yet having arrived. Though understanding is *time*, it has no relation drawn by another.[12] Only recognizing it as coming and going, no skin bag[13] has seen through it as *being time* of *abiding in position*—how much less could there be a time of *passing through the barrier?* Even recognizing *remaining in position*, who can express the preservation of *already being such?* Even if they have long expressed it as *such*, still everyone gropes for the appearance of its countenance. If we leave ordinary people's being *being time* at that, then even enlightenment and nirvana are only *being time* which is merely the appearances of going and coming.

In sum, it cannot be ensnared or arrested—it is the manifestation of *being time*. The celestial monarchs and celestial beings manifesting in the regions right and left are *being time* now exerting their whole strength. The other myriad *being times* of water and land are now manifesting exerting their whole strength. The various species and objects that are *being time* in darkness and light are all the manifestation of their whole strength, they are the passage of their total strength. If they were not the present *passage of whole strength*, not one single thing would become manifest, there would be no passage— you should study it this way. You should not have been learning about passage as like the wind and rain's going east and west. The *whole world* is not *inactive*, it is not *neither progressing nor regressing*: it is *passage.*

Passage is, for example, like spring: in spring there are numerous appearances—this is called *passage*. You should learn that it *passes through* without any external thing. For example, the *passage* of spring necessarily *passes through* spring. Though *passage* is not spring, because it is the *passage* of spring, *passage* has *accomplished the Way* in this *time* of spring. You should examine thoroughly in whatever you are doing. In speaking of *passage*, if you think that the objective realm is outside and the phenomenon which *passes through* passes a million worlds to the east through a billion eons, in thinking thus you are not concentrating wholly on the study of the Buddha Way.

Yakuzan, at the direction of the Zen master Sekitō, went to call on the Zen master Baso. He said, "As far as the Buddhist canon is concerned, I pretty much understand its message—what is the living meaning of Zen?" When Yakuzan asked this, Baso said, "Sometimes I have him raise the eyebrows and blink the eyes. Sometimes I don't have him raise the eyebrows and blink the eyes. Sometimes having him raise the eyebrows and blink the eyes is it, sometimes having him raise the eyebrows and blink the eyes is not it." Hearing this, Yakuzan was greatly enlightened. He said to Baso, "When I was with Sekitō, I was like a mosquito climbing on an iron ox."

What Baso says is not the same as others. *Eyebrows and eyes* must be *mountains and oceans*, because *mountains and oceans* are *eyebrows and eyes*. That *having him raise* must see the *mountains*, that *having him blink* must have its source in the *ocean*. *It* is conditioned by *him*, *he* is induced by causation.[14] *Not it* is not *not having him*, *not having him* is not *not it*. These are all *being time*. The mountains are *time*, the oceans are *time* too. If they were not *time*, the mountains and oceans could not be. You should not think there is no *time* in the *immediate present* of the mountains and oceans. If *time* disintegrates, mountains and oceans too disintegrate; if *time* is indestructible, mountains and oceans too are indestructible. On this principle *the morning star* appears, *the Buddha* appears, *the eye* appears, *the raising of the flower* appears. This is *time*. If it were not *time*, it would not be thus.

Zen Master Kisei of Sekken was a religious descendant of Rinzai, and was the heir of Shuzan. One time he said to the community, "Sometimes the intent arrives but the expression doesn't arrive: sometimes the expression arrives but the intent doesn't arrive. Sometimes intent and expression both arrive, sometimes neither intent nor expression arrive." *Intent* and *expression* are both *being time; arriving* and *not arriving* are both *being time.* Though *the time of arrival is incomplete,* yet *the time of nonarrival has come. Intent* is a donkey, *expression* is a horse; the horse is considered the expression, the donkey is considered the intent. *Arriving* is not *coming; not arriving* is not *yet to come.* This is the way *being time* is. *Arriving* is blocked by *arriving,* not blocked by *not arriving. Not arriving* is blocked by *not arriving,* not blocked by *arriving. Intent* blocks *intent* and sees *intent; expression* blocks *expression* and sees *expression. Blocking* blocks *blocking* and sees *blocking. Blocking* blocks *blocking*—this is *time.*[15] Though *blocking* is used by *other things,* there is never any *blocking* which blocks *other things.*[16] It is *oneself meeting other people,* it is *other people meeting other people,* it is *oneself meeting oneself,* it is *going out* meeting *going out.* If these do not have *time,* they are not *so.*

Also, *intent* is the *time* of *the issue at hand; expression* is the *time* of *the key of transcendence. Arriving* is the *time of the whole body; not arriving* is the *time* of *one with this, detached from this.* In this way should you correctly understand and *be time.*

Though the aforementioned adepts have all spoken as mentioned, is there nothing further to say? We should say *intent and expression half arriving too is being time; intent and expression half not arriving too is being time.* There should be study like this. *Having him raise his eyebrows and blink his eyes is half being time; having him raise his eyebrows and blink his eyes is amiss being time. Not having him raise his eyebrows and blink his eyes is half being time; not having him raise his eyebrows and blink his eyes is amiss being time.*[17] To investigate thus, coming and going, investigating arriving and investigating not arriving, is the *time* of *being time.*

1240

Notes

1. "Three-headed and eight-armed" is the form of a titan, representing wrath.
2. The idealized or glorified body of Buddha, representing higher development of humanity, is referred to as being sixteen feet tall standing and eight feet high seated.

3. "Staff and whisk," "pillar and lamp," are often used in Zen lore to stand for objects or phenomena in general.

4. "Hundred grasses," or hundred plants, is a conventional term for all things or all forms.

5. "Understanding" and "not understanding" refer, respectively, to the realm of phenomena and appearances and the realm of noumenon or emptiness. Clarifying and sharpening relative understanding while at the same time being aware of the ultimate inconceivability of existence in itself is a Zen art.

6. Seigen, Ōbaku, Baso, and Sekitō were all famous Chinese Zen adepts of the eighth to ninth centuries.

7. "Going into mud and water" is a standard expression for entering the world, often used to refer to one who has transcended the world, then willingly acting in the world for an instructive purpose.

8. Rinzai said, "In this naked mass of flesh is a true human with no position or rank, always coming in and going out through the senses. Those who have not yet witnessed it, look!"

9. "Remaining in the normal position," or abiding in the normative state, is a phrase from the *Hokke* scripture often used by Dōgen. It means in effect that emptiness of absolute identity or unconditional existence does not negate relative identity or existence.

10. Rat and tiger are used to name particular times in the twelve-hour day of Sino-Japanese calendry, and as signs of the zodiac are also assigned to years in the twelve-year cycle.

11. "Leftovers being leftovers" seems to refer to noumenon and phenomena in terms of their separate identities as different aspects or facets of the totality of interdependent origination. Half-exhaustive investigation would be that of either noumenon (absolute emptiness) or phenomena (the realm of appearances and differentiation), the exhaustive investigation of either one being that of half being-time, as being-time is the totality of noumenon and phenomena.

12. Var. lect. "another time."

13. "Skin bag" means the mortal or physical being.

14. The living meaning of Zen ("it") as being time is conditioned, in its manifestation, by the person: the person is manifest according to causation (karma). This passage thus can be taken to mean that though the essence of Zen is in everyone, its expression, or realization, depends on personal cultivation.

15. Here "block" means being within a particular being-time; hence it says that states or things "block" themselves—this is in the sense of their being in, or being, their respective being-times.

16. The being in a particular being-time also defines ("is used by") other

things by relativity: an individual being-time does not interfere with the being-time of anything else, however.

17. Again, emptiness and relative existence are each "one half"—if there is one-sided clinging to emptiness ("not raising the eyebrows") or existence ("raising the eyebrows"), this is "amiss."

The Eight Awarenesses of Great People

(Hachidaininkaku)

Ultimately, Buddhism is supposed to be practical, and its traditional reservation about philosophy is that in the excitement of intellectual exercise there is a tendency to forget that the teachings are meant to be applied. One of the great Buddhist teachers of China put it in these terms: first comes understanding, without which action is blind; then comes action, without which understanding is ineffective; finally understanding and action become one.

"Don't do any evil, do what is good, and purify the mind—this is the teaching of all Buddhas." This ancient formulation of Buddhism sums up the message of the final three chapters of *Shōbōgenzō* to be presented in this volume. Together they illustrate three fundamental phases or elements of Zen found throughout the whole of the Buddhist teachings: detachment, integration, and harmonization of detachment and integration.

The Eight Awarenesses of Great People, ostensibly written for mendicants but applying to lay people as well, may be considered a general outline of the main elements of Buddhist practice concerning detachment. The result of nirvana, is sometimes referred to as coolness, dispassion, noncontentiousness. The peace and mind and clarity thus realized are one facet of liberation.

The Eight Awarenesses of Great People

The Buddhas are great people. As these are what is realized by great people, they are called the awareness of great people. Realizing these principles is the basis of nirvana. This was the final teaching of our original teacher, Shakyamuni Buddha, on the night he passed away into final extinction.

1. Having few desires

Not extensively seeking objects of desire not yet attained is called having few desires.

Buddha said, "You monks should know that people with many desires seek to gain a lot, and therefore their afflictions are also many. Those with few desires have no seeking and no craving, so they don't have this problem. You should cultivate having few desires even for this reason alone, to say nothing of the fact that having few desires can produce virtues. People with few desires are free from flattery and deviousness whereby they might seek to curry people's favor, and they also are not under the compulsion of their senses. Those who act with few desires are calm, without worry or fear. Whatever the situation, there is more than enough—there is never insufficiency. Those who have few desires have nirvana."

2. Being content

To take what one has got within bounds is called being content.

Buddha said, "O monks, if you want to shed afflictions, you should observe contentment. The state of contentment is the abode of prosperity and happiness, peace and tranquility. Those who are content may sleep on the ground and still consider it comfortable; those who are not content would be dissatisfied even in heaven. Those who are not content are always caught up in sensual desires; they are pitied by those who are content."

3. Enjoying quietude

Leaving the clamor and staying alone in deserted places is called enjoying quietude.

Buddha said, "O monks, if you wish to seek the peace and happiness of quietude and nonstriving, you should leave the clamor and live without clutter in a solitary place. People in quiet places are honored by the gods. Therefore you should leave your own group as well as other groups, stay alone in a deserted place, and think about extirpating the root of suffering. Those who like crowds suffer the vexations of crowds, just as a big tree will suffer withering and breakage when flocks of birds gather on it. Worldly ties and clinging sink you into a multitude of pains, like an old elephant sunk in the mud, unable to get itself out."

4. Diligence

Diligently cultivating virtues without interruption is called diligence, pure and unalloyed, advancing without regression

Buddha said, "O monks, if you make diligent efforts, nothing is hard. Therefore you should be diligent. It is like even a small stream being able to pierce rock if it continually flows. If the practitioner's mind flags and gives up time and gain, that is like drilling for fire but stopping before heat is produced—though you want to get fire, fire can hardly be gotten this way."

5. Unfailing recollection

This is also called keeping right mindfulness; keeping the teachings without loss is called right mindfulness, and also called unfailing recollection.

Buddha said, "O monks, if you seek a good companion and seek a good protector and helper, nothing compares to unfailing recollection. Those who have unfailing recollection cannot be invaded by the thieving afflictions. Therefore you should concentrate your thoughts and keep mindful. One who loses mindfulness loses virtues. If one's power of mindfulness is strong, even if one enters among the thieving desires one will not be harmed by them. It is like going to the front lines wearing armor—then one has nothing to fear."

6. Cultivating meditation concentration

Dwelling on the teaching without distraction is called meditation concentration.

Buddha said, "O monks, if you concentrate the mind, it will be in a state of stability and you will be able to know the characteristics of the phenomena arising and perishing in the world. Therefore you should energetically cultivate and learn the concentrations. If you attain concentration, your mind will not be distracted. Just as a household careful of water builds a dam, so does the practitioner, for the sake of the water of knowledge and wisdom, cultivate meditation concentration well, to prevent them from leaking."

7. Cultivating wisdom

Developing learning, thinking, and application, the realization is wisdom.

Buddha said, "O monks, if you have wisdom, you will have no greedy attachment. Always examine yourselves and do not allow any heedlessness. Then you will be able to attain liberation from ego and things. Otherwise, you are neither people of the Way nor laypeople—there is no way to refer to you. True wisdom is a secure ship to cross the sea of aging, sickness, and death. It is also a bright lamp in the darkness of ignorance, good medicine for all the ailing, a sharp axe to fell the trees of afflictions. Therefore you should use the wisdom of learning, thinking, and application, and increase it yourself. If anyone has the illumination of wisdom, this is a person with clear eyes, even though it be the mortal eye."

8. Not engaging in vain talk

Realizing detachment from arbitrary discrimination is called not engaging in vain talk; when one has fully comprehended the character of reality, one will not engage in vain talk.

Buddha said, "O monks, if you indulge in various kinds of vain talk, your mind will be disturbed. Even if you leave society you will still not attain liberation. Therefore you should immediately give up vain talk which disturbs the mind. If you want to attain bliss of tranquility and dispassion, you should extinguish the affliction of vain talk."

These are the eight awarenesses of great people. Each one contains the eight, so there are sixty-four. If you expand them, they must be infinite; if you summarize them, there are sixty-four. After the final speech of the great teacher Shakyamuni, made for the instruction of the Great Vehicle, the ultimate discourse at midnight on the fifteenth day of the second month, he didn't preach anymore and finally became utterly extinct.

Buddha said, "You monks always should single-mindedly seek the path of emancipation. All things in the world, mobile and immobile, are unstable forms which disintegrate. Stop now and don't talk anymore. The time is about past, and I am going to cross over into extinction. This is my last instruction."

Therefore students of the Buddha definitely should learn these principles. Those who do not learn them, who do not know them, are not students of Buddha. These awarenesses are the Buddha's treasury of the eye of true teaching, the sublime heart of nirvana. The fact that many now nevertheless do not know them and few have read or heard of them is due to the interference of demons. Also, those who have cultivated little virtue in the past do not hear of or see them.

In the past, during the periods of the true teaching and the imitation teaching, all Buddhists knew them, and practiced and studied them. Now there are hardly one or two among a thousand monks who know the eight awarenesses of great people. What a pity—the decline in the degenerate age is beyond compare. While the true teaching of the Buddha is still current in the world and goodness has not yet perished, one should hasten to learn them. Don't be lazy. It is difficult to encounter the Buddha's teaching even in countless eons. It is also difficult to get a human body. And even if one gets a human body, it is preferable to live as a human where it is possible to see a Buddha, hear the teaching, leave the mundane, and attain enlightenment. Those who died before the Buddha's final extinction didn't hear of these eight awarenesses of great people, and didn't learn them. Now we have heard of them and learn them—this is the power of virtue cultivated in the past. Now, learning and practicing them, developing them life after life, we will surely reach unexcelled enlightenment. Explain them to people the same as Shakyamuni Buddha.

1253

The Four Integrative Methods of Bodhisattvas

(Bodaisatta shishōhō)

Bodhisattvas are people committed to the welfare, liberation, and enlightenment of all living beings; to dwell in detachment and cling to nirvana hampers this commitment, so they carry transcendence one step further. *The Four Integrative Methods of Bodhisattvas* restates a traditional Buddhist formulation representing nonselfish ways of being in the world. For bodhisattvas, absorption in the commitment of all bodhisattvas, becoming aware of the link of all beings and the eternal work of enlightening, is in itself a gateway of liberation from narrow selfish concerns.

The Four Integrative Methods of Bodhisattvas

The four integrative methods of bodhisattvas are giving, kind speech, beneficial action, and cooperation.

This *giving* means not coveting; not coveting is not being greedy. In worldly terms it is said that not being greedy means not flattering. Even if one should rule four continents, to provide education and civilization in the correct way is just a matter of not being covetous. For example, it is like the treasures one relinquishes being given to strangers. To offer flowers from distant mountains to a Buddha, to give away treasures from one's past life to living beings—in terms of teaching as well as in terms of things, in each are inherent virtues involved in giving.

There is a principle that even if it is not one's own thing, that does not hinder giving. It doesn't matter how insignificant the thing is—the principle is that the effort must be genuine. When one leaves the Way to the Way, one attains the Way. When attaining the Way, the Way is necessarily being left to the Way. When goods are left to goods, the goods unfailingly become giving. Self gives to self, other gives to other. The causal power of this giving reaches afar, throughout the heavens and human world, and even reaches the realized sages and saints. The reason for saying this is that, having become the recipient of giving and having formed an affinity, the Buddha said on this account, "When a person who gives comes into a group, the people first look at that person. Know that heart implicitly comes across."

Therefore one should give even a single phrase or a single verse of the teaching. It becomes a good seed in this life and other lives. One should give even a single coin or a single blade of grass of resources—it causes roots of goodness in this age and other ages to sprout. Teaching too is treasure, material resources too are teaching. It must depend on the will and aspiration.

In fact, there are cases where one person effected the well-being of another by giving his whiskers, and someone gained kingship after having presented sand to a Buddha. They didn't crave the thanks of others, they just did what they could. Setting up a ferry or building a bridge is also transcendent generosity of giving.

When one learns giving well, being born and dying are both giving. All productive labor is fundamentally giving. Entrusting flowers to the wind, birds to the season, also must be meritorious acts of giving. The principle testifying to King Ashoka's offering of half a mango to a group of hundreds of monks being great giving should also be studied well by those who receive. It is not only a matter of exerting physical effort; one should not miss the right opportunity.

Truly it is because the virtues of giving are inherent in oneself that one has now attained oneself. The Buddha said, "It may even be used oneself—how much the more can one give it to one's parents, spouse, and children." So we know that even using something oneself is a portion of giving; giving to one's parents, spouse, and children must also be giving. If one can give away even a mote of dust as charity, even though it is one's own doing, one should quietly rejoice in it, because one has correctly passed on one of the virtues of the Buddhas,

because one has begun to practice one of the principles of bodhisattvas.

What is difficult to transform is the mind of living beings: this
giving is to intend, from having put forth a single chattel and thus
begun to transform the mind of living beings, to transform it even as
far as attainment of enlightenment. In the beginning, it must be done
by giving. For this reason in the beginning of the six transcendent
ways is the transcendent way of giving. One should not calculate the
greatness or smallness of the mind, nor the greatness or smallness of
the thing. Nevertheless, there is a time when the mind transforms
things, and there is giving in which things transform the mind.

Kind speech means that in looking upon living beings one should
first arouse a mind of kindness and love and should utter caring, kind
words. It is the absence of harsh speech. In ordinary social convention
there is the etiquette of asking if someone is well or not; in Buddhism
there is the expression "take care" and the ethical conduct of asking
how someone is. To speak with the thought in one's heart of kindly
minding living beings as one would a baby is kind speech.

Those with virtue one should praise; those without virtue one
should pity. Once one has taken to kind speech, one will gradually
increase kind speech; therefore hitherto unknown and unseen kind
speech will appear. As long as one is alive now, one should gladly
speak kindly; then one will never regress, life after life. The conquer-
ing of enemies and the harmonization of rulers is based on kind
speech. To hear kind speech to one's face gladdens the countenance
and pleases the heart; hearing kind speech indirectly makes a deep
impression on the mind. You should know that kind speech comes
from a kind heart, and a kind heart has good will as its seed. One
should learn that kind speech has the power to turn the heavens. It is
not just praising the able.

Beneficial action means to employ skills beneficial to living beings, high and low. For example, one watches over the road far and
near, working out means to benefit others. One should pity even an
exhausted turtle and take care of an ailing sparrow. When one has
seen an exhausted turtle or an ailing sparrow, one doesn't want their
thanks—one is simply moved to helpful action.

Fools think that when benefit to others is put first, one's own benefit will be reduced. It is not so. *Beneficial action* is one principle; it is
universally benefiting self and others. An ancient ruler got out of the

bath three times and spat out his food three times to go to the aid of others. He was not unwilling to educate the people of another country. So one should help equally those who are inimical and those who are friendly. It is to benefit self and others alike. If one acquires this heart, even in the plants and trees, wind and water, the principle of beneficial action being inherently nonregressive will indeed be beneficially acted out. One should wholeheartedly strive to rescue the ignorant.

Cooperation means nonopposition. It is not opposing oneself and not opposing others. It is like a human Buddha being the same as a human. Because of assimilation to the human world, we know a Buddha must assimilate to other worlds. When one knows cooperation, self and others are one thusness. Their music, song, and wine accompanies people, accompanies celestial beings, accompanies spirits. People keep company with music, song, and wine, and music, song, and wine keep company with music, song, and wine. People keep company with people, celestials keep company with celestials, spirits keep company with spirits—there is such logic. It is the learning of cooperation.

For example, a task of cooperation is a manner, is a standard, is an attitude. After regarding others as self, there must be a principle of assimilating oneself to others. Self and others are endless with time.

An ancient philosopher said, "The ocean doesn't refuse water—therefore it has been able to become so immense. Mountains don't refuse earth—that is why they can be so high. An enlightened ruler doesn't refuse people—therefore his community can become populous." Know that the ocean's not refusing water is *cooperation*. Know further that the virtue of the water not refusing the ocean too is complete. For this reason water gathers and becomes an ocean, earth accumulates and becomes a mountain. We implicitly know that because the ocean doesn't refuse the ocean it forms an ocean and creates its immensity. Because the mountain doesn't refuse the mountain, it forms a mountain and makes its height. Because an enlightened ruler doesn't reject people, he forms a community of them. A sovereign does not reject people. Though the sovereign doesn not reject people, that does mean there are no rewards and punishments. But though there are rewards and punishments, there is no rejecting people.

In ancient times of pristine honesty, nations had no rewards or punishments. That is because the rewards and punishments of those times were not on a part with now. Even now there must be people who seek the right way even without reward. This is beyond the conception of the ignorant man. Because an enlightened ruler is wise, he doesn't reject people. People always form a nation—though they have a mind to seek an enlightened ruler, because there are few who thoroughly know the reason an enlightened ruler is an enlightened ruler, they only rejoice in not being rejected by an enlightened ruler but don't know how to not reject an enlightened ruler themselves. Therefore, because there is the logic of cooperation in both enlightened rulers and in ignorant people, cooperation is the practical undertaking of the bodhisattva. One should face everyone with a mild countenance.

1243

BIRTH AND DEATH
(Shōji)

Birth and Death, which is undated in the *Shōbōgenzō*, integrates transcendence with being in the world. The theme is a reflection of the basic principle that existence is empty and emptiness is existence, which is put into practice by neither grasping nor rejecting, being free from both craving and aversion.

In a well-known Zen story a monk comes to a Zen master, who asks him where he has come from. "The South," replies the monk. The master asks the monk about Buddhism in the South, a region abounding in Zen centers; the monk answers, "There's a lot of discussion going on." The master says, "How can that compare with me planting the fields here and making rice balls to eat?" The monk, who apparently did not see anything enlightening or liberating about this, said, "What can you do about the world?" The master said, "What do you call the world?"

In the final analysis, according to the Zen teachings, it is not that the world binds people, it is people who bind themselves to the world. Bondage and delusion do not come from the world itself, but from ideas and attitudes regarding the world, from people's relation to the world. Therefore the question of what can be done about the world calls forth the question of what people think and feel the world to be.

BIRTH AND DEATH

"Because there is Buddha in birth and death, there is no birth and death." Also, "because there is no Buddha in birth and death, one is not deluded by birth and death." These are the words of two Zen teachers called Kassan and Jōsan. Being the words of enlightened people, they were surely not uttered without reason. People who want to get out of birth and death should understand what they mean.

If people seek Buddha outside of birth and death, that is like heading north to go south, like facing south to try to see the north star: accumulating causes of birth and death all the more, they have lost the way to liberation. Simply understanding that birth and death is itself nirvana, there is nothing to reject as birth and death, nothing to seek as nirvana. Only then will one have some measure of detachment from birth and death.

It is a mistake to assume that one moves from birth to death. Birth, being one point in time, has a before and after; therefore in Buddhism birth is called unborn. Extinction too, being one point in time, also has before and after, so it is said that extinction is nonextinction. When we say "birth" there is nothing but birth, and when we say "extinction" there is nothing but extinction. Therefore when birth comes it is just birth, and when extinction comes it is just extinction. In facing birth and extinction, don't reject, don't long.

This birth and death is the life of the Buddha. If we try to reject or get rid of this, we would lose the life of the Buddha. If we linger in this and cling to birth and death, this too is losing the life of the Buddha; it is stopping the Buddha's manner of being. When we have no aversion or longing, only then do we reach the heart of the Buddha.

However, don't figure it in your mind, don't say it in words. Just letting go of and forgetting body and mind, casting them into the house of Buddha, being activated by the Buddha—when we go along in accord with this, then without applying effort or expending the mind we part from birth and death and become Buddhas. Who would linger in the mind?

There is a very easy way to become a Buddha: not doing any evil, having no attachment to birth and death, sympathizing deeply with all beings, respecting those above, sympathizing with those below, not feeling aversion or longing for anything, not thinking or worrying—this is called Buddha. Don't seek it anywhere else.

THE ECSTASY OF ENLIGHTENMENT
Teachings of Natural Tantra

ORIGINS OF TANTRIC BUDDHISM

Tantrism is widely known as the most elaborate and colorful form of Buddhism. It is considered by many to be the most sophisticated form of Buddhism, while viewed by some as the most degenerate. It is certainly the most controversial. In modern times, Tantrism is the principal mode of Buddhism in Tibet, Nepal, Bhutan, Ladakh, and Mongolia, as well as a major tradition of Buddhism in Japan.

In the past, Tantric Buddhism was also practiced in India and China, and probably in what are now Afghanistan, Indonesia, and Malaysia. Tantrism was absorbed by Taoism in China, by Hinduism and Sufism in India, by Sufism in Afghanistan, and by Hinduism and Sufism in Indonesia and Malaysia.

The main source of Tantric Buddhism, from which the movement emanated over such a vast area of Asia, was the extraordinarily rich cultural basin of old Bengal. Now comprising Bangladesh and part of India, the Bengal region was just east of Magadha, the original homeland of Buddhism. A major center of trade since ancient times, the Bengali cultural basin was connected with many different regions, including the Greek and Roman spheres, by both land and sea routes. It is one of the oldest strongholds of Buddhism.

Numerous ethnic and linguistic groups have inhabited the region of old Bengal since ancient times, and many more were to immigrate there over the ages. This process resulted in a diverse population, with many different traditions of thought and behavior. When Bengal was eventually integrated into Aryan and Muslim polities, this endemic cultural pluralism survived, engendering a spirit of religious tolerance that withstood even the most violent political agitations and pressures. There can hardly be any doubt that Tantrism played a major role in this aspect of Bengali cultural resilience.

The Buddhist presence in Bengal was very old and well established when Tantrism emerged as a distinct movement. According to the famous seventh-century Chinese pilgrim Hsuan-tsang, Gautama Buddha, himself, visited several places in Bengal and taught there. While there is no concrete corroboration of this claim, it cannot be considered unlikely.

There is, after all, no surviving concrete contemporaneous corroboration of anything about Buddhism in the lifetime of Buddha himself. There was no Buddhist art in Buddha's time, and no Buddhist literature. But it is well established that Buddha did travel around during nearly fifty years of teaching activity, and Bengal was a highly accessible neighbor to Buddha's native Magadha. The linguistic differences between the majority languages of Magadha and Bengal were at most dialectical.

Even if Gautama Buddha himself did not visit Bengal personally, given the status of Bengal as a trade center, and the known support for Buddhism among the merchant class in India, it would seem reasonable to consider it likely that Buddhism did, indeed, enter the Bengali region from very early times.

The first concrete monumental evidence of Buddhist presence in Bengal appears to be a stone plaque inscription assigned to the Maurya period (c. 325–183 B.C.E.). Two votive inscriptions on the railing of a Buddhist stupa are dated from the second century B.C.E. According to the Buddhist historian Taranatha, Buddhist communities were established in east Bengal from the time of the great Maurya emperor Ashoka (c. 273–232 B.C.E.).

Ashoka united nearly all of India, including Baluchistan and Afghanistan, under the Maurya rule. He is known to have sent Buddhist missionaries all over the Indian subcontinent, as far south as Sri Lanka, and as far west as Anatolia, Syria, Egypt, and Greece. Considering the fact that Buddhism is even believed to have reached as far as Ireland at this time, via the sea route from the Mediterranean, it is hardly thinkable that Bengal would not have been within the scope of this vast missionary effort.

Early Buddhist literature, although of uncertain date because of its derivation from oral tradition, mentions Bengal as a center of maritime trade and of Buddhist activity from olden times. The *Mahavamsa* refers to a prince named Vijaya who made a voyage from Bengal to Sri Lanka with a retinue of seven hundred. The *Mahaniddesa* acknowledges Bengal as an important center of overseas trade, and so does the remarkable *Milindapanho, Questions of Menander,* which is believed to record conversations of a Buddhist elder with a Graeco-Buddhist king. It is well known that Buddhism spread through Central Asia and into China along the Silk Road trade routes, and there can hardly be any doubt that knowledge of Buddhism also went along with other forms of international communication in other regions as well.

The dialogue with Menander would have taken place in the West, on the other side of the Indian subcontinent, where the empire of Alexander the Great collided with that of Chandragupta Maurya. Mention in this context would reflect the far-flung fame of Bengal in those ancient times. The *Divyavadana* also includes north Bengal within the domain of the Buddhist *majjimadesa* or "Middle Country," the classical homeland of Buddhism.

The reputation of old Bengali Buddhism becomes even clearer in the early centuries of the common era. An inscription dated back to the second or third century includes Vanga, in the heartland of Bengal, among the countries that "gladdened the hearts" of the teachers of the Buddhist Sthaviravada, or School of the Elders. Other countries mentioned include Kashmir in the north, Gandhara (now in Afghanistan and Pakistan) in the west, China in the north and east, and Sri Lanka in the south, suggesting the immensity of the realm of Buddhist culture within which Bengal was included as a major center.

A seventh-century Chinese pilgrim, I-ch'ing, even states that a temple for Chinese Buddhists was established in Bengal under royal patronage in the second century. As this was a time when Buddhism was still in an early phase of establishment in China, this would indicate the international importance of old Bengal as a primary source of the teaching.

In the fifth century C.E., the Chinese traveler Fa-hsien found Buddhism flourishing in Bengal. He reports more than twenty Buddhist establishments in Tamralipti, a major trade center, where he spent two years copying Buddhist scriptures and iconographic art. Archaeologists have discovered numerous examples of Bengali Buddhist statuary and epigraphic records from the fifth and sixth centuries. These artifacts include figures of Maitreya, the Future Buddha, and the bodhisattvas Manjusri and Avalokitesvara, all important images of Mahayana Buddhism. An early sixth-century grant also records the founding of a Mahayana community in Bengal by the great master Shantideva.

The famous seventh-century Chinese pilgrim Hsuan-tsang gives extensive accounts of Buddhist establishments in Bengal, confirming the currency of both Hinayana and Mahayana Buddhism. Hsuan-tsang's own tutor at the great Buddhist university of Nalanda, at that time the head of the monastery, was from a noble Bengali family. Several kings of the Candra dynasty, which ruled in east Bengal from the sixth to the eighth centuries, were also devout Buddhists, and the Buddhist complex at Harikela in east Bengal was a renowned center of learning during this era.

It was largely under the illustrious Pala dynasty (c. 750–1200) that Tantrism emerged as a major movement in old Bengali Buddhism, profoundly influencing the development of Buddhism in Tibet. The Pala dynasty ruled not only Bengal, but at times included parts of Bihar, Assam, and Orissa as well. The famous Buddhist university of Nalanda in Bihar, absorbed into the Bengali political and cultural sphere, reached the height of its glory under Pala rule.

Another major Buddhist complex, Vikramalashila, was founded by Dharmapala (c. 775–810), the second Pala king. With six colleges, one hundred and fourteen teachers, over a hundred temples, and accommodations for three thousand students, Vikramalashila outshone even Nalanda. Large numbers of seekers from Tibet and Nepal, as well as various parts of India, gathered there to study Buddhism.

In the time of the third Pala king, Devapala (810–847), the king of the Shailendra dynasty of Southeast Asia requested (and received) a grant of revenue from five villages to support a monastery at Nalanda. The powerful Shailendra king, who ruled in Java, Sumatra, and Malaya, wanted to establish a center in the Buddhist heartland where students from his own domain could go to study. The magnificent Buddhist monument of Borobodur in central Java was built by the Shailendras, its grand design testifying to the prestige of the Buddhist teaching.

Thus the influence of Buddhism under the patronage of the Bengali Palas extended over a vast area, from Tibet and Nepal to Indonesia. The Sanskrit alphabet used by Kobo Daishi, the founder of Tantric Buddhism in eighth-century Japan, who brought it from China, also clearly points to a Bengali cultural origin, with a recognizable resemblance even to the letters used for modern Bengali and Assamese. At that time there were three major trade routes connecting Bengal with China, including the Tufan-Nepal route through Tibet.

Many important figures of Tibetan tradition were educated in the Bengali Buddhist tradition, and a number of native Bengalis also played important roles in the establishment of Buddhism in Tibet. There are supposed to have been 84 Tantric Siddhas, or adepts, born in Bengal between the 10th and 12th centuries. Perhaps it is not coincidental that this period immediately follows the rise of the Five Houses of classical Zen in China, and coincides with the brilliant Sung dynasty literary articulation of Zen. It also coincides with the rise of Complete Reality Taoism in China, a neo-Taoist movement that resembles both Zen and Tantric Buddhism.

Tantra and Other Religions

Bengali Tantric Buddhism also undoubtedly influenced the development of Shaivite Nathism. Some of the Buddhist Siddhas are also considered Natha Siddhas, illustrating the nondogmatic nature of Tantrism. Tantric Buddhist theory and practice were also adopted by several Vaishnavite sects. Traces of Tantric Buddhism can also be seen in the teachings of famous mystic poet Kabir, as well as in the Sikhism of Guru Nanak. Like some Taoists and Sufis, some of the Tantric Suddhas were also famed as alchemists.

It appears that elements of Bengali Tantric Buddhism may have also been adopted by Sufis from the Islamic tradition. When the Hindu Sena dynasty supplanted the Palas in Bengal, elitist Brahminical reaction against egalitarian Tantric Buddhist ideas and practices led to suppression of Buddhism. When Turki Muslims subsequently supplanted the Senas, it is said, Buddhists welcomed Islam, which was similarly casteless and egalitarian in spirit, and many formally converted to the new religion.

Ancient cordiality between Muslims and Tantric Buddhists has survived up to the present in Ladakh, "Little Tibet," in spite of recent outside agitation. The Dalai Lama of Tibet has also said that the Tibetan Muslims have kept the best of Tibetan culture.[a]

There were apparently Sufis in Bengal before the Turki ouster of the Hindu Senas. It may not be coincidental that the first Afghan Sufi to use the love motif, so characteristic of Tantric Buddhism, lived in the 11th and 12th centuries, not long after the greatest flourishing of the Bengali Siddhas, in an area where Tantric Buddhism had also been thriving. The illustrious 13th-century Jalaluddin Rumi, known for his love poetry, was originally from Balkh, in Afghanistan. It is well established that there was contact between this region and Buddhist Bengal during the Pala dynasty.

The Chishti order of dervishes, which originated in the 10th century and specialized in the use of music to induce ecstasy, is mentioned in connection with Bengal. The Chishti order was an offshoot of the Sufi Khajagan, whose fourth master, Abdul Khaliq Gujduvani (d. 1190), may have learned the technique of "prayer of the heart," it is thought, from Buddhists of the Hindu Kush who practiced recitation of mantras.[b]

Mantric practice is a characteristic of Tantric Buddhism, and Bengal and the Hindu Kush area are known to have been in contact during the Pala dynasty. Musicians of the Chishti order have been respected for many centuries throughout the Indian subcontinent, where the influence of this order has lasted to the present day.

The Shattari branch of the Naqshbandi order, also descended from the Khajagan, is also mentioned as having been active in Bengal. The Shattaris were known for a rapid method of spiritual illumination; this peculiarity is also associated with certain Zen and Tantric Buddhist teachings, although the methods used are not necessarily the same.[c]

Sufis from the Suhrawardi order, which was founded in the 12th century and employed both ecstatic and quiescent exercises, are also known to have worked in Bengal. Many of them are said to be buried there. Use of ecstasy and quiescence to facilitate subtler perceptions are also characteristic of Tantric Buddhism, as seen in the songs of the Bengali Siddhas.

The modern heirs of the Tantric Siddhas in Bengal are the Bauls, who like their spiritual ancestors are fundamentally nonsectarian, popular, often considered unorthodox like the Tantrists, and also use vernacular songs rather than intellectual dogma to convey their teachings.

Tantric Practice

There are countlessly many forms of Tantric practice, by the nature of its use of the materials of everyday life, including both the inner resources of the mind and body as well as the outer resources of the intellectual, cultural, and material environment. While customary observances of Tantrism, as well as other forms of Buddhism, may at times become locally stereotyped, there remains overall a broad external diversity in every form of Buddhism, including Tantra. Beneath this methodological diversity lies the esoteric unity of the fundamental continuum of Buddhism.

The unity of the continuum of Buddhism is recapitulated within Tantra, just as Hinayana Buddhism is recapitulated with Mahayana Buddhism. Tantra is part of a unified continuum with Hinayana and Mahayana Buddhism, and it also contains and consummates a unified continuum of all three phases of Buddhism within the specifically Tantric mode of expression and practice.

Typical misperceptions of Tantra result from obscuration of this continuum through obsession with the outer forms. When the observer is obsessed with local and temporal forms of any of the stages, be it Hinayana, Mahayana, or Tantric Buddhism, the fundamental unity of the continuum is obscured.

In the context of Tantric Buddhism, the principles of Hinayana and Mahayana Buddhism are personified as supernal beings, or represented by letters or abstract images. The practices are carried out in the process of the individual's mental relationship to this esoteric world. Those who only observe from outside, or those within tradition who have forgotten what they are doing, may see or experience this kind of practice as a form of idolatry, apparently quite different from the religious models of exoteric Buddhism. From a unitarian pan-Buddhist point of view, however, the differences are only external.

This is why there is no religious bigotry in Tantric Buddhism. Recognizing the value of each phase of philosophy and practice in its own proper time in the evolution of the individual and society, the Tantric outlook is able to integrate the whole range of Buddhist teachings and practices. In the same way, the Tantric outlook is able to appreciate and employ teachings and practices of other religions or systems of culture and thought ambient within the host communities and civilizations of the esoteric Buddhist world.

All the ranges of Buddhism, including the various ranges of Tantra, are implicitly represented in the practical songs, the *carya-giti*, of the old Bengali Tantric adepts or Siddhas. While it is necessary to defer the greater part of the illustration to commentary on the songs themselves, some sense of the practicalities of the three stages of Buddhism can be gained from comparison of certain basic exercises.

The continuum of the three successive levels of Buddhism might be described as purification, integration, and re-creation.

The first level of Buddhism addresses the problem of mental clarification, dissolving gross attachment to the notional world. The purpose of this type of exercise is to seek insight into objective truth by overcoming the subjective emotional, perceptual, and intellectual biases that are based on ignorant selfishness and cultural conditioning. This is the stage in which personal nirvana is to be realized.

The second level addresses the problem of harmonizing unbiased insight into objective truth with the everyday world of historically conditioned social, intellectual, and perceptual convention. The purpose of this type of exercise is to discover and uncover objective truth everywhere, hidden in ordinary life beneath a veneer of appearances formulated of frozen perceptions. This is the stage in which the nirvanic quintessence of both persons and things is realized.

The third stage finally goes beyond duality in perception of absolute and relative. Everything in relative and imaginary reality reminds the Tantric Buddhist of absolute truth, and this guides the understanding and expression of both material and abstract dimensions of life.

In the first stage, living is a form of responsibility; in the second stage, living is a form of duty; in the third stage, living is a form of artistry, encompassing responsibility and duty in creative devotion. Living in all its many aspects becomes a practical art of expressing a constructive relationship with absolute truth in the context of all life.

Tantra is the consummation of the wedding of absolute and relative knowledge, of insight and compassion. As the simultaneous realization of the transcendence and integration is learned in the first two stages of Buddhism, continuity with Tantra is also reflected in the first two stages, just as the first two stages are also expressed within the total context of Tantra.

In the Hinayana teaching of the Pali *Dhammapada*, Buddha says, "Just as many kinds of garlands can be made from a heap of flowers, so also much good can be done by a mortal being."[1] In the unitarian Mahayana teaching of the hybrid Sanskrit *Saddharmapundarika-sutra*, Buddha says, "All productive activities and means of livelihood are not at variance with the character of reality." Tantric Buddhism is a fully developed manifestation of these realizations. "All forms are forms of Buddha; all sounds are voices of Buddha."

The integrity of the whole range of Buddhism, and its recapitulation in Tantra, can be seen in the symbolism of the pan-Buddhist personification of universal compassion, Avalokitesvara. The name of this personification is sometimes translated "Lord Who Looks Down," or sometimes "Lord Who Regards the Cry of the World." In the West, this figure is best known by the Chinese name Kuan-yin, commonly called the Goddess of Mercy. The impersonal meaning of the name is "capacity of objective observation."

All pan-Buddhists and Tantrists mediate on Avalokitesvara at some time. The integration of Buddhist enlightenment with the world, and the intrinsic unity of Buddhism underlying a diverse range of method that encompasses other religions as well, is poetically explained in the description of the teaching of the bodhisattva Avalokitesvara found in the unitarian *Avatamsaka-sutra* or *Flower Ornament Scripture.*

> I know a way of enlightening practice called "undertaking great compassion without delay," which sets about impartially guiding all sentient beings to perfection, dedicated to protecting and guiding sentient beings by communicating knowledge to them through all media.
>
> Established in this method of enlightening practice undertaking great compassion without delay, I appear in the midst of the activities of all sentient beings without leaving the presence of all Buddhas, and take care of them by means of generosity, kind speech, beneficial actions, and cooperation.
>
> I also develop sentient beings by appearing in various forms. I gladden and develop them by purity of vision of inconceivable forms radiating auras of light, and I take care of them and develop them by speaking to them according to their mentalities, and by showing conduct according to their inclinations, and by magically producing various forms and teaching them doctrines commensurate with their various interests, and by inspiring them to begin to accumulate good qualities, by showing them projections according to their mentalities, by appearing to them as members of their own various races and conditions, and by living together with them.[2]

The syncretism attributed to Tantric Buddhism is a result of application of these principles. It cannot be considered in itself a degeneration, as ultraconservative sectarians and externalist scholars have ordinarily considered it. There is the possibility of degeneration in the practice of each and every phase of Buddhism, not only Tantra. Buddhist texts, both Hinayana and Mahayana, are often explicit on this point.

There are different characteristic deteriorations of each of the three phases of Buddhism, but in spite of their differences in expression, they are fundamentally based on the same set of weaknesses of human psychology. Ignorance or nihilism may take the form of extreme quietism on the level of Hinayana Buddhism, whereas it may take the form of decadence on the level of Mahayana Buddhism or adventurism on the level of Tantric Buddhism. Greed may manifest itself as vanity on one level, officiousness on another level, and ambitiousness on a third level. Aggression may appear in the form of prudishness, in the form of proselytism, or in the form of authoritarianism; or in a combination of all three of these forms.

The deteriorations of religious forms consequent upon approaching them with greed, aggression, and ignorance are not limited to Tantric Buddhism, or to any particular religion.

Tantra and Sexuality

Apart from idolatry and hybridization of various kinds attributed to Tantric Buddhism, the most commonly assailed feature of this form of Buddhism is the conscious transformation of sexuality into religious experience. Although this aspect of Tantric Buddhism is no different from any other form of Buddhism in being susceptible to misunderstanding, misuse and degeneration, that is a different matter from saying that it is inherently degenerate. The latter opinion is more a reflection of the mentality of those who hold it, or of external misperception, than it is of the Tantric art of love.

It is an unfortunate fact, nonetheless, that the name of Tantra has been used to conjure up images of promiscuous orgies. Exaggerations and degenerations aside, such images appear to be derived in the main from Brahmanical paranoias about race and caste mixing.

The natural ecstasy of Tantric Buddhist love is of an entirely different qualitative range than that of ordinary sexual feeling. It is incomparably more refined, and more subtly ecstatic, leaving a more stable impression on the quality of life, resulting in a more permanent mental enhancement, than the temporary satisfaction of ordinary sensuality. For some, in fact, it is a purely psychic or spiritual practice, without a physical counterpart; and for some it is purely symbolic, representing a metaphysical experience.

The esoteric significance of sexual union in Buddhism, and also the invisibility of this level of understanding and experience to the vulgar eye, are explained at some length in the final book of the pan-Buddhist *Flower Ornament Scripture,* in the story of the visit of the pilgrim Sudhana, "Wealth of Good," to the woman Vasumitra, "Friend of the World."

According to the story, the pilgrim is directed to Vasumitra in the course of a long journey to call on spiritual benefactors. Vasumitra is not a sectarian Buddhist, but a devotee of the god of light. The pilgrim is sent to her, however, by a Buddhist nun, who is further described as having attained an enlightening liberation characterized by removal of all vain imaginings. This manner of setting up the visit illustrates the sense of order in Buddhist practice, the need for purification and clarification before integration and re-creation.

According to the Buddhist nun, Vasumitra lives in a city called Ratnavyuha, "Array of Jewels," in a country called Durga, "Difficult to Approach." These details illustrate both the promise and the perils of this level of experience.

When the pilgrim had made his way to the place where Vasumitra lived, people tried to discourage him from visiting her. This illustrates the superficial mind focused only on external forms. According to the story in the scripture, the people who tried to dissuade the pilgrim from visiting the woman were those "who did not know of Vasumitra's virtues or the scope of her knowledge." They said to Sudhana, "What has someone like you—with senses so calm and subdued, so aware, so clear, without confusion or distraction, your gaze focused discreetly right before you, your mind not overwhelmed by sensations, not clinging to appearances, your eyes averted from involvement in all forms, your mind so cool and steady, your way of life profound, wise, oceanic, your mind free from agitation or despondency—what have you to do with Vasumitra?"

This passage underscores Sudhana's level of preparation before visiting Vasumitra, as well as the appearance of incongruity to those who do not perceive the integrity of Vasumitra or the possibility of Sudhana's reintegration.

There were others, however, who in fact "knew the excellence of the virtues of Vasumitra, and were aware of the scope of her knowledge." These people encouraged the pilgrim Sudhana and gave him precise directions, adding, "You have really made a gain if you ask about Vasumitra. You surely seek Buddhahood; you surely want to make yourself a refuge for all sentient beings; and you surely want to transform the notion of purity."

This passage represents awareness of a higher level of purity, in the world but not stained by worldly vanities. The esoteric aspect of this level of Buddhism is not necessarily a matter of secrecy, as the story illustrates, but an issue of perception and knowledge. The spiritual eye sees what the mundane eye does not.

When the pilgrim finally meets Vasumitra, he finds that she is not only physically beautiful, but that she also "was well versed in all arts and sciences," she had "learned to use the magic of true knowledge," and she had "mastered all aspects of the expedient means of enlightening beings." The image is not one of a sexual temptress, but of a paragon of enlightening integration of the absolute and the relative.

Finally, in conversation with the pilgrim, Vasumitra reveals the secrets of spirituality in intimate union. "I have attained an enlightening liberation called 'ultimately dispassionate,' " she says, explaining the means and end of her universal adaptation; "To gods, in accord with their inclinations and interests, I appear in the form of a goddess of surpassing splendor and perfection; and to all other types of beings I accordingly appear in the form of a female of their species, of surpassing splendor and perfection. And all who come to me with minds full of passion, I teach them so that they become free of passion. Those who have heard my teaching and attain dispassion achieve an enlightening concentration called 'realm of nonattachment.' "

This is a degree of profound satisfaction and spiritual transport unattainable by mundane emotions and gross sensuality. Vasumitra goes on to explain, "Some attain dispassion as soon as they see me, and achieve an enlightening concentration called 'delight in joy.'

"Some attain dispassion merely by talking with me, and achieve an enlightening concentration called 'treasury of unimpeded sound.'

"Some attain dispassion just by holding my hand, and achieve an enlightening concentration called 'basis of going to all buddha-lands.'

"Some attain disposition just by staying with me, and achieve an enlightening concentration called 'light of freedom from bondage.'

"Some attain dispassion just by gazing at me, and achieve an enlightening concentration called 'tranquil expression.'

"Some attain dispassion just by embracing me, and achieve an enlightening concentration called 'womb receiving all sentient beings without rejection.'

"Some attain dispassion just by kissing me, and achieve an enlightening concentration called 'contact with the treasury of virtue of all beings.'

"All those who come to me I establish in this enlightening liberation of ultimate dispassion, on the brink of the stage of unimpeded all-knowledge."[3]

Vasumitra finally explains that she was inspired to seek supreme perfect enlightenment by Manjusri, the supernal bodhisattva who represents both wisdom and knowledge, transcendental insight into emptiness, as well as formal mastery of art and science.

Thus, the scriptural story illustrates the principles of both the theory and practice of Tantra, showing how this manifestation of Buddhism may be externally controversial because of the different perceptions of observers, while inwardly coherent as an expression of fully integrated Buddhist spirituality.

Songs of the Adepts

The Tantric songs of the old Bengali adepts translated here are thought to date from the 10th and 11th centuries. This collection is currently believed to be the only full length text in the Old Bengali language extant. In translating it from the original Old Bengali, I have made use of Nilratan Sen's critical edition of *Caryagitikos*, which includes a late Sanskrit commentary in Bengali script by Munidatta, thought to be of the 15th century; and Tarapad Mukhopadhyāy's critical edition in his study *Old Bengali Language and Text*. The translator's commentaries are intended to expound the meanings of the songs, which are often in symbolic "twilight language," in the overall context of pan-Buddhism, specifically to illustrate the continuity of Tantra with other forms of Buddhism.[4]

The Ecstasy of Enlightenment

1

LUI

The body is a tree, with five branches;
When the mind is unstable, time enters in.
Firmly determine the Greater Bliss;
Ask the Teacher, says Lui, and know!
What is the use of meditation at all?
One dies bound to pleasure and pain.
Give up the bondage of desire,
the hope for keenness of sense;
Draw the wings of emptiness
close to your sides.
Lui says, "I am seen in meditation,
Seated on the seat of inhalexhalation."

The body is a tree, with five branches;
When the mind is unstable, time enters in.

The image of the body as a tree is elaborated by the Chinese Zen Buddhist Lan-hsi in his *Treatise on Meditation:* "Ordinary people are like trees: putting the manure of greed and lust on the thin soil of folly and delusion, planting seeds of ignorance, transplanting shoots of form, feeling, perception, conditioning, and consciousness, producing buds of active habit-ridden consciousness, growing roots of attachment and stems of flattery and deceit, sprouting leaves of jealousy and envy, creating trees of affliction, causing flowers of infatuation to bloom, forming fruits of greed, aggression, and ignorance."[5]

In Lui's verse, the "five branches" of the tree of the body may be taken to stand for the limbs and head; or they may be understood to refer to the "five clusters" of form, feeling, perception, conditioning, and consciousness, which are commonly used in Buddhist literature to represent a mortal being, as also in Lan-hsi's essay. "When the mind is unstable, time enters in" because the body is governed by the mind and is therefore affected, even afflicted, by fluctuations in the mind, which bring the whole being under the sway of time.

Aristotle is reported to have said, "The soul is not within the body; rather the body is within the soul, because the soul is more extensive than the body, and greater in magnitude."[6] Were the term "mind" in the Buddhist sense substituted for Aristotle's "soul," this statement could have come from India, in explanation of the primary Buddhist emphasis on care and cultivation of mind. The philosophers and physicians of Taoism, which is much like Tantric Buddhism, also regard instability and hyperactivity of the mind to be direct causes of physical unwellness and deterioration.

Firmly determine the Greater Bliss;
Ask the Teacher, says Lui, and know!

The Greater Bliss is subtle transport, beyond the ordinary senses of joy and sorrow. Although it is a natural phenomenon, this is nevertheless sporadic in people subject to ordinary social and psychological conditioning. Therefore it is not accessible as a constant resource unless and until it is deliberately stabilized. This is why there is, in the stage of ultimate realization, no contradiction between natural and attained enlightenment.

"Ask the Teacher, says Lui, and know." This simple exhortation contains many meanings. On the surface is the sense of the need for guidance. In practice it is necessary to "ask the teacher" in order to know, because the confused or unenlightened mind cannot guide itself to enlightenment. Underlying this is the sense of what "teacherhood" is all about. It is properly for the sake of enlightening knowledge alone that one goes to a teacher; not for imagined blessings or graces, let alone lesser goals.

The emphasis on knowing highlights the necessity of direct, firsthand personal experience on the way to enlightenment. The aim is not to be rescued, to be saved, to be convinced, to be converted, to be forgiven, to be absolved, to believe, to have faith, but to *know*. It is through this knowledge, this personal experience of the spiritual euphoria of enlightenment, that one can attain salvation, certainty, and serenity.

What is the use of meditation at all?
One dies bound to pleasure and pain.

After Prince Siddhartha gave up his royal inheritance to seek permanent peace of mind, he followed two Hindu yoga teachers. The first one taught him to reach several stages of meditation, in the highest of which there is no longer any pain or pleasure. The second one taught him to reach a series of stages of abstraction, the most refined being described as neither perception nor nonperception.

Siddhartha found that these yogic experiences seemed to last for very long periods of time, in subjective terms. Yet they inevitably dissolved, leaving the seeker back in the world, now with a profound longing and sorrow at the loss of celestial states. Thus it was that Siddhartha came to realize that these practices and experiences were not eternal spirituality itself, but rather temporal methods of cultivating different perspectives. Siddhartha's subsequent detachment from all mental states, both ordinary and extraordinary, ultimately led to his liberation.

This point was later reemphasized in Zen Buddhism, to remedy centuries of devolutionary sectarian cultism dependent upon attachment to limited theories, practices, and altered states of mind. The Tantric adept Lui here expresses the same stage, known in Universalist Buddhism as "abandoning the raft," or letting go of the means when the end has been realized.

In the idea that meditation is a means, not an end, is implicitly echoed the principle that to enter into meditation practice in the wrong frame of mind is useless and even harmful. Seeking personal power, or thrilling experiences, or self-deceptive reality-avoidance, or obsessiveness in general, are unsuitable bases for meditation. Lui warns people not to become wrongly attached to meditation; he also reminds people to scrutinize their own motives and actions. Seekers need to ask themselves what they are really thinking of meditating for in the first place.

Give up the bondage of desire, the hope for keenness of sense;
Draw the wings of emptiness close to your sides.

Desire is part of our inherited instinctive constitution, as a mechanism of survival and evolution. Desire can also be influenced and cultivated beyond survival value by habit and conditioning. Bondage to desire, preoccupation with craving for intense experience, makes the individual and community especially vulnerable to exaggerated selfishness, aggression, heedlessness, and short-sightedness.

To give up the bondage of desire is to be able to experience and understand desire without compulsiveness, without augmentation of craving. This is a way to be more objective about desire, and therefore less under the control of associated feelings such as hope, fear, elation, and disappointment.

Ironically, perhaps, attempts to control desire may in fact have the reverse effect of magnifying desire in the mind of someone deliberately trying to control it. This is why Buddhists resort to perception of "emptiness" to transcend the bondage of desire without laboring to extinguish desire itself.

By viewing desire and its objects as conditional, emphemeral phenomena, and viewing repetitious thinking about desire as self-delusion, Buddhists "draw the wings of emptiness close to their sides," transcending the bondage of desire even in the very midst of desire.

To those already obsessed with desire and its fulfillment and frustration, this way of managing desire can seem negative or nihilistic. When the mind is already set on its own preoccupations in that way, the felicitous outcome on the "other side" of liberation from obsession is not even thinkable. The Buddhist goal of realizing emptiness is actually a better happiness, as illustrated in the ancient *Dhammapada*. Buddha himself presents the pattern of spiritual regeneration following upon mortification or transcendence of the lower self: "Do not indulge in negligence, do not be intimate with attachment to desire. The vigilant one, meditative, gains great happiness."[7]

Liu says, "I am seen in meditation,
Seated on the seat of inhalexhalation."

This verse may seem, at a glance, to contradict the earlier verse questioning the use of meditation. It must be realized, however, that the earlier verse defines the realizations upon which wholesome meditation and lucid vigilance can be practiced.

The term "inhalexhalation" is a coinage intended to imitate the original technical expression, underlining the sense of the breathing as one continuous cycle in two phases. This is considered a useful exercise for concentrating a scattered mind and preparing it to perceive reality more objectively.

In ancient Buddhism, mindfulness of breathing and mindfulness of impermanence were referred to as two *amrta-dvara* or "doors of immortality" leading to nirvana, or clearing of the mind. Mindfulness of breathing was considered the better door in the sense that by nature it contains the other door within it.

The Indian meditation master Prajnatara spoke of both application and realization of this practice in these terms, five hundred years before Lui: "Breathing in, I do not dwell on the elements of mind or body; breathing out, I do not get involved in myriad things."

Zen Buddhists of the Far East, whose teachings resemble those of these Vajrayana Siddhacaryas of Bengal, consider Prajnatara (fifth century C.E.) their twenty-seventh Indian patriarch. Chinese records say he was from "Eastern India," which would include the area of what had been Magadha when Buddha was born there a thousand years before Prajnatara, and the Bengali Pala dynasty when Lui sang there five or six hundred years later. Buddha's mother-tongue, Magadhi, and Lui's "Old Bengali" language are directly related.

Thus it is possible to see, in more than one dimension, the historical continuity of Buddhism in its first homeland over a period of at least fifteen hundred years, unbroken through what conventional scholarship generally designates Hinayana, Mahayana, and Vajrayana Buddhism.

2

KUKKURI

> Having milked the turtle, the pitcher holds no more;
> The crocodile eats the tree's tamarind.
> Listen to the courtyard being swept, o mistress;
> A thief has stolen the earrings in the middle of the night.
> Father-in-law gone to sleep, the bride is awake;
> The earrings have been taken by a thief—
> where does one go to look for them?
> By day, the bride is scared of the crows;
> When scared at night, she goes to Kamarupa.
> Kukkuri sings of such practice:
> It enters the heart of one in a million.

Having milked the turtle, the pitcher holds no more;
The crocodile eats the tree's tamarind.

The turtle that withdraws its head and limbs and shuts itself up in its shell for safety was anciently used as an image of the practice of withdrawal of the senses from external stimulation. Sometimes this is used for stress reduction, for mental and physical health. Sometimes the practice is applied to the effort to recollect a scattered mind, or to abstract processes of thoughts and judgment from the influence of immediate stimuli.

When withdrawal is overused, or indulged in for escapist purposes, the results are stultifying rather than restorative. The first line of this couplet expresses this by saying, in effect, that there is a limit to which the "turtle" exercise can be optimally employed ("milk" also means "utilize" in Old Bengali, much as it can mean "exploit" in modern English).

The crocodile is the picture of ferocity, the tamarind a leguminous tree with a pulpy fruit. This presents a counterpoint to the passivity of withdrawal, actively sinking one's teeth into the knotty problems of real life. A Zen proverb says, "The level field of equanimity is littered with the skulls of the dead; it is only the experts who can get through the forest of thorny problems."

Listen to the courtyard being swept, o mistress;
A thief has stolen the earrings in the middle of the night.

The mistress is formless insight, listening is attention. The courtyard being swept is the spontaneous passing away of random thought and feelings.

The first line represents a concrete exercise in clearing the mind of inward chatter. The thief is natural bliss, or the bliss of naturalness (sahajananda); the earrings are artificialities. The middle of the night is formless, silent mental equipoise. The second line describes the exercise taking effect.

Father-in-law gone to sleep, the bride is awake;
The earrings have been taken by a thief—
where does one go to look for them?

The father-in-law stands for conventionally structured thinking, bound by rules of conditioned habit that are ultimately arbitrary yet rigidly maintained. The bride stands for nondiscursive insight, seeing immediately and directly, thus always fresh and new.

When the "father-in-law" of authoritarian conventional thinking has "gone to sleep" in the quiescence of cessational meditation, then the "bride" of nonconceptual knowing can "waken" and operate without interference in observational meditation.

When acquired superficialities have been dropped through the experience of naturalness ("the earrings have been taken by a thief"), there is no obstacle to looking back into the mystery of the essence and source of consciousness ("where does one go to look?").

By day, the bride is scared of the crows;
When scared at night, she goes to Kamarupa.

Daytime stands for the world of differences. Silent, formless insight is "drowned out" by the clamor of the worldly mind, with its internal bantering and chattering, whose crude stimulation distracts and dulls the faculty of finer sense.

Night stands for nirvana, or the experience of the absolute. Kama-rupa, a place name that literally means "Form of Desire," stands for a locus on the subtle energy body, and spiritual bliss.

When experience of the absolute in nirvanic quiescence goes so deep as to put one in danger of slipping into complete annihilation, the subtle awareness of formless insight maintains the "ember" of life in the medium of spiritual ecstasy.

This is the meaning of the classic Zen verse that says, "It shines right at midnight, and does not appear at dawn."

Kukkuri sings of such practice:
It enters the heart of one in a million.

The Siddha concludes by reminding his hearers that what he is sing-ing of is a practical process, not just philosophical or literary conceits. Bodhidharma, the founder of Zen, said, "There are many who see the Way; there are few who practice it." The *Flower Ornament Scripture*, a root source of Far Eastern Tantric Buddhism, emphasizes this point strongly:

> Like a person skilled in medicine
> who cannot cure his own disease:
> so are those who are learned
> but do not apply the teaching.
> Like someone counting others' treasures
> without half a coin of his own:
> so is the one who is learned
> who does not practice the teaching.
> Like one who is born in a royal palace
> yet freezes and starves,
> so are those who are learned
> but do not practice the teaching.[8]

[3]

VIRUBA

> A single wine-making woman enters two houses;
> Using fermenting agents, she makes the wine.
> In natural calm, she makes the wine;
> Who ages not nor dies is firm of body and mind.
> Seeing the sign on the tenth door,
> The buyer came of his own accord.
> Sixty-four pitchers are given in display;
> Once a customer's gone in, there's no coming out.
> One small container, with a slender tube;
> Viruba says, "Make movements calmly."

A single wine-making woman enters two houses;
Using fermenting agents, she makes the wine.

The wine-making woman is wisdom, the two houses are samsara and nirvana. Samsara is the mundane world, and nirvana is absolute truth, or transcendent inner peace. The fermenting agents are developmental practices, the wine-making is the process of awakening, and the wine is the spiritual euphoria of realization.

According to the *Flower Ornament Scripture* a bodhisattva, who is someone in the process of enlightening self and others, has both a face of nirvana and a face of samsara. The insight of Buddhas penetrates both the relative and the absolute, producing two kinds of knowledge. Thus "the wine-making woman enters two houses" and "makes the wine."

In natural calm, she makes the wine;
Who ages not nor dies is firm of body and mind.

Insight has to be stabilized before it can be employed constructively. A classical Zen Buddhist image for this is the flame and glass of a lamp. The flame is like insight, the glass is like calmness; without stable calmness, access to insight fluctuates like an unsheltered candle in the wind.

"Who ages not nor dies" is the Buddha-nature, which is believed to be the natural and inherent essence of living beings.

T'ien-t'ai and Hua-yen Buddhism also calls this "mind in its aspect of suchness" in contrast to "mind in its aspect of repetitious arousal." In Taoist hygiene theory, which has close affinities to Tantric Buddhism, detachment from fluctuations of thought and feeling in favor of calm immersion in the essence of mind itself is considered a restorative "elixir" that reduces both physical and mental stress, thus fostering health and longer life.

Seeing the sign on the tenth door,
The buyer came of his own accord.

According to Munidatta's commentary, the "tenth door" is the "door of Vairocana," who is the Adi-Buddha, or primordial Buddha, the essence and function of cosmic consciousness represented by the sun and its rays of light. The *Flower Ornament Scripture* features the "Tower of Vairocana," containing infinite infirmities within it, symbolizing the awakening of the whole mind.

Munidatta comments that "seeing the sign on the tenth door" means "seeing the sign of great joy, pleasure, and delight," which corresponds to the experience of the first of the ten stages of enlightenment expounded by the comprehensive *Flower Ornament Scripture*, in which one begins to rise above mundane entanglements by means of the intensity of joy in contemplating the realization of Buddhahood.

Absorbed into the life attitude, the experience of spiritual joy at the thought of enlightenment, leads one naturally and spontaneously into the path of refinement. Thus Viruba sings that the "buyer," that is, the spiritual seeker, "came of his own accord."

Sixty-four pitchers are given in display;
Once a customer's gone in, there's no coming out.

According to convention, worldly arts and sciences are traditionally said to be sixty-four in number. "Sixty-four pitchers" may be taken to refer to the sum total of worldly knowledge. These are "given in display" in the sense that things of the world are not permanently there, only temporarily.

Once we are born in the world, we inevitably die; "there's no coming out" alive. Any aspect of the world or worldly knowledge could become a dead-end obsession, for anyone who remained heedless of the transitory and mutable nature of mundane phenomena.

One small container, with a slender tube;
Viruba says, "Make movements calmly."

The small container with a slender tube is the human body, with focus on the respiratory system. As explained earlier, mindfulness of breathing is a traditional method of cultivating concentration and calmness. This helps the individual to live in the world constructively without being unduly influenced by external pressure and confusion.

The quality of the breathing is taken as a barometer of mental state. Rapid, shallow breathing, for example, would be expected to coincide with some sort of mental agitation, whereas slow, deeper breathing would be expected to coincide with calmness. Therefore, while the breathing slows as the mind slows, conversely the mind can also be calmed by breathing more calmly.

Thus, while the last line of the verse can be taken as a general recommendation to balance activity with calmness, it is also a specific direction for mindful breathing. In practice, these two meanings reinforce one another, and ultimately coincide.

In more advanced meditation, the "slender tube" can also be understood to mean the "central channel" visualized along the course of the spinal cord of the physical body. The "movements" of opening, energizing, and clearing the channel in meditation must be made with great care. Generally speaking, this is only possible after the mind-breath continuum is already calmed.

[4]

GUNTARI

> Pressing the three channels, the yogini gives an embrace;
> Lotus and lightning mix together in the afternoon.
> Yogini, I cannot live a moment without you;
> Kissing your face, I sip the lotus sweet juice.
> After casting off, the yogini is no longer affected;
> Leaving the source of mind, she's soared to ecstasy.
> The key has been turned in the lock
> of the passage of breath;
> The moon and the sun spread their wings.
> Guntari says, "I am strong in making love;
> A man inside a woman, perpetually erect."

Pressing the three channels, the yogini gives an embrace;
Lotus and lightning mix together in the afternoon.

In Tantric yoga, the body is visualized as consisting of a network of
energy channels and concentration points. This exercise facilitates
transcendence of the physical body while retaining creative capacity,
without lapsing into nihilistic indifference.

The "three channels" are the right, left, and center channels, forming the main trunk of this network. The right and left channels are
called channels of perception and dalliance, the central channel is
called the channel of purification. One form of inner exercise involves mentally circulating the experiences fostered in the channels
of perception and dalliance into the channel of purification, where
they are clarified and resolved.

According to Munidatta, the yogini (female yogi) symbolizes *nairatmya* or selflessness, and the pressing of the three channels by the
embrace of the yogini means making them free of manifestation.
Selflessness means relativity, in Buddhist terms, in the sense that
nothing that can be apprehended exists in and of itself. This realiza-

tion is the ultimate "clearing" of the energy channels, whose existence is relative to the mind, visualized as actual in order to counteract the grossness of ordinary bodily sense.

Lotus and lightning symbolize insight and skill in means, which are the two major complementary pragmatic facets of enlightenment. These two "wings" of Buddhism are also represented by female and male. Sexual intercourse symbolizes the perfect harmonization of intuitive insight into the essential nature of ultimate reality with practical knowledge of the characteristics of mundane actualities.

The afternoon represents the combining of light and darkness, which symbolizes the integration of perceptions of relative and absolute realities, and the discursive and nondiscursive cognitions that take place through these experiences. Thus the "afternoon" is the proper "time" of the "mixing" of the "lotus and lightning."

Yogini, I cannot live a moment without you;
Kissing your face, I sip the lotus sweet juice.

The ancient Chinese *Tao Te Ching* says, "When people are born they are supple, and when they die they are stiff. When trees are born they are tender, and when they die they are brittle. Stiffness is thus a companion of death, flexibility is a companion of life."[9]

In Buddhist terms, the selflessness, or emptiness, of all things is expressed and realized as fluidity; nothing is static, everything is an evolving process. Were this not so, everything would come to a standstill, and there would be no room for expression of creative energy.

Kissing the face of the yogini means personally experiencing liberation from views by realizing their relativity to mental states that are themselves relative. The lotus sweet juice is the elixir of immortality, another name for nirvana, or cessation of confusion.

After casting off, the yogini is no longer affected;
Leaving the source of mind, she's soared to ecstasy.

Here Munidatta further defines the yogini as "the yogini of selflessness, representing the thought of enlightenment." After "casting off" entanglement, consciousness is fluid but no longer under the influence of externals.

This nonattachment does not mean remaining stagnant, insensitive, or inactive. Outwardly unburdened by things, inwardly not clinging to stillness, from stillness the thought of enlightenment rises in spiritual transport.

The Chinese Zen master Lin-chi said, "I do not grasp the ordinary or the holy outside, and I do not dwell on the fundamental inside; I see all the way through, and no longer experience confusion."

The key has been turned in the lock
of the passage of breath;
The moon and the sun spread their wings.

As mentioned earlier, the practice of mindfulness of breathing is one of the two "doors to immortality" or gateways to nirvana, including within it the other "door," which is mindfulness of impermanence.

The moon and the sun stand for two kinds of *bodhicitta* or "thought of enlightenment," the fundamental inspiration of Buddhism. The moon represents the *samvrti-bodhicitta* or worldly thought of enlightenment, and the sun represents the *paramartha-bodhicitta* or absolute thought of enlightenment. The worldly thought of enlightenment is based on consciousness of impermanence and conditionality, while the absolute thought of enlightenment is based on direct sensing of the transcendent peace of nirvana.

Thus the couplet says, in effect, that both ordinary thought of enlightenment and transcendent thought of enlightenment are activated through the practice of mindfulness of breathing, when the stage of unobstruction is reached.

This couplet provides pragmatic directions for attaining the state of mind represented by the embrace of the yogini and the intercourse of lotus and lightning.

Guntari says, "I am strong in making love;
A man inside a woman, perpetually erect."

Making love symbolizes the uniting of mystical insight with temporal knowledge and action. The "man" represents *upaya*, expedient means, and the "woman" represents *prajna*, deep insight, or *sunyata*, emptiness of absoluteness.

The "man inside a woman" illustrates the practical principle that expedient means in the true Buddhist sense operate only within the scope of authentic insight. This image also illustrates the metaphysical principle underlying expediency of action, that ways and means are conditional and temporary, thus empty of inherent ultimacy or absoluteness.

That the man is, nonetheless, "perpetually erect" signifies that "emptiness" does not mean nothingness. It is precisely in the fluidity of true emptiness that the creativity of acting on the thought of enlightenment comes to life.

[5]

CATILA

> The flow of existence is impenetrably deep,
> its current is swift;
> Both banks are muddy, the middle can't be fathomed.
> Catila builds a bridge for the sake of Truth;
> People going to the Other Side cross over in safety.
> The tree of illusion's cut asunder, then the pieces joined;
> The strong axe of nonduality is fashioned in nirvana.
> Climbing the bridge, go neither right nor left;
> Enlightenment is close, not far away.
> Any of you people who would go across,
> Ask Catila, the unsurpassed master.

The flow of existence is impenetrably deep,
its current is swift;
Both banks are muddy, the middle can't be fathomed.

As we are swept along by the current of events, we don't really know why; we are constantly occupied with response and adaptation to ever-changing circumstances. We do not know where we came from to begin with, and we do not know where we will go when we perish from this earth; when we try to grasp the origin or the ending of our sense of self, we find they slip from the grip of our perception. And when we try to fathom the process of life in the meanwhile, life in all its possibilities and potentials for better and for worse, we find that it is beyond the power of our conception to fully comprehend.

The way of looking at the human situation illustrated in this couplet is an ordinary method of cultivating the *bodhicitta* or thought of enlightenment. It is not that Buddhism is a pessimistic philosophy, even at the elementary level, as has sometimes been concluded on the basis of fragmentary observation. This type of exercise is not abstract philosophy, but a process of considering the difficulties of our predicament in a broad yet concentrated manner, in order to stimulate our superlative adaptive capacity to develop ourselves even beyond the needs of the immediate conditions.

This "liberation" is not just for personal enjoyment or fulfillment, according to Buddhist philosophy, but for freeing energy and intelligence from short-term individual survival to long-term, far-reaching needs of humanity, our fellow beings, and our environment as a whole.

In Taoist spiritual alchemy, the individual development is referred to as taking over the process of creative evolution, and its reinvestment in the welfare of the world is called partnership in the process of creative evolution.

Catila builds a bridge for the sake of Truth;
People going to the Other Side cross over in safety.

The use of a bridge to symbolize the Buddhist teaching is also common in China and the Far East. The mundane world and conventional reality is called "this side" or "this shore" and transcendence, nirvana, and ultimate truth is called the "other side" or the "farther shore."

The adept says that he "builds" this bridge, underscoring the principle that a way across is a temporal expedient, a conditional construction.

The purpose of the bridge is not to get people out of the world, but to conduct them to a completely different perspective on the world. Because of the pliability of consciousness, outside the force-field of conventional usage it is exposed to incalculable dangers from the influences of the environment and the psychological residue in subconscious storage. The bridge is constructed so as to enable people to arrive at transcendence in safety, not swept away by the forcefulness of powerful emotions, ecstatic visions, or other extraordinary experiences occurring to the consciousness no longer defended by the boundaries of customary views.

The tree of illusion's cut asunder, then the pieces joined;
The strong axe of nonduality is fashioned in nirvana.

The total path of Buddhism does not end at transcendence of the world, but includes reintegration. The Chinese Zen master Pai-chang said, "A Buddha is just someone who leaves bondage, then comes back within bondage to be a Buddha for others."

In terms of Buddhist Yoga, phenomena have three natures: absolute, relative, and conceptual. The nature of things as conceived (*parikalpita*) is the subjective description projected on things; this is the root and substance of illusion.

To cut the tree of illusion asunder means distinguishing the conceptual nature of things from the relative and absolute natures of things, realizing the unreality of mere description, and letting go the mental grasp on the images of the conceptual description to "see through" to the absolute.

This discerning transcendence of illusion, however, is not the end of the Buddhist path, as the present couplet illustrates. After having "cut the tree of illusion asunder," then one "rejoins the pieces." By cutting through the illusion that description is itself reality, the practitioner acquires the freedom to operate constructively within the realm of convention, no longer bound by the limits of conditioned thought.

This is the meaning of the nonduality of samsara and nirvana, which is the basis of Universalist and Tantric Buddhism. This nonduality is inaccessible, however, to the mind still enmeshed in its own conceptual descriptions. Only in the inner silence of nirvana is it possible to directly experience nonduality. Zen proverb says, "Let go both hands over a cliff; after dying completely, come back to life; then nothing can deceive you."

Climbing the bridge, go neither right nor left;
Enlightenment is close, not far away.

Using the esoteric imagery of the energy channels to interpret "right" and "left," the first line of this couplet warns the practitioner not to linger in perception or dalliance on the way over. Extraordinary perceptions and experiences may occur as the mind goes beyond the bounds of conventional conditioning. Enthusiasts may become fascinated by these phenomena, thus losing the way to real freedom and enlightenment. Therefore this kind of warning is normal in Buddhist meditation lore.

One of the lures of extraordinary perceptions and experiences is the sense of enhancement, which gives rise to the notion of enlightenment as an accumulation of such attainments. This results in a kind of disorientation that obstructs realization of penetrating insight into the essential. Thus it is said that enlightenment is not far away, in the sense that insight is not something acquired from outside. The Japanese Zen master Dogen wrote, "Why abandon a seat in your own house to idly roam in the dusty realms of alien countries?"

Any of you people who would go across,
Ask Catila, the unsurpassed master.

The bridge stands for method, liberative techniques by which the human mind is freed from arbitrary limitations. Such bridges are constructed by people who have already made the crossing, based on their consequent knowledge of the goal and their subsequent use of available materials to construct means for others to cross over. In order to use a particular method, it is therefore necessary to follow directions, that is, to follow it correctly, in accordance with its expert design.

[6]

BHUSUKU

> Of what is taken and discarded, what remains?
> Encircled by clamor, he scatters to the four quarters.
> Its own flesh is the deer's enemy;
> Bhusuku the hunter will not let it go for a moment.
> The deer neither touches grass nor drinks water;
> The deer doesn't know the doe's abode.
> The doe speaks, the deer listens: "You, deer!
> Abandon this forest and be a wanderer."
> As it sprints away, the hooves of the deer cannot be seen;
> Bhusuku says so, but it enters not the ignorant mind.

Of what is taken and discarded, what remains?
Encircled by clamor, he scatters to the four quarters.

What is taken and discarded is the mortal body. This first line represents contemplation of impermanence. The Japanese Zen master Dogen taught, "If you would be free of greed, first you must leave selfishness behind. In order to leave selfishness behind, the contemplation of impermanence is the foremost mental discipline."

The encircling clamor is the continual fluctuation of the environment, including the ups and downs of fortune and the vagaries of human behavior. Scattering to the four directions means freeing the mind from this knot of anxiety by dissolving the feeling of subject versus object and realizing the ungraspability of things in themselves.

Its own flesh is the deer's enemy;
Bhusuku the hunter will not let it go for a moment.

Desires of the flesh can lead people to unreasonable actions with undesirable consequences. Habitual desires can bind people into limited and limiting routines of behavior. Unchecked by reason, obsession with personal desires is potentially self-destructive. In the *Dhamma-pada*, Buddha says, "Whoever overcomes this clinging vulgar craving in the world, so hard to get over, has sorrows fall away, like drops of water from a lotus."[10]

The hunter is the inner observer, watching for heedless obsessive-ness, ready to shoot it down wherever it is found. This represents self-watching, a basic Buddhist exercise. Through the practice of self-watching, one comes to understand how much energy one spends on vanity and futility. This realization can then be used to cultivate a capacity of conscious inner self-regulation.

The deer neither touches grass nor drinks water;
The deer doesn't know the doe's abode.

The deer refraining from fodder and water represents the mind turn-ing away from involvement in habitual routine attachments, which obstruct direct realization of objective truth. The deer not knowing where the doe abides symbolizes the inability of the ordinary condi-tioned senses and culturally formulated intelligence to know empti-ness. The *Sandhinirmocana-sutra* says, "Someone in ignorance who clings to the signs of the world because of overwhelming interest in perceptual and cognitive signs thus cannot think of, or assess, or be-lieve in the ultimate nirvana that obliterates all signs so that reifica-tion ends."[11]

The doe speaks, the deer listens: "You, deer!
Abandon this forest and be a wanderer."

The speaking of the doe is the manifestation of emptiness in imper-manence and ungraspability; the listening of the deer represents in-wardly silencing conceptual description reifying things. When the intelligence comes to understand that nothing can be grasped or pos-sessed, it is induced to let go of its holdings and thus free itself from thralldom to the realm of the senses. The *Sandhinirmocana-sutra* says, "Those who pursue thoughts cannot think of, or assess, or be-lieve in the character of the ultimate truth that is beyond the sphere of all thought and deliberation."[12]

As it sprints away, the hooves of the deer cannot be seen;
Bhusuku says so, but it enters not the ignorant mind.

Sprinting away represents transcending the world. Leaving no tracks means that transcendence is not an act of rejection, not a program of ascetic denial, but a departure from subjective views and illusions. Attachment to detachment is not freedom; even less so is attachment to masochistic self-indulgence in the name of mortification.

Yet even though this is authoritatively stated, the point is not understood by the ignorant, who prefer to follow tracks. When the emperor of China, a lavish patron of Buddhist churches, asked the founder of Zen what the highest meaning of the holy truths is, the Zen founder replied, "Empty, nothing holy." When the emperor failed to understand, the Zen founder left the country; but as a later commentator said, "How could he avoid the growth of a thicket of brambles?" This is Bhusuku's point. As a contemporary Indian saying has it, "Buddha told people not to worship anything, and then they began to worship him."

KAHNA

> The road was blocked by the vowels and consonants;
> See that, Kahnu was saddened.
> Where can Kahnu go to make an abode?
> He is unattached to any object of mind.
> The three of them, they three are separate;
> Kahnu says, "The world is broken!"
> Whatever has come has gone;
> In the forest of lingering attachment, Kahnu was sad.
> Kahnu is here, nearby, in the city of the Victor;
> Kahnu says, "Infatuation doesn't enter my mind."

The road was blocked by the vowels and consonants;
Seeing that, Kahnu was saddened.

The vowels and consonants represent conventionalized cognition and understanding, structured by language and conceptualization. These "block the road" in the sense that when they capture all of our attention, they obstruct formless intuitive perception and understanding.

To be "saddened" by this recognition is to realize the limitations of conditioned mental constructions. As in the case of other exercises in observation of limitation, the purpose here is to arouse the *bodhicitta* or thought of enlightenment.

Where can Kahnu go to make an abode?
He is unattached to any object of mind.

Intelligent contemplation of impermanence is a basic Buddhist practice exercised for the purpose of cultivating nonattachment, as a means of freeing the mind from the compulsive force of habitual involvement in objects of thought and feeling. The *Diamond-sutra* says, "One should activate the mind without dwelling on anything."

The three of them, they three are separate;
Kahnu says, "The world is broken!"

This couplet represents another method of meditation. Here the "three" are the organs, objects, and consciousnesses of the senses. The practitioner develops a keen inner sense of emptiness through meditating on the relativity of sense organs, sense objects, and sense consciousnesses.

To arrive at the inconceivable state of nonconceptual cognition, one contemplates organs of sense without consciousness or object, consciousness of sense without organs or objects, and objects of sense without organs or consciousnesses. Because all experience consists of combinations of these three, no one of them can be grasped in itself. Since no one can be grasped in itself, what is there to combine?

Naturally, it must be kept in mind that this is an exercise in attention, not philosophical rhetoric. The use of logic is not to arrive at conceptual resolutions, but to maneuver the attention in such a way as to focus inconceivable insights beyond the domain of discursive thought.

Whatever has come has gone;
In the forest of lingering attachment, Kahnu was sad.

Having entered the domain of extraordinary perceptions and intimations of spiritual experience, so as to be free of clinging attachment to relative phenomena, however abstract or ethereal they may be. A Zen proverb says, "It is comparatively easy to rise higher with every step; it is harder to let go of each state of mind." Kahnu's "sadness" mimes the condition of one who had become infatuated with a temporary spiritual state, and therefore experiences its passing as a loss.

Kahnu is here, nearby, in the city of the Victor;
Kahnu says, "Infatuation doesn't enter my mind."

The final couplet illustrates the condition of one who has gone beyond infatuation with all phenomena, both mundane and transmundane.

The Victor is an epithet of a Buddha, one who has overcome delusion. The domain of enlightenment is "nearby" in our innermost mind and our objective environment everywhere. The Chinese Zen master Kuei-shan said, "As long as feelings do not stick to things, how can things hinder you?"

[8]

KAMBALAMBARA

> The boat of compassion is filled with gold;
> There is no place to keep any silver.
> Sail, Kamali, up to the sky!
> When life is gone, how can it return?
> When the peg is uprooted and the rope unraveled,
> Sail off, O Kamali, having asked a true guide.
> Riding on the prow of the boat,
> he seeks in the four directions;
> Without an oar, how can he row?
> The boat is pressed on either side, left and right;
> On the way the Great Ecstasy has been found.

The boat of compassion is filled with gold;
There is no place to keep any silver.

Silver represents the relative thought of enlightenment, which is intellectual understanding of the human predicament and the consequent aspiration to rise above it. Gold represents the absolute
thought of enlightenment, which is intuitive gnosis of ultimate
truth.

Buddhism distinguishes three kinds of compassion. There is sentimental compassion, which is personal and emotional, taking the
troubles of oneself and others at face value. Then there is dreamlike
compassion, which is austere and visionary, regarding human problems as results of illusion. Finally there is objectless compassion,
which is natural, spontaneous, and unbiased by emotionalized conceptions of persons as objects of compassion.

This couplet sings of objectless compassion, which can only come
about through experiential realization of the absolute truth, transcending psychologically conditioned notions and sentiments. This
is why the adept says that the boat of compassion is filled with gold

and has no more room for silver. Here he echoes the teaching of Nagarjuna, the seminal Buddhist writer on emptiness, who stated that true emptiness *is* true compassion.

Sail, Kamali, up to the sky!
When life is gone, how can it return?

Kamali is a vernacular or familiar form of the poet's name. He urges himself to "sail up to the sky," in the sense of rising above views of the world, to realize emptiness.

Here it is important to distinguish between the usage of the word "sky" as representing emptiness (*sunyata*), which Buddhists consider ultimate truth, and its usage in terms such as "absorption in the plane of the sky" (*gagana-tala-samadhi*), which represent exercises in abstraction.

The key to determining which meaning is intended is in the second line of the couplet. Prince Siddhartha did not attain liberation and enlightenment and become Buddha until he gave up pursuing yogic trances as aims in themselves, realizing that they are still impermanent.

Here the Tantric adept also points out that this life is our only chance for enlightenment, a manner of teaching also common to Zen masters of the Far East. Later Lamaism notwithstanding, there is even a Tibetan proverb that says, "No one has the power to be born again and again."

The self-exhortation method of meditation represented here is another feature of this teaching that is also practiced in Zen. A model example in the classic *koan* collection *No Barrier* relates that every day Zen master Ruiyan would call to himself and answer himself; then he would say to himself, "Be awake, be alert!" "Yes!" "From now on, don't be fooled by anyone!" "Yes! Yes!"

When the peg is uprooted and the rope unraveled,
Sail off, O Kamali, having asked a true guide.

The peg is a false sense of permanence and stability. The unraveling of the rope represents analytic meditation such as that explained in the preceding song by Kahnu.

A man walking at night sees a piece of rope in the road. In the dark, he thinks it is a snake, and is frightened. This stands for the conceptualized nature of things; we conceive things to be such and so, describe them thus in our minds, and react to our own descriptions.

On closer examination, it is not a snake; it is only a piece of rope. This stands for the relative nature of things. This is the realm of conditional existence as is, apart from what we may imagine subjectively.

On yet closer analysis, the "rope" is actually a name for a bundle of fibers twisted together, perceived and used as a single entity. This stands for the absolute nature of things, the sense in which nothing exists of itself, but only as a temporary association of interdependent elements.

This rope metaphor is a classical contemplation method of Buddhist Yoga, designed to dissolve the opacity of concrete pseudo-absoluteness projected on objects by the unreflective mind still in the stage of naive realism. It is referred to elsewhere in these Tantric songs, and is also widely represented in Far Eastern Buddhism, especially T'ien-t'ai "stopping and seeing" practices, and certain types of Zen *koan* meditation.

Riding on the prow of the boat,
he seeks in the four directions;
Without an oar, how can he row?

Seeking in the four directions refers to meditation on the sense in which things conditionally exist, the sense in which things do not absolutely exist, the sense in which things neither exist nor do not exist, and the sense in which things both exist and do not exist.

This exercise is also basic to T'ien-t'ai Buddhism, and is found in Zen *koans.* Although the setup used may often take the form of logical propositions, the purpose of the practice is not philosophical or rhetorical, but psychological. It is a guide to meditation method, which the Tantric adept here likens to an oar propelling a boat onward, as the technique propels inner perception in its progress toward refinement.

The boat is pressed on either side, left and right;
On the way the Great Ecstasy has been found.

Pursuing the "four direction" meditation, "either side, left and right," can be understood to refer to existence and nonexistence. Combining this with the "energy channel" meditation spoken of earlier and evidently alluded to here, the left and right channels, of dalliance and perception, can be used as receptacles of the experiences witnessed in the process of the "four direction" meditations, each step of which provokes specific different experiences.

The inner visionary representations of these experiences, as they are registered in the channels of perception and dalliance, are then pressed into the central channel, that is the channel of purification, where they are resolved, clarified, and purified.

The Great Ecstasy that is found in the purification channel is the subtle bliss of disentanglement and liberation characteristic of the realization of emptiness.

The "way" here has two levels of meaning, both indicated by the esoteric terminology. Emptiness is the "Middle Way" between attachment and rejection, affirmation and denial. The middle channel of purification thus symbolically stands for the realization of emptiness, by which the mind is purified of biased views.

Concretely, in Tantric practice, it technically stands for the inner visualization in which the contemplation of emptiness is carried out and formless insight is subtly registered in the mind-body continuum.

This is beautifully illustrated in a Zen *koan* in the famous collection known as *The Blue Cliff Record*. One day a Zen master "went wandering in the mountains." When he returned, a disciple asked him where he had been. "Wandering in the mountains," he said. "Where did you go?" the disciple asked. "First I went pursuing the fragrant grasses," replied the master; "then I returned following the falling flowers." The disciple said, "How springlike!" But the master said, "Cooler than autumn dew dripping on the lotus."

In terms of inner visualization meditation, wandering in the mountains means psychic experience within the energy network visualized in the place of one's own physical body. The fragrant grasses and the falling flowers refer to the channels of perception and dalliance. The disciple's reaction is still in the vein of dalliance ("warm"), so the master corrects him in the vein of purification ("cool").

[9]

KAHNU

> The pillar, so firm, is broken;
> The various fastenings encircling it are torn away.
> Kahnu makes love, drunk with wine;
> In the lotus forest of spontaneity, he is extremely happy.
> As when an elephant bull makes love to a cow,
> So does suchness rain like the elephant's sweat.
> The six courses are all inherently pure,
> Unstained in the least by being and nonbeing.
> The treasure of the ten powers is collected in the ten
>   directions;
> Tame the elephant of ignorance, by being unaffected.

The pillar, so firm, is broken;
The various fastenings encircling it are torn away.

This couplet illustrates a meditative exercise in transcending subjectivity, applied to both body and mind. In meditating on the body, one mentally reduces one's physical existence to elements, seeing thereby through the death of the self. In meditating on the mind, the temporally acquired mentality is "deconstructed" by analyzing the cultural, social, and personal factors that have conditioned and formed it.

Kahnu makes love, drunk with wine;
In the lotus forest of spontaneity, he is extremely happy.

Making love symbolizes union with emptiness. Inebriation symbolizes having nothing hanging on one's mind, having one's mind off things. Wine stands for the subtle euphoria of nirvana.

The lotus forest of spontaneity is the experience of life after nirvana. Extreme happiness refers to the condition of one who has escaped the prison of artificialities.

As when an elephant bull makes love to a cow,
So does suchness rain like the elephant's sweat.

Suchness, *tathata* in both Sanskrit and Bengali, means actuality as directly witnessed without conceptualization. Because it is not limited by the filtration of conceptual processing, the experience called "suchness" gives the impression of extraordinary richness and abundance.

The six courses are all inherently pure,
Unstained in the least by being and nonbeing.

The six courses are states of mind represented by animals, ghosts, denizens of hell, human beings, celestial beings, and antigods. Animals symbolize ignorance and folly, ghosts symbolize cupidity and greediness, antigods symbolize aggression and hatred, human beings symbolize socialization, and celestial beings symbolize meditative states. These six are often conventionally used to stand for the whole range of conditioned states, and in various combinations may be employed to describe psychological complexes.

Ordinarily the path of Buddhism is first represented as transcendence of these six courses of conditioning. In the Buddhist practice known as stopping or cessation, the mind ceases its active occupation with conditioned states. In the complementary practice known as seeing or contemplation, the compulsiveness of six courses is undermined by viewing them as inherently empty of absolute existence by the very fact of their dependence on conditions.

In accord with the two meditative modes of stopping and seeing, or cessation and contemplation, the meaning of "pure" is twofold. In the state of stopping or cessation of thought, everything seems clear, because there is no judgment and comparison. In the process of seeing and contemplating the ultimate nature of things, insight penetrates the vanity of subjective imagination, while intellect comprehends the inevitable end of all that is caused.

Because conditioned phenomena depend on other things, they have no absolute intrinsic existence of their own; thus they are "unstained by being." Insofar as they do exist relatively when causal conditions coalesce, phenomena are not absolutely nonexistent either, so they are "unstained by nonbeing." This is one way Buddhism defines the Middle Way, which is none other than true emptiness.

The treasure of the ten powers is collected in the ten directions;
Tame the elephant of ignorance, by being unaffected.

The ten powers are powers of knowledge characteristic of complete Buddhas. Together, they are referred to as the consummate all-knowledge or omni-science of Buddhas, which they use to enlighten others. The first one is knowledge of what is true and what is not. Second is knowledge of the results of actions. Third is knowledge of various interests. Fourth is knowledge of various realms. Fifth is knowledge of different faculties, higher and lower.

The sixth power is knowledge of all destinations, or consequences of various different ways of life. Seventh is knowledge of all states of meditation and concentration, including how they get polluted, how they are purified, and how to enter into them and emerge from them. Eighth is knowledge of past history. Ninth is knowledge of others' conditions. Tenth is knowledge of ending contamination, which means being free from psychological affliction in the midst of all experience, mundane or supramundane.

The ten directions represent the totality of the relative universe, including both mental and material aspects. The treasure of the ten powers of knowledge is "collected" in the ten directions in the sense that the relative universe is the "mine" from which these knowledges are extracted.

By the same token, the relative universe "conceals" these knowledges from the eye that only looks at superficial appearances and fails to descry underlying patterns. For this reason it is said that the fundamental substance of illusion and enlightenment is one and the same; the difference between folly and wisdom lies in how the individual handles it.

This is a basic perspective of Mahayana Buddhism, and a primary meaning of Tantra, which is translated into Chinese as "fundamental continuity." The relative thought of enlightenment is cultivated on the basis of this understanding, and the absolute thought of enlightenment is awakened through perception of this continuity.

A key to overcoming the basic ignorance of self-contained subjectivity, and thus perceiving the "fundamental continuity" and there beginning the process of disinterring the ten knowledges from throughout the universe, is suggested in the final line of the adept's song—"by being unaffected." When the blinding force of automatic judgment and emotional reaction is undermined by intelligent non-participation, then attention can be stabilized and greater objectivity can be realized. This process is also called "stopping and seeing."

10

KAHNU

> Outside the city is your hut, Gypsy woman;
> You go on touching the Brahmin scholar.
> Hey, Gypsy woman! I'll be with you; live with me!
> Kahnu the hated is a naked mendicant.
> A single lotus with sixty-four petals;
> Climbing onto it, the destitute Gypsy woman dances.
> O Gypsy woman, I ask you about true being;
> In whose boat, O Gypsy, do you come and go?
> The Gypsy woman sells her mandolin, and has no wicker
>   basket;
> She's discarded her dancer's paraphernalia right in front of
>   you.
> O Gypsy woman, I'm a naked mendicant!
> From you I have gotten a garland of bones.
> Breaking the tank, the Gypsy woman eats the lotus root;
> I kill the Gypsy woman, I take life.

Outside the city is your hut, Gypsy woman;
You go on touching the Brahmin scholar.

The Gypsy woman symbolically stands for the ultimate selflessness (inherent identitylessness) and emptiness (inherent nonabsoluteness) of temporal phenomena. This subtle spiritual perception is "outside the city," beyond the limits and bounds of the edifice of conventional reality as construed by the historically and culturally conditioned thought habit and worldview. This is why the *Sandhinirmocana-sutra* says that, "The ultimate truth transcends all objects of thought and deliberation."

The Gypsy woman is an "outcaste," rejected by the orthodox Brahmin scholar of conventional thinking. "Someone in ignorance who clings to rhetoric," continues the *Sandhinirmocana-sutra*, "because of an overwhelming interest in words, thus cannot think of, or assess, or believe in the pleasure of holy silence with inner tranquility."[13] And yet the "scholar's" edifice of thought, being itself relative and conditioned, has no absolute existence of its own; in Buddhist terms, it is ultimately "empty." So the "Gypsy woman" of emptiness "keeps on touching" the "Brahmin scholar" of form.

Hey, Gypsy woman! I'll be with you; live with me!
Kahnu the hated is a naked mendicant.

To realize communion with objective emptiness, the Buddhist first becomes inwardly empty; thus "I'll be with you; live with me!" This is not, however, to escape reality, but rather to face reality more directly; more directly, that is, than is possible through a rigidly self-limiting framework of fixed assumptions and descriptions. This is a matter of recovering original freedom of perspective and potential from herd-instinct conformism to coercive training and unexamined habit.

Such is the nature of convention, nevertheless, that conformism is part of its operation. Thus a certain price is to be paid for departure from the circle of familiarity and acceptance. Here that price is summed up in the word "hated." This is not necessarily intended literally, although it is not unknown for hatred to be visited upon the unconventional. In a more subtle sense, "hated" means that one's integrity is not dependent upon the views of others.

The naked mendicant is the mind that is not clothed by worldly thought habit and not employed by worldly compulsion. The famous Sung dynasty Chinese Zen master Yuan-wu, writing about the same time as these Bengali Siddhas, often used the expression "bare and untrammeled, naked and free" to describe the state of the mind not veiled by presumption or preconception and not clouded by inner or outer conversation.

A single lotus with sixty-four petals;
Climbing onto it, the destitute Gypsy woman dances.

Sixty-four is the total number of wordly arts and sciences; the total number of erotic arts is also said to be sixty-four. One lotus with sixty-four petals represents the mind-body continuum and its manifold, complex capacities.

Destitution symbolizes nonattachment, which means freedom from obsessiveness. This characterizes the realization of selflessness and emptiness, which stand for the fluidity of the liberated mind.

The "Gypsy" dancing illustrates the dynamic nature of selflessness and emptiness. These terms, in their practical dimensions, do not denote negative states of suppression or withdrawal, but rather the renewable, constructive ability to operate without unconsciously losing perception and creativity to the lull of repetitious habit.

Imagery of enlightening beings with many faces, hands, and implements frequently appears in Tantric and other Buddhist art, reflecting the versatility and richness of human development believed to be possible in the aftermath of psychological, intellectual, and spiritual liberation.

O Gypsy woman, I ask you about true being;
In whose boat, O Gypsy, do you come and go?

According to the *prajnaparamita* teaching, matter is emptiness, and emptiness is matter; the same is true, furthermore, of sensation, perception, conception, and consciousness. Thus being and emptiness are identified, metaphysically and intuitively, as a basis for practical exercises, contemplation and insight.

On one level, being is the "vehicle" in which "emptiness" is conveyed, to the contemplative eye seeing into metaphysical reality. On another level, the "unidentified" mind that does not cling to anything possessively has a pragmatic kind of "emptiness" in it, even while in the midst of material forms, sensations, perceptions, conceptions, and consciousness. As in the Taoist image of the "empty boat," this inner emptiness, in Buddhist terms, is what the classical Zen master Lin-chi called "not taking on the delusions of others."

In terms of Buddhist Yoga, all these phenomena have relative existence, but their existence as we picture and define them to ourselves is subjective and conditional. So this existence is nonexistent in absolutely objective reality. By detachment from its conceptual description of things, the mind is enabled to perceive and conceive in ways not defined in that description; and it is also enabled to sense absolute emptiness intuitively.

The question "in whose boat do you come and go" implies that emptiness should not be sought in abstract nothingness outside or other than existence, or in quietism separated from the world. This theme is common to universalist Buddhism, both in the scriptures and the works of the schools.

The question "whose boat" also suggests that in order to liberate the mind from arbitrary restrictions due to historical conditioning, it is imperative to know what that conditioning is. This Buddhist self-analysis includes individual and collective or interactive dimensions of personal and social evolution and development, as shown in illustrative stories about conditions in past lives and other worlds frequently found in classical and vernacular Buddhist literature.

The Gypsy woman sells her mandolin, and has no wicker basket;
She's discarded her dancer's paraphernalia right in front of you.

Abandoning instruments, implements, and paraphernalia symbolizes abandoning the means when the end has been reached. This happens "right in front of you" in the sense that now your perception of truth is not limited by the medium of symbol and method, but is experienced as direct witness.

O Gypsy woman, I'm a naked mendicant!
From you I have gotten a garland of bones.

Having divested oneself of psychological and intellectual holdings, one's perceptions and intuitions are not obscured by an overlay of arbitrary thought-habit, and one's energy and attention are not in the employ of worldly ambitions. From the experiential realization of emptiness, the superficial "flesh" of subjective illusions is stripped away, leaving the bare "bones" of objective truth.

Breaking the tank, the Gypsy woman eats the lotus root;
I kill the Gypsy woman, I take life.

According to Nagarjuna, the master expositor of emptiness, the Buddhas have declared that departure from all views is emptiness, but those who take emptiness for a view cannot be cured. Thus the doctrine of emptiness says that things are not as we think them to be, and yet they are not nothing.

When the contemplation of emptiness slips unconsciously into nothingness, the regenerative potential of the emptiness experience is nullified. This pseudo-emptiness, while subjectively comfortable, is ultimately destructive to social, psychological, and spiritual integrity. In that sense, of "emptiness" taken to an extreme, the "Gypsy" breaks the vessel of life and consumes the root of life. So the adept "kills the Gypsy woman" and thus "takes life." In Zen terms, first one "breaks up the home and scatters the family," then one "comes to understand how to make a living."

11

KRISHNA

> The energy in the channels is strong, suspended in space;
> The unbeaten drum is played in the call of the valiant one.
> Krishna the naked yogi has entered into practice;
> In uniformity he moves freely through the city of the body.
> The vowels and consonants are bell-anklets on the feet;
> The sun and moon are ornamental bangles.
> Abandon lust, hatred, and folly;
> Take supreme liberation, a garland of pearls.
> Killing mother-in-law, sister, and sister-in-law at home,
> Killing mother, Krishna has become a naked mendicant.

The energy in the channels is strong, suspended in space;
The unbeaten drum is played in the call of the valiant one.

The channels here are the energy channels visualized in the body, as explained earlier. When the energy in the channels is strong, that means the visualization is fully developed. "Suspended in space" means that the visualization of the energy channels is based on emptiness, and also that it supercedes ordinary awareness of the physical body and surroundings.

The call of the valiant one is what is commonly referred to as the "lion's roar," meaning the Buddhist teaching of emptiness, which overcomes all illusions, as a valiant warrior overcomes enemies. The drum is also a common symbol of Buddhist teaching; in this case it is said to be played "unbeaten" in the sense that emptiness, being intrinsic to relativity and not anything in itself, is therefore not relative to anything.

Krishna the naked yogi has entered into practice;
In uniformity he moves freely through the city of the body.

The yogi's nakedness represents freedom from attachment, having no psychological holdings. If one enters into Tantric practice greedy for secrets and powers, that will prevent enlightenment. Thus it is necessary for the yogi to be "naked" as a prerequisite to success in this practice.

Mental "travel" through the body is part of Tantric visualization practice, utilizing the network of energy channels centered on the three main channels. When the attention alights on different points, this stimulates different psychic experiences; "uniformity" here refers to psychological equanimity, which enables the yogi to "move freely" through the energy body without getting hung up on any particular experience.

The vowels and consonants are bell-anklets on the feet;
The sun and moon are ornamental bangles.

The vowels and consonants represent energy and matter, the universe of form and structure. The sun and moon are absolute and relative thought of enlightenment, formless awakening of mind based on intuition of absolute truth and formal awakening of mind based on analysis of relative truth. Both the life of the ordinary world (vowels and consonants) as well as the life of spiritual development (sun and moon) are experienced as adornments from the point of view of the ethereal essence of consciousness centered in emptiness.

Abandon lust, hatred, and folly;
Take supreme liberation, a garland of pearls.

Lust, hatred, and folly are traditionally described as the "three poisons" at the root of unnecessary human suffering. Liberation from these three poisons is a basic aim of Buddhism; this is repeated even after the exalted vision of the preceding couplet because lust, hatred, and folly can also be generated from ignorant attitudes toward "spiritual" experience, just as they can derive from an ignorant relation to life experience in the material world.

Killing mother-in-law, sister, and sister-in-law at home,
Killing mother, Krishna has become a naked mendicant.

Killing is a standard symbol for realization of impermanence, for detachment, and for transcendence. This couplet follows up on the preceding. The ninth-century Chinese Zen master Linchi said, "If you want to attain objective vision and understanding, just do not take on the confusion of others. Whatever you meet, inwardly and outwardly, immediately kill. If you meet Buddha, kill Buddha; if you meet a Zen master, kill the Zen master; if you meet a saint, kill the saint. If you meet your parents, kill your parents; if you meet your relatives, kill your relatives. Only then can you attain liberation, and penetrate through to freedom, without being constrained by things." The use of language which, however symbolic, is nevertheless harsh and even shocking, is a technique common to Tantric and Zen Buddhism, used to jar the consciousness out of the self-hypnotic mental lethargy known in Buddhist Yoga as "the lull of words."

[12]

KRISHNA

> I play a game of chess on the board of compassion;
> The true teacher, by enlightenment, has overcome
> the power of the world.
> The deuce is removed, the king is slain;
> By the instruction of the teacher,
> Krishna is near the winner's circle.
> Breaking through the front line, I slay the pawns;
> Mounting an elephant, I stir up five people.
> The king is extinguished by wisdom;
> With certainty, the power of the world is overcome.
> Krishna says, "I give a good gambling stake;
> Surveying the sixty-four squares on the chessboard, I take it."

I play a game of chess on the board of compassion;
The true teacher, by enlightenment, has overcome
  the power of the world.

The board of compassion is the world as it is experienced by the liberated Buddhist who can no longer be confused by things of the world. The exercise of free compassion is metaphorically represented as "play" because it is a spontaneous expression of transcendental independence. The Japanese Zen master Hakuin wrote, "Enlightening beings of the higher vehicle do not dwell in the state of result they have realized; from the ocean of effortlessness, they radiate unconditional great compassion. . . . This is what is called coming back within going away, going away within coming back."[14]

The deuce is removed, the king is slain;
By the instruction of the teacher,
  Krishna is near the winner's circle.

The "deuce" stands for dualistic thinking; removing the deuce means overcoming illusory dualism. The "king" is ego-centrism; slaying the king means overcoming self-centered habits of thinking, behaving, and processing experience. The winner's circle is the realm of enlightenment.

Nonduality and objectivity are characteristics of compassion in the Buddhist sense of the word, as illustrated by Zen master Hakuin: "Powerful enlightening beings spin the wheel of the principle of nonduality of light and dark. In the midst of the red dust, ashes on the head and mud on the face, they act freely in the company of sound and form; like a lotus blossom whose color and fragrance become fresher and clearer in fire, they go into the marketplace extending their hands, acting for others. This is what is called being on the road without leaving home, leaving home without being on the road."[14]

Breaking through the front line, I slay the pawns;
Mounting an elephant, I stir up five people.

The front line is the surface of things, or things as they seem to be. The pawns are the constituent elements of things. Breaking through the front line and slaying the pawns means seeing through the outward aspects of things by penetrating analysis of the elements of events.

According to Munidatta, the elephant stands for mindfulness of things as they really are, and the five people stand for the five clusters (form, feeling, perception, habit, and consciousness), and the objects of the five elementary senses. Knowing things as they really are uproots the notion of selfhood in the five clusters and the overmastering influence of the objects of the five senses.

The king is extinguished by wisdom;
With certainty, the power of the world is overcome.

The word for wisdom used here, *mati,* also means intelligence and understanding, both in Sanskrit and Old Bengali. The "king," can also be translated "the idol," highlighting its symbolic meaning. One point of saying that the "king" or dominant egotism is extinguished by wisdom or intelligence is to counter the notion that selflessness refers to a zombie-like state achieved by simple mortification, or a condition of compulsive servility engineered by operant conditioning.

In practical terms, the egoistic orientation is not undermined by bullying, abasement, or suppression of individuality. These procedures, which are often found in authoritarian cults, actually tend to harden the shell of the ego, as it perversely aggrandizes itself through abasement, supposing this to be holiness.

In the same way, the "power of the world," the allure, facination, or distraction of material senses, is not to be definitively overcome by procedures whose essential technique is denial or isolation from the world. In terms of practical philosophy, this means that "emptiness" is not nothingness; it is not realized by bludgeoning oneself senseless, or by puzzling oneself witless, but by certitude of insight into absolute truth.

"With certainty" means "certainly," describing the annihilation of king ego-centrism by means of wisdom. In Zen as well as Tantric symbolism, this intelligence, this wisdom, is symbolized by an inconceivably sharp sword.

Krishna says, "I give a good gambling stake;
Surveying the sixty-four squares on the chessboard, I take it."

The "good gambling stake" given by the one who has already overcome the world and attained freedom is the rededication of purified, liberated, and enlightened thought, word, and deed to the liberation of others.

According to Buddhist teaching, there are people whom even Buddhas cannot help. Dedication to the liberation of others cannot, therefore, be practically undertaken in the spirit of expectation. This pertinent fact of life is encapsulated in the playful reference to the bodhisattva enterprise as a "gamble."

The sixty-four squares of the board symbolically represent the sum total of the arts and sciences, or the whole potential accessible to humankind. The adept returning to the world after liberation "surveys" the sixty-four squares to observe the total context of human activities and possibilities, and see what move might be made where, with what effects.

Based on this knowledge, both general and particular, the adept then "takes" the "move," even "takes" the whole board, acting appropriately to each setting, regarding all sixty-four squares as having value, actual or potential.

13

KRISHNA

> The Three Refuges are made a boat
> by the One with Eight Children;
> His own body compassion,
> emptiness is his wife.
> Having crossed over the ocean of existence,
> it is like an illusion, a dream;
> The central current is deeply considered
> during the crossing over.
> With the Five Tathagatas as oars,
> Krishna's body crosses the net of illusion.
> Scent, texture, taste, however they may be,
> Are like dreams without sleep.
> Mind the sailor, emptiness the boat,
> Krishna has gone off, with great bliss.

The Three Refuges are made a boat
by the One with Eight Children;
His own body compassion,
emptiness is his wife.

In Sanskrit the Three Refuges are called Buddha, Dharma, and Sangha. On one level, these terms refer to an enlightened exemplar (Buddha), an enlightening teaching (Dharma), and a harmonious communion of people (Sangha) attuned to the teaching. On the level of personal realization, the Buddha is the awakened mind, the Dharma is objective reality, and the Sangha consists of all living beings.

The One with Eight Children is what is called *amalavijnana* in Sanskrit, meaning "Pure Consciousness." According to Buddhist psychology this subtends eight consciousnesses: five basic sense consciousnesses, cognitive consciousness, intellect, and a repository or storage consciousness. As differentiations of function, these eight consciousnesses may be pictured as deriving from the ninth, or pure consciousness; so this pure consciousness is referred to as "the one with eight children."

The *Sandhinirmocana-sutra* says of this pure consciousness, "It is the basis of the adornments of the enlightened. Its pathways are mindfulness and knowledge, its vehicles are great tranquility and subtle observation. Its entrances are the great liberations of emptiness, signlessness, and wishlessness, and its adornments are infinite virtues."[15]

The boat is a symbol of a vehicle or means of deliverance, of liberation. It is pure consciousness that brings the Three Refugees to life and makes them into a way to freedom. Without this living element, "Buddha" is an icon, "Dharma" is a doctrine, and "Sangha" is a business or social club. The *Sandhinirmocana-sutra* explains, "With supremely pure awareness, the awakened one is attached neither to the mundane nor to the supramundane. He proceeds according to formless truth, and dwells in the abode of the enlightened."[16]

The consummation of enlightenment is conventionally described as a wedding of insight and compassion, or wisdom and skill in expedient means. In these terms, insight and wisdom refer to the fluid or ethereal aspect of emptiness, while compassion and skill in means refer to the concrete or localized manifestation of emptiness, which is the relativity of existence. Realization of emptiness, in the Buddhist sense, therefore implies liberation from absolutist fixations, which enables the mind thus awakened to operate more freely.

Hence the wedding of compassion and emptiness means the capacity to be present and active in the world without becoming imprisoned in the process. This is the description of the Buddhist ideal of the bodhisattva or enlightening being, who is in the world but not of the world.

Having crossed over the ocean of existence,
it is like an illusion, a dream;
The central current is deeply considered
during the crossing over.

The word "illusion" is used here, as often in Buddhist literature, in the manner of magicians, for whom the word means a deception of the senses. The effect depends upon the brain's habit of selecting, organizing, and interpreting data into familiar representations; the magician or illusionist deceives the audience by manipulating attention, directing and diverting it in order to produce calculated effects in the minds of observers.

A dream is also usually considered a subjective perception of something that is not objectively there, an organization of neurological activity or data into a representation of experience. Whether a dream is thought of as a random release of energy, as a reflection of everyday life, or as a mirror of unconscious urges, what Buddhist literature generally refers to by the image of a dream is the phenomenon of experiencing what seems to be actually real and yet is not.

The metaphors of the illusion and the dream, as used in Buddhist teaching, thus refer to the mentally constructed nature of the world as we conceive of it. We do not perceive objective reality directly and wholly; our brains select, edit, and organize the data of our senses into conceivable, manageable representations. It is in this sense, in reference to how we construe things, that Buddhist scripture says that the world is only mind, or only consciousness, or only representation.

The particular ways in which individual and collective minds construe information are historically conditioned by culture, society, and personal experience. Born into a particular culture in a particular time, one learns to perceive the world, and to think about it, in a manner conforming to that culture in that time. In a condition of "total immersion" from infancy and therefore having no basis of comparison, one subconsciously absolutizes the world one learns to perceive.

Even as one matures within a particular culture, there is no obvious way of knowing that this "world" is an interpretation, a mental construction. The internalized worldview filters experience in such a way as to exclude disruptive incongruity, preserve its own structure intact, and maintain the continuity of the habit of thought into which it has been conditioned. It is only after "having crossed over," or having gotten past the boundaries of self-reflection, having ceased to absolutize a worldview, that one can see its subjective nature, its illusion-like or dream-like quality.

This realization might be described as a kind of liberation, but it is not yet enlightenment. In penetrating the illusion of objectivity in subjective absolutism, there is a peril of swinging from a relative extreme of attachment to an opposite extreme of rejection. Then the result is not freedom from delusion, but simply disillusion; instead of releasing creative vision and potential, it breeds destructive cynicism and nihilism.

That problem of extremism, often mentioned in Buddhist technical literature, is why "the central current is deeply considered during the crossing over." No longer able to cling to the world as absolute, nevertheless one does not deny the world as relative. Neither does one deny the actuality of all sorts of views of the world, and their effects on people's minds and behavior, however unrealistic any particular views may be. Integrating these perspectives without bias is the Middle Way, the "central current." In Mahayana Buddhism, this is often referred to in general pragmatic terms as "neither grasping nor rejecting."

With the Five Tathagatas as oars,
Krishna's body crosses the net of illusion.

Tathagata is another word for a Buddha, referring to attainment and expression of objective reality. The Five Tathagatas are the so-called Dhyani Buddhas or Meditation Buddhas: Vairocana, Ratnasambhava, Amoghasiddhi, Akshobhya, and Amitayur. These names are associated with specific aspects of enlightened knowledge and are invoked in Tantric meditation methodology.

Vairocana, "The Illuminator" or "Cosmic Sun," associated with cognition of the essential nature of the cosmos, is visualized in the forehead. Ratnasambhava, "Made of Jewels," associated with cognition of equality, is visualized in the right shoulder. Amoghasiddhi, "Impeccable Accomplishment," associated with practical knowledge, is visualized in the left shoulder. Akshobhya, "The Immovable One," associated with mirrorlike cognition, is visualized in the heart. Amitayur, "Infinite Life," associated with precise observational cognition, is visualized in the throat.

This visualization practice involves a different way of experiencing the body, or the sense of physical being, through positive transformation of its mental basis. Certain symbolic gestures, sounds, prayers, thoughts, images, and color associations may also be used to help the actualization of transformation. In this way, as the personal experience of being is refined, the mind-body complex is propelled beyond the confines imposed by the illusion of absoluteness.

Scent, texture, taste, however they may be,
Are like dreams without sleep.

The similarity of ordinary sense experience to that of dreams lies in the general process of representation, and in the habit of taking representation for reality. Just as we ordinarily don't know we are dreaming when we are dreaming, Buddhists say, we ordinarily don't realize we are reacting to subjective views when we think we are experiencing objective reality.

When we are awake (in the ordinary sense of the word), our brains normally have greater control over the images they hold than they do when we are asleep. While our waking brains may be able to control images, in the sense of keeping them steady, they do not necessarily have control over this control. That is to say, the way in which our brains organize and maintain our pictures of the world is a product of both biological and social inheritance and conditioning.

In this sense, as we are we ultimately have no more "control" over our experience of ourselves and our world, and no more contact with objective reality, in the state in which we think we are "awake" than we do when we are asleep and dreaming. This is why Buddhists try to become more conscious, more awake; not just because dreams are not real, but because the full potential of human intelligence and creativity only becomes accessible when consciousness emerges from the shell of fixation on imagined realities and preoccupation with preconceptions.

Deliberate transformation of consciousness, performed by Tantric Buddhists in both waking and dreaming meditation, is an exercise in will and attention, undertaken in order to overcome the power over the mind exerted by the automatic repetition of inherited and conditioned worldviews.

Mind the sailor, emptiness the boat,
Krishna has gone off, with great bliss.

Through insight into emptiness and conscious restructuring of experience, the mind is emancipated from slavery to instinct and conditioning, and develops the capacity of autonomy and free will. In Zen Buddhism, this capacity is called the director, or the host; in Tantric Buddhism, this may be referred to as the *vajradhara*, the thunderbolt-bearer, holder of power.

Were it not for fluidity, which is the quality of emptiness, the mind would have no means of conscious transformation and creative development. Were there no direction, which is the nature of will, fluidity would degenerate into vulnerability, irresoluteness, and lack of meaning and purpose.

Thus it is with "mind the sailor" and "emptiness the boat" that the adept has "gone off" beyond the range of worldly illusions, with the "great bliss" of having first escaped from a suffocating prison, and then found an inexhaustible source of treasures.

14

DOMBI

> Between the Ganges and the Yamuna, there runs a river:
> Submerged in it, the outcaste yogini effortlessly
> reaches the other shore.
> Sail on, Gypsy, sail on; there's been a delay on the way.
> At the lotus feet of the true teacher,
> you will go again to the city of the Victorious.
> The five oars are put down, a rope is tied
> to the back of the boat;
> With the sky for a pot, I bail water,
> so it doesn't get in through the cracks.
> The moon and sun are the mast
> upon which creation is unfurled and wrapped up;
> The two courses, left and right, do not appear good;
> let one sail on at will.
> Without a penny, without a dime,
> one reaches the other side effortlessly.
> Whoever is in a chariot can get no further—
> spitting water, he drowns.

Between the Ganges and the Yamuna, there runs a river:
Submerged in it, the outcaste yogini effortlessly
reaches the other shore.

The Ganges and Yamuna (Jamna) Rivers (which run through Bengal) represent the right and left energy channels in the psychophysical body visualized in meditation, also called the channels of perception and dalliance. The river that runs between the Ganges and Yamuna stands for the central channel, which is the channel of purification.

The yogini (yogini is the feminine form of yogi) symbolizes emptiness and selflessness. The yogini is an "outcaste" in that she is not acceptable to those who are attached to their ingrained ideas of things and their images of themselves. Since ordinary society is based on conventions commonly accepted as true, the mind limited to social training cannot accommodate the insight into the emptiness of absoluteness in worldviews.

The *Sandhinirmocana-sutra* explains the self-limiting nature of this "outcasting" reflex in the course of one of its typically scientific discourses on ultimate truth and its inaccessibility to the conditioned mentality: "Someone in ignorance who clings to the signs of the world because of overwhelming interest in perceptual and cognitive signs thus cannot think of, or assess, or believe in the ultimate nirvana that obliterates all signs so that reification ends."[17]

The "submerging" of the outcaste yogini in the central channel of purification means that the practitioner is not focused on fostering meditative perceptions (right channel), or on dallying with their contents (left channel), but on resolving and clarifying experience (central channel). Thus the yogini reaches the "other shore" of liberation "without effort," disentangled from all mental construction.

Sail on, Gypsy, sail on; there's been a delay on the way.
At the lotus feet of the true teacher,
you will go again to the city of the Victorious.

In the *Saddharmapundarika-sutra* or Lotus Scripture, one of the greatest treasures of Ekayana (Unitarian) Buddhism, the Buddha teaches that *nirvana*, which apparently had been the goal, is actually just a temporary stopping place, an "illusory citadel," on the way to the complete knowledge and vision of Buddhas.

The *sutra* says that a large number of followers who thought they had already attained the ultimate were offended by this statement and left the Buddha's presence. Others remained, admitting that they now realized they had thought themselves saintly when they were actually just decrepit. These people were now able to learn more advanced and comprehensive teachings from Buddha.

This "schism" is one of the great dramas of Buddhism, illustrating an essential truth about history as well as individual development. The exhortation to "sail on, sail on," here addressed by the singer to herself, echoes the Buddha's inspiration to progress, not allowing oneself to stagnate after reaching the deep quiescence experienced in attaining nirvana and merging with emptiness, as illustrated in the first couplet.

This next step, progressing beyond nirvana, called "stepping forward from the top of the hundred foot pole" in Zen, must be taken with care. Freedom implies responsibility. The "true teacher" is truth teaching; the "lotus" is the awakening of the unified, whole mind, the "feet" are the bases of this awakening, the traces of truth by which enlightenment is guided.

The Victor is another name for Buddha, who has mastered the self and in this sense "conquered the world." The city of the Victor is the realm of enlightened experience. Attainment of enlightenment is sometimes referred to as "arrival," in view of the factual transition from a deluded state to an awakened state; but it is also commonly called "return," in the sense that this enlightenment is considered true normalcy, the true "home" of the human essence. Thus enlightenment may also be called restoration, or reversion; so the inspiration says "you will go again."

The five oars are put down, a rope is tied
to the back of the boat;
With the sky for a pot, I bail water,
so it doesn't get in through the cracks.

The five oars are the "five Tathagatas," the five Dhyani Buddhas or Meditation Buddhas used in visualization meditation, as explained earlier. When the enlightened cognitions associated with these Buddhas have been awakened, the practice of deliberate visualization is relinquished. The means are superceded when the goal is reached; thus it is said that "the five oars are put down."

Awakening is followed by stabilization of the realization. This is symbolized by the "rope tied to the back of the boat." In Zen Buddhism, this process of stabilization and maturation is called "nurturing the embryo of sagehood." Initial realization is likened to an infant, which must be nurtured and protected in order to fulfill its potential of wholesome growth and development.

The actual practice of nurturing and protecting the newly awakened mind is depicted in the second line of this couplet. Here, "water" symbolizes disturbance by objects, the "sky" stands for inner calmness and emptiness. With this "pot" the "water" of disturbance, that may otherwise "get in" through the "cracks" or gaps in attention, is "bailed out," keeping the mind clear and unruffled.

The moon and sun are the mast
upon which creation is unfurled and wrapped up;
The two courses, left and right, do not appear good;
let one sail on at will.

The moon stands for the worldly thought of enlightenment, the thought of enlightenment arising from understanding the relative nature of the world. The sun stands for the absolute thought of enlightenment, the thought of enlightenment arising from insight into inconceivable absolute reality.

When these two are pictured as points, their connection is pictured as a line; the "unfurling" of creation is contemplation of relative reality, the "wrapping up" of creation is contemplation of absolute reality. Going back and forth, from contemplation of the relative to contemplation of the absolute, and from contemplation of the absolute to contemplation of the relative, is a meditative practice designed to lead to the capacity for poise in the center between these extremes, the so-called Middle Way.

The Middle Way is the path the Buddhist seeks to tread, and it is for this purpose that the contemplation of two levels of truth is practiced. Thus "the two courses, left and right, do not appear good." The practitioner leans neither toward the mundane nor toward the absolute, and is thus able to "sail on at will," free of encumbering bias.

Without a penny, without a dime,
one reaches the other side effortlessly.
Whoever is in a chariot can get no further—
spitting water, he drowns.

In the *Vajracchedika Prajnaparamita-sutra,* Buddha says that he did not acquire anything by complete perfect enlightenment. In one sense, this is understood to mean that the awakening and development of Buddhahood is awakening and development of existing potential, not something added. In another sense, it means that enlightenment cannot manifest or develop in the mind while it is occupied by acquisitiveness, or possessiveness.

Ironically enough, intense effort at religious exercises may, in reality, be a manifestation of greed, disguised as spiritual seeking. Devotion may be nothing more than proprietary sentiment. That is why the unencumbered one "without a penny, without a dime" arrives at the "other shore" of transcendence "without effort," while the super-ficial one who cleaves to an apparatus as truth itself cannot go beyond its limits or avoid its inevitable failure.

15

SHANTI

> On discerning analysis of essence,
> the imperceptible cannot be observed.
> Whoever goes on a straight path
> will never turn back.
> From shore to shore, samsara is not a straight path, you fool!
> Little child, don't forget a word—the royal path is steep!
> You find no limit to the depth of the sea
> of illusion and delusion:
> No boat or raft is seen ahead;
> you're mistaken not to ask a guide.
> In the trackless expanse of emptiness,
> nothing can be seen;
> you do not entertain doubt as you go.
> Here eight great adepts attain fulfillment,
> going on the straight path.
> Abandoning both left and right paths,
> Shanti speaks succinctly;
> The river bank has no weeds, no rough ground—
> one may go on the way with eyes closed.

On discerning analysis of essence,
the imperceptible cannot be observed.
Whoever goes on a straight path
will never turn back.

Analytic meditation is one method of arriving at emptiness. There are various ways of practicing this type of meditation, including both linear and nonlinear modes of contemplation.

An example of a method in the linear mode is given in the *Heroic Progress Scripture:* "Examine the nature of earth: in its gross form, it is the gross element earth; in its fine form, it is subtle atoms, even subatomic particles next to nothing. On analysis of the most minute form of matter, it is found to be composed of seven parts; when you go even further to break down subatomic particles, this is real emptiness."

An example of a method in the nonlinear mode is in the Zen *koan* "The Wheelmaker" in the classic collection *No Barrier:* "The original wheelmaker made wheels with a hundred spokes. Suppose you take away both sides and remove the axle; what does this clarify?"[18]

A straight path, in Buddhist terms, is a technical term with more than merely moralistic meaning. The *Scripture Spoken by Vimalakirti* says, "A straightforward mind is a site of enlightenment, because it has no falsehood or artificiality." The special sense of straightforward is "direct," meaning direct perception of truth without subjective distortion. Using the same terminology, the illustrious Sixth Grand Master of Zen said, "If you are purely and wholly straightforward in mind everywhere, whatever you are doing, you do not move from the site of enlightenment, which actually becomes the Pure Land. That is called absorption in one practice."

From shore to shore, samsara is not a straight path, you fool!
Little child, don't forget a word—the royal path is steep!

Samsara literally means "revolving," and connotes mundane existence, or the world. In Chinese Buddhism, the term is translated as "revolving," "flowing and revolving," and "birth and death." Later Taoism also borrowed this terminology, without externalizing the imagery. Ch'en Ying-ning, a modern Taoist, explains, "The ocean of birth and death is people's thoughts. Random thoughts come from nowhere in an instant, occurring and passing away, impossible to stop altogether. The occurring of a thought is 'birth,' the passing away of a thought is 'death.' In the space of a single day, we are born and die thousands of times! So 'transmigration' is right in front of us—we don't have to wait until we die to experience it."[19]

From shore to shore, therefore, from birth to death or beginning to end, fluctuating thoughts are not a straight path. The "royal path," or the way to real enlightenment, cannot be pursued willy-nilly; to attain right orientation it is necessary to get over the obstacles to understanding created by our mental habits, and perceive reality directly.

You find no limit to the depth of the sea
of illusion and delusion:
No boat or raft is seen ahead;
you're mistaken not to ask a guide.

The apparent objectivity of the perceived "world" as constructed by our brains for navigational purposes is an illusion; the notion that this and nothing else is real or true is a delusion. We find no limit to their depths because the contents of illusion and delusion are self-contained and self-conditioned; the eye of illusion sees only illusions, the eye of delusion sees only delusions. This is encapsulated in the Zen proverb, "When Mr. Chang drinks wine, Mr. Lee gets drunk."

This is the reason for guidance. Even if someone wants to get over illusion and delusion, subjectivity still blinds the mind wrapped up in preconceptions, expectations, hopes, and fears. The possibility of seeing a viable way out is affected by the mental conditioning and emotional state. Thus it is a mistake—indeed, the very same mistake as the original delusion—to rely on what is found through a search based on subjective supposition, without seeking perspective from an objective source of perception and knowledge.

In the trackless expanse of emptiness,
nothing can be seen;
you do not entertain doubt as you go.
Here eight great adepts attain fulfillment,
going on the straight path.

In the *Madhyamika-karika*, Nagarjuna explains that according to the Buddhist usage, "emptiness" means departure, or detachment, from all views. He adds that the Buddhas have also said that those who take emptiness for a view are incurable. Therefore the statement "nothing can be seen" is not a description or a prescription but a test. The orthodox usage means that there is no reification, whereas the deteriorated understanding is literal.

The teaching of Buddhist Yoga states that it is the fact possible to cultivate a state of mind in which no objects appear. This is not regarded as a true state per se, but as a demonstration of a kind of relativity. There are technical terms for this state, and in orthodox schools it is always rigorously distinguished from emptiness. The objectless state is *empty*, in Buddhist terms, but it is not *emptiness*. Those who understand this distinction both intellectually and experientially are capable of further progress.

Pragmatic dimensions of emptiness are expounded in different ways throughout the Buddhist canon. The image of tracklessness appears in the ancient *Dhammapada*, in the section on the Arhat, or Worthy, where Buddha says, "Those whose compulsions are gone, who are not addicted to consuming, whose sphere is emptiness, signlessness, and liberation, are hard to track, like birds in the sky."[20]

Similar imagery and practice were also taught in Zen Buddhism. The 17th-century Japanese master Shigetsu said, "First getting rid of clinging to ego even in the midst of energy and matter, you attain our original state of egolessness. Then you must also know that phemonena have no selfhood either. Once you realize there is no self in persons or things, then you walk in emptiness even in the midst of your daily activities. This is called traveling the bird's path."

The symbolism of the "eight great adepts" who attain fulfillment in this way can refer to the eight consciousnesses or the eight awakenings of great people.

The eight consciousnesses are comprised of five sense consciousness, the cognitive consciousness (*manovijnana*); the intellect/mentality (*manas*), which includes emotion and judgment; and the "repository" consciousness (*alayavijnana*), in actuality largely subconscious, where all sorts of inherited, experienced, and generated data are stored. The practice of nonreification—departure from all views, or emptiness—purifies the total apparatus of the "eight consciousnesses" of stultifying accumulations of clinging habit.

The eight awakenings of great people are related to this idea, as means of clarification of consciousness and attainment of nirvana. First is having few desires. Buddha said, "People with many desires seek to gain a lot, and therefore their afflictions are also manifold. Those with few desires neither seek nor crave, so they do not have these problems. You should cultivate having few desires even for this reason alone, to say nothing of the fact that having few desires can produce virtues. People with few desires are innocent of using flattery and deviousness to curry the favor of others, and they are not under the compulsion of their senses. Those who act with few desires are calm, without anxiety or fear. Whatever the situation, there is more than enough—there is never insufficiency. Those who have few desires have nirvana."

Second is being content. Buddha said, "If you want to shed afflictions, be content. Contentment is the abode of prosperity and happiness, of peace and serenity."

Third is enjoying quietude. Buddha said, "If you wish to seek the peace and happiness of quietude and noncontrivance, leave the clamor and live an uncluttered life in an uncrowded place. . . . Those who like crowds suffer the vexations of crowds, just as a big tree will suffer withering and breakage when flocks of birds gather on it. Worldly ties and clinging sink you into a multitude of pains, like an old elephant stuck in the mud unable to get itself out."

Fourth is diligence. Buddha said, "Nothing is difficult if you make diligent effort, so you should be diligent. Even a small stream can go through rock if it flows continually."

Fifth is unfailing recollection, or keeping right-mindfulness. Buddha said, "If you seek a good companion, if you seek a good protector and helper, nothing compares to unfailing recollection. Those who have unfailing recollection cannot be invaded by draining afflictions, so you should concentrate your thoughts and keep mindful. One who loses mindfulness loses virtue. If one's power of mindfulness is strong, one will not be harmed even if one enters among draining desires."

Sixth is concentration in meditation. Buddha said, "If you concentrate the mind, it will be in a state of stability, and you will be able to discern the characteristics of phenomena that come to be and pass away in the world."

Seventh is cultivating insight. Buddha said, "If you have insight, you will have no greedy attachment. Always examine yourselves and do not allow any heedlessness. Then you will be able to attain liberation from ego and objects. . . . Genuine insight is a secure ship to cross the sea of aging, ailing, and dying. It is a bright lamp in the darkness of ignorance, it is good medicine for the unwell, and it is a sharp axe to fell the trees of afflictions. So you should use the insight gained by learning, reflection, and application, and develop it in yourself. Anyone who has the illumination of wisdom is a person with clear eyes, even the mortal eyes."

Eighth is not engaging in vain talk. Buddha said, "If you indulge in various kinds of vain talk, your mind will be disturbed. Then you will not attain liberation even if you leave society. Therefore you should immediately give up vain talk, which disturbs the mind. If you want to attain the bliss of tranquillity and dispassion, you should extinguish the affliction of vain talk."

Buddha is said to have articulated these eight awarenesses on the night he passed away into final extinction. According to this tradition, in his last reminder to his followers he said, "Always seek the path of emancipation with a single mind. All things in the world, mobile and immobile, are unstable forms that disintegrate."

Each of these eight awarenesses contains the other; so their integrated awakening is also represented by the number sixty-four. Sixty-four has already appeared in these songs; it stands for the totality of the eight awarenesses in Hinayana Buddhism, the totality of worldly arts and sciences in Mahayana Buddhism, and the totality of erotic arts in Vajrayana Buddhism.

Hinayana Buddhism deals with transcendence, Mahayana deals with nonduality, and Vajrayana deals with creativity. Thus the three phases of Buddhism are interrelated in an orderly continuity. These are all in the realm of relative means, nevertheless, and not absolute ends; so the seeker is warned not to "entertain doubt," not to linger or dally, neither grasping nor rejecting, on the journey through the traceless void.

Abandoning both left and right paths,
Shanti speaks succinctly;
The river bank has no weeds, no rough ground—
one may go on the way with eyes closed.

Graduating from exercises in perception and dalliance, entering into clarity, one attains lucidity and directness. On the "other shore" beyond the stream of confusing thoughts and feelings, clarity if spontaneous, and its growth is natural, with no need of artificial cultivation.

This stage is captured in a Chinese Zen poem composed around the same time as the Bengali song:

Now, when study's complete, it is like before.
When even the finest thread is shed,
then you reach unknowing.
Let it be short, let it be long—stop cutting and patching;
Whether it's high or whether it's low, it will level itself.

The abundance or scarcity of the house
is used according to occasion;
roaming serenely in the land,
one goes where his feet take him.

In the *Dhammapada*, Buddha says of this stage, "By what track can
you lead the trackless one, the enlightened one, with infinite vision,
the one whose victory is not overturned, whose victory none in the
world can approach? By what track can you lead the trackless one,
the enlightened one, with infinite vision, whom no ensnaring craving
can carry away?"[21]

This couplet can also be interpreted from the standpoint of the
sudden method, which nevertheless does not contradict the gradual-
ist interpretation. The sudden or immediate method of practice in
Sanskrit Tantric tradition is *Mahamudra* or Great Symbol meditation, which resembles a type of Zen meditation.

The Yuan dynasty Zen master Yuansou gives a fairly typical version of this mode of practice: "Real Zennists set a single eye on the
state before the embryo is formed, before any signs become distinct.
This opens up and clears the mind so that it penetrates the whole
universe. . . . Now there is nothing in the universe, nothing mundane
or transmundane, to be an object, an opposite, a barrier, or an impedi-
ment to you."[22]

The Sung dynasty master Yuan-wu said, "The penetrating spiritual
light and vast open tranquility have never been interrupted since beginningless time. The pure, uncontrived, ineffable complete true
mind does not act as a partner to objects of material sense, and is not
a companion of myriad things."[23]

[16]

MAHIDHARA

> In three bursts, the black cloud of mystic sound rumbles;
> Hearing it, the fearsome devil and all his cohorts flee.
> Intoxicated, the elephant of mind runs;
> In thirst, it churns the endless sky.
> Sin and virtue both torn away, the chain is broken
>   from the tethering post.
> Urged on by the sky, the mind has entered nirvana.
> Drunk on ambrosia, one ignores the whole triple world;
> To the master of the five objects, there's no opposition
>   to be seen.
> The heat of the rays of the scorching sun
>   pervade the courtyard of space;
> Mahidhara says, "Submerged herein,
> nothing do I see."

In three bursts, the black cloud of mystic sound rumbles;
Hearing it, the fearsome devil and all his cohorts flee.

The classical Zen master Pai-chang explained the three stages of Buddhism in these terms: "The words of the Teachings all have three successive steps; elementary, intermediate, and final good. . . . The elementary good is teaching that the immediate mirroring awareness is your own Buddha. The intermediate good is not to keep dwelling in the immediate mirroring awareness. The final good is not to make an understanding of nondwelling either."

Pai-chang also expounds this three-step process in greater detail: "When you no longer have clinging attachment, and yet you dwell in nonattachment, considering that correct, this is the elementary good. This is abiding in the subdued mind. . . .

"Once you are no longer grasping and clinging, and yet you do not dwell in nonattachment either, this is the intermediate good. This is the Half Word Teaching. This is still the formless realm; though you avoid falling into the ways of escapists and maniacs, this is till a meditation sickness. . . .

"When you no longer dwell on nonattachment, and do not even make an understanding of not dwelling either, this is the final good. This is the Full Word Teaching. You avoid getting stuck in the formless realm, you avoid lapsing into meditation sickness, you avoid getting stuck in the way of bodhisattvas, and you avoid falling into the state of the king of demons."

Tao-hsin, the Fourth Grand Master of Zen in China, explained the three stages of realization in this manner: "A bodhisattva in the beginning stage first realizes that all is empty. After that, one realizes that all is not empty. This is nondiscriminatory insight. This is the meaning of 'form itself is emptiness.' It is not an emptiness that is the result of annihilation of form; the very nature of form is empty.

"Bodhisattva practice has emptiness as its realization. When beginning learners see emptiness, this is seeing emptiness, not real emptiness. Those who cultivate enlightenment to the point where they attain real emptiness do not see emptiness or nonemptiness; they have no views."

Intoxicated, the elephant of mind runs;
In thirst, it churns the endless sky.

This couplet may have three levels of interpretation. On the ordinary level, referring to the deluded state, it represents the mind besotted by imagination and desire. Impulsive and hasty, this mad mind confuses all clarity.

On the level of confusion seeking enlightenment, these lines represent an abnormal state of excitement. In classical Zen, the "leakage of words" happens when the marvel is spoken so clearly that the unripe intellect loses sight of process. In thirst for attainment of a bewilderingly attractive prospect, the immature mind creates more confusion by subjective desire and consequent haste.

On the level of awakening, this couplet is interpreted to represent the mind ecstatic from the effect of the teaching becoming oblivious to superficial discriminations, soaring untrammeled into the infinity of blissful consciousness beyond the structures of mundane habits of thought.

Sin and virtue both torn away, the chain is broken
   from the tethering post.
Urged on by the sky, the mind has entered nirvana.

A classical Buddhist joke, which nevertheless has a most serious point, says that the true ignoramus is one who hears of transcending good and bad and thinks that means it is good to be bad. Stupid as it may seem when presented in this way, the idea that liberation from "sin and virtue" means license and abandon remains subconsciously in the minds of people trained to think in these terms, even if they have intellectually rejected some or all of the norms according to which they were socialized.

In Buddhist terms, the point where "sin and virtue" are "both torn away" is when the individual is mature enough not to need threats and promises to act with conscience. This is not a rejection of social or moral values; it is the development of a real conscience, based on consciousness rather than indoctrination. No longer chained to an internalized external system of automated response (which is subject to breakdown under conditions of contradiction and other forms of duress and distress), one is now able to act on reality instead of ideology.

The extinction of confusion in nirvana is referred to in Buddhist Yoga as the highest expedient. It is this experience that clears the mind in the way that enables one to come face to face with truth and reality in a direct relationship inaccessible to doctrine, imagination, or intellectual speculation. The irony of nirvana is that while one may be inspired to seek it through fear and hope, or aversion and desire, ultimately nirvana cannot be attained as long as one remains within the domain of fear and hope and aversion and desire.

That is why the song says that the mind has entered nirvana "urged on by the sky," for nirvana is truly attained through actual realization of emptiness, symbolized by the sky, which contains all things without being stained by them.

Drunk on ambrosia, one ignores the whole triple world;
To the master of the five objects, there's no opposition to be seen.

Ambrosia means nirvana; drunkenness means detachment from thought. The triple world refers to the realm of desire, the realm of form, and the formless realm. Ignoring the whole triple world is not literal, as drunkenness is not literal; it means being unattached, aloof from all objects in the three realms.

This aloofness and nonattachment does not imply negation or suppression of experience. As the song says, "To the master of the five objects, there's no opposition to be seen." The five objects are objects of the five senses. When the mind is not subject to their influence, there is no need to oppose the senses to be free. The classical Zen master Kuei-shan said, "As long as feelings do not stick to things, how can things hinder you?"

This couplet can be interpreted to represent the spiritual "death and rebirth" process of liberating the mind from worldly influences by "ignoring" the whole world in nirvanic "drunkenness," and then, after that, returning to the world with self-mastery to secure the freedom of mind in the midst of worldly things.

This process is illustrated in the story of a wayfarer who went to a Zen master and said, "Who is not a companion of myriad things?" The master said, "I'll tell you when you can swallow the water of the West River in one gulp." At this the wayfarer attained enlightenment.

The Zen exercise of "not being a companion of myriad things" is a practical equivalent of the Tantric "drunk on ambrosia, ignoring the whole triple world." The Zen awakening of the immediate mirroring awareness, "swallowing the water of the river in one gulp," is the experiential equivalent of the Tantric "mastery of the five objects, without opposition to be seen."

The heat of the rays of the scorching sun
  pervade the courtyard of space;
Mahidhara says, "Submerged herein,
  nothing do I see."

The sun is enlightened consciousness, the heat of its rays is the certitude of enlightened insight, evaporating the mists of illusion. The courtyard of space is emblematic of the vastness of the enlightened perspective, the pervasion of the sunlight represents the completeness and comprehensiveness of enlightened perception.

Zen master Yuan-wu wrote, "The penetrating spiritual light and vast open tranquility have always been there. The pure, uncontrived, ineffable, complete mind does not act as a partner to objects of material sense, and is not a companion of myriad things. When the mind is always as clear and bright as ten suns shining together, detached from views and beyond feelings, cutting through the ephemeral illusions of birth and death, this is what is meant by the saying 'Mind itself is Buddha.' "[24]

[17]

VINA

The moon is joined to the gourd of the sun,
making a mandolin;
The ascetic has fashioned an unstrummed stem and disc.
Play, friend, the lyre of Heruka;
The sound of the strings of emptiness,
compassion does enjoy.
Contemplating the arrays of vowels and consonants,
The supreme elephant equanimously awaits an opening.
When the edge of the palm presses the instrument's spring,
The notes of the thirty-two strings all emanate.
The Thunderbolt Bearer dances, the Goddess sings;
The Buddha-drama is unparalleled.

The moon is joined to the gourd of the sun,
making a mandolin;
The ascetic has fashioned an unstrummed stem and disc.

The moon, the relative thought of enlightenment, is joined to the sun, the absolute thought of enlightenment, making an instrument of awakening. The ascetic also means the central channel of the psychic nerve system, the channel of purification. It is the process of purification that joins the sun and moon, the relative and absolute thought of enlightenment. Centered and cleared, awakened consciousness is not caused to vibrate, or resonate, by external impacts; so the instrument is "unstrummed."

Play, friend, the lyre of Heruka;
The sound of the strings of emptiness,
compassion does enjoy.

Heruka is a symbolic personification of the Dharma or reality that underlies the teaching. The reality and the teaching it engenders are summarized in emptiness and compassion. The Heruka is a "wrathful" form, representing active destruction of ignorance, the liberative quality of the compassion of emptiness.

Liberative compassion is realized through emptiness, for it is by the experience and realization of emptiness that compassion is enabled to rise above sentimentality. Sentimental compassion is intrinsically limited and limiting. Emptiness is not realized in nihilism or cynicism but rather in fluidity and openness. Thus, the experiential realization of emptiness makes it possible to perceive and express objective, impartial compassion.

Contemplating the arrays of vowels and consonants,
The supreme elephant equanimously awaits an opening.

Discerning the structure of the world of conventionally conditioned vision and understanding as reflected in routine habits of thought, the self-possessed mind calmly watches for the gaps, through which other dimensions of reality can be perceived and employed.

When the edge of the palm presses the instrument's spring,
The notes of the thirty-two strings all emanate.

According to the teaching of the *Lotus* scripture, thirty-two is the number of manifestations of Avalokitesvara, the multifaceted personification of compassion, whose name literally means "the power of objective observation."

The capacity to project different personalities in compassionate response to situational needs is a characteristic of the *bodhisattva*, who has taken autonomous control of the mind-body instrument.

The number thirty-two also refers, in the context of Tantric Buddhism, to the network of energy channels visualized in the body of spiritual experience. This network is conceived of as an internal counterpart to thirty-two marks of distinction on the idealized external image of a Buddha. Interpreted in this sense, the couplet refers to the activation of the energy network after the mind has been cleared by going through the "opening" in the "vowels and consonants" of conceptual thought.

The Thunderbolt Bearer dances, the Goddess sings;
The Buddha-drama is unparalleled.

The Thunderbolt Bearer represents the created universe, expedient means, and structured knowledge; the body, speech, and mind of the cosmic Buddha in its manifest aspect. The Goddess represents space, formless insight, and emptiness; the body, speech, and mind of the cosmic Buddha in its occult aspect.

The Buddha-drama of the interplay of the Thunderbolt Bearer and the Goddess is "unparalleled" because it features the entire cosmos, abstract and concrete, in its all-inclusive cast. The mind of the practitioner absorbed in this drama becomes merged, imbued, and identified with the cosmic realities of Buddhahood.

18

KRISHNAVAJRA

> I traverse the three realms without effort;
> I sleep in the play of great bliss.
> No matter what your conduct, Gypsy woman,
> You're a ragged mendicant in the midst of respectable people.
> Everything is destroyed by you, Gypsy woman!
> Work left undone, the moon is eclipsed.
> Some people may call you ugly,
> But the wise never leave you.
> Krishna sings, "You act the outcaste woman;
> There is no immoral woman better than the Gypsy!"

I traverse the three realms without effort;
I sleep in the play of great bliss.

The "three realms" are the realm of desire, the realm of form, and the realm of formless abstraction. These include all possible mundane and heavenly states of mind. "Traversing" means not dwelling, recognizing that one is a temporary traveler in this world, not a permanent resident. "Without effort" means free from artificiality, without contrivance.

"Sleep" stands for detachment from the images of the world, "great bliss" for the serene spiritual transport this detachment engenders. "Play" represents the experience of life without the burden of self-importance.

No matter what your conduct, Gypsy woman,
You're a ragged mendicant in the midst of respectable people.

The *Hrdaya-sutra* or *Heart Scripture* says, "Form is not different from emptiness, emptiness is not different from form; form is itself emptiness, emptiness is itself form." The "conduct" of the "gypsy woman" is the form of emptiness; in whatever form emptiness appears, it is still emptiness. The "respectable people" are the outward forms of the known world, the "ragged mendicant" is the inner essence that is beyond the reach of conceptualization.

Everything is destroyed by you, Gypsy woman!
Work left undone, the moon is eclipsed.

As Nagarjuna wrote, "Emptiness is departure from all views." What is "destroyed" by the "gypsy woman" of emptiness is the sense of fixity and absoluteness that seems like a characteristic of the external world. Seen in reality as a characteristic of subjective habit, assumption, and conditioning, this illusion of absoluteness is thereby "destroyed."

In the religious field, Munidatta defines the "gypsy woman" of emptiness as *asampradaya,* which can mean nonsectarian, or not having an established doctrine, traditional belief, or usage. This is "departure from all views," in recognition of the fact that established doctrines, traditional beliefs, and customary usages are locally and temporally conditioned phenomena, not timeless absolutes; and therefore of relatively local, temporal, and conditional worth, not absolute, unqualified value.

According to the *Sandhinirmocana-sutra,* the classic textbook of Buddhist Yoga, those who see the absolute truth "can and do dismiss the forms of practices," and they "can and do shed bondage to forms." This is the sense of the expression "work left undone." According to the *Flower Ornament Scripture,* "As soon as they attain the eighth stage, Immovability, enlightening beings become freed from all efforts and attain the state of effortlessness, freed from physical, verbal, and mental striving, freed from stirring cogitation and flowing thoughts, and become stabilized in a natural state of development."

The "moon," as the mundane or relative thought of enlightenment, serves to orient the intellectual and emotional faculties toward enlightenment in the "dark night of ignorance," that is, even while still in the realm of ordinary conventional conditioning. As such, it may involve attraction and aversion, both intellectual and emotional. When the absolute thought of enlightenment is subsequently awakened by the experience of emptiness, its direct, unmediated authenticity "eclipses" the moon of relative understanding.

Some people may call you ugly,
But the wise never leave you.

When people fear or reject the teaching of emptiness, they usually are thinking of it in a nihilistic way, or they feel their imaginary self, personal predilections, and subjective biases are being threatened. There is no real comparison, however, accessible to the mind wrapped up in its own subjectivity, as the *Sandhinirmocana-sutra* explains: "A man accustomed to pungent and bitter flavors all his life cannot think of, or assess, or believe in the sweet taste of honey and sugar. Someone in ignorance who has an overwhelming interest in desires because of passionate craving, and is therefore inflamed with excitement, thus cannot think of, or assess, or believe in the marvelous bliss of detachment and inward effacement of all sense data."

Krishna sings, "You act the outcaste woman;
There is no immoral woman better than the Gypsy!"

Emptiness is "outcaste" in that it does not fit into conventional thinking; it is a "woman" in being pregnant with all things. The nature of emptiness is not "immoral" in the relative sense of being "unconventional," but in the absolute sense of being nonconventional, or inconceivable.

This is why the bliss of realization is called "spontaneous" or "natural." It is not just an exaggerated state induced by concentration. As a classical Zen master Lin-chi said, citing an even more ancient maxim, "Even if there were something beyond nirvana, I would say it is like a dream, or an illusion."

19

KRISHNA

> Being and nirvana—tabor and drum.
> Mind and breath—rattle and cymbal.
> Hail, hail! The drum is sounded!
> Krishna's going to marry the Gypsy!
> Getting married, the Gypsy devours birth;
> Her dowry consists of unexcelled truth.
> Day and night are passed in lovemaking;
> The night is spent among yoginis.
> Whoever is devoted to the Gypsy woman
> Will not let go for a moment,
> intoxicated with naturalness.

Being and nirvana—tabor and drum.
Mind and breath—rattle and cymbal.

Return to the Source, a famous contemplative treatise by Fatsang, one of the main expositors of Hua-yen or Flower Ornament Buddhism, expresses the normative doctrine of the nonduality of being and nirvana in these terms: "In ultimate truth, things are empty and quiescent in their fundamental nature; in conventional truth, things seem to exist yet are empty. The ultimate and conventional, purely empty, are null and groundless."[25]

This is a pattern for contemplation of the integration of being and nirvana, of the relative and the absolute. The treatise goes on to define the pragmatic experience of this contemplation further: "Once relating cognition is stilled, objects related to are empty. Mind and objects not constraining, essence pervades, empty and open."

The second line of the Bengali couplet follows up with a method of stilling the discriminatory mind to perceive the nonduality of being and nirvana. This is summed up in the relationship of mind and breath. *The Secret of the Golden Flower,* a Zen Taoist compendium of meditation methods, says, "The breath is one's own mind; one's own mind does the breathing. Once mind stirs, then there is energy. Energy is basically an emanation of mind. Our thoughts are very rapid; a single random thought takes place in a moment, whereupon an exhalation and inhalation respond to it. Therefore inner breathing and outer breathing accompany each other like sound and echo. In one single day you breathe countless times, so you have countless random thoughts. When the luminosity of spirit has leaked away completely, you are like a withered tree, like dead ashes.

"So should you have no thoughts? It is impossible to have no thoughts. Should you not breathe? It is impossible not to breathe. Nothing compares to making the affliction itself into medicine, which means to have mind and breath rest on each other."[26]

Hail, hail! The drum is sounded!
Krishna's going to marry the Gypsy!

Buddhist teaching is commonly symbolized as a drum in scripture. In particular, the drum's characteristics of inner hollowness with outer responsiveness represent emptiness. Since the point of the teaching is realization of emptiness, here the Tantric adept Krishna presents the image of the drum as signaling marriage with "the Gypsy," or union with emptiness.

Getting married, the Gypsy devours birth;
Her dowry consists of unexcelled truth.

Birthlessness, or nonorigination, is one of the most important technical terms of universalist Buddhism. The attainment of the stage of immovability and nonregression is said to be contingent upon realization of the "birthlessness" or "nonorigination" of all phenomena, graphically represented here as the "Gypsy devouring birth."

The *Sandhinirmocana-sutra* explains this elusive perception in these terms: "What is the essencelessness of the birth of things? It is the dependently originated character of things. Why? Because they exist dependent on the power of other conditions and do not exist of themselves. This is called essencelessness of birth."

The "dowry of unexcelled truth," or realization of the absolute truth, is also defined more explicitly in the same *sutra:* Buddha says,

"I also allude to ultimate essencelessness revealed by the selflessness of things when I say that all things have no origination or extinction and are fundamentally quiescent and inherently nirvanic. This is because the ultimate essencelessness revealed by the selflessness of things is the eternal and constant real nature of all things, permanent and uncreated, having no relation to any defilements."[27]

Day and night are passed in lovemaking;
The night is spent among yoginis.

Lovemaking day and night represents constant intercourse with emptiness, both rationally (day) and intuitively (night). Spending the night among yoginis (female yogis) represents intimacy with subtle mystical insights and epiphanies in the extraordinary ranges of consciousness accessible to the opened mind.

Whoever is devoted to the Gypsy woman
Will not let go for a moment,
intoxicated with naturalness.

Someone asked an ancient Zen master, "What about when someone who has realized enlightenment returns to confusion?" The Zen master replied, "A broken mirror does not shine again; fallen leaves do not return to the branches." Somone who is "devoted to the Gypsy woman," someone who has realized emptiness and is free from the bondage of rigid views and absolutist thinking, can no longer be deluded by illusion. Sloughing off restricted habits of thought implanted by conditioning and accident, the mind regains its natural spontaneity, expansive and buoyant, unencumbered by artificialities.

20

KUKKURI

I am without hope, an ascetic husband;
My pleasure cannot be told.
It's opened up, O Mother, the confinement room's
    been found;
The one I look for here is not here at all.
The first conception is of the seeds of our desires;
Examining the arteries, attend the phantom shape.
When our youth is fulfilled,
We're uprooted and collected to our fathers.
Kukkuri says, "This world is quiet;
Who awakes here is a hero."

I am without hope, an ascetic husband;
My pleasure cannot be told.

Zen is based on enlightenment, but a cardinal rule of Zen is not to
anticipate enlightenment. The reason for this approach is that the
anticipation contains subjective wishes, desires, and imaginations,
which impede the clarification of the mind. Therefore, as Kukkuri
says in the first line of this couplet, the ascetic practice of one who
would mate with emptiness lies in entertaining no hope, even while
acting in a purposeful manner.

This is much more difficult than torturing oneself in expectation
of transcendental rewards. The difficulty is not that of gross hardship,
but of subtlety and balance. Being without hope in this sense does not
mean cynicism or despair; it is a sort of waiting without anticipation.
Because the experience of emptiness is literally inconceivable, the
spiritual transport engendered cannot be described in terms of ordinary sensation or feeling; hence the "pleasure cannot be told."

It's opened up, O Mother, the confinement room's been found;
The one I look for here is not here at all.

The mother stands for egolessness, the confinement room is the innermost mind. When the essence of mind is known as it is, the self as ordinarily conceived or imagined is not there. That secondary, acquired self is not the natural essence of mind, but is composed of conditions, habits, and products of mind.

This couplet represents the practice known in Zen and neo-Taoism as "turning the light around." The syncretic Zen Taoist meditation text called *The Secret of the Golden Flower* says, "If you can look back again and again into the source of mind, whatever you are doing, not sticking to any image of person or self, then this is 'turning the light around wherever you are.' This is the finest practice."[28]

The first conception is of the seeds of our desires;
Examining the arteries, attend the phantom shape.

The first conception refers to the physical body; the phantom shape is the psychic or energetic body, which is engendered by concentration and visualization. The arteries are the psychic energy channels used to structure visualization. *The Secret of the Golden Flower* says, "What is most wondrous is when the light has crystallized in a spiritual body, gradually becoming consciously effective."[29] Attending the phantom shape is taught in the aftermath of emptiness realization, to go beyond the "great death" of nirvana without coming back to gross materialism.

When our youth is fulfilled,
We're uprooted and collected to our fathers.

On the ordinary level, this recollection fortifies the resolution to learn how to shift attention from the relative to the absolute, and how to shift energy from the physical body to the psychic body.

The 13th-century Japanese Zen master Dogan said, "Students should think of the fact that they will surely die. This truth is indisputable. But even if you do not think about that fact, for the time being you should at least determine not to pass the time in vain."

The Secret of the Golden Flower says, "From the point of view of the universe, human beings are like mayflies. From the point of view of the Way, even the universe is as an evanescent reflection."[30]

On the literal level, therefore, this couplet refers to the state of cause of practice. On the symbolic level, however, it refers to the state of effect of practice. When immaturity is ended, naive realism and overweening self-importance are shed, illusions are undermined, and perennial truth is seen.

Kukkuri says, "This world is quiet;
Who awakes here is a hero."

The traditional order of Buddhist practice is to realize the emptiness of person first, then to realize the emptiness of phenomena after that. The word "quiet," when it is used in an overtly nonobjective sense, is sometimes employed to express the subjective experience of some-one in a state of profound abstraction. More often it is used to express the underlying emptiness of all things, to emphasize the fact that the clamor of the world is created, and to represent inner perception of "leisure within hurry," the absolute within the relative.

In simple terms, the critical point to see and reflect upon is the practical fact that the world itself is not our confusion, or the source of our confusion; we ourselves create the confusion in our relation-ship with the world. We then become locked into this confusion when we relate to our relationship with the world as if it were the world itself.

The meaning of seemingly arcane Buddhist expressions like "non-doing," "noncontrivance," and "nonreification" becomes clear in this context, when it is realized that the shackles of stultifying routine, needing repetition for cohesion, can therefore be "undone" by being "nondone."

21

BHUSUKU

> In the dark of night, the mouse is about;
> It eats nectar—the mouse gathers food.
> Kill, o yogi, the pilfering mouse,
> So that its comings and goings break off.
> Digging into the world, the mouse digs a well;
> The restless mouse knows it exists for destruction.
> The black mouse knows no direction;
> Mental reality travels the sky.
> Then the mouse is restless;
> The true teacher's enlightenment will quiet it down.
> When the mouse's scurrying is cut off,
> Bhusuku says that bondage ends then.

In the dark of night, the mouse is about;
It eats nectar—the mouse gathers food.

In the midst of activity, the mind is influenced, and taxed, not only by the environment, but also by subtle, subconscious streams of thought and feeling scurrying around in the back of the mind, affecting perceptions, reactions, and patterns of energy flow unawares. This subliminal activity is usually only noticed in attentive stillness.

Kill, o yogi, the pilfering mouse,
So that its comings and goings break off.

Zen master Hung-chih said, "If you want to be even-minded and peaceful, you must put an end to the subtle pounding and weaving in the mind. Do you want to not grumble? You must cut it off and cast it down. Then you can see through it all."

Digging into the world, the mouse digs a well;
The restless mouse knows it exists for destruction.

When it becomes consciously aware of its own instability and ultimate transcience, the fluctuating mind itself generates the relative thought of enlightenment.

The black mouse knows no direction;
Mental reality travels the sky.

Unenlightened thought does not correspond to objective conditions; mental reality is projected in the vacuum between subject and object.

Then the mouse is restless;
The true teacher's enlightenment will quiet it down.

Were thought and feeling actually linked to objective reality, there would be no uncertainty. As long as thought and feeling continuously feed themselves and each other, and also feed on themselves and each other, in self-conditioning closed-circuit channels, there is ongoing unrest. Indeed, because the entire process is one of self-reflection, cessation of the routine is felt, and feared, as a threat of annihilation. Only by authentic enlightenment, seeing through the vanity of self-reflection and attaining to truthfulness of self-understanding, is it possible to experience the genuine repose of naturalness.

When the mouse's scurrying is cut off,
Bhusuku says that bondage ends then.

In the *Dhammapada*, Buddha says, "Knowing the extinction of conditioning, you know the uncreated."[31] Zen master Hung-chih said, "When your state is thoroughly peaceful and your life is cool and serene, then you will see the emptiness of the ages, where there is nothing to be troubled with, nothing that can obstruct you."

22

SARAHA

> One constructs being and nirvana by oneself;
> In vain do people fetter themselves.
> I don't know the inconceivable yogi;
> How can birth and death exist?
> Where there is birth, there is death;
> Living and dying have no difference.
> Whoever is apprehensive of birth and death here
> Should desire the rejuvenating elixir.
> Whoever roams the universe, even the heavens
> Never becomes free of old age and death.
> Whether action's caused by birth, or birth by action,
> Saraha says, the Truth is inconceivable.

One constructs being and nirvana by oneself;
In vain do people fetter themselves.

Buddha said, "It is by oneself that evil is done, it is by oneself that one is afflicted. It is by oneself that evil is not done, it is by oneself that one is purified. Purity and impurity are individual matters; no one purifies another."[32]

I don't know the inconceivable yogi;
How can birth and death exist?

The emperor of China asked the founder of Zen, "What is the ultimate meaning of the holy truths?" The Zen founder replied, "Empty, nothing holy." The emperor asked, "Who are you?" The Zen founder replied, "I don't know."

The "inconceivable yogi" is the Buddha-nature, or true self, which is not the socially conditioned personality, or the idea of self or image of the ego. Because this nature is not identical to the subjective stream of consciousness, it does not come and go.

Where there is birth, there is death;
Living and dying have no difference.

Whatever is born must die; this is the nature of transitory existence. Buddhists therefore seek liberation from psychological subjection to impermanent things. According to the *Dhammapada*, Buddha said, "What attachment is there when one has seen these white bones as like gourds discarded in autumn?"[33]

Whoever is apprehensive of birth and death here
Should desire the rejuvenating elixir.

The Sufi master Hadrat Ali said, "The world is a transitory abode, not a permanent abode. And the people in it are of two sorts: one who sells his soul and ruins it; and one who ransoms his soul and frees it."[34] Buddha said, "What mirth is there, what joy, while constantly burning? Shrouded in darkness, why not seek a light?"[35]

Whoever roams the universe, even the heavens
Never becomes free of old age and death.

Buddha said, "There is nowhere in the world—not in the sky, nor in the sea, nor in the depths of the earth—where death will not overcome you."[36] The Sufi master Ali said, "Whoever capitulates to the perishing of this world and the next perishes in them."[37]

Whether action's caused by birth, or birth by action,
Saraha says, the Truth is inconceivable.

The *Flower Ornament Scripture* says, "All consequences are born from actions; like dreams, they're not truly real. They continually die away, moment to moment, the same as before and after. Of all things seen in the world, only mind is the host; by grasping forms according to interpretation, it becomes deluded, not true to reality. All philosophies in the world are mental fabrications; there has never been a doctrine by which one could enter the true essence of things."[38]

23

SHANTI

> Carding the cotton fiber by fiber,
> Card and card the fibers to ultimate isolation.
> Even then Heruka is not attained;
> Why not contemplate it, Shanti says.
> Carding the cotton, I feed it to the void;
> With the void, I exhaust myself.
> In a multitude of paths, no two ways are to be seen;
> Not even a hairtip enters, Shanti says.
> Neither action nor agency—the reason for this,
> According to Shanti, is self-understanding.

Carding the cotton fiber by fiber,
Card and card the fibers to ultimate isolation.

This couplet refers to analytic meditation. By reducing everything to elements and conditions, the mind is disabused of the illusion of things existing in and of themselves.

Even then Heruka is not attained;
Why not contemplate it, Shanti says.

The experience of emptiness realized by analytic reduction is called "mere emptiness," or "empty emptiness," or "partial emptiness." It is also called "empty thusness." Beyond this is the experience called "nonempty emptiness," or "nonempty thusness." In this way illusion is shattered.

Carding the cotton, I feed it to the void;
With the void, I exhaust myself.

Analytic meditation reduces phenomena to emptiness. Understanding the emptiness of all things, one realizes the emptiness, or ultimate unreality, of the personality and ego structure as conditioned by relating to the world of objects as objective reality itself.

In a multitude of paths, no two ways are to be seen;
Not even a hairtip enters, Shanti says.

The Zen classic known as *The Blue Cliff Record* says, "In one there are many kinds; in two there is no duality." In his popular work *Skeletons*, the medieval Japanese Zen master Ikkyu wrote, "Although there are many paths up the base of the mountain, we see the same moon on the high peak." The enormous diversity of Buddhist teachings and practices is based on the application of the principle of *upaya-kausalya*, or "skill in means," according to which the teaching must be adapted to specific needs. Without suitable adaptation, the essential liberative quality of the teaching is lost; doctrine becomes dogma, training becomes conditioning.

The unity of the end, in contrast to the diversity of the means, is also emphasized in Buddhist Yoga, as explained in the *Sandhinirmo-cana-sutra*: "The selflessness of phenomena in the ultimate sense in true thusness is not said to have a cause, is not causally produced, is not created. This is ultimate truth. Having realized this ultimate truth, one no longer seeks any other ultimate truth. There is only the stability of the true nature of things, the abiding of the realm of reality, which is constant and perpetual whether or not Buddhas appear in the world."[39]

This scriptural passage also explains Shanti's statement that "not even a hairtip enters." Nothing can be added to the absolute unity of ultimate truth, nothing can divide it. Zen literature says of the absolute that "wind cannot penetrate it, water cannot wet it." The Zen collection *No Barrier* speaks of attuning the mind to ultimate truth in these terms: "Better to let go of everything, from space on, for such subtle secrecy that nothing can get in."

Neither action nor agency—the reason for this,
According to Shanti, is self-understanding.

Self-understanding includes understanding the nature and character of mental construction. Only thus is it possible to distinguish subjectivity from objectivity. The *Flower Ornament Scripture* says, "Eye, ear, nose, tongue, body, mind, intellect, senses: by these, one always revolves, yet there is no one and nothing that revolves. The nature of things is fundamentally birthless, yet they appear to have birth; herein there is no revealer, and nothing that's revealed. Eye, ear, nose, tongue, body, mind, intellect, senses: all are void and essenceless, but the deluded mind conceives them to exist. Seen as they truly are, all are without inherent nature. The eye of reality is not conceptual; this seeing is not false. Real or unreal, false or not false, worldly or unworldly—there's nothing but descriptions."[40]

24

BHUSUKU

> The lotus blooms at full midnight,
> Thirty-two yoginis are thereupon uplifted.
> The moon is made to go on the path of the central channel;
> Through the jewel, naturalness is expressed.
> The moon goes to nirvana;
> The lotus plant conveys its juice through the stalk.
> The bliss of cessation is formless and pure;
> Whoever realizes this is enlightened.
> "I have realized it by union," Bhusuku says,
> "In the desire for the great ecstasy of natural bliss."

The lotus blooms at full midnight,
Thirty-two yoginis are thereupon uplifted.

Midnight symbolizes inner silence, the quieting of the internal talk. The same image is also used in Zen Buddhism, and in Taoist inner alchemy. This silence allows room for the blossoming of latent or dormant mental capacity that is otherwise usually drowned out by inner conversation.

In terms of visualization practice, the lotus blossom is commonly used as a pedestal or foundation of imagery evoked for contemplation. The perfection of this visualization only becomes possible on a background of inner silence, for otherwise the mind is too preoccupied, scattered, and distracted to hold an image steady enough for practical use.

In terms of the first-mentioned level of interpretation, the uplifting of the thirty-two yoginis represent the unfolding of spiritual sutleties. In terms of visualization practice, the thirty-two yoginis stand for the system of energy channels and nodes, which can be activated after the perceptual bias of coarse consciousness is stilled in the "midnight" of inner silence.

The moon is made to go on the path of the central channel;
Through the jewel, naturalness is expressed.

In visualization practice, the moon is placed above the lotus blossom; this stands for the thought of enlightenment. Certain letters or images, containing the meanings that inspire the thought of enlightenment, may also be visualized on the moon. Then the moon is "absorbed" into the body, conveying the sense of internalization of the inspiration. Then the "jewel," the precious essence of mind, now being freed from the dross of worldliness by the thought of enlightenment, is able to express its natural spirituality.

The moon goes to nirvana;
The lotus plant conveys its juice through the stalk.

Abstractly, the moon going to nirvana represents the thought of enlightenment culminating in perfect peace of mind. Concretely, in visualization practice, this follows on the previous couplet, representing the image of the moon, aglow with the conscious energy of inspiration, rising up the central channel to the node of Nirvana at the center of the crown of the head. The rising of the energy, producing inner bliss, is graphically represented by the rising of the juice through the stalk of the lotus.

Chinese Taoists using visualization systems of energy channels and nodes similar to that used in Tantric Buddhism sometimes refer to the center of the crown as the Nirvana (*Ni-wan*) point, and the center of the brain as the Nirvana Chamber. This latter also corresponds to the preliminary location of the point called Most Hidden (*Akhfaa*) in the Five Subtleties system of the Sufis, who warn against experimentation and make it clear that these are not actual physical locations, but are used as concentration points for purposes of mental orientation.[d]

The bliss of cessation is formless and pure;
Whoever realizes this is enlightened.

The bliss of cessation is the subtle transport of nirvana. The great Sung dynasty Zen master Yuan-wu wrote, "Let go of all your previous imaginings, opinions, interpretations, worldly knowledge, intellectualism, egoism, and competitiveness; become like a dead tree, like cold ashes. When you reach the point where feelings are ended, views are gone, and your mind is clean and naked, you open up to realization."[41]

"I have realized it by union," Bhusuku says,
"In the desire for the great ecstasy of natural bliss."

This yoga, or "union," is also called return to the source. It is a restoration of natural primal unity, rather than a contrived compromise of fundamentally dissident aspects of mind. Because this union is not contrived, it is literally inconceivable; its reality is experienced in the "great ecstasy," or "aloof standpoint" of "teacherless knowledge," direct inner cognition.

This yoga of union with the original buoyancy of the spontaneous natural mind is explained by the celebrated Sung dynasty Zen master Hung-chih in terms of both process and attainment; "When you are open and naturally aware, clean and naturally clear, you are capable of panoramic consciousness without making an effort to grasp perception, and you are capable of discerning understanding without the burden of conditioned thought. You go beyond being and nothingness, and transcend conceivable feelings. This is only experienced by union with it; it is not gotten from another."[42]

25

SHABARA

High, high the mountain; there dwells a mountain girl,
Wearing peacock feathers and a necklace of gunja berries.
Mad mountain man, crazy Shabara, please do not make a
  ruckus;
Your own wife is called the Beauty of Naturalness.
The mountain girl roams the forest by herself,
A thunderbolt bearer in earrings.
The mountain savage fills the bed of the triple world,
a nice bed covered with great ecstasy.
The savage lover and the selfless consort pass the night
  in love.
I chew the betel of mind with the camphor of great ecstasy;
Taking empty selflessness to heart, I pass the night in bliss.
The bow of the teacher's words
strikes with the arrow of one's own mind;
With one arrow shot, pierce through,
pierce through to ultimate nirvana.
The savage is maddened with profound rage;
Gone into the clefts of the peaks, how can the savage
  be found?

High, high the mountain; there dwells a mountain girl,
Wearing peacock feathers and a necklace of gunja berries.

The mountain girl represents *sunyata*, emptiness, and *nairatmya*, selflessness or identitylessness. The mountain and its height stand for transcendence beyond worldly views. Peacock feathers allude to the colors associated with visualization practice. *Gunja*, overtly referring to a type of berry, also means "murmuring" and "meditation," thus alluding to repetition of mantras and meditations. The fact that the girl is "wearing" the feathers and necklace represents the fact that formal practices are still externals, expedient means, not the realization of emptiness itself.

Mad mountain man, crazy Shabara, please do not make a ruckus;
Your own wife is called the Beauty of Naturalness.

The name of the adept, Shabara, literally means a mountaineer, a barbarian, a savage. This image, especially with the added description of madness and craziness, alludes to what is beyond convention. The mad mountain man is asked not to make a ruckus in the sense that transcendence of convention is not accomplished by destroying convention or trying to be unconventional (postures which are still attached to convention, albeit by opposition), but by realizing the nature of convention as convention and not absolute reality. The inherent emptiness of convention, which means being empty of absoluteness, is symbolized by the mountaineer's own wife, the "beauty of naturalness."

In its natural state, relative reality, in itself, is innocent of the restrictions of conceptualized reality. The *Sandhinirmocana-sutra* says, "The ultimate essencelessness revealed by the selflessness of things is the eternal and constant real nature of all things, permanent and uncreated, having no relation to any defilements."[43] So there is no need to "make a ruckus" to be free, for existence and emptiness inherently interpenetrate, already "married" in natural reality.

The mountain girl roams the forest by herself,
A thunderbolt bearer in earrings.

The forest of delusion is inherently empty; this realization itself shatters illusions.

The mountain savage fills the bed of the triple world,
a nice bed covered with great ecstasy.
The savage lover and the selfless consort pass the night in love.

In Zen terminology, initial realization of emptiness is referred to as "sitting atop a hundred-foot pole." In the classic *No Barrier*, an ancient master is quoted as saying, "Atop a hundred-foot pole, one should step forward to manifest the whole body throughout the universe." It is as though union with emptiness were like cleaning a vast mirror, in which the whole universe is then reflected.

The "great ecstasy" with which the "bed of the triple world" is covered refers to the ethereal nondiscursive consciousness of the mind freed from its prison of conditioned conceptualizations. The mountain savage and the selfless consort passing the night in love represents the oneness of existence and emptiness realized by freeing the mind from the belief in conceptual description as objective reality.

I chew the betel of mind with the camphor of great ecstasy;
Taking empty selflessness to heart, I pass the night in bliss.

In Buddhist practice, ecstasy is instrumental; it is not pursued or experienced as an end in itself. A result of cessation of internal talk, it is then used to dissolve the habit of compulsive conceptualization. This enables the practitioner to "take empty selflessness to heart" by direct perception of "the ultimate essencelessness revealed by the selflessness of things," attained by "knowledge that is not conditioned by words, not thinking in conformity with words, free from the lull of words." As before, the "night" represents, from the point of view of practice, the state of mind in which words and concepts are inoperative; and, from the point of view of realization, the ultimate truth to which no words or concepts can actually apply.

The bow of the teacher's words
strikes with the arrow of one's own mind;
With one arrow shot, pierce through,
pierce through to ultimate nirvana.

The instructions of the teacher provide impetus and direction, but it is the mind of the practitioner that must "fly." Along the way there are many obstacles; it is necessary to penetrate them resolutely in order to arrive at the aim.

The savage is maddened with profound rage;
Gone into the clefts of the peaks, how can the savage be found?

The "profound rage" of the "savage" represents the mental revolution, referred to technically in Sanskrit as *paravrtti*, "turning back" or "recoiling," in which the mind turns away from the illusions of the world to realize transcendence. In *The Blue Cliff Record*, a Zen master says, "With my staff across my shoulder, I pay no heed to people; I go straight into the myriad peaks."

26

LUI

> Being does not exist, nonbeing does not work;
> Who believes in such an enlightenment?
> The Way, Lui says, is inscrutable to conception;
> Sporting in the triple world, I cannot be detected.
> He to whom color, character, and figure are not known—
> How can he discourse on scriptural knowledge?
> You will present me with questions, "Whose?" "What?"
> Like the moon in the water, it is neither real nor false.
> Lui says, "As long as I will be,
> The one with whom I am will be unseen."

Being does not exist, nonbeing does not work;
Who believes in such an enlightenment?

This couplet expresses the Middle Way. In the Buddhist perspective, "being does not exist" in the specific sense that what exists only conceptually or relatively does not exist absolutely. "Nonbeing," on the other hand, "does not work" because it is inert. The *Sandhinirmocana-sutra* explains the fallacy of a nihilistic interpretation of emptiness: "If people have not yet been able to accumulate stores of superior virtue and knowledge, and are not simple and direct by nature, and still persist in clinging to their own views even though they have the power to think discerningly and to discard and affirm, when they hear such a teaching, they are unable to truly understand what I say with hidden intent. Even if they believe in such a teaching, they make a rigid literal interpretation of the meaning, saying that all things definitely have no essence, definitely are not originated or extinguished, definitely are fundamentally quiescent, and definitely are inherently nirvanic. Because of this, they acquire a view of nothingness, or a view of nonexistence of characteristics, in regard to all things. Because they get the idea of nothingness, or the idea of nonexistence of characteristics, they deny all characteristics, saying they are nonexistent; they deny the characteristic of mere conceptualization, the characteristic of dependence, and the real characteristic of all things."[44]

Having dismissed both extremes of being and nonbeing, the Siddha Lui then asks, "Who believes in such an enlightenment?" This question directs the attention to the mind that conceives of "being" and "nonbeing." This mind, which can become fixated on the notions of being or nonbeing, can by the same token detach itself from these views to attain the subtle poise of the center, the Middle Way.

The Way, Lui says, is inscrutable to conception;
Sporting in the triple world, I cannot be detected.

The *Sandhinirmocana-sutra* says, "Someone in ignorance who clings to the signs of the world because of overwhelming interest in perceptual and cognitive signs thus cannot think of, or assess, or believe in, the ultimate nirvana that obliterates all signs so that reification ends."[45] The early Zen master Tao-hsin wrote, "Those who cultivate the Way and attain real emptiness do not see emptiness or nonemptiness; they have no views."

The "triple world" ordinarily refers to the totality of conditioned existence, specifically the realms of desire, form, and formless abstraction. Munidatta here takes the term to mean body, speech, and mind. Either way—and there is no real contradiction between these two interpretations—"sporting in the triple world" refers to freedom of action. The liberated one "cannot be detected" in the sense that there is no fixation on any object, and no identification with things. As a Zen proverb describes this freedom, "The gods offering flowers find no road to strew them on, demons and outsiders secretly spying cannot see."

He to whom color, character, and figure are not known—
How can he discourse on scriptural knowledge?

This couplet follows on the preceding to counter the drift toward denial, as repudiated in the quotation from scripture cited in the comments on the first couplet. Realization of emptiness does not mean destruction or disappearance of characteristics. In Zen terms, misconstrued emptiness results in a kind of ignorance in which one "calls a pitcher a bell," or "points to a deer and says it's a horse."

You will present me with questions, "Whose?" "What?"
Like the moon in the water, it is neither real nor false.

"Whose" questions the subject in relation to the object, "what" questions the object in relation to the subject. The "moon in the water" is a reflection, representing the relation, or relativity, of the reflecting subject and reflected object; "neither real nor false" means neither absolutely existent nor absolutely nonexistent. Here again the mind of the practitioner is directed toward the Middle Way by detachment from one-sided views.

Lui says, "As long as I will be,
The one with whom I am will be unseen."

In Buddhist terms, the sense of identification with acquired habits of thought and attitude is a false self. The real self is the Buddha-nature, which is "permanent, pure, blissful self." As long as the false self is the center of subjective operation, the true self remains obscure.

The uncovering of the true self is also directly connected to the uncovering of the true nature of phenomena. The Japanese Zen master Dogen wrote, "Studying Buddhism is studying the self; studying the self is forgetting the self. Forgetting the self is being enlightened by all things." As long as subjective attitudes and ideas reign, the objective nature of things is obscured.

Viewed in another way, this final couplet sums up by illustrating the identity and distinction of existence and emptiness. In terms of essence, subject and object are both empty of absoluteness, yet in terms of characteristics, subject and object are not without apparent factuality. "As long as I will be, the one with whom I am" alludes to essential identity on the level of absolute truth, while being "unseen" refers to experiential distinction on the level of relative truth.

27

BHUSUKU

> The clouds of compassion pervade endlessly,
> Smashing the duality of being and nonbeing.
> Up in the middle of the sky, wondrous;
> Behold, Bhusuku, the natural essence.
> When quiet, one's own mind gives a cry of cheer,
> On hearing which the web of the senses is rent.
> In ecstasy have I realized purity of objects,
> Like the moon shining in the sky.
> In this triplex world, this much indeed's essential;
> Bhusuku the Yogi opens up the darkness.

The clouds of compassion pervade endlessly,
Smashing the duality of being and nonbeing.

Compassion, in the Buddhist sense, is not just emotional feeling; it is at once the orientation and energy of living Buddhist philosophy. The commonweal for which the Buddhist strives is twofold, mundane and transmundane. Mundane weal refers to the peace and happiness of the world, while transmundane weal refers to liberation from slavery to ego and things.

If apparent reality were a fixed absolute, there would be no possibility of freedom or change, and therefore no inspiration, no leeway, and no use for Buddhistic compassion. If apparent reality had no psychological reality, on the other hand, everyone would already be liberated and would have no needs; so there would be no reason, no need, and no scope for Buddhistic compassion.

By realizing the emptiness of absoluteness in conditioned states, the Buddhist is enabled to be compassionate without the limitation of strictly personal emotion. By realizing the relative and psychological realities of conditioned states, the Buddhist is motivated to extend compassion without the limitation of personal aloofness. Thus the nonduality of being and nonbeing is realized in the experience and exercise of objective compassion.

Up in the middle of the sky, wondrous;
Behold, Bhusuku, the natural essence.

The middle of the sky represents emptiness, specifically in terms of its identity to the Middle Way beyond the duality of being and nonbeing, the essential nature of all things.

It is in this sense that the *Flower Ornament Scripture* says, "Sentient beings and phenomena are null and void in essence, like space, with no location. Attaining this spacelike knowledge, one is forever free from grasping and clinging; like space, it has no variation and is unobstructed in the world."

Speaking of the inner clarification that prepares the mind to perceive the essential nature of things, the same scripture also says, "If you want to know the realm of Buddhahood, make your mind as clear as space; detach from subjective imaginings and from all grasping, making your mind unimpeded wherever it turns." It is important to realize, from a practical point of view, that this is not the same experience as the exercise of absorption in space, or *gaganatalasamadhi*, which is sometimes practiced by Buddhists as part of a method of loosening subjective attachment to conditioned perceptual and conceptual biases.

This pragmatic distinction is made clear by the 13th-century Zen master Dogen, who wrote, "Those who claim to have fulfilled Zen study and assume the rank of teacher, while they hear the voice of the nature of things and see the forms of the nature of things, yet their bodies and minds, their experiences of object and subject, just continue to rise and fall in the pit of confusion. What this is like is *wrongly thinking that the nature of things will appear when the whole world we perceive is obliterated, that the nature of things is not the present totality of phenomena.*"[46]

When quiet, one's own mind gives a cry of cheer,
On hearing which the web of the senses is rent.

Quieting the habitually ruminating mind allows room for intuitive understanding to surface into consciousness in a functional manner. This breaks routine fixation on the surface appearances of externals.

The 11th-century Zen master Yuan-wu wrote, "Just still the thoughts in your mind. It is good to do this right in the midst of disturbance." This makes it clear that this quietude is an inner method of releasing potential, not a habit of eremitic quietism. Neither does it refer to a temporary forced stilling of thought trains, but something more profound, as Yuan-wu also explained in his writings: "Let go of all your previous imaginings, opinions, interpretations, worldly knowledge, intellectualism, egoism, and competitiveness. Become like a dead tree, like cold ashes. When you reach the point where feelings are ended, views are gone, and your mind is clean and naked, you open up to realization."

In ecstasy have I realized purity of objects,
Like the moon shining in the sky.

In ecstasy, beyond conceptual thought, the eye of direct perception sees things as they are without subjective projections or interpretations. Purity, in Buddhist metaphysics, means emptiness of inherent identity. Here, the moon shining in the sky represents awareness of essential emptiness. The *Flower Ornament Scripture* says, "In each moment of mind are infinite lands produced; by the spiritual power of the enlightened, all are seen as pure."

In this triplex world, this much indeed's essential;
Bhusuku the Yogi opens up the darkness.

It is realizing the essential emptiness of what we consider the world itself, whether in the realm of desire, the realm of form, or the realm of formless abstraction, that ultimately disperses the impermeable darkness of naive material realism. In the *Dhammapada*, Buddha says, "It is better to live one day seeing the ultimate truth than to live a hundred years without seeing the ultimate truth."[47]

28

ARYADEVA

Where the wind of the senses has vanished from the mind,
I don't know where my self has gone.
Wonderful—the drum of compassion is sounding!
Aryadeva reigns without support.
It appears like the light of the moon;
The mind, transforming, enters unresisting therein.
Giving up worldly habits of fear and hate,
Seeking, seeking, scrutinize emptiness.
Aryadeva has destroyed everything;
He wards off fear and hate from afar.

Where the wind of the senses has vanished from the mind,
I don't know where my self has gone.

The visceral or instinctive sense of selfhood, revolving around desire and fear, attraction and aversion, in pursuit of self-gratification and self-preservation, is intimately connected to, or one might say a quality of, the relationship of the organism to the sensory environment. The sociopsychological sense of selfhood also involves desire and fear, attraction and aversion, self-gratification and self-preservation, but with greater complexity of subject matter, including much that is of a more subtle nature than the subject matter of instinctive or visceral self-consciousness.

In contemporary terms, for example, self-esteem is spoken of almost as if it were a material substance; and indeed it can actually involve material substances in the overall composition of its subject matter. Whether one considers the abstract psychological patterns or the actual content of attention in the concrete operation of these patterns, the relationship between the core of consciousness and the data of the senses is crucial to the nature and quality of the experience of the empirical self.

In Buddhist thought, this much is considered to be well-established fact. But in terms of Buddhist philosophy and psychology, which are not two separate fields, representations of facts of this nature are not made for acceptance as dogma, but for practical structure in meditation. So it is not a philosophical problem, but a meditative task, involving a very specific kind of introspection, that the Siddha presents in the second line of the couplet: When the subject matter of self-consciousness is discounted, where is the self?

Wonderful—the drum of compassion is sounding!
Aryadeva reigns without support.

In one of the most famous of Zen stories, a seeker asked the founder of Zen, "Please enable me to attain peace of mind." The Zen founder responded, "Bring me your mind, and I will set it at peace." The seeker said, "When I search for my mind, I cannot grasp it." The Zen founder said, "I have set your mind at peace."

When one carries out the meditation described in the first couplet, the attention bypasses all objects, sensory or abstract, ultimately to find nothing graspable. This ungraspability is one classical definition of emptiness, and this particular exercise is a well-known method of inducing the experience of emptiness. When the climax or consummation is reached, when ungraspability is no longer just a concept but a direct experience, instead of falling into an abyss the mind opens up into an inconceivable realm, which the ancients used to call *thusness.*

Thusness is the actual substance of objective compassion, what Buddhists and neo-Taoists sometimes call the "wondrous existence" that is identical to "true emptiness." It is at once inconceivable and undeniable; for this reason, allusion to the experience may often appear paradoxical from an ordinary point of view.

To merge with thusness, according to an eminent Zen master of ancient times, one must realize that "you are not it; it is you." An earlier Zen master said, "A sage has no self, but there is nothing that is not the self." This is the stage of "forgetting the self to be enlightened by all things," and the time when artificiality is dropped to merge consciously with the natural.

Not dwelling on anything external or internal, the mind is "without support." That means it is not leaning on anything. Centered and aware, this undistracted mind "reigns" over its faculties as an autonomous overseer.

It appears like the light of the moon;
The mind, transforming, enters unresisting therein.

This couplet represents the mind being liberated from the limitations imposed by absorption in matter, form, and habits of thought. In terminology commonly associated with Zen, Munidatta describes the experience illustrated here as the mind-king attaining mindlessness and merging with pure radiance, as discriminatory thought loses its influence. With the mind absorbed in naturalness, he continues, the darkness of discriminatory thinking is dissolved; this is "entering unresisting into the light."

Giving up worldly habits of fear and hate,
Seeking, seeking, scrutinize emptiness.

The *Flower Ornament Scripture* says, "What happens to all fears with the attainment of the stage of joy, fears such as fear of not surviving, fear of ill repute, fear of death, fear of states of misery, fear of intimidation by groups, is that all such fears leave. Why is that? Inasmuch as the very concept of self is gone, there is no self-love, much less any love for material things."[48] When there is no fear, there is no aversion; the defensiveness of the ego is gone.

This state of mind is not a product of ordinary sentiments like boldness or indifference, nor is it an outcome of the abnegation of self secretly treasured as real. Rather, it is a result of the realization of emptiness, experientially impressed upon the psyche as a result of first-hand search and discovery. Here the Siddha uses the word *biara*, "examine, scrutinize," from Sanskrit *vicara* (an intellectual function active in the first stage of meditation), further describing it as deliberate and purposeful, underscoring the fact that realization of "emptiness" comes about through penetrating insight, and has nothing to do with ignoring reality.

Aryadeva has destroyed everything;
He wards off fear and hate from afar.

Destroying everything is a familiar representation of realizing the emptiness, the voidness of inherent selfhood, in all things. This "wards off fear and hate from afar" in that the transcendence experienced through emptiness is not suppression of states of mind that have already arisen, but rather dissolution of the very basis of compulsive reaction to conditions. This pragmatic distinction is made clear in the saying of Bunan, a Japanese Zen master of the 17th century, that "It is easy to be detached from things; it is harder to be inaccessible to things."

[29]

SARAHA

> No dot, no crescent; no sun, no moon—
> The Mind King is free of everything.
> Going straight ahead, straight ahead,
> don't take a turn on the road!
> Enlightenment is near at hand;
> don't go to a distand land!
> The protective band is on your wrist; don't get a mirror.
> Self is realized by oneself, in one's own mind.
> Roaring on the Other Shore,
> In the midst of bad people he goes on aloof.
> Of the canals and watercourses to the left and right,
> Saraha says, "My dear, the straight way appeals!"

No dot, no crescent; no sun, no moon—
The Mind King is free of everything.

The dot and crescent, orthographical marks indicating nasalization and thus associated with the sacred syllables *Om* and *Hum,* symbolically represent the sun and moon, which in turn represent formless and formal cognition, absolute and relative thought of enlightenment. Here the Siddha refers directly to the absolute itself, beyond all possibility of representation and expression.

The extraordinary Sung dynasty Zen master Fo-yen said, "Only when you have arrived at the state where there is no delusion and no enlightenment are you comfortable and saving energy to a maximum degree."[49] This is the aim to which the Bengali adept Saraha refers in this introductory couplet. This allusion is not made simply as a statement of an ideal or a goal, but more immediately as an indication of orientation.

Going straight ahead, straight ahead,
don't take a turn on the road!
Enlightenment is near at hand;
don't go to a distant land!

One of the apparent paradoxes commonplace to universalist Buddhism is the principle that enlightenment is not an attainment. In terms of objective reality, this means that truth is so of itself and is not an intellectual construction. In terms of subjective reality, this means that the capacities of the enlightened mind are not acquired but uncovered, not produced but developed. The ultimate directness, in these terms, the straight path *par excellence,* is actual pragmatic realization, disinterment, so to speak, of what has always been there. As Fo-yen said, "Buddhism is a most economical affair, conserving the most energy; it has always been present, but you do not understand."[50] Realizing this in life experience is the straight way.

The protective band is on your wrist; don't get a mirror.
Self is realized by oneself, in one's own mind.

This couplet underscores the teaching that enlightenment is not obtained from outside. In the *Dhammapada,* Buddha is reported to have said, "I have overcome all, I know all, I am unaffected by all things. Leaving everything behind, having ended craving, I am freed. Having understood on my own, to whom should I attribute it?"[51] The famous Sung dynasty Zen master Ta Hui wrote, "Buddha means awake, being aware everywhere and always. Seeing Buddha everywhere means seeing your own inherent natural Buddha in the fundamental wellspring of your self."[52]

Roaring on the Other Shore,
In the midst of bad people he goes on aloof.

The Other Shore is transcendence; roaring means that this is not quietism. In Zen terms, those who have attained true transcendence and liberation are able to "enter into the realms of both Buddhas and devils," whereas quietists are "only able to enter the realm of Buddhas, not the realm of devils." In other words, the contrived detachment of the quietist is dependent upon an artificially controlled environment, whereas the authentic transcendence of the self-realized is independent of the surroundings. It is axiomatic in Buddhism, furthermore, that the enlightened enter in among the unenlightened to fulfill the purpose of enlightenment.

Of the canals and watercourses to the left and right,
Saraha says, "My dear, the straight way appeals!"

The canals and watercourses to the left and right refer to the network of psychic energy channels and focal points utilized in contemplative visualization exercises. The straight way, metaphysically speaking, is the Middle Way, beyond being and nothingness; psychophysically speaking, it is the central channel of purification, beyond perception and dalliance. Here the Siddha insists on the central realization, warning the seeker not to cling to either being or nothingness, either materialism or quietism; and not to wander "tripping" in psychic states, bemused by perception and dalliance.

DHENDHANA

> My house has no neighbor on settled land.
> There is no rice in the pot—I am ever the guest.
> Samsara goes on whirling around;
> How can milk, after milking, go back into the teat?
> The bull gave birth; the cow is sterile.
> The jar's being milked, all day and night.
> The intelligent one is ignorant.
> The thief is a policeman.
> Day after day, the jackal fights with the lion;
> Few understand the song of Dhendhana's verse.

My house has no neighbor on settled land.
There is no rice in the pot—I am ever the guest.

Realizing that the secondary "self" resulting from social and psychological conditioning is not an absolute reality, one ceases to identify oneself in terms of the surroundings. This is "having no neighbors," or, in Zen terms, "not keeping company with myriad things."

Realizing that things of the world are impermanent, one ceases to think of personal possessions as appurtenances of the self. This is having "no rice in the pot." Being nevertheless in the temporal world, all the while realizing the transitoriness of the empirical self as well as of all things, one is in the world without being of the world; this is being "ever the guest."

Samsara goes on whirling around;
How can milk, after milking, go back into the teat?

Samsara is the flux of conditioned states, in which what goes before influences what comes along afterward. On one level, samsara means the flow of thoughts in self-conditioning patterns of habit. If the mind goes along with the flow, it will not be possible to return to the source.

The bull gave birth; the cow is sterile.
The jar's being milked, all day and night.

One method of meditation on emptiness considers the relativity of cause and effect. If a cause is only a cause relative to its effect, then the effect must coexist with the cause; but if the effect is already there, the cause cannot be the cause of that effect, and the effect cannot be the effect of that cause. Similarly, considering that nothing temporal exists of itself but depends on conditions, how can those conditions themselves exist in order to produce something?

It is important to understand that these meditations are not philosophy as understood in the conventional Western sense. Nor are they mysterious oriental paradoxes to be entertained intellectually. Meditations of this kind are designed to enable the mind to register the limitations of linear thinking.

The apparent paradox of an "effect without a cause" is called "inconceivable existence," here symbolically represented as a "bull giving birth." The apparent paradox of a "cause without an effect" is called "true emptiness," here symbolically represented as a "sterile cow."

Such imagery is common in Zen tradition, wherein it is not used for bafflement or destruction of reason (as touted by certain popularizers of irrationalism who confuse mystification with mysticism) but for encapsulating directions for those meditation practices that lead to direct experience of the inadequacy of linear thinking. This makes it possible to transcend the limitations of conditioned thought without abnormally suppressing or warping the intellect.

According to Munidatta, "milking the jar," taking something out of the vessel rather than putting something in, represents actual realization of essencelessness, or emptiness of intrinsic nature. In the *Sandhinirmocana-sutra*, Buddha explains, "When I say all things have no essence, I am alluding to three kinds of essencelessness: essencelessness of characteristics, essencelessness of birth, and ultimate essencelessness.

"What is the essencelessness of characteristics of all things? It is their conceptually grasped character. Why? Because the characteristics are defined by artificial names, not by inherent definition. Therefore this is called the essencelessness of characteristics.

"What is the essencelessness of birth of things? It is the dependently originated character of things. Why? Because they exist dependent on the power of other conditions and do not exist of themselves. Therefore this is called the essencelessness of birth.

"What is the ultimate essencelessness of things? It means that things are said to be essenceless because of the essencelessness of birth; that is to say the fact of dependent origination is also called ultimate essencelessness. Why? I reveal the pure object of attention in things to be ultimate essencelessness. Dependency is not a pure object of attention, so I also call it ultimately essenceless."53

The intelligent one is ignorant,
The thief is a policeman.

Conventional intelligence, insofar as it is dealing with the conceptually grasped characteristics of things, is therefore ignorant of the absolute nature of things. Insofar as the conventional intellect grasps things and appropriates them into its preconditioned worldview, it is a thief. On the other hand, when intelligence is used to analyze things to understand their conditionality, recognize their transitoriness, and arrive at the emptiness of inherent nature, inspiring the thought of enlightenment, it thus prevents appearances from occasioning delusion; so the "thief" turns out to be a "policeman."

Day after day, the jackal fights with the lion;
Few understand the song of Dhendhana's verse.

The jackal is clinging, compulsive, conditioned thinking and conceptualization; the lion is realization of emptiness, insight into absolute truth. The meaning of the jackal fighting with the lion is explained in the *Sandhinirmocana-sutra* in these terms: "People produce explanations of the dependent and real natures based on the characteristics of the conceptualized nature, saying they are such and such, in accord with how people conceptualize them. Because the explanations condition their minds, because their awareness conforms to the explanations, because they are lulled by the explanation, they cling to their conceptualizations of the dependent nature and the real nature as such and so.

"Because they cling to their conceptualizations of the dependent and real natures, this condition produces the dependent nature of the future, and due to this condition people may be defiled by afflictions, actions, or birth, and forever rush around in repetitious cycles, with no rest, suffering pains and vexations, going through all kinds of psychological states."[54]

The jackal fights with the lion because it feels threatened with annihilation. This is why "few people understand," as the Siddha says. As a Zen proverb has it, "The roar of the lion bursts the brains of the jackal."

[31]

DARIKA

> By the practice of nonseparateness
> of emptiness and compassion,
> physically, verbally, and mentally,
> Darika sports on the Other Shore of the sky.
> The inscrutable mind is in great ecstasy;
> Darika sports on the Other Shore of the sky.
> What are mantras to you? What are Tantras to you?
> What are meditation and elucidation to you?
> In the effortless play of nondependence
> is indescribably ultimate nirvana.
> Considering sorrow and happiness one,
> the knower enjoys the senses;
> Mind above everything,
> Darika feels neither self nor nonself.
> O King, O King, O King! The other kings are bound!
> By the kindness of Lui's lotus feet, Darika's attained
> the twelfth stage.

By the practice of nonseparateness
of emptiness and compassion,
physically, verbally, and mentally,
Darika sports on the Other Shore of the sky.

Body, speech, and mind, or thought, word, and deed, are referred to in Tantric Buddhism as the Three Mysteries; in essence of the same nature as the universe itself, the three mysteries are the medium through which the individual identifies with the cosmic Buddha.

The "other shore of the sky" is the state of the practitioner gone beyond realization of emptiness *qua* emptiness. The *Flower Ornament Scripture* describes this as being "empty, signless, wishless, yet with compassion and kindness," and being "in the world with great forbearance, having acquired detachment; having existinguished the flames of afflictions and stilled worldly cravings, coursing in the nonduality of things as like reflections, illusions, dreams, yet showing compassion."

In terms of the structure of meditation, this is illustrated in the T'ien-t'ai "stopping and seeing" practice, wherein one first contemplates the conditional nature of things in order to enter into contemplation of their ultimate emptiness, then contemplates the conditional nature of things in order to re-emerge from emptiness into relativity. Going back and forth between contemplation of these two facets of conditionality, finally one attains the central balance of the Middle Way.

The classical Zen master Pai-chang said, "A Buddha is just someone outside of bondage who comes back inside of bondage to be a Buddha in this way; someone beyond birth and death, someone on the other side of mystic annihilation, who comes back to this side to act thus as a Buddha." He also said, "A Buddha does not remain in Buddhahood; this is called the real field of blessings." Such is the "nonseparateness of emptiness and compassion" to which the Siddha refers in this couplet.

The inscrutable mind is in great ecstasy;
Darika sports on the Other Shore of the sky.

The inscrutable mind is gone beyond both form and emptiness. Pai-chang said, "Just don't be obstructed by being or nothingness, and do not abide in nonobstruction, and have no knowledge or understanding of nonabiding. This is called spiritual power. When you do not even cling to this spiritual power, it is called having no spiritual power, so you are like the saying, 'Footsteps of a bodhisattva with no spiritual power cannot be found.' This is someone beyond Buddha, most inconceivable."

What are mantras to you? What are Tantras to you?
What are meditation and elucidation to you?
In the effortless play of nondependence
is indescribably ultimate nirvana.

This couplet speaks of transcending the means when the end is attained, but the first line also provokes the question of one's relation to the teaching to begin with. For those who approach it with ambition, greed, or other impure egotistic motives, the teaching is said to be "golden chains." The T'ang dynasty Zen master Lin-chi also said, "Although gold dust is precious, when it gets in your eyes it blinds you."

Zen master Yen-t'ou, a contemporary of Lin-chi, explained this point quite clearly: "The moment you prize anything, it has turned into a nest, a dodge. The ancients called this clothing sticking to the body, an ailment most difficult to cure. When I was traveling in the past, I called on teachers in one or two places; they just taught day and night concentration, sitting until your buttocks grow callouses, yet all the while your mouth is drooling. From the start they sit in the utter darkness in the belly of the primordial Buddha and ignorantly say they are sitting in meditation, conserving this attainment. At such times, there is still desire there!

"Have you not heard the saying, 'When independent and unimpassioned, you yourself are Buddha'? An ancient remarked, 'If you poison the milk, even clarified butter is deadly.'

"This is not something you attain by hearing, not something you reach or abide in, not something in your forms! Don't misperceive what is merely a gate or a door."[55]

Considering sorrow and happiness one,
the knower enjoys the senses;
Mind above everything,
Darika feels neither self nor nonself.

The early Zen master Seng-ts'an, considered the Third Patriarch of Chinese Zen, wrote, "The Great Way is without difficulty; just avoid discriminating." He also wrote, "If you want to gain the way of oneness, don't be averse to the six sense fields. The six sense fields are not bad; after all they're the same as true awakening." The enjoyment of the senses that is not limited by aversion to pain or sorrow and attraction to pleasure or happiness is the experience of enlightened knowledge and perception. Neither identifying nor rejecting, the mind is beyond the world even in the midst of the world.

O King, O King, O King! The other kings are bound!
By the kindness of Lui's lotus feet, Darika's attained
the twelfth stage.

When the "central government" of the mind is independent and autonomous, it cannot be overwhelmed by temporary states; it can employ its faculties without being confused or deluded by their operations.

The kindness of lotus feet refers to compassionate, enlightened guidance. Lui, many of whose own Tantric songs appear in this collection, was evidently Darika's teacher.

The twelfth stage is the supreme realization of Buddhism. The highest stage of bodhisattvahood is the tenth, which is called "Cloud of Teaching." Above this, the eleventh stage, is basic buddhahood, called "Equal Enlightenment." Beyond this is the twelfth stage, the final goal, called "Sublime Enlightenment."

[32]

BHADE

> So long have I been self-deluded;
> Now I've understood, enlightened by a true teacher.
> Now the Mind King is my lord;
> It rolls into the sea of the sky.
> I see the ten directions all empty;
> Outside mind there is neither sin nor virtue.
> Told by a Vajrayana master the hiding place of liberation,
> I have supped on the water of the sky.
> Bhade says, "Misfortune has come!
> I have devoured the Mind King!"

So long have I been self-deluded;
Now I've understood, enlightened by a true teacher.

Self-delusion, keeping the mind in confinement within subjective opinion, bias, and sentiment, is the factor that makes an outside source of guidance necessary. Without a source of objective insight, subjectivity processes everything in terms of its existing predilections and prejudices.

Even when there is a true teacher at hand, subjective biases based on truthless elements like wishful thinking can distort or obstruct reception of truthful input. For this reason it is also necessary for the seeker to reach forward from a deeper level than the psychological self. Part of reaching forward in this way is seeking truth by inner reality, without preconceptions of what outward form it may take.

Now the Mind King is my lord;
It rolls into the sea of the sky.

Enlightenment by a true teacher, understanding that the acquired self is not the real Buddha-nature, one is able to distinguish the temporal from the primal and become conscious of the essence of mind. When attention is successfully focused on this essence, it is not confined by the realms of desires, forms, and abstractions. The sea of the sky stands for the realization of emptiness that ensues, as well as the feeling that this experiential realization engenders. The experience, which is like a total perception, is not a blackout or a blank, but it does feel like slipping into a boundless openness. This can be thrilling at first, but when the experience is properly digested, it leads to spontaneous natural ecstasy.

I see the ten directions all empty;
Outside mind there is neither sin nor virtue.

One of the major awakenings of the Japanese Pure Land saint Ippen took place as he watched children at play, spinning tops. Watching them spin for a time and then fall still, Ippen reflected that the good and evil of the world is like a top; spin it and it turns, don't spin it and it stops.

In his *Ten Mysterious Gates*, the great Flower Ornament Buddhist master Chih-yen wrote, "Good and bad are according to the operation of mind, so it is called creation by operation of the mind. Since there is no separate realm of objects outside of mind, we say 'only mind.' If it operates harmoniously, it is called nirvana; that is why the scripture says, 'Mind makes the Buddhas.' If it operates perversely, it is samsara; that is why the scripture says, 'The triple world is illusory; it is only made by the mind.' "[56]

The *Dhammapada* begins with Buddha's sayings, "Everything has mind in the lead, has mind in the forefront, is made by mind. If one speaks or acts with a corrupt mind, misery will follow as the wheel of the cart follows the foot of the ox.

"Everything has mind in the lead, has mind in the forefront, is made by mind. If one speaks or acts with a pure mind, happiness will follow like a shadow that never leaves."[57]

Told by a Vajrayana master the hiding place of liberation.
I have supped on the water of the sky.

An ancient Zen master said, "Let your hiding place have no traces, but do not hide in tracelessness." The hiding place that has no traces is the innermost essence of mind not fixed on objects; this is "the hiding place of liberation." The tracelessness in which one should not hide is attachment to detachment, or in extreme cases oblivion; as a Zen proverb says, "Stagnant water cannot contain the coils of a dragon." Therefore the Siddha says he has supped on the water of the sky, the fluid living energy of emptiness, freedom, release.

Bhade says, "Misfortune has come!
I have devoured the Mind King!"

Abiding in the state of the Mind King results in what is called "mirroring awareness." While this is a fundamental initiatory experience, and subsequently a basic tool, of Zen and Mahamudra practice, the same provisions apply to this as to all expedient teachings of Buddhism.

Classical Zen master Pai-chang said, "To speak of the mirror awareness is still not really right; by way of the impure, discern the pure. If you say the immediate mirrorlike awareness is correct, or that there is something else beyond mirroring awareness, both are delusion. If you keep dwelling in the immediate mirrorlike awareness, this too is delusion, referred to as the error of naturalism."

With typical Vajrayana skill, Bhade expresses all of these meanings. A Zen proverb says, "Ascending from earth to sky is easy; coming down to earth from the sky is hard."

33

KRISHNACARYA

> The arm of emptiness, striking with suchness,
> Has brought everything back to the capital of illusion.
> He slumbers unaware of difference between self and other;
> Krishna the naked mendicant has gone to sleep in
>   naturalness.
> Without consciousness or sense, he's in a deep sleep;
> Having done everything successfully, he's aslumber in
>   felicity.
> In a dream I have seen the emptiness of triplex existence,
> Turning back beyond coming and going.
> The master Jalandhari will be a witness;
> The top scholars notice no bias in me.

The arm of emptiness, striking with suchness,
Has brought everything back to the capital of illusion.

The *Sandhinirmocana-sutra* says, "Inasmuch as the conceptualized characteristics in transient appearances, on which are based the conceptualizations that are the sphere of discrimination, are not actually true, therefore this inherent essencelessness, true thusness in which phenomena have no identity, the pure focus of attention, is called ultimate reality."[58]

Illusion is seen to be illusion on emptying the mind and seeing thusness without preconceptions. The *Sandinirmocana-sutra* also says, "The characteristic of conceptual grasping can be known through the association of names and characterizations. The characteristic of dependent origination can be known through the conceptual clinging superimposed on dependent existence. The perfect characteristic of reality can be known by not clinging to conceptions superimposed on dependent existence."[59]

He slumbers unaware of difference between self and other;
Krishna the naked mendicant has gone to sleep in naturalness.

Slumber, sleep, and unawareness represent a state of mind unencumbered by preoccupation with superficial appearances. Nakedness symbolizes purity of mind, mendicancy symbolizes nonattachment, or purity of heart, being in the world but not of it. The Yuan dynasty Zen master Yuansou said, "The mind of people of the Way is straight as a bowstring. Simply because they are not burdened by ideas of others and self, of right and wrong, of sacred and profane, of better and worse, or by deception, falsehood, flattery, or deviousness, they spontaneously gain access to the substance of mind that dwells on nothing."[60]

Without consciousness or sense, he's in a deep sleep;
Having done everything successfully, he's aslumber in felicity.

Before Buddha was enlightened, he learned to attain a state of abstract trance referred to as "neither perception nor nonperception." This was supposedly considered, in his day, the most exalted state one could attain. Buddha went beyond this to a state called "cessation of all perception and sensation," but he realized that this is still not really nirvana, not spiritual liberation.

The *Sandhinirmocana-sutra* says, "Even if enlightening beings are versed in the mysteries of mind, intellect, and consciousness based on knowledge of reality, nevertheless the Buddha does not consider them to be versed in all the mysteries of mind, intellect, and consciousness. If enlightening beings inwardly truly do not see clinging or clinging consciousness, do not see repository or repository consciousness, do not see accumulation, do not see mind, do not see the eye, form, or eye-consciousness, do not see ear, sound, or ear-consciousness, do not see nose, scent, or nose-consciousness, do not see tongue, flavor, or tongue-consciousness, do not see body, feeling, or body-consciousness, do not see intellect, phenomena, or conceptual consciousness, then they are called enlightening beings well versed in ultimate truth."[61]

Having no consciousness or sense, in the context of universalist and Tantric Buddhism, is not meant literally, but alludes to realization of ultimate truth, generally referred to as emptiness and thus commonly depicted or approached by negations. In terms of personal experience, this couplet speaks of consciousness experienced as "radiant" rather than bent on itself, sensing all things as if "lighting" the universe, rather than leaping around, or mucking about, from one object, or one narrow focus, to another.

In a dream I have seen the emptiness of triplex existence,
Turning back beyond coming and going.

The first line of this couplet describes perception of emptiness in the relativity of subject and object. Dreaming is not only a symbol of this particular aspect of relativity; in Buddhist Yoga, the phenomenon of dreaming is also considered a demonstration or proof of relativity and the emptiness of phenomena as conceptually grasped.

In the second line, "turning back" refers to the mental revolution whereby one ceases to view subjectively projected conceptualizations as objectively intrinsic characteristic of things. This enables one to place the attention on a level of reality that is "beyond coming and going" in the sense that consciousnes is not fixated on transient appearances.

The master Jalandhari will be a witness;
The top scholars notice no bias in me.

Jalandhari, a Siddha or adept, seems to have been the teacher of Krishnacarya; the reference here is not, however, to formal authority, but to objective knowledge. Emptiness, in the Buddhist sense, has been defined by one Hindu scholar as freedom from prejudice. When one actually witnesses emptiness experientially, then cultural and intellectual biases cannot be maintained; there is then no conflict or contradiction, furthermore, between intellectual understanding and intuitive insight. Able to deal effectively with the ordinary world while at the same time spiritually and psychologically liberated by realization of emptiness, one attains the supreme balance of the Middle Way.

34

TARAKA

> I have no self; how can there be attachment?
> In the Great Symbol, desire is broken down.
> Realize naturalness; don't forget, O Yogi!
> You'll be completely released, be however you are.
> So far so good;
> On the road of naturalness, Yogi,
> don't remain in confusion.
> Castration and hernia are known when swimming;
> How can what is beyond the range of words be explained?
> Taraka says there's no chance here—
> Whoever understands, there's a rope around his neck.

I have no self; how can there be attachment?
In the Great Symbol, desire is broken down.

The Great Symbol, Mahamudra in Sanskrit, is the Tantric equivalent to Zen Buddhism. They are no different in essence, though techniques may vary within both traditions. Based on the immaculate mind, the essential great symbol practice is like the exercise of the "mirroring awareness" often referred to by the classical Zen master Pai-chang, who lived in the eighth and ninth centuries. This is when Old School Tibetan Buddhism, the Nyingma, including Mahamudra practice, was established in Tibet.

In practical terms, "having no self" means not being imprisoned in subjectivity. This is the experience, commonly referred to in Buddhist literature, of shedding the duality of subject and object in direct perception. The 17th-century Zen master Bunan wrote, "Just see directly and hear directly. When seeing directly, there is no seer; when hearing directly, there is no hearer." He also wrote, "One who sees, hears, feels, and knows without subjectivity is called a living Buddha." That is what this means.

The 13th-century Zen master Dogen expressed this practical process brilliantly in his famous essay *The Issue at Hand*, wherein he
wrote, "To act upon and witness myriad things with the burden of
the self is delusion; to act upon and witness the self in the advent
of myriad things in enlightenment." He also wrote, "The study of
Buddhism is study of the self. To learn about the self is to forget the
self. To forget the self is to be enlightened by all things."[62]

The Mahamudra or Great Symbol experience is also called the
Sagara-mudra-samadhi, or absorption symbolized by the ocean. This
refers to an oceanic, all-at-once consciousness of the totality of everything. This state of mind shatters attachment to subjective discrimination, so attention is not fixated on particular objects. Thus it is that
"desire is broken down," because there is an overwhelming sense of
unity and fullness of experience, leaving no room for wishful thinking at all.

Realize naturalness; don't forget, O Yogi!
You'll be completely released, be however you are.

Zen master Bunan said, "To acquiesce to the teaching of enlightenment as it is, directly abandon all things, merge with the body of
thusness, and experience peerless peace and bliss, is no more than a
matter of whether or not you think of yourself." He also wrote, "Become dead while alive, completely, then whatever you do, as you
will, is good."

So far so good;
On the road of naturalness, Yogi,
don't remain in confusion.

The 13th-century Zen master Lan-hsi, one of the first in Japan, wrote
of the difference between natural enlightenment and artificial confusion in a seminal treatise on Zen meditation: "Your own light of wisdom is clear and bright of itself, but when obscured by false ideas
you lose this and therefore create illusions." Sho-itsu, another 13th-
century Zen master instrumental in the establishment of this teaching in Japan, expressed naturalness in this way: "Zen is not conception or perception; if you establish an idea, you turn away from the
source. The Way is beyond cultivated effects; if you set up accomplishment, you lose the essence."

Castration and hernia are known when swimming;
How can what is beyond the range of words be explained?

Trying to pursue spiritual practices through the agency of ego-centered artificiality does not eliminate moral and psychological weaknesses and defects; it actually makes them even more evident, sometimes more dramatic and more exaggerated, than in the context of the hypocrisy of ordinary life.

One aspect of such a problematic approach to spiritual studies is the attempt to reduce the transcendental to cliches, or to encompass the inconceivable within preconceptions. This manner of study is not only spiritually impotent and sterile; because of the conceit it engenders, it causes egoism to protrude even more grotesquely than it does on the level of mundane social, emotional, and intellectual life.

This is why the state of realization to which these Tantric Siddhas are pointing is called naturalness.

Taraka says there's no chance here—
Whoever understands, there's a rope around his neck.

An ancient Japanese Buddhist poem says, "There is no way in all the world; even in the remote mountains, the deer cries in autumn." The Zen classic known as *The Blue Cliff Record* says, "Even if you can grasp it before it is spoken of, still this is remaining in the shell, wandering in limitation; even if you penetrate at a single phrase, you still won't avoid insane views on the way." The same work also says, "One who can take action on the road is like a tiger in the mountains; one immersed in worldly understanding is like a monkey in a cage."[63]

35

SARAHA

> The body is a boat, mind is the rudder;
> Hold the helm, guiding the vessel,
> by the instruction of a true teacher.
> Hold the rudder with a steady mind—
> There's no other way to the other shore.
> A boatman pulls a boat by a rope;
> Give it up and go by naturalness alone.
> There's terror on the road; brigands are strong.
> All is told in the fluctuation of the world.
> To the shore, he goes upstream in the swift current:
> Saraha says, "It is proved in the sky."

The body is a boat, mind is the rudder;
Hold the helm, guiding the vessel,
by the instruction of a true teacher.

According to the *Dhammapada*, Buddha said, "The mind is restless, unsteady, hard to control. The wise one makes it straight, like a fletcher straightens an arrow." Buddha also made it clear that mere external asceticism, or physical discipline, does not in itself lead to enlightenment: "What good is matted hair to you, idiot? What good is hide clothing? While your inward state is a tangle, you polish your exterior."[64]

The importance of a *true* teacher, a guide external to one's subjective imaginations, wishes and expectations, was emphasized by both Tantric Siddhas and Zen masters. They even abandoned the institutionalization of forms when this obstructed the perception of truth and truthfulness.

According to the famous Taoist wizard called Ancestor Lu, who is associated with amalgamating Taoism with Zen, "If you do away with writings but still stick to a teacher's tradition, this very teacher's tradition becomes a source of obstruction. You should by all means examine clearly and go to visit adepts who can transmit the profound marvel. If you don't find such a person, you will suffer from obstruction all your life.

"Generally speaking, beginners have dreams about the Way; once they make a mistake in choosing a teacher and are given false teachings, they are confused and cannot attain enlightenment. They follow false teachings all their lives, thinking them to be true guidance. Their bodies and minds become imprisoned, so that even if real people point out true awakening to them, they may repudiate it and turn away.

"Once they have tasted fanciful talk, they sell falsehood by falsehood, and believe falsehood through falsehood."[65]

Hold the rudder with a steady mind—
There's no other way to the other shore.

In the *Dhammapada,* Buddha says, "Like a fish out of water, cast on dry ground, this mind flops around trying to escape the realm of bedevilment.

"The mind is mercurial, hard to restrain, alighting where it wishes. It is good to master this mind; a disciplined mind brings happiness.

"Let the wise one watch over the mind, so hard to perceive, so artful, alighting where it wishes; a watchfully protected mind brings happiness.

"The mind travels afar, acts alone, is incorporeal, and haunts a cave; those who will control it escape the bonds of bedevilment."[66]

A boatman pulls a boat by a rope;
Give it up and go by naturalness alone.

The *Flower Ornament Scripture* says, "It is like a boat going to the ocean. Before it reaches the ocean, it is dragged with much effort, but once it reaches the ocean it is propelled without effort by the wind. The distance it travels on the ocean in one day is farther than it could be dragged by force in even a hundred years.

"In the same way, enlightening beings, having stored provisions of roots of goodness and boarded the ship of the Great Vehicle, reaching the great ocean of practice of enlightening beings, arrive at all-knowledge in a moment by effortless knowledge, which could not be reached even in countless eons by their former practices involving effort."[67]

There's terror on the road; brigands are strong.
All is told in the fluctuation of the world.

The Zen-Taoist wizard Ancestor Lu said, "The obstacle of bedevilment may arise in the mind, may attach to objects, may operate through other people, or may pertain to the body. Bedevilments arising in the mind are ideas of self and others, ideas of glory and ignominy, ideas of gain and loss, ideas of right and wrong, ideas of profit and honor, ideas of superiority. These are dust on the pedestal of the spirit, preventing freedom.

"Bedevilment in the body is when it is invaded by illness, hunger, cold, satiation, pain, and pleasure. When one becomes comfortable, one becomes lazy, repeating vicious circles into which one becomes trapped and bound."[68]

To the shore, he goes upstream in the swift current:
Saraha says, "It is proved in the sky."

The "swift current" is the flow of conditioned states, thoughts, and feelings. Going "upstream" in the current means transcending these states, thoughts, and feelings even in their very midst, not going along with the force of their momentum, but focusing on the "shore" of ultimate truth. The aim, at this point, is realization of emptiness, so the Siddha says that it is "proved in the sky."

[36]

SARAHA

> When your mind is split by sleep,
> it's your own fault.
> Enjoying the instruction of the teacher,
> how can you remain a vagrant?
> Wondrous, the sky born of hum!
> When you've taken a Bengali wife,
> your conceptions are destroyed.
> Mysterious, the illusion of being—it shows others versus self;
> This world is a bubble—in naturalness the self is empty.
> Leaving the nectar, you've swallowed the poison;
> control of mind comes from oneself.
> By understanding what about my own people and others
> may I put up with vicious in-laws?
> Saraha says, "Better an empty cowpen—
> what use have I for a vicious bull?
> Destroying the world on my own,
> I enjoy myself at will."

When your mind is split by sleep,
it's your own fault.
Enjoying the instruction of the teacher,
how can you remain a vagrant?

In the Zen Buddhist practice of koan meditation, and in the Pure Land Buddhist practice of incantation, it is necessary to reach continuity that is unbroken even by sleep, unification of mind not split even in sleep, before the breakthrough of satori (in Zen) or Rebirth (in the Pure Land) can take place. Not being interrupted or diverted by sleep does not mean sleeplessness; what it signals is the transition from deliberate effort to spontaneity.

When the mind is split by sleep, this indicates that the practice of concentration is still deliberate. When the work is internalized as a natural process, in contrast, sleep does not divert the mind. The Siddha says that when the mind is split it is "your own fault" because it is your own deliberate effort that is interrupted. This is somewhat subtle, and can be understood only through personal experience.

The image of the vagrant is from the *Saddharmapundarika-sutra* or Lotus Sutra, one of the major revelations of universalist Buddhism. The vagrant is the son of a wealthy man who leaves home and falls into poverty, becoming a migrant laborer. When at last he is reunited with his father, the son does not recognize him. Only after employing his son and testing him for probity does the father at last reveal his identity and finally bequeath all his wealth to his son.

The father in this story represents the Buddha-nature, which the scripture declares is the original endowment inherent in everyone. The wanderings of the son represent the confusion into which the mind, unaware of its inherent Buddha-nature, falls. When the son returns and is employed on his father's estate, this represents exertion of effort in practice. When the father reveals their relationship and bequeaths his fortune to his son, this represents return to the original natural Buddha-nature and the realization of awakening.

In Zen Buddhism, the image of the vagrant as a migrant laborer is often used to represent those who try to attain enlightenment by subjectively motivated striving, ignorant of the intrinsic Buddha-nature. Here the Siddha presents an analogous image, again emphasizing the transition from deliberateness to spontaneity.

Wondrous, the sky born of hum!
When you've taken a Bengali wife,
your conceptions are destroyed.

The mantric syllable *hum* is the "seed letter" of the Buddha Akshobhya, whose name means "Immovable." According to the Ten Stages teaching of the *Flower Ornament Scripture*, immovability is attained in the eighth stage, which is the stage at which the practitioner transcends effort to attain effortlessness. Thus the Siddha artfully continues his teaching on spontaneity.

The *Flower Ornament Scripture* says, "As soon as they attain the eighth stage, Immovability, enlightening beings become freed from all efforts and attain the state of effortlessness, freed from physical, verbal, and mental striving, freed from stirring cogitation and flowing thoughts, and become stabilized in a natural state of development."[69] It also describes those in this state as "wholly detached from mind, intellect, consciousness, thought, and ideation. Unattached, not grasping, equal to space, having entered into the nature of openness." Such is the "wondrous (inconceivable) sky born of *hum*."

The "Bengali wife" is another symbol of emptiness. As explained earlier, in Tantric Buddhism the wife ordinarily stands for *shunyata*, or emptiness, while the husband ordinarly stands for *upaya*, or method. Bengal was not culturally Hinduized or Sanskritized until comparatively late in its history, and even then never completely. This was the homeland of many Tantric adepts, and may have indeed been the original homeland of Tantric Buddhism.

The name Sanskrit, used for the cultivated language of Hinduism, means "compounded," and therefore is a convenient symbol for artificial convention, in the usage of those not socially and intellectually dominated by Sanskrit culture. Gautama Buddha himself, whose native Magadhi language was a forerunner of the Bengali language used by the Vajrayana Siddhas in these songs, was one of the first to abandon the ritual constrictions of Sanskrit language and Hindu cultural convention. If we understand "emptiness" as a window to reality beyond artificial conventions of thought and perception, "Bengali" is thus a marvelously apt symbol of the "culture" or "homeland" of the "wife" that is *shunyata*, "departure from all views."

Mysterious, the illusion of being—it shows others versus self;
This world is a bubble—in naturalness the self is empty.

The illusion of others versus self refers to ignorance of the fact that the totality of all living beings is one single being, one single organism. It also refers to the artificial division between subject and object, created by the projection of subjective discriminations which are then reified as independent objective realities.

Buddhist teachings often refer to the world, including the empirical self, as like a bubble. This is said in view of its transitory, evanescent, insubstantial nature. But there is also more to this image. The *Shurangama-sutra* says, "Space is born within great awareness, like a bubble from the ocean." Here, "space" means that which contains the universe. The classical Zen master Pai-chang said, "Space is symbolized by the bubble; the ocean represents essence. The essence of inherent radiant awareness is greater than space, and so it is said that space is born within great awareness like a bubble from the ocean."

Since the self, here meaning the acquired psychological self, is a mental construct, its artificial boundaries dissolve in the state of naturalness, or effortless spontaneity. This is realized through the "inherent radiant awareness" of which Zen master Pai-chang speaks.

Leaving the nectar, you've swallowed the poison;
control of mind comes from oneself.
By understanding what about my own people and others
may I put up with vicious in-laws?

The teaching of emptiness is traditionally said to be both nectar and poison. It is nectar when it is accurately understood and thus releases the mind from bondage. It is poison when it is misconstrued and thereby leads to nihilism, antinomianism, or schizoid reification of "emptiness" as something apart from existence.

Zen master Pai-chang said, "The universally equal teaching of the Mahayana is like nectar, and also like poison. If you can digest it, it is like nectar; but if you cannot digest it, it is like poison. When reading scriptures and studying the teachings, if you do not understand the living word and the dead word, you will certainly not penetrate the meanings and expressions in them." The Indian master Nagarjuna, considered the ancestor of both Zen and Vajrayana, wrote, "Emptiness seen wrongly destroys the weak-minded, like a mishandled snake or a misperformed spell."

The true teaching of emptiness, correctly understood and realized in actual experience, is the understanding that enables one to tolerate others, even the vicious, and their illusions, without self-righteousness. The *Flower Ornament Scripture* says, "Enlightening beings are able to see the things of the world this way: all things, existent and nonexistent, they realize are illusions; living beings and lands are made by various actions. Entering the realm of illusion, they have no attachment therein; thus attaining skillfulness, they are tranquil, free from folly."[70] The same scripture also says of this understanding, "Realizing the world is empty, they do not destroy the things of the world."

Saraha says, "Better an empty cowpen—
what use have I for a vicious bull?
Destroying the world on my own,
I enjoy myself at will."

"Better an empty cowpen than a vicious bull" means that it is better not to grasp anything than to mistake something relative for an absolute. As usual in this literature, the female, here the "cow," represents emptiness, while the male, here the "bull," represents method, "skill in means." If religious forms are perverted to serve egotistic ambitions ("vicious bull"), as often happens in cultic movements and religious politics, it is better to have nothing to do with them at all.

Thus the Siddha speaks of "destroying the world," realizing emptiness, the absolute truth transcending all worldly concepts, "on my own," outside the realm of mundane establishments posing as religious bodies. In this way one attains personal experience of liberation, "enjoying myself at will," rather than becoming more entangled and fettered than ever by submitting to authoritarian institutions. And this is what the original Tantric adepts actually did.

[37]

KAHNU

> For one whose mind-field is rubbish and junk,
> The Tantric works are a necklace of bricks.
> Say, how can nature be told of,
> Where body, speech, and mind do not enter?
> In vain does a guru teach a disciple;
> How can what is beyond speech be told?
> As much talk, so much rubbish;
> The teacher is dumb, the student is deaf.
> How can Kahnu tell of the winner's treasure?
> As the deaf and dumb understand.

For one whose mind-field is rubbish and junk,
The Tantric works are a necklace of bricks.

If the mind is full of garbage, like desire for recognition, desire for power over others, desire for ascendancy, desire for self-esteem, or even simple thrill-seeking, religious practice only exaggerates these negative characteristics. Zen master Pai-chang said, "The world that is bound becomes and decays, but what the power of concentration holds will leak out to another realm, totally unawares."

Say, how can nature be told of,
Where body, speech, and mind do not enter?

This is another warning for those who are attached to ritual, doctrine, and meditation in the very same manner as attachment to any mundane thing. Pai-chang said, "How can you carve and polish emptiness to make an image of Buddha? How can you say emptiness is blue, yellow, red, or white? As it is said, 'Reality has no comparison, because there is nothing to which it may be likened; the embodiment of reality is not constructed and does not fall within the scope of any classification.' That is why it is said, 'The essence of the sage is nameless and cannot be spoken; it is impossible to linger in the empty door of truth as it really is.' Just as insects can alight anywhere but the flames of a fire, people's minds can relate to anything but transcendental insight."

In vain does a guru teach a disciple;
How can what is beyond speech be told?

Pai-chang said, "When you call on teachers to seek some knowledge or understanding, this is the demon of 'teachers,' because it gives rise to verbalization and opinion." He also said, "Just detach from all sound and form, and do not dwell in detachment either; and do not dwell in intellectual understanding. This is practice."

As much talk, so much rubbish;
The teacher is dumb, the student is deaf.

Pai-chang said, "If one should say, 'I am capable of explaining, I am able to understand; I am the teacher, you are the disciple,' this is the same as demonic suggestion." Zen master Yuansou said, "There is no real doctrine at all for you to chew on or squat over. If you will not believe in yourself, you pick up your baggage and go around to other people's houses looking for Zen, looking for the Way, looking for mysteries, looking for marvels, looking for Buddhas, looking for Zen masters, looking for teachers."[71]

How can Kahnu tell of the winner's treasure?
As the deaf and dumb understand.

Zen master Ju-ching said, "You must strip off your eyes so that you see nothing at all; then after that, there is nothing you don't see. . . . You must block your ears shut so that you hear nothing at all; then after that, there is nothing you don't hear."

In *The Blue Cliff Record*, Zen master Yuan-wu says, "Even if your whole body were an eye, you still wouldn't be able to see It. Even if your whole body were an ear, you still wouldn't be able to hear It. Even if your whole body were a mouth, you still wouldn't be able to speak of It. Even if your whole body were a mind, you still wouldn't be able to perceive It.

"Now, leaving aside 'whole body' for the moment, if you had no eyes, how would you see? Without ears, how would you hear? Without a mouth, how would you speak? Without a mind, how would you perceive? If you can unfurl a single pathway here, you'll be a fellow student with the ancient Buddhas."[72]

[38]

BHUSUKU

This world is nonexistent from the start;
it appears to be by mistake.
How can one who is startled by the rope-snake
be bitten by the fiber rope in reality?
Wondrous Yogi, don't dirty your hands!
With such behavior, if you are awake in the world,
your habitual desires will fall away.
It is like a mirage, a fairy city, a reflection in a mirror—
In the midst of the whirlwind, be yourself firm as a rock.
Like the son of a sterile woman playing many kings of sports,
Space is swollen by oil from sand, by the horns of a hare.
The Warrior says clearly, Bhusuku says clearly,
"All is such of its own nature:
If you are ignorant and confused,
ask a teacher of truth and find out."

This world is nonexistent from the start;
it appears to be by mistake.
How can one who is startled by the rope-snake
be bitten by the fiber rope in reality?

In terms of the metaphysics of Buddhist Yoga, to which this couplet overtly refers, "this world" means the world as we represent it to ourselves in our thoughts, according to conditioned mental predilections and habits. In technical Sanskrit, this is called the *parikalpita-svabhava,* or the nature of things as conceptualized. This projected nature of things is traditionally symbolized by the fearful misperception of a length of rope as a snake. Pursuing this illustration, the "rope" stands for *paratantra-svabhava,* the dependent nature of things. The fact that the rope is not a rope of itself, but a bundle of fibers, is called the *parinishpanna-svabhava*, the perfect, absolute, or real nature of things.

The *Sandhinirmocana-sutra*, a classic of Buddhist Yoga, explains, "People produce explanations of the dependent and real natures based on the characteristics of the conceptualized nature, saying they are such and such, in accord with how people conceptualize them. Because the explanations condition their minds, because their awareness conforms to the explanations, because they are lulled by the explanation, they cling to their conceptualizations."[73]

The comprehensive pan-Buddhist *Flower Ornament Scripture* illustrates this principle by the image of the mind as an artist. Mistaking the conceptualized nature of things for objective reality is delusion. Zen master Pai-chang Cheng wrote, "An artist draws a picture of hell, depicting hundreds and thousands of scenes; setting down his brush, he looks it over, and feels a shiver run through him." The scripture says, "Of all things seen in the world, only mind is the host; by grasping forms according to interpretation it becomes deluded, not true to reality."

According to an ancient story frequently alluded to in Chinese Zen teachings to explain the significance of this point, once a man at a banquet lifted his wine goblet and saw in it the reflection of a bow hanging on the wall behind him. Mistaking it for a little snake in the wine, yet unable to stop his momentum, he went ahead and drank the wine; then he became sickened, thinking he had swallowed a viper. Later, when he saw the bow on the wall and realized what had really happened, he knew the "snake" was a product of his own imagination, and immediately recovered his health.

Wondrous Yogi, don't dirty your hands!
With such behavior, if you are awake in the world,
your habitual desires will fall away.

To "dirty your hands" means grasping and clinging to illusions and delusions. Zen master K'en-t'ang wrote, "In a village where the wells are poisoned, the water should not even be tasted; with even a single drop, the whole family dies."

"If you are awake in the world" indicates that nonattachment, not "dirtying your hands," does not mean escapism or nihilism, but understanding the real nature of the world. Zen master Wu-men wrote,

"If no idle matters hang on your mind, then it is a good season in the human world."[74]

With this realization, habitual desires "fall away" even while in the world, because they are rooted in subjectivity, not in objectivity. Zen master Dogen wrote, "Minding already gone, 'mindless' does not quite describe it. In this life, purity is foremost."[75]

It is like a mirage, a fairy city, a reflection in a mirror—
In the midst of the whirlwind, be yourself firm as a rock.

The *Flower Ornament Scripture* says, "The world is like a mirage, differentiated because of conceptions; knowing the world is ideation, one is freed from delusions of thought, view, and mind. Just as people think a mirage in the heat is water, yet the water does not exist and the wise should not seek it, the same is true of sentient beings: worldly states are all nonexistent, like mirages, existing in the perception—this is the realm of the unobstructed mind."[76] Zen master Dogen wrote, "The autumn colors of the thousand peaks are dyed with seasonal rain; how could the hard rock on the mountain follow along with the wind?"[77]

Like the son of a sterile woman playing many kinds of sports,
Space is swollen by oil from sand, by the horns of a hare.

The son of a sterile woman, oil pressed from sand, and the horns of a hare, are all images commonly used in Zen as well as Tantric Buddhism. They do not represent absolute nonexistence, or illogic or irrationality, as has been claimed by misguided Zen popularizers; they symbolize the identity of true emptiness and inconceivable existence. The *Flower Ornament Scripture* says, "Enlightening beings examine all things, clearly realize all are like phantoms, and carry out phantomlike practice, never giving it up. . . . Buddhas liberate phantom beings with great kindness and compassion. The liberation is also phantomlike; they teach them by phantom power."[78]

The Warrior says clearly, Bhusuku says clearly,
"All is such of its own nature:
If you are ignorant and confused,
ask a teacher of truth and find out."

Zen master Fen-yang wrote, "Few believe in the Buddha in their own mind; unwilling to take responsibility for it, they suffer a lot of cramps. Arbitrary ideas, greed and anger, the wrappings of afflictions, all are conditioned on attachment to the cave of ignorance."[79]

Zen master Fo-yen said, "The Way is not only evident after explanation and demonstration, because it is always being revealed naturally. Explanation and demonstration are expedients used to enable you to realize intuitive understanding; they are only temporary byways. Whether you attain realization through explanation, or enter in through demonstration, or reach the goal by spontaneous sensing through individual awareness, ultimately there is no different thing or separate attainment. It is just a matter of reaching the source of mind."[80]

39

KAHNU

> Emptiness is filled by the nature of mind;
> Don't be saddened by detachment from the clusters.
> How can you say Kahnu is not there?
> Day by day he penetrates the triple world.
> The ignorant one is distressed on seeing
> the perishing of what is seen,
> But how can a broken wave
> make the ocean run dry?
> Being ignorant, people do not look closely—
> They do not see the cream there within the milk.
> No one who leaves the world comes back here;
> Kahnu the Yogi revels in such an existence.

Emptiness is filled by the nature of mind;
Don't be saddened by detachment from the clusters.

This couplet emphasizes the perennial insistence that "emptiness," in Buddhist usage, is a technical term and is not meant in the ordinary literal sense of absence, nonexistence, or removal of something existent. The "clusters" are the components of the mortal being, as traditionally defined in Buddhist practical philosophy: form, sensation, conception, synergy, and consciousness. Not being "saddened by detachment from the clusters" means realizing that detachment from transitory things, in Buddhist practice, is not based on nihilistic rejection but on the emptiness of absoluteness; so nothing real is destroyed in the process; nothing is lost, except delusion.

How can you say Kahnu is not there?
Day by day he penetrates the triple world.

This couplet emphasizes the pragmatic implications of the principle that realization of emptiness and nonattachment, in the Buddhist sense, does not mean, and does not led to nihilism or quietism. Zen master Pai-chang said, "Buddhahood is not inactivity; it is not passivity, or quiescence in the darkness." Pai-chang also said, "Cultivating mundane causes while in the sanctified state, a Buddha enters among sentient beings, becoming like them in kind to invite, lead, teach, and guide them. Joining those hungry spirits, limbs and joints afire, one expounds transcendental wisdom to them, inspiring them with the will for enlightenment. If one just remained in the sanctified state, how could one go there and talk with them?

"Buddha enters into various classes and makes a raft for sentient beings; like them, he feels pain, unlimited toil and stress. When a Buddha enters a painful place, he too feels pain, the same as sentient beings. A Buddha is not the same as sentient beings only in that he is free to go or to stay."

The ignorant one is distressed on seeing
the perishing of what is seen,
But how can a broken wave
make the ocean run dry?

The mind constricted by discriminatory thinking sees persons and things as isolated existences in themselves, rather than as part of a totality comprising all beings and things. By shifting attention to the totality, in contrast, one sees that a "broken wave," an isolated individual, event, or phenomenon, which arises and passes away, is part of an "ocean" of universal interdependence. The former mode of consciousness is called the aspect of mind that is born and dies; the latter is called the aspect of mind that is true to suchness.

Being ignorant, people do not look closely—
They do not see the cream there within the milk.

In terms of phenomena, the "milk" here refers to external appearances, while the "cream" refers to inner essence. In terms of mind, the "milk" refers to conditioned consciousness, while the "cream" refers to the essence of consciousness. Cream within milk means Buddha-nature within the human mind.

No one who leaves the world comes back here;
Kahnu the Yogi revels in such an existence.

Zen master Hua-yen was asked, "How is it when greatly enlightened people return to confusion?"

The Zen master replied, "A broken mirror does not shine again; fallen leaves cannot climb up a tree."

Zen master Dogen wrote:

> The wind is still throughout the world,
> birds cry, the mountains are quiet.
> The crossroads are bright as daybreak,
> the doors of the senses cool as autumn.
> Half sitting where there is no doubt,
> one sees illusion in a floating reflection.[81]

40

BHUSUKU

> The tree of nature pervades the triple world;
> O space-like intrinsic essence, who is released from caste?
> Just as drinking water spilled into water
> cannot be distinguished,
> So does the mind-jewel merge
> into the sky.
> Where there is no self, how can there be other?
> The origin nonexistent, birth and death have no being.
> Bhusuku says, "Wondrous!" The Warrior says, "Wondrous!"
>   All is essentially thus!
> Going and not coming back,
> therein is neither being nor nonbeing.

The tree of nature pervades the triple world;
O space-like intrinsic essence, who is released from caste?

The triple world—consisting of the realm of desire, the realm of form, and the formless realm—is by nature empty of instrinsic essence or absolute reality. There is no exception to emptiness in all the world, but the nonexistence of absoluteness does not erase the existence of relativity. Indeed, they are one and the same—relativity *is* emptiness. The great master Nagarjuna, ancestor of both Zen and Tantric Buddhism, wrote in his seminal verses on the Middle Way, *yah pratitya-samutpadah sunyatam tam pracaksmahe,* "Interdependent origination, we declare, is itself emptiness."

For this reason, even though Buddhism is casteless, and the original Tantric movement went further than any other form of Buddhism in overcoming or breaking through the tyranny of caste prejudice, especially in Bengal, yet caste divisions were generally maintained socially and politically by Hindu power structures; nevertheless realized Buddhists were psychologically and spiritually freed by their inner understanding.

This spiritual realization is concentrated in the question "Who is released?" This encapsulation is not simply an allusion to selflessness (the ultimate unreality of the secondary, psychologically and socio-culturally conditioned ego); it is a meditation exercise, looking into the innermost essence of mind. This is what Zen Buddhists call "turning the light around and looking back," which is also part of the old Tibetan practice of Mahamudra, the Great Symbol.

Just as drinking water spilled into water
cannot be distinguished,
So does the mind-jewel merge
into the sky.

The "mind merging with the sky" refers to the practice and realization that Zen-inspired neo-Taoists call "absolute nonresistance." The Taoist master known as Preserver of Truth said, "In the beginning of study of the Way, it is necessary to sit calmly, collect the mind, and detach from objects, so the mind does not possess anything. By dwelling in nonpossessiveness, one does not cling to anything, spontaneously entering into absolute nonresistance. The mind then merges with the Way."[82]

This type of practice also has precedent in ancient classical Taoism, as noted in the book of the Huainan Masters: "What sages learn is to return their nature to the beginning, and let the mind travel freely in openness. What developed people learn is to link their nature to vast emptiness and become aware of the silent infinite."[83]

Where there is no self, how can there be other?
The origin nonexistent, birth and death have no being.

The 17th-century Zen master Bankei said, "If you don't think of being superior to others, you won't be inferior to them."

A common Buddhist dictum often quoted in Zen texts says, "When the mind is excited, all things arise; when the mind is quiet, all things quiesce." The third patriarch of Zen wrote, "When the one mind does not conceive, all things are error-free."

The *Blue Cliff Record* poses the question, "Right now, where do seeing and not seeing, hearing and not hearing, speaking and not speaking, knowing and not knowing, come from?" This is not a rhetorical or philosophical question, but a meditation exercise. The Taoist master called Preserver of Truth said, "Concentrating on the absolute, practice being unborn."[84]

This exercise also has its precedent in classical Taoism, according to the Huainan Masters: "Sages send the spirit to the capital of awareness and return to the beginning of myriad things. They look at the formless and listen to the soundless. In the midst of profound darkness, they alone see light; in the midst of silent vastness, they alone have illumination."[85]

Bhusuku says, "Wondrous!" The Warrior says,
"Wondrous!" All is essentially thus!
Going and not coming back,
therein is neither being nor nonbeing.

The term *arhat,* used for a Buddhist saint who has overcome the world and attained nirvana, is sometimes interpreted as deriving from *ari-han,* "killer of the enemy." The image of the warrior, who fights egoism and delusion, is common in Buddhist texts. Here, the Siddha Bhusuku is referring to himself.

In the *Sandhinirmocana-sutra,* "one-pointedness of mind" is defined as "realizing that images concentrated on are only consciousness; or, realizing this, to meditate on suchness." The statement that "all is essentially thus" means seeing things as they really are, undistorted by subjective projections based on conditioned conceptualizations.

"Going and not coming back" refers to "departure from all views," as Nagarjuna has defined emptiness, leaving behind all biased notions; and because emptiness is relativity, here there is neither absolute being nor absolute nonbeing. Such is the transcendent Middle Way.

[41]

KANKANA

> When the void joins the void,
> All things then arise.
> I am perfectly aware of the four moments;
> By stopping in between, there is supreme awakening.
> Dot and crescent have not entered the mind;
> While seeking one, the other's lost.
> Knowing where you come from,
> You remain centered, totally unencumbered.
> Kankana says, in tumultuous sounds,
> "All has been smashed by the roar of suchness!"

When the void joins the void,
All things then arise.

The two "voids" are mind and objects. When the mind is empty of preconceptions and sees actuality void of subjective projections, everything is *suchness*. The *Flower Ornament Scripture* says, "No view is seeing that can see all things. If one has views about things, this is not seeing anything." It also says, "People wrongly conceptualize things spoken of in conventional terms; knowing the world is all birthless, this is seeing the world."

I am perfectly aware of the four moments;
By stopping in between, there is supreme awakening.

The "four moments" are the moment before a thought arises, the moment of imminent arising, the moment of actual arising, and the moment of passing away. Mindfulness of these four moments is the basis of one of the meditation practices of T'ien-t'ai Buddhism, among the parent schools of Zen. "Stopping in between" means not dwelling on any of these moments, even while aware of them. By this technique, the extra dimensions of consciousness that are beyond thought per se become accessible. The classical Zen master Ma-tsu said, "When successive thoughts do not await each other, and thought after thought dies out moment to moment, this is called the oceanic meditation. It takes in all truths, just as hundreds of thousands of different streams all return to the ocean."

Dot and crescent have not entered the mind;
While seeking one, the other's lost.

Dot and crescent stand for sun and moon, which represent the absolute and relative thought of enlightenment. This couplet alludes to the state of realization, transcending aspiration. If one focuses only on the absolute, one becomes oblivious to the relative; if one focuses only on the relative, one has no sense of the absolute.

According to a koan in the classic collection *Annals of the Empty Valley*, Zen master Ch'ing-yuan asked the illustrious Sixth Patriarch of Zen, who was famous for the natural wisdom known in Zen as teacherless knowledge, "What should be done to avoid falling into stages?" The Patriarch asked back, "What have you done?" Ch'ing-yuan said, "I don't even practice the holy truths." The Patriarch retorted, "Then what stage do you fall into?" Ch'ing-yuan said, "Since I don't even practice the holy truths, what stage would I fall into?" The Patriarch said, "Right! Keep it well."

Remarking on this, the later master Pao-en said, "Utterly forgetting human convention, what's the need of second thoughts? Shattering the mass of doubt, how does it require a single remark? Who is the one who finds the marvel free in all ways, not lingering in the mystic gate?" This bespeaks the realization to which the Bengali Siddha Kankana alludes in this couplet.

Knowing where you come from,
You remain centered, totally unencumbered.

Ma-tsu said, "The triple world is only mind; all forms are impressions of a single truth. Whatever form you see, you are seeing mind. Mind is not mind of itself; there is mind because of form. . . . What is born in the mind is called form; when you know that form is empty, then birth is unborn. If you understand this mind, then you can dress and eat according to the times, nurturing the embryo of sagehood. What further concern is there?"

The Second Patriarch of Zen asked the Founder of Zen, "My mind is not at peace; please give me peace of mind." The Founder replied, "Bring me your mind, and I will make it peaceful." The Second Patriarch said, "When I search for my mind, I cannot find it." The Founder said, "I have pacified your mind."

The *Diamond Cutting Wisdom Scripture* says, "Past mind cannot be grasped, future mind cannot be grasped, present mind cannot be grasped."

The *Flower Ornament Scripture* says, "Mind discriminates worlds, but that mind has no existence. The enlightened know this truth, and thus see the body of Buddha."[86] It also says, "No view is called seeing, the birthless is called beings. Whether views or beings, knowing they've no substantial nature, the seer dismisses entirely the subject and object of seeing; not destroying reality, this person knows the Buddha."[87]

Kankana says, in tumultuous sounds,
"All has been smashed by the roar of suchness!"

Smashing everything by the roar of suchness means realizing what is referred to in Buddhist Yoga as the "selflessness of things in true suchness." The selflessness of things means there is no inherent identity in things, as their definitions and identities are actually projected mental constructions.

The *Flower Ornament Scripture* says, "If one can know this real body's quiescent character of true thusness, one can see the truly enlightened transcending the path of speech. Things expressed in words cannot disclose the character of reality; only through equanimity can one see things, including the Buddha."[88]

The same scripture says, "There is no creator or created; they only arise from habitual conceptions. How can we know it is so? Because other than this, naught is. All things have no abode; no definite locus can be found. The Buddhas abide in this, ultimately unwavering."[89]

KAHNU

> The mind is a tree, the five senses its branches:
> Desires are its plentiful leaves and fruits.
> He cuts with the axe of a supreme teacher's words;
> Kahnu says, "The tree won't grow again!"
> Pure and impure water make the tree grow;
> The wise one who obeys the teacher cuts it.
> The fool who knows not to cut or split the tree
> Accepts its existence when it's rotted and fallen.
> Void is the tree at its best, space the axe:
> Cut the tree, so that the root does not sprout.

The mind is a tree, the five senses its branches:
Desires are its plentiful leaves and fruits.

Zen master Lan-hsi wrote, "Ordinary people are like trees: putting the manure of greed and lust on the thin soil of folly and delusion, planting seeds of ignorance, transplanting shoots of the five clusters; they produce buds of habit-ridden consciousness, growing roots of attachment and stems of egoism toward others, bringing forth branches of flattery and deceit, sprouting leaves of jealousy and envy, creating trees of affliction, causing the flowers of infatuation to bloom, forming fruits of the three poisons of carving, antagonism, and stupidity. When the tasks of name and gain are done, they sing the songs of desires."

He cuts with the axe of a supreme teacher's words;
Kahnu says, "The tree won't grow again!"

Once upon a time there were seven princesses, known as the Seven Sagacious Women. One day, on the occasion of a seasonal flower festival, when great crowds of people were hurrying to the parks to enjoy themselves, one of the Seven Sagacious Women said to the others, "We should not go along like everyone else to frolic in the realm of the senses for mundane pleasures. We should go to the forest of corpses."

The other women said, "There are corpses rotting everywhere there; what is good about that?"

The first woman said, "Let's just go; there will be something good."

When they got to the forest, the woman pointed to a corpse and asked the other women, "The corpse is here; where has the person gone?"

Reflecting on this, the women all attained enlightenment.

Pure and impure water make the tree grow;
The wise one who obeys the teacher cuts it.

According to Zen master Pai-chang, the introductory teaching of Buddhism is for "weeding out impure things," while the advanced teaching is for "weeding out pure things." He explains, "When traces do not appear on either side, then there is neither lack nor sufficiency, neither profane nor holy, neither light nor dark. This is not having knowledge, yet not lacking knowledge; it is not bondage, not liberation."

Obsession with "pure things" can delude people even more deeply than attachment to "impure things," because of the blinding demon of self-righteousness. Pai-chang also said, "Just do not be affected by greed for anything, even being or nonbeing. When it comes to the matter of untying bonds, there are no special words or phrases to teach people. If you say there are some particular verbal expressions to teach people, or that there is some particular doctrine to give people, this is called heresy and demonic suggestion."

Pai-chang further describes spiritual progress in terms of successive attachments and detachments, ultimately transcending obsession with both impure things and pure things: "To dwell on evil when encountering evil is called the enlightenment of sentient beings. To dwell on goodness when encountering goodness is called the enlightenment of Buddhist disciples. Not dwelling on either side, good or bad, and yet not making nondwelling an understanding, is called the enlightenment of bodhisattvas. Only when you neither dwell on anything nor make an understanding of nondwelling can this finally be called the enlightenment of Buddhas."

The fool who knows not to cut or split the tree
Accepts its existence even when it's rotted and fallen.

One who does not know how to analyze the body to overcome gross self-centered obsession with sensation and emotional experience clings to self-importance even in the face of undeniable evidence of fragility and mortality.

Void is the tree at its best, space the axe:
Cut the tree, so that the root does not sprout.

Lan-hsi wrote, "Is there anyone who can pull the tree out by the roots with a single hand, and plant it on a ground where there is neither light nor shade, making a shadowless tree? This must be someone with great power, who has the same root as heaven and earth, the same body as all things."

Zen master Dogen said, "Having pruned away the tree on the moon, tonight I don't long for any tonight of yore. When a foreigner comes, a foreigner is reflected; when a native comes, a native. This is the boundless pure light of the full moon night."[90]

[43]

JAYANANDI

> Like a mirror looked at in dreams,
> So the delusion that intervenes.
> When the mind is freed of delusion,
> Then comings and goings are gone.
> It is not to be burned, nor soaked, nor cut off;
> See how illusion recurs in delusion again and again.
> The body is like a shadow illusion;
> It is beyond the two extremes.
> Suchness of mind is inherently pure;
> Jayanandi says directly, "There is no other."

Like a mirror looked at in dreams,
So the delusion that intervenes.

The mirror looked at in dreams symbolizes arbitrary subjectivity unconnected to objective reality. What this mirror reflects is conditioned mental habit, the predilections and preoccupations of the self, constructing pictures from bits of stored impressions. The projections of subjective bias, mistaken for objective realities, are delusions that screen the mind from truth. In the words of a Buddhist proverb often quoted in Chinese Zen, "Cataracts in the eye make flowers in the sky."

When the mind is freed of delusion,
Then comings and goings are gone.

The eighth-century Zen master Ma-tsu said, "True suchness of mind is like a clear mirror reflecting forms. The mirror represents the mind; the forms represent all things. If the mind grasps at things, it gets involved in external conditions; this is the meaning of birth and death. If the mind does not grasp at things, this is the meaning of true suchness."

He also said, "The path does not require cultivation; just do not be polluted. What is pollution? As long as you have a mind that is born and dies, with artificial contrivance, all of it is pollution. If you want to realize the path directly, the normal mind is the path. What is the normal mind? It has no artificiality, no affirmation, no grasping or rejection, no nihilism or eternalism, no profanity or holiness." This approach to enlightenment is just like the *sahaja* or "natural" path of the Bengali adepts.

The *Flower Ornament Scripture* says, "Having risen above all views, whether mundane or transcendental, yet able to know the truth, one becomes a great illuminate."

It is not to be burned, nor soaked, nor cut off;
See how illusion recurs in delusion again and again.

Illusion cannot be "burned, soaked, or cut off" precisely because it is illusory and not actually real. On the persistent habit of entertaining illusions about delusions, the *Flower Ornament Scripture* says, "Ignorant creatures, because of continually slipping into erroneous views, because of minds shrouded by the darkness of ignorance, because of being puffed up with pride, because of conceptions, because of mental fixations of desires caught in the web of craving, because of hopes pursued by actions in the tangle of deceit and falsehood, because of deeds connected with envy and jealousy producing mundane states, because of accumulation of actions rife with passion, hatred, and folly, because of the flames of mind ignited by anger and resentment, because of undertaking of actions bound up with delusion, because of seeds in the mind, intellect, and consciousness bound to the flows of lust, existence, and ignorance, therefore produce sprouts of subsequent mundane life."[91]

The body is like a shadow illusion;
It is beyond the two extremes.

The two extremes are being and nonbeing; illusion neither exists nor does not exist. It does not exist absolutely, but it does exist mentally. The *Flower Ornament Scripture* says, "When great enlightening beings see all worlds as like illusions, they do not see beings born or dying, they do not see countries born or passing away, they do not see phenomena born or perishing."[92] It further explains, "The world is like a mirage, differentiated because of conceptions; knowing the world is ideation, one is freed from delusions of thought, view, and mind."[93]

Suchness of mind is inherently pure;
Jayanandi says directly, "There is no other."

The *Sandhinirmocana-sutra* says, "With supremely pure awareness, the Buddha was attached neither to the mundane nor the supramundane. He proceeded according to formless truth and dwelt in the abode of the enlightened ones. He had arrived at equality with all the enlightened ones and had reached the point of nonobstruction and the state of unchangeability."[94]

The Zen master Hsia-t'ang said, " 'Buddha' is a temporary name for what cannot be seen when you look, what cannot be heard when you listen, whose place of origin and passing away cannot be found when you search. It covers sound and form, pervades sky and earth, penetrates above and below. There is no second view, no second person, no second thought. It is everywhere, in everything, not something external. This is why the single source of awareness is called 'Buddha.' "[95]

44

DHARMA

Lotus and Lightning have become friends;
The outcaste woman's burned in the yoga of equality.
The house of the Gypsy woman is afire;
Sprinkle water with the moon.
There are no scorching flames, smoke does not appear;
By way of the highest peak, one enters into the sky.
The idols Vishnu, Shiva, and Brahma are burnt;
Nine times the royal grant deed's been burned.
Dharma says, "Clearly we know—
The water's risen in the five pipes."

Lotus and Lightning have become friends;
The outcaste woman's burned in the yoga of equality.

Lotus and lightning stand for emptiness and compassion, insight and skill in means, represented as female and male. The harmonious combination of emptiness and compassion, the integration of insight and skill in means, characterizes the realization of Buddhist enlightenment. In these terms, the burning of the outcaste woman (emptiness) in the yoga (union) of equality refers to the realization of emptiness as the essential nature of being, not as an independent or isolated "void" existing of itself.

In terms of Tantric sexual yoga, the friendship of lotus and lightning symbolizes the union of female and male. In this context, the "outcaste woman" represents the central channel of the esoteric energy body visualized in meditation, the channel of purification. The "burning" stands for the blazing of the bliss of climactic sexually generated energy. This burns away the conceptual complications that ordinarily clutter the conditioned consciousness. This "burning" takes place in "equality" in the sense that it makes the practitioner indifferent to transitory thoughts. It also means that in order to be effective for spiritual purposes, this practice must be based upon, and carried out in, a state of equanimity.

The house of the Gypsy woman is afire;
Sprinkle water with the moon.

The Gypsy woman, or washerwoman (dombi), symbolizes the cleared central channel of purification. The woman's house represents the body, and the physical world; on another level, it represents the psychic state of the central channel of the energy body. In terms of the house symbolizing the body and the physical world, the fact that the house is "afire" alludes to the impermanence of the body and the world. In terms of the internal symbolism, the house afire represents the central channel energized by the blaze of ecstasy.

The moon stands for the relative thought of enlightenment. To sprinkle water on the fire with the moon means, on the level of external symbolism, to realize the transitory nature of the body, its capacities, and the physical environment as a whole. This is the means of maintaining a balance of detachment in the midst of ecstatic bliss. On the level of internal symbolism, sprinkling water with the moon means inwardly realizing the relative nature of the experience of bliss, thus maintaining equanimity even in ecstasy.

In both esoteric and exoteric Buddhism, this gesture of balance is standard practice whenever there is opening of access to extraordinary experiences or capacities. This prevents psychological aberration and spiritual deterioration through instinctive grasping and exaltation of the ego.

There are no scorching flames, smoke does not appear;
By way of the highest peak, one enters into the sky.

The absence of scorching flames and smoke alludes to maintenance of balanced equanimity and inward calmness in the midst of ecstasy. The highest peak represents orgasmic climax; entering this way into the sky means using this natural bliss to clear the mind of conceptual clingings and complications, including fantasy and longing, in order to perceive emptiness, as "departure from all views."

The idols Vishnu, Shiva, and Brahma are burnt;
Nine times the royal grant deed's been burned.

In psychological and spiritual terms, the burning of these idols refers to transcendence of concepts of destruction, subsistence, and creation. As the *Diamond Cutting Wisdom Scripture* says, "Past mind cannot be grasped, future mind cannot be grasped, present mind cannot be grasped."

The burning of the grant deed nine times symbolizes a nine-step process of transcending proprietary attachments. On one level of interpretation, the "nine times" refer to the classic nine stages of meditation, from the first stage, which is characterized by attention, examination, joy, bliss, and singlemindedness, through the ninth stage, which is characterized by cessation of all sensation and perception. Nirvana, in the Buddhist sense, is beyond this ninth stage; so the "grant deed" of proprietary attachment is "burned" nine times, symbolizing ultimate transcendence through and beyond these nine stages.

On another level of interpretation, the number nine derives from three times three, referring to entry, abiding, and exit of three stages—detachment, not abiding in detachment, and not making an understanding of nonabiding. In Zen terms, this is referred to as "nine pounds of tortoise hair," alluding to the nine stages as well as the ultimate transcendence.

Dharma says, "Clearly we know—
The water's risen in the five pipes."

The five pipes are the five basic senses; the water is conscious energy. "Clearly we know" alludes to awareness of the senses clarified by the purification process.

Zen master Dogen said, "Everyone holds a luminous jewel, all embosom a precious gem; if you do not turn your attention around and look within, you will wander from home with a hidden treasure. Have you not heard it said, 'In the ear, it is like the great and small sounds in an empty valley, none not complete; in the eye, it is like myriad images under a thousand suns, none able to avoid casting shadows'? If you seek it outside of sense experience, you will hinder the living meaning of Zen."[96]

As the order of these Tantric couplets by Dharma illustrates, this comes after clarification and purification. Zen master Dogen also said, alluding to the same caveat, "Unless the cold pierces through our bones once, how can we have the apricot blossoms perfuming the whole world?"[97]

45

BHUSUKU

> Crossing over, the diamond boat travels the lotus canal;
> Afflictions have been carried away by the Bengali Nonduality.
> Today Bhusuku's become a Bengali,
> Having taken an outcaste for his wife.
> The five ports are burnt,
> the realms of the senses destroyed:
> I do not know
> where my mind has gone.
> I've no more gold or silver;
> Compassion to those around me remains.
> I have appropriated the whole treasury;
> There is no difference in living and dying.

Crossing over, the diamond boat travels the lotus canal;
Afflictions have been carried away by the Bengali Nonduality.

The diamond and lotus are the two universes of phenomena and noumena, formal knowledge and formless insight, compassion and wisdom. Their conjunction produces the completeness of enlightened experience.

The sexual symbolism of the boat and canal are obvious; the precondition of "crossing over" alludes to the aforementioned precondition of purification.

Bengali culture is a synthesis of non-Aryan and Aryan cultures; here this historical "Bengali Nonduality" symbolically represents union of emptiness and form, or absolute and relative truth, the quintessence of enlightenment.

Today Bhusuku's become a Bengali,
Having taken an outcaste for his wife.

Bhusuku, the man, symbolizes formal knowledge and skill in means; the outcaste wife symbolizes formless insight and emptiness. Becoming a Bengali represents synthesis of these two aspects of enlightenment in a completely integrated whole.

The five ports are burnt,
the realms of the senses destroyed:
I do not know
where my mind has gone.

The five ports are the senses; burning symbolizes ecstasy, and resulting nonattachment. Destruction of the realms of the senses symbolizes transcendence of the senses; "I do not know where my mind has gone" alludes to transcendence of egocentric experience of the senses.

I've no more gold or silver;
Compassion to those around me remains.

Gold and silver represent the absolute and relative thought of enlightenment; these are means of orientation and practice. When enlightenment itself is fully realized, the thought of enlightenment is held no more; the means are relinquished on attainment of the end.

The compassion of the enlightened is called objectless or unconditional compassion; this means that the objects of this compassion are not selected by subjective design, or based on preconceived conditions. Thus it is spontaneous compassion; so the couplet does not say that it is exercised, but that it "remains."

I have appropriated the whole treasury;
There is no difference in living and dying.

The whole treasury is complete enlightenment, sometimes referred to in Buddhist literature as the land of jewels. That "there is no difference in living and dying" refers to realization of nonduality of samsara and nirvana. The *Flower Ornament Scripture* says, "Just as space never increases or decreases whether all worlds become or disintegrate, because space has no birth, similarly the enlightenment of Buddhas has no increase or decrease whether there is attainment of

enlightenment or not, because enlightenment has no signs or coun-
tersigns, no unity and no variety." It also says, "Like birthlessness is
the emergence of Buddha, like deathlessness the nirvana of Buddha:
all words and similes end—all purposes are achieved, beyond compare."

46

SABARA

Void upon void; axe the third house with the mind.
The girl who is egolessness at heart is well
protected while awake.
Untie, release the vexatious knot of illusion and delusion!
Frolicking in great ecstasy, the Wild Man has taken
the Void to wife.
Look here! My third house is like space!
How splendid! The cotton is in bloom!
Beside the third house is the moonlight;
Darkness opened, space blossoms.
The millet is ripened, the wild man and woman are drunk;
All day long the savage feels naught, senseless
in great ecstasy.
The fourth abode is built of basketwork;
Hoisted up on it, the savage has been cremated,
while a virtuous she-jackal cries.
The one intoxicated with the world has died,
offering to the dead made in the ten directions;
Look—the savage has become inert,
his wildness at an end.

Void upon void; axe the third house with the mind.
The girl who is egolessness at heart is well
protected while awake.

Void upon void stands for the emptiness of emptiness, called *sunyata-sunyata* or *sunyata-atisunyata* in Sanskrit. This is the fourth emptiness in the *prajna-paramita* teaching.

The third house is thus the third emptiness, which is inner and outer emptiness, or emptiness of the internal and external. The fourth emptiness is used to "axe" or "empty" the experience to which the third emptiness alludes, resulting in more subtle and more completely integrating liberation and enlightenment.

Nagarjuna, the specialist on emptiness wrote that "ultimate truth cannot be expressed without resorting to conventional usage; nirvana cannot be attained without arriving at ultimate truth." In resorting to conventional usage, Tantric Buddhism may use concepts or terminology of Hinduism or other religions. This gives some the impression of syncretism, but in its genuine form it is actually pure Buddhism, in the act of applying this particular principle.

In the context of multifaceted Bengal, use of selected Hindu structures would be normal for Tantric Buddhists. Pursuing this potential in the interpretation of this couplet, the "third house" would be the third stage of life, enjoyment of connubial bliss. Aligning this with Buddhism yields an allusion to the third emptiness, emptiness of the internal and external. In terms of Tantric Buddhist practice, this illustrates the principle that realization of inner and outer emptiness is a necessary concomitant of engagement in the transformation of connubial bliss into spiritual practice.

The fourth stage of life, in conventional Hindu usage, is the stage of liberation, when one leaves society to contemplate the eternal and prepare for physical death. Aligned with the fourth emptiness of Buddhism, this yields an illustration of the principle of parinirvana, ultimate extinction.

The girl who is egolessness at heart is the essence of emptiness. Always symbolized by a female, here emptiness is represented as a girl to emphasize the sense of innocence, as the void upon void of the emptiness of emptiness is innocent of any notion, even of emptiness. That is the true nature of egolessness.

The Buddhist principle of emptiness is thoroughly rational, but the rational principle coincides with direct experience and intuitive insight. Without the inner formless insight into essence, the outer formal knowledge of the principle of emptiness cannot be effective. Therefore it is said that the girl is well protected while awake, just as true emptiness as such can only be realized by conscious experience.

Untie, release the vexatious knot of illusion and delusion!
Frolicking in great ecstasy, the Wild Man has taken
the Void to wife.

This couplet uses conventional terminology of Hinayana, Mahayana, *and* Vajrayana Buddhism all together to construct a colorful illustration of the principle that "nirvana cannot be attained without arriving at ultimate truth." Thus the "wild man" of free use of expedient means needs to marry the "void" and be released in the "ecstasy" of transconceptual insight in order to realize the aim of ultimate truth and attain liberation from vexation, bondage, illusion and delusion, in nirvana.

Look here! My third house is like space!
How splendid! The cotton is in bloom!

Seeing the third house to be like space again refers in another way to realization of the emptiness of inner and outer emptiness. The cotton blooming is an artful expression that illustrates, in addition to its code meaning, the Buddhist principle of "resorting to conventional usage to express absolute truth."

The word used here in old Bengali for "cotton" is *kapasu.* Using this word rather than the more common *tula* signals uncommon usage, alerting the reader to something else, or some other meaning. The expression "blooming" is a hint to uncovering this meaning, in its sense of "splitting open."

Dividing *kapasu* into two, making *ka-pasu,* yields the meaning "next to *ka.*" In the Sanskrit and Bengali alphabets, "next to *ka*" is *kha.* In the Sanskrit language, from which Hindu and Buddhist Bengali is derived, *kha* means "space." This is a standard symbol for emptiness in Mahayana and Tantric Vajrayana Buddhism. Thus "cotton blooming" stands for the uncovering of the absolute truth of emptiness within the conventional realities of the world.

Use of such a symbolic device, at once artful and yet calm and free of emotional extreme, in a context full of erotic imagery, represents the actual feeling of the experience of emptiness within the experience of artful living.

Beside the third house is the moonlight;
Darkness opened, space blossoms.

The moonlight beside the third house is awareness of the fourth emptiness in the midst of the experience of the third emptiness. The opening of the darkness symbolizes the voiding of voidness, realization of the emptiness of emptiness. The blossoming of space then illustrates the experience of oneness of samsara and nirvana, wherein everything is pure.

The millet is ripened, the wild man and woman are drunk;
All day long the savage feels naught, senseless
in great ecstasy.

Millet is a cheap grain, signifying plainness and nonadornment, the simplicity of experience in itself, without pretense and artificial rationalization. The ripening of the millet of experience, and its fermentation and distillation into intoxicating liquor, symbolize the development of intense insight into the essence of reality. Intoxication represents the liberation of the mind from the confines of the apparent world as known to ordinary consciousness. Absence of feeling and sense in great ecstasy alludes to the indescribable nature of this transcendental insight and the experience it yields.

The fourth abode is built of basketwork;
Hoisted up on it, the savage has been cremated,
while a virtuous she-jackal cries.

The relative flimsiness of basketwork stands for the impermanence of the body and the individual life in the world. This is the reason, in conventional terms, for entrance into the fourth stage of life, liberation, in preparation for physical death.

The relative airiness of basketwork stands for experience of the ultimate emptiness of the conditional world, both subjective and objective, both inside and outside ourselves. In Buddhist terms, this is the fourth emptiness, void upon void. This is also the basis of parinirvana.

The cremation of the savage in the fourth abode represents the transcendence of subtle residual attachments to the experience of unity of samsara and nirvana. It also represents parinirvana.

The she-jackal of empty egolessness cries when the savage of expedient means is cremated, because "without resorting to conventional usage, ultimate truth cannot be expressed."

The one intoxicated with the world has died,
offering to the dead made in the ten directions;
Look—the savage has become inert,
his wildness at an end.

This is a touching description of the end of a Buddha's life on earth, representing the end of a teaching cycle, and the distribution of the Buddha's relics, symbolizing the residual influence of the teachings. Until their future rebirth as a living word, these teachings become a dead word, inert relics with no power to act on their own.

Notes

1. Cleary, T. *Dhammapada: The Sayings of Buddha* (New York: Bantam Books, 1995), p. 21.
2. Cleary, T. *The Flower Ornament Scripture: A Translation of the Avatamsaka-sutra* (Boston: Shambhala Publications, 1993), p. 1276.
3. *The Flower Ornament Scripture*, pp. 1270–1273.
4. For the sake of the general reader, I have omitted diacritical marks in transcribing Sanskrit names and terms.
5. Cleary, T. *The Original Face: An Anthology of Rinzai Zen* (New York: Grove Press, 1978), p. 41.
6. Cleary, T. *Living a Good Life: Advice on Virtue, Love, and Action from the Ancient Greek Masters* (Boston: Shambhala Publications, 1997), p. 15.
7. *Dhammapada*, pp. 14–15.
8. *The Flower Ornament Scripture*, pp. 306–307.
9. Cleary, T. *The Essential Tao* (San Francisco: HarperSanFrancisco, 1991), p. 57.
10. *Dhammapada*, p. 108.
11. Cleary, T. *Buddhist Yoga: A Comprehensive Course* (Boston: Shambhala Publications, 1995), p. 10.
12. *Buddhist Yoga*, p. 10.
13. *Buddhist Yoga*, p. 10.
14. Cleary, T. *Kensho: The Heart of Zen* (Boston: Shambhala Publications, 1997), p. 75.
15. *Buddhist Yoga*, p. 1.
16. *Buddhist Yoga*, p. 1.
17. *Buddhist Yoga*, p. 10.
18. Cleary, T. *Unlocking the Zen Koan* (Berkeley: North Atlantic Books, 1997), p. 42.
19. Cleary, T. *Immortal Sisters: Secrets of Taoist Women* (Berkeley: North Atlantic Books, 1996), p. 8.
20. *Dhammapada*, p. 35.
21. *Dhammapada*, p. 62.
22. Cleary, T. *Zen Essence: The Science of Freedom* (Boston: Shambhala Publications, 1989), p. 76.

23. *Zen Essence*, p. 26.
24. *Zen Essence*, p. 26.
25. Cleary, T. *Entry into the Inconceivable: An Introduction to Hua-yen Buddhism* (Honolulu: University of Hawaii Press, 1983), p. 162.
26. Cleary, T. *The Secret of the Golden Flower* (San Francisco: HarperSanFrancisco, 1991), pp. 23–24.
27. *Buddhist Yoga*, p. 29.
28. *The Secret of the Golden Flower*, p. 37.
29. *The Secret of the Golden Flower*, p. 13.
30. *The Secret of the Golden Flower*, p. 13.
31. *Dhammapada*, p. 125.
32. *Dhammapada*, p. 56.
33. *Dhammapada*, p. 51.
34. Cleary, T. *Living and Dying with Grace* (Boston: Shambhala Publications, 1995), pp. 23–24.
35. *Dhammapada*, pp. 50–51.
36. *Dhammapada*, p. 45.
37. *Living and Dying with Grace*, p. 68.
38. *The Flower Ornament Scripture*, p. 300.
39. *Buddhist Yoga*, p. 18.
40. *The Flower Ornament Scripture*, p. 299.
41. *Zen Essence*, p. 31.
42. *Zen Essence*, p. 61.
43. *Buddhist Yoga*, p. 29.
44. *Buddhist Yoga*, p. 34.
45. *Buddhist Yoga*, p. 10.
46. Cleary, T. *Shobogenzo: Zen Essays by Dogen* (Honolulu: University of Hawaii Press, 1986), p. 39.
47. *Dhammapada*, p. 41.
48. *The Flower Ornament Scripture*, p. 704.
49. Cleary, T. *Instant Zen: Waking up in the Present* (Berkeley: North Atlantic Books, 1994), p. 74.
50. *Instant Zen*, p. 80.
51. *Dhammapada*, p. 113.
52. *Zen Essence*, p. 53.
53. *Buddhist Yoga*, p. 28.
54. *Buddhist Yoga*, p. 30.
55. *Instant Zen*, p. 129.
56. *Entry into the Inconceivable*, p. 145.
57. *Dhammapada*, pp. 7–8.
58. *Buddhist Yoga*, p. 37.
59. *Buddhist Yoga*, pp. 24–25.

60. *Zen Essence*, p. 79.
61. *Buddhist Yoga*, p. 21.
62. *Shobogenzo*, p. 32.
63. Cleary, T. and Cleary, J. C. *The Blue Cliff Record* (Boston: Shambhala Publications, 1977), p. 240.
64. *Dhammapada*, p. 127.
65. Cleary, T. *Vitality, Energy, Spirit: A Taoist Sourcebook* (Boston: Shambhala Publications, 1991), p. 95.
66. *Dhammapad*, p. 17.
67. *The Flower Ornament Scripture*, p. 767.
68. *Vitality, Energy, Spirit*, p. 91.
69. *The Flower Ornament Scripture*, p. 765.
70. *The Flower Ornament Scripture*, pp. 880–881.
71. *Zen Essence*, p. 79.
72. *The Blue Cliff Record*, p. 489.
73. *Buddhist Yoga*, p. 30.
74. *Unlocking the Zen Koan*, p. 95.
75. Cleary, T. *Rational Zen: The Mind of Dogen Zenji* (Boston: Shambhala Publications, 1993), p. 44.
76. *The Flower Ornament Scripture*, p. 881.
77. *Rational Zen*, p. 43.
78. *The Flower Ornament Scripture*, p. 885.
79. *Zen Essence*, p. 16.
80. *Zen Essence*, p. 51.
81. *Rational Zen*, p. 63.
82. Cleary, T. *Practical Taoism* (Boston: Shambhala Publications, 1996), p. 3.
83. Cleary, T. *The Book of Leadership and Strategy: Lessons of the Chinese Masters* (Boston: Shambhala Publications, 1992), p. 112.
84. *Practical Taoism*, p. 27.
85. *The Book of Leadership and Strategy*, p. 113.
86. *The Flower Ornament Scripture*, p. 291.
87. *The Flower Ornament Scripture*, p. 378.
88. *The Flower Ornament Scripture*, p. 379.
89. *The Flower Ornament Scripture*, p. 381.
90. *Rational Zen*, p. 57.
91. *The Flower Ornament Scripture*, p. 707.
92. *The Flower Ornament Scripture*, p. 871.
93. *The Flower Ornament Scripture*, p. 881.
94. *Buddhist Yoga*, p. 1.
95. *Zen Essence*, p. 74.
96. *Rational Zen*, p. 59.
97. *Rational Zen*, p. 53.

Supplementary Notes

(a) cf. Kamenetz, Rodger, *The Jew in the Lotus* (San Francisco: HarperSan-Francisco, 1994), p. 213.

(b) cf. Scott, Ernest, *The People of the Secret* (London: Octagon Press, 1983), pp. 261–262.

(c) On the main Sufi orders and their ways, see Shah, Idries, *The Way of the Sufi* (London: Octagon Press, 1968).

(d) On the system of subtleties, see Shah, Idries, *The Sufis* (New York: Doubleday, 1964), p. 430; and Shah, Idries, *A Perfumed Scorpion* (London: Octagon Press, 1978), pp. 89–90.

Select Bibliography

Bagchi, Jhunu. *The History and Culture of the Palas of Bengal and Bihar.* New Delhi: Abhinav Publications, 1993.

Chatterji, Suniti Kumar. *The Origin and Development of the Bengali Language.* London: George Allen & Unwin, 1970.

Chattopadhyay, Bhaskar, ed. *Culture of Bengal through the Ages: Some Aspects.* Burdwan, West Bengal: University of Burdwan, 1988.

Cleary, Thomas. *Buddhist Yoga: A Comprehensive Course.* Boston: Shambhala Publications, 1995.

———. *Dhammapada: The Sayings of Buddha.* New York: Bantam Books, 1995.

———. *Entry into the Inconceivable: An Introduction to Hua-yen Buddhism.* Honolulu: University of Hawaii Press, 1983.

———. *The Flower Ornament Scripture.* Boston: Shambhala Publications, 1984, 1986, 1987, 1989, 1993.

———. *Unlocking the Zen Koan.* Classics of Buddhism and Zen, vol. 4. Boston: Shambhala Publications, 2001.

———. *Rational Zen: The Mind of Dogen Zenji.* Classics of Buddhism and Zen, vol. 3. Boston: Shambhala Publications, 2001.

———. *The Secret of the Golden Flower.* San Francisco: HarperSanFrancisco, 1991.

———. *Shōbōgenzō: Zen Essays by Dōgen.* Classics of Buddhism and Zen, vol. 2. Boston: Shambhala Publications, 2001.

———. *Vitality, Energy, Spirit: A Taoist Sourcebook.* The Taoist Classics, vol. 3. Boston: Shambhala Publications, 2000.

———. *Zen Essence: The Science of Freedom.* Classics of Buddhism and Zen, vol. 1. Boston: Shambhala Publications, 2001.

Cleary, Thomas and J. C. Cleary. *The Blue Cliff Record.* Boston: Shambhala Publications, 1977.

Dudjom Rinpoche. *The Nyingma School of Tibetan Buddhism*. Boston: Wisdom Publications, 1991.

(Mukhapadhyāy) Mukherji, Tarapad. *The Old Bengali Language and Text*. Calcutta: Calcutta University, 1967.

Scott, Ernest. *The People of the Secret*. London: Octagon Press, 1983.

Sen, Nilratan, ed. *Caryagitikos*. West Bengal: Dipali Sen, 1978.

Sen, Sukumar. *An Etymological Dictionary of Bengali: c. 1000–1800*. Calcutta: Eastern Publishers, 1971.

Shah, Idries. *The Way of the Sufi*. London: Octagon Press, 1968.

Yoshida, Keikoh. *Kon-Tai Ryobu Shingon Kaiki*. Kyoto: Heirakuji Shoten, 1971.

BQ 9258 .C54 2005 v.2

Classics of Buddhism and Zen